WORKING V

WORKING WITH FACULTY WRITERS

Edited by

ANNE ELLEN GELLER AND
MICHELE EODICE

UTAH STATE UNIVERSITY PRESS
Logan

© 2013 by University Press of Colorado

Published by Utah State University Press
An imprint of University Press of Colorado
5589 Arapahoe Avenue, Suite 206C
Boulder, Colorado 80303

 The University Press of Colorado is a proud member of
the Association of American University Presses.

The University Press of Colorado is a cooperative publishing enterprise supported,
in part, by Adams State University, Colorado State University, Fort Lewis College,
Metropolitan State University of Denver, Regis University, University of Colorado,
University of Northern Colorado, Utah State University, and Western State Colorado
University.

Cover design by Dan Miller
Cover illustration © Valentina Razumova / Shutterstock

ISBN: 978-0-87421-901-2 (paperback)
ISBN: 978-0-87421-902-9 (e-book)

Library of Congress Cataloging-in-Publication Data

Working with faculty writers / edited by Anne Ellen Geller and Michele Eodice.
       pages cm
   Includes bibliographical references and index.
   ISBN 978-0-87421-901-2 (pbk.) — ISBN 978-0-87421-902-9 (e-book)
1. Academic writing—Study and teaching (Higher) 2. Academic writing—Vocational
guidance. 3. Writing centers—Administration. 4. English language—Rhetoric—Study
and teaching (Higher)—Authorship. 5. English language—Rhetoric—Study and
teaching (Higher)—Research. 6. Report writing—Study and teaching (Higher). 7.
Education, Higher—Aims and objectives. 8. Universities and colleges—Administration.
9. College teachers—Tenure. I. Geller, Anne Ellen, 1969- editor of compilation. II.
Eodice, Michele, 1957- editor of compilation.
   P301.5.A27W67 2013
   808'.04720711—dc23
                              2013019563

CONTENTS

FOREWORD

Bob Boice

As tradition would have it, elite scholars might overlook this collection of chapters by expert practitioners of writing instruction and faculty development. Elite scholars might believe that writing is inspired, not blocked, or that it is done well only alone without intervention. But this collection of real-life accounts of experiences in little-known methods of helping graduate students and professors work more effectively as teachers and writers is needed despite the fact that many are in denial of it. These practical accounts offer up-close observations of how struggling academics can be coached by specially educated experts. More faculty developers should be sharing their useful observations amongst others doing similar work, rather than publishing in journals where few people read their articles carefully. Readers looking for assessed practices and ideas for helping their novice or still struggling colleagues, including dissertators, will become valued by their institutions for having learned creative ways of moving past blocking-related feelings that they are over-scheduled and too busy to complete enough writing/publication for tenure—or even to teach for student comprehension and involvement. This practical mode of faculty development (simply coaching faculty writers in proximity) helps make academic writing, and, surprisingly, even teaching, less difficult and more effective in my experience (Boice 2000).

Much of my earlier research on writers and their barriers to scholarly productivity led me to think about the other aspects of a faculty member's life, such as teaching. I propose two unusual ideas here for helping ourselves in both domains: First, I claim that we can profit by learning the positive lessons taught in treating writing/teaching blocks. Second, we can write and teach more effectively as story tellers who balance contemporary advice with forgotten accounts of the earliest discoverers of our new, higher minds.

Two pioneers in understanding the potential of our higher minds and creativity are Charles Darwin and Sigmund Freud. They address forgotten factors that impact our usual blocks in terms of creative thinking.

Darwin was first to realize the limitations of our freedom from natural selection that effectively removed us from survival pressures like predation, allowing humans leisure time and curiosity-based innovations that have built our higher minds. And Freud found that we block when we rush writing. He particularly noticed that when we will not let go and allow our uncreative solutions to mesh with creative applications, we give up on civilization and live in neurotic ways.

Since then, creative blocks have been deemed unscientific concepts that either don't exist or else can't be taken seriously. Misunderstanding the concepts of blocking and fluency leads to strictly deterministic views of the mind that proscribe proven methods of self-controlled, mentally balanced ways of writing that remove tendencies toward painful and even maddening blocks. Studies show that learning to do two different things at the same time does indeed replace writing blocks with fluent, more brilliant and novel solutions; so do the equally effective tactics of coaching analogous economies of teaching (Boice 2011). They do so by replacing excessive anxieties and well-intentioned over-preparations of teaching materials with a conceptual, image-based focus on main points.

So in fact, writing and teaching often fail to be effective and inspirational out of what at first seems the fault of our creative blocks. But not until I used the leisure of my early retirement to observe exemplary, versus blocking new teachers in front of classrooms did I see the connection with writing. That is, I found that modeling calm, image-based, nonverbal skills weekly for these struggling new faculties helped do more than teach them a set of textbook strategies for engaging their students. Those new faculty who fared best at unblocking had each realized that their most important changes went beyond learning new skills (Boice 2011); they also came to appreciate their blocks as useful warnings of weak habits instead of just punishments for not having learned what they had been taught. Is that finding nothing but relabeling blocks to obscure the real reasons—suspected by critics—like laziness (Boice 2000)? I say no! Some finally unblocked teachers and writers complained of occasional returns to painful, anxious sessions and admitted they still didn't enjoy these creative efforts. But those blockers who decided blocks were fair warnings to change their mental habits in difficult tasks requiring intensely focused attention, were thereafter happy, eager writers who increased their productivity. These important changes of mind were not easy to put into hard numbers, even though they rank along with my proven findings.

I could go on with other casual impressions of blocking symptoms like avoidance and procrastination, but I think my point is already clear:

I've come to appreciate the kinds of collected experiences by those of us who carry out this important but oft-unappreciated effort. I thus see the special appeal of a book like this one. I suspect that many insights await our attentiveness, and that although this book focuses on faculty as writers, I hope I have invited you to think also of faculty as teachers. Creative practice and reflection in each realm, can, I've found, improve the other (Boice and Branch, n.d.). Thank you for letting me share my thoughts as I endorse this important collection. I encourage you, dear reader, to immerse yourself in each of the unique chapters anon. You never quite know where you will find useful alternative ideas like those I've mentioned, but I'm certain the impressive quality of thinking and selection shown by these two editors will reward your reading.

REFERENCES

Boice, R. 2000. *Advice for New Faculty: Nihil Nimus.* Needham, MA: Allyn-Bacon.
Boice, R. 2011. "Going Beyond Usual Teaching and Writing Improvements with Coached Changes in Imagination and Creativity." Plenary address delivered at the Annual Conference of the Professional and Organizational Development Network in Higher Education, Atlanta, GA, October 27.
Boice, R., and V. Branch. N.d. "Writing Block." In process.

ACKNOWLEDGMENTS

As with all writing, we would like to acknowledge influences from texts and colleagues, influences that expand our thinking and improve our efforts. Special thanks to Michael Spooner and the staff at Utah State University Press and the University Press of Colorado for making the process seem smooth and easy. We also found helpful the feedback from editors, peer reviewers, and other readers.

The forty-four authors of sixteen chapters represent an influential group of scholars and practitioners from whom we have learned a great deal; we have enjoyed our collaboration with them and look forward to working together in the future. We also appreciate Bob Boice's attention to this project.

Thanks go to St. John's University and the University of Oklahoma for sponsorship of our project. Anne's work was supported by a 2012 St. John's University Summer Support of Research Award, the 2011 Summer Faculty Writing Institute in Paris, and the ongoing, year-round community of the Faculty Writing Initiative. A subvention approved by OU Provost Nancy Mergler and OU Vice President for Research Kelvin Droegemeier contributed to the production of this book. Graduate students participating in Camp Completion and faculty writing groups at OU provided inspiration for this collection.

Finally, support from Kami Day, Moira Ozias, Joan Geller, Gino DiIorio, Natalie Byfield, Robin Wellington, and Maura Flannery kept us fed and loved throughout the process.

WORKING WITH FACULTY WRITERS

INTRODUCTION

Anne Ellen Geller

Here's one image of the faculty writer: She's in an office where book-shelves line the walls. She's hunched over a desk. Perhaps she wears glasses. She is typing, and her eyes move back and forth from her text to the books and data scattered around her. Occasionally, she furrows her brow. Or she stretches her shoulders and rubs her neck. She is alone. The scene is quiet. The only aspect of this dominant image that has changed in the nearly twenty years since I began my own doctoral pro-gram is that the purring electric typewriter with a waving sheet of paper and clicking keys is now a silent, shiny, silver Apple laptop.

But there are other images of the faculty writer available to us. She is reading aloud from her draft to a small group of cross-disciplinary colleagues who are nodding and taking notes. She is describing her goals to a writing or editorial coach. Perhaps she has carried her lap-top out of her office to a common space on campus, like a writing cen-ter or coffee shop, and she is working to the rhythm of the typing of colleagues around her. Or maybe she is at a lunch event sponsored by her campus's center for teaching and learning. There, she and other faculty discuss the process of publishing scholarly articles, and she feels less discouraged by the revise and resubmit response she received by e-mail that morning.

One image, the first static one, signifies the idealized individual fac-ulty writer, who struggles alone, is brilliant alone, and succeeds alone. The other images represent the more realistic social aspects of writing, the individual writer working alone *and* within communities. These images celebrate the value of supportive and challenging colleagues, and point to the desire faculty have to learn from one another and from those with more experience and expertise about what it takes to successfully develop and sustain a scholarly agenda and a publishing career. The solitary and social acts depicted in these images are all nec-essary and integral to the life of the successful scholarly writer, but the truth is that within the academy we still tend to valorize the first image.

One of our hopes in putting together this collection is to make certain readers know that many in higher education have developed productive writing programs for all faculty (and future faculty). Often these programs allow faculty—and graduate students—to meet and support one another across disciplinary and departmental boundaries, to come to new insights about their own disciplinary writing and their own writing processes, and, sometimes, to develop new insights about their students' writing.

We have also had other reasons to bring together this collection. For example, we want to share what we have come to know from our own work with faculty writers, and we wish to contribute to the growing body of knowledge about how writers work and what supports their work. We want to offer a timely, early twenty-first century response to historical and contemporary issues related to the production of writing in the academy during the "late age of print" (Striphas 2009; Bolter 2001); and, in that context, we want to highlight what can be done to promote and sustain all writing in the academy, whether that means student writing (undergraduate and graduate) or faculty writing. With the ever-increasing pressure on faculty to be productive researchers and writers, we thought it was time to share best practices with all who hope to effectively support faculty writers, and this is a book for anyone who wants to learn more about developing and assessing such support. We hope those who use these chapters to develop faculty writing programs strive to keep those initiatives closely linked to initiatives for student writing, for we believe it is this connection that leads to a true culture of writing across a campus.

Our best practices of supporting faculty writing are more important now than they have ever been. For decades universities have struggled to develop and sustain a culture of writing, and now, in a time when the very definition and concept of text production is changing, there are both more possibilities for this support and more challenges. One of the challenges is the pressure of accountability. A culture of assessment has taken hold in higher education, and as intellectual labor is counted and measured throughout our institutions, we want to embrace—and help others embrace—realistic and authentic ways to speak not just for the texts faculty produce (or the number of texts faculty produce) but also for how institutions commit to making the process and work of writing visible and valued.

Finally, we want to demonstrate a commitment to "making a book," for we believe these ideas are important enough for a book. Lindsay Waters put it well: "At the heart of book making is the gathering, the tying together of materials into a package, a unity that the person or group of people pulling together are prepared to have judged" (Waters 2004, 80). With the forty-four authors who have contributed the chapters you are about to read, including our foreword by Bob Boice, and with our editor, we feel certain we are offering, in a sense, a book about how faculty make other books (and articles and grant proposals)—a meta level investigation of the process of scholarly writing. Each author holds different institutional power and brings a different institutional perspective to working with writers in the academy and many of these chapters are coauthored so those perspectives are directly in conversation even within chapters. The book as a whole develops a series of interconnected analyses, meditations, and critiques on what it means to be writers, readers, teachers, and learners in higher education.

WHO WE ARE AND WHAT WE DO

As researchers of writing and as writing program administrators, Michele Eodice and I have both intentionally committed our professional lives to writers and their texts. While teaching undergraduate writing classes, while advising graduate students, or while mentoring the writing consultants in the writing centers we've directed, we've tried to be curious experts who never tire of talking with writers about their writing and their writing processes. And with this stance we've learned a great deal from the many writers in our lives.

Michele and I also share years of experience of working with faculty who are teaching with writing; we have developed many ways to reach faculty to help them develop the habits of mind they need to link writing with learning. We have helped faculty create effective writing assignments and strengthen the ways they engage with, respond to, and assess student writing. We discovered early on, through our writing center and writing across the curriculum work, that it was nearly impossible to talk with faculty about how they taught with writing without hearing something about who they themselves were and had been as writers. (Christopher Thaiss and Terry Zawacki [2006] also experienced this in their assessment research at George Mason University reported in *Engaged Writers/Dynamic Disciplines.*) The more Michele and I explicitly took this approach—being open to talking with faculty about their own writing—the more we recognized how much faculty from across the disciplines crave writing community. We knew many other writing program administrators and teaching center professionals had these same experiences and had developed thoughtful and successful approaches to supporting faculty writing.

Over the time we conceived of this collection, Michele and I each developed our institutions' faculty writing support programs. At St. John's, where I am an Associate Professor in English and the Director of Writing Across the Curriculum in the Institute for Writing Studies, I collaborate with the Center for Teaching and Learning (CTL). With a group of interested faculty, Maura Flannery, the faculty director of the CTL and I have nurtured a Faculty Writing Initiative, which has, at this point, provided twenty well-attended on-campus faculty writing retreats within three years and a series of workshops, often facilitated by experienced St. John's faculty, on topics such as "Revise and Resubmit," "Peer Review," "Developing Edited Collections," and the upcoming "Tools for Writing." At St. John's Faculty Writing Initiative events, cross-disciplinary faculty have empathetically listened to a colleague who has had an article rejected and is processing what feel like mean-spirited peer reviews and they have enthusiastically celebrated with a colleague who is passing around his newly published book so everyone can "ooh" and "ahh" and touch the text. At one lunch, a junior faculty person described the linguistic bias of a journal editor who she felt made assumptions about her text on the basis of her name. These are powerful and informative experiences for all present. Similar conversations have taken place at the St. John's Summer Faculty Writing Institute, which brings twenty cross-disciplinary faculty to our Paris or Rome campus for a combined writing retreat and writing across the curriculum workshop (Geller 2011). There, for example, a psychology faculty member received feedback from her peers as she worked to get the results of her research into a form she could circulate to the popular press. Within months of distributing this newly created document she was quoted in an *Essence* magazine article.

At the University of Oklahoma, Michele leads a unit that includes the writing center and writing across campus initiatives, connecting most closely with the teaching center. With this structure, she works at the intersections of writing and learning, writing and teaching, and scholarly writing, as faculty participate in workshops and writing groups to enhance their own writing process and progress. In each of our faculty writing support programs we've created opportunities for faculty to give one another advice on writing issues like drafting and revision, but also on less openly talked about topics like perseverance and time management. We've seen great value in junior faculty learning from senior faculty, but we've also seen senior faculty turn to their junior colleagues. We've listened as faculty from across disciplines learn about new publication outlets or grant opportunities from one another when the silo-ization of the academy would have likely meant that without our faculty writing support programs these faculty might never have met let alone talked about their scholarly projects and interests. Much of this collection touches on the ways that simply getting faculty to "walk across the hall" has contributed to their writing esteem and the culture of writing at their institutions. At each of our institutions we are fortunate enough to have physical space devoted to writing and writers. Though these spaces are used primarily by student writers, they were deliberately designed so they could also host faculty writers. We believe there is great value in students and faculty seeing one another's writing and witnessing one another in the act of writing.

As Michele and I have traveled to conferences and to other institutions to facilitate workshops, give invited talks, and provide external evaluations of programs, we have heard of small-scale and large-scale programs we admire. For example, Plymouth State University, in New Hampshire, has a longstanding "guilting bee," a group of faculty who meet to both support one another's writing and to "guilt" one another—with a collegial spirit—into getting writing done. Queen Mary, University of London's Thinking Writing Program, hosts Urban Writing Retreats for faculty and doctoral students across the disciplines. And Temple University's Writing Center offers writing retreats in a variety of configurations—on weekends, in the evening, or during spring and summer semester breaks. When we have described our own faculty writing support programs, or described those we know about, faculty across the disciplines at other institutions have told us that they wish they had a local faculty writing support program in place. They often ask us, What would we need to start a program like that here? What would it take to fund it? How could we convince our administration that writing support for faculty would be valuable? Thus, we hope this book will help more institutions imagine how to develop writing support for their faculty, many of whom might feel they would be stigmatized locally if they were to ask for such support without being able to provide models of how it can work effectively and why it is important for all faculty. We've also imagined that this project could lead writing program directors, center for teaching and learning directors, deans, and provosts to ask their faculty what they need in a writing support program, and we hope these chapters offer readers some sense of why needs assessment is integral to providing faculty with what they need most.

WHY SUPPORT FACULTY WRITERS?

The academy's "publish or perish" phenomenon is relatively new, given the history of higher education in the West, and it remains largely associated with twentieth century demands for legitimizing tenure decisions based on some measurement of quantity and quality of publications. Even with different levels of demand for research (scholarly publication) across institutional types, and knowing that "publish or perish" continues to create a "paper glut," (Siegel and Baveye 2010) measuring scholarly output remains a staple of the academic marketplace. As William Savage notes in "Scribble, Scribble Toil and Trouble: Forced Productivity in the Modern University," before junior faculty have completed their first book, they must account for their second book, "and the inquiry about its status assumes that work is in progress or implies that it should be. The request for a peek at the opus indicates a certain impatience on the part of administrators awaiting tangible results" (Savage 2003, 41). Savage points out: "The fact that questions are asked annually conveys to their recipient the importance of the enterprise. That the answers may have direct bearing on raises and promotions bespeaks the carrot-and-stick philosophy of the modern academy" (41). Every author in this book understands how work with faculty writers has very real material consequences.

As institutions compete with each other for resources and rankings, research output begins to count more—and more is expected of faculty. The demands for publication will be tempered or inflamed by the varied goals of an institution. Lindsay Waters, an editor at Harvard University Press, offers a critique: he likens the "meteoric rise in scholarly publication" to an economic bubble ready to burst (Waters 2004, 19). He fears that too many in the academy "now believe scholarship is only about jobs and promotion" (75).

We want to meet the readers of this book and their writing groups where they are at in terms of writing. So this collection offers ways to work with faculty writers that maintain their autonomy, dignity, and individual professional goals, without ignoring the very real demands on their time and intellectual capital. As the chapter descriptions below will reveal, part-time faculty, full-time faculty, and graduate students can all benefit from writing support, as can faculty in teaching oriented, research oriented, and administrative positions. To think otherwise is to reinforce the biases and stereotypes of the academy we wish to work against. Also, faculty writing is writ large in this collection. A number of faculty and administrators (including deans) have attended St. John's University writing retreats to work at writing some might consider "non-academic." But whether they were working on newsletter articles or blog entries or memoirs intended only for their family members, and whether their texts will be read by their staff or their grandchildren or their university press editors, we have been firm in welcoming all faculty writers and all faculty writing. Because of this, the atmosphere has been welcoming, supportive, and curious.

Over twenty years ago Bob Boice, distinguished author of this collection's foreword, reported from his research that fewer academics than we realize actually write and publish, yet the academy "has been shamefully slow to help its own, especially to make writing for publication easier and more democratic" (Boice 1990, 9). Perhaps, Boice suggested, "we subscribe to Social Darwinism, supposing only the fittest survive" (7). And, he pointed out, we reinscribe that belief again and again for "those who dominate our journals openly claim that they are among the few who have had 'the right stuff' to master the rules of writing for publication" (8). More recently, Wendy Belcher, who has coached many graduate student and faculty writers and written from her experiences, told the story of a party where she met an academic who described literally belting himself to his chair to get his writing done. She says that from her experiences working with academic writers, and from the research she knows, she was not entirely surprised by this academic's story. She writes: "What has most struck me about these confessions is how many faculty believe they are unique in their writing dysfunction" (Belcher 2009a, 185).

Many faculty have never thought of themselves as writers. Instead, they think of themselves as readers or problem solvers or project managers or scientists. They "talk, do research, go to conferences, teach, figure things out, reason, analyze, argue" (Elbow and Sorcinelli 2006, 19). But within the academy, most must combine these professional identities with the identity of "writer." As Peter Elbow writes, if professors "don't write things, they don't get to be professors" (Elbow and Sorcinelli 2006, 19). Yet research shows "the skills, orientations and pressures that lead to initiating writing or writing-related activity are qualitatively different from the skills, orientations, pressures or supports that lead to their continuation and completion" (Moore 2003, 340).

In researching "professors as writers" (Boice 1990) we have learned a great deal about faculty writing processes and habits, as well as what leads to faculty members' academic writing successes or failures. We know quite a bit about how faculty write together (Day and Eodice 2001). Resources describe how faculty writers navigate writing for funding and publication across their careers (Germano 2001; Moxley 1992; Moxley and Taylor 1997; Rocco and Hatcher 2011). Research shows that in addition to keeping a regular individual writing schedule (Belcher 2009b; Boice 1990; Bolker 1998), having time and space to write (Elbow and Sorcinelli 2006; Farr et al. 2009; Geller 2011; Grant 2006; McGrail, Rickard, and Jones 2006; Murray and Newton 2009), and feeling part of a supportive community of writing peers (Eodice and Cramer 2001; Friend and González 2009; Grant 2006) are also key to faculty productivity. In fact, a meta-analysis of seventeen studies published between 1984 and 2004 that examined the effects of writing courses, writing support groups, and writing coaches reveals that "all interventions led to an increase in average publication rates for the participants" (McGrail et al. 2006, 19) and "benefits of all models included an increase in confidence, skills and teamwork" (34).

A number of chapters in this collection are written from the perspective of facilitators who are working, explicitly or implicitly, to understand how faculty "do" their own writing as they mentor their students "doing" writing. As Michael Carter has stated: "Having faculty in the disciplines identify ways of *doing* and associated ways of *writing* reveals the extent to which writing is critical to the ways of *knowing* valued in the disciplines" [our emphasis] (Carter 2007, 404). This *doing, writing, knowing* continually activates a campus culture of vibrant intellectual exchange and, when made visible, provides meta-awareness of what it takes to actively and collaboratively contribute to both the consumption and production of knowledge. Beyond gains in scholarly productivity and the development of new attitudes toward their own writing, we believe writing support for faculty can also draw explicit attention to the relationship between faculty writing and their students' learning through writing. And yet there is much more for us to learn about the interrelationship between doing scholarly writing as a researcher-writer and teaching writing as a researcher-teacher.

SUPPORTING WRITING, TEACHING, AND LEARNING IN COLLEGES AND UNIVERSITIES

Both local needs and global expectations have shaped how support is given to writers in college and university settings. And the most common response to the desire to help writers in higher education—or the mandate to do so—has long been for institutions to create writing centers, institutional spaces that offer one-to-one tutoring and workshops facilitated by peer or professional staff. Without providing a full history of writing centers, it is safe to say that their emergence over the twentieth century coincides with the enrollment of first generation students, military veterans, women, and non-mainstream students—those who did not fit earlier admissions qualifications based on preparation, income, race, or linguistic parity (see Boquet 1999; Carino 1995; Lerner 2003).

Even if writing centers began only as a response to a perceived need for improved student writing, writing centers have always sought—and have often found—a larger institutional role influencing academic culture. With the writing across the curriculum, writing to learn, writing in the disciplines, and communication across the curriculum movements, programmatic structures tended to coalesce around writing centers as sites for universal writing support. At some institutions, that universal support has extended to writing support for faculty. There is also a longstanding tradition of writing groups (Moss et al. 2004; Gere 1987) in and around higher education. Whether structured institutionally or informally and whether comprised of students or faculty, writing groups have always provided opportunities for the interdisciplinary exchange of ideas and the formation of community. Thus, most institutions of higher education have some history of attention to writing and writers and have directed resources toward individuals and the community, whether through curricular or extra-curricular programming.

The emergence of institutionalized writing support (writing centers, writing across the curriculum) for students and faculty shares a history with the emergence of faculty development initiatives and teaching centers. According to Connie M. Schroeder, the "relatively young field" of "professional and organizational development" is still forming its identity (Schroeder 2011, xi). Professional development offered by teaching and learning centers has been synonymous with instructional support: the teaching aspect of faculty work was seen as what needed attention and resources. But teaching centers' focus on the proverbial three-legged stool—of research, teaching, and service—means they can, with some ease, support faculty writing with attention to how the writing process informs and is informed by all other aspects of faculty life.

A variety of institution types are represented in the chapters that follow, and the chapter authors spend their scholarly and professional lives in a variety of locations—from teaching and learning centers to writing across the curriculum, and communication across the curriculum programs to writing centers. We believe this diversity is necessary to illuminate the sites, the resources, and the type of leadership needed to embed support for faculty writers into the academic community in sustainable ways. Overall, this collection reveals the range of locations and models of support for faculty writers, explores the ways these might be delivered and assessed, delves into who faculty writers are, and who they might be, and considers the theoretical, philosophical, and pedagogical approaches to faculty writing support, as well as its relationship to student writing support.

SECTION 1: LEADERSHIP AND LOCATIONS

What sometimes keeps an institution from supporting faculty writing is the simple question of who would provide the support. (What that often means, of course, is whose budget will pay for the support and whose staff will provide the support.) As described throughout this introduction, student writers on most campuses can readily find writing support through the courses offered by writing programs or in writing centers where they can physically sit with peer writing tutors or meet online to virtually discuss works in progress. We know successful student writing centers and writing programs have been shown to change the writing culture of an institution. But again and again we've heard writing directors responsible for supporting students' writing lives describe the faculty (or dissertation writers) who seek support for their extended writing projects as a problem—a problem that will eat up already scarce resources.

Those involved with early writing across the curriculum programs in the 1970s and 1980s (e.g., those funded by the National Endowment for the Humanities) often turned attention to faculty writing even as they focused on supporting faculty teaching writing. Many of these initiatives were informed by beliefs and practices of the National Writing Project—that "teachers of writing must write, as well as read and talk about the teaching of writing" and that teachers should have "the rare opportunity of coming together as a community of writers over a sustained period of time, freed from the demands of teaching, to write and to share their pieces with other teachers of writing in regularly scheduled editing/response groups" (Gray 2000, 143–44). But as writing across the curriculum and writing in the disciplines programs have become more curricularized, and as funding for all institutional programs tightens, the resources and time for bringing groups of faculty together to write and respond to one another's writing have become a luxury. Faculty are, instead, brought together for intensive workshops focused only on teaching with writing, with attention to assignment design, response, and assessment.. The first chapter of this collection, Chris Anson's "Beyond the Curriculum: Supporting Faculty Writing in WAC Programs" reviews the history of faculty writing support offered by writing programs as a way of providing context for the spectrum of programming currently offered by writing programs. Anson also considers what writing programs might now want to research and learn as part of their more recent investments in writing support initiatives for faculty.

There has been enough need—and desire—for faculty writing support that both writing programs and centers for teaching and learning, in addition to administrative offices (provosts' offices, for example), more and more often facilitate and fund such endeavors, often informally. But because the question of who should be responsible for support for faculty writing and faculty writers remains a perennial institutional issue, we devote quite a bit of space in this collection to chapters that address and complicate this question. Even centers for teaching and learning, with their faculty focused missions, sometimes do not, or cannot because of budgetary, time, and staffing constraints, conceive of themselves as support centers for faculty scholarship and writing. If centers for teaching and learning are, and have been, tasked with supporting both new and experienced teachers as they reflect on teaching practices, facilitating departmental and institutional curricular development and outcomes assessment, and overseeing the integration of technology into education across their institutions, some might ask how they can have the extended time and resources to support faculty writing and faculty writers. In "The Scholarly Writing Continuum: A New Program Model for Teaching and Faculty Development Centers," Brian Baldi, Mary Deane Sorcinelli, and Jung H. Yun describe a continuum of faculty writing support programs that might be offered by a center for teaching and learning and describe how a campus's customized program should grow from needs assessment. They also overview research on faculty writing support programs to articulate the reasons a faculty development center would want to support faculty writers in multiple ways.

Perhaps focusing on the question of *who* should support faculty writers keeps us from more difficult questions that deserve our attention. At the heart of Lori Salem and Jennifer Follett's "The Idea of a Faculty Writing Center: Moving from Troubling Deficiencies to Collaborative Engagement" is the question, How might we support faculty writers while also facilitating institutional self-examination and sponsoring equitable and reasonable expectations for faculty writers? Salem and Follett ask us to imagine faculty writing centers that would proceed from an informed understanding of literacy communities and literacy practices rather than from missionary stances that risk reinscribing unexamined institutional beliefs and expectations about faculty publication. And it is in a chapter about the University of Virginia Professors as Writers (PAW) program that we find an enactment of the critical reflection Salem and Follett theorize. In "Talking about Writing: Critical

Dialogues on Supporting Faculty Writers," Gertrude Fraser and Deandra Little shape their chapter as a critical dialogue to model their own efforts to be reflective practitioners and to promote their belief that faculty writing is a reflective practice. By describing the PAW program of small grants and workshops, from its development through qualitative assessment of the program, the coauthors offer a series of unexpected program outcomes. They set both expected and unexpected outcomes in the context of their differing institutional lenses and in the context of research that examines the intersections between organizational and faculty development orientations within the academy and research on faculty writing and faculty productivity.

SECTION II: WRITING GROUPS/RETREATS/RESIDENCIES

When institutions provide support for faculty writers and their writing, it is often in the form of individual consulting or counseling. Emory University's Center for Faculty Development and Excellence, for example, established an Author Development Program, which offers editorial consultations to faculty (Brown 2006). Or, an institution might contract with individual writing consultants or consulting companies, who then offer courses or online support for faculty. What we know is that faculty seeking writing support will likely search it out, even if an institution does not provide it, finding friends, psychotherapy, or academic coaches useful.

But most of the programs described and evaluated in this collection go beyond supporting individual writers' needs to argue for the additional value of writing community. Writing retreats, writing support groups, and designated geographical (or theoretical) writing spaces for faculty (like the faculty writing retreat and WAC workshop in Rome and Paris described in Geller or the "Faculty Writing Place" described in Baldi, Sorcinelli and Yun in this collection) all create space and time for faculty to write and also offer opportunities for faculty to reflect on and share their processes, struggles, and successes. This section offers models of this type of faculty writing support and also shows how engaged assessment of programs that work with faculty writers can educate everyone on our campuses about the complex practices and social processes of writers.

As Wendy Weiner (2009) states, "assessment is not going away," but when we consider how many institutions offer a variety of formal and informal support for faculty writing, it is surprising how little has been published considering what interventions work well and why. What writing support best creates scholarly communities of practice? What would we find out if we were to trace the longer-term effects of faculty participation in writing support programs? Would we see that writing residencies have long-term impact on the teaching of writing or instructional practices more generally? Although many chapters in this collection include assessment and evaluation data, the chapters in this section offer explicit examples of assessment of writing support initiatives and the models they provide offer both inspiration and guidelines for others who will eventually need to assess whatever programs they put into place or who will need evidence of the value of writing support to make a case for supporting faculty writers.

In "How Teaching and Learning Centers Can Support Faculty as Writers," Tara Gray, A. Jane Birch, and Laura Madson describe thirteen years of successful structured programming at New Mexico State University and Brigham Young University to argue that the teaching center is the unit that should take the lead in support for faculty and graduate student writing because facilitating writing programs will help teaching centers reach all of their goals, including their teaching goals. In "Faculty Writing Groups: Writing Centers and Third Space Collaborations," Angela Clark-Oates and Lisa Cahill employ the idea of third space to explain why they believe faculty writing groups create a space beyond writing centers and beyond classrooms (and perhaps even beyond teaching centers) where disciplinary faculty can consider both their own writing lives and students' writing lives. They claim that by creating writing groups that address the needs of faculty writers writing centers can connect faculty writing processes with student writing processes and can therefore have a greater effect on changing the culture of writing on college and university campuses.

Using survey and interview data in "Supporting a Culture of Writing: Faculty Writing Residencies as a WAC Initiative," Jessie L. Moore, Peter Felten, and Michael Strickland research the impact of five years of summer faculty writing residencies at Elon University, cosponsored by the Center for the Advancement of Teaching and Learning and the Writing Across the Curriculum Program and offer recommendations for designing faculty writing support programming that fosters scholarly writing about teaching and WAC initiatives.

In "Assessing the Effects of Faculty and Staff Writing Retreats: Four Institutional Perspectives," Ellen Schendel, Susan Callaway, Violet Dutcher, and Claudine Griggs, four writing center directors at four different institutions, collaborate on a multi-institutional study of the relationship between the desired outcomes they've identified for faculty writing support and the long term consequences of short term faculty writing retreats for those who participate in them. These co-authors also use their assessment to consider the type of follow-up support faculty most need and describe the newest faculty-as-writers initiatives they've developed.

Two chapters that capture the experiences of writing group members follow. The seven coauthors of "Feedback and Fellowship: Stories from a Successful Writing Group" collaborate to describe a long-standing cross-disciplinary writing group at Texas A&M. Virginia Fajt, Fran I. Gelwick, Verónica Loureiro-Rodríguez, Prudence Merton, Georgianne Moore, María Irene Moyna, and Jill Zarestky, a group of all women faculty, from disciplines ranging from mathematics and Hispanic studies to veterinary pathobiology and civil engineering reflect on their work together in the context of literature on learning communities and communities of practice. By focusing on aspects of this group's success, this chapter offers some important recommendations for improving the effectiveness of feedback in cross-disciplinary writing groups and suggestions we believe will help other institutions' groups achieve this type of longevity. And, in "Developing a Heuristic for Multi-disciplinary Faculty Writing Groups: A Case Study," Trixie G. Smith, Janice C. Molloy, Eva Kassens-Noor, Wen Li, and Manuel Colunga-Garcia provide a case study of an established faculty writing group at a Research 1 university. Using organizational psychology, linguistics and systems theory, the core faculty members of this group and the writing center director of the sponsoring center reflect on the relationships within this long-standing group as well as the reading and response practices of the group.

SECTION III: ISSUES AND AUTHORS

There is little doubt, as I have noted throughout this introduction, that the academy can, however unintentionally, make the process of scholarly research, writing and rewriting, and publication seem like luck or magic or talent rather than the laborious, recursive process it is. Who faculty and graduate students are when they take part in writing support programs may not always be who they are striving to be either professionally or as writers. Institution-type can also inform the intellectual work participants choose to prioritize in a writing support program. In "Guiding Principles for Supporting Faculty as Writers at a Teaching-Mission Institution," Michelle Cox and Ann Brunjes turn our attention to community colleges and universities where teaching and service are privileged over publication to show that writing retreats at teaching intensive institutions must be distinct from those held at research intensive institutions. Cox and Brunjes explain how the week-long Teacher-Scholar Summer Institute at Bridgewater State University helps to foster a culture of writing on campus and provide faculty development related to writing pedagogy. By combining the two aims, and providing stipends for participants (funded institutionally and through grant funds), the institute embraces and supports faculty members' full identities as scholars and teachers. Drawing on identity theory and including Institute evaluation data from focus groups and follow-up interviews, Cox and Brunjes offer a model adaptable for other teaching intensive schools.

In the business of higher education *who* is eligible for faculty writing support is sometimes a question. At St. John's the Faculty Writing Initiative is open to all faculty—full-time and part-time, as well as to graduate students. Michele and I believe it is unfortunate that some institutions allocate their faculty writing support to tenure-stream and tenured faculty only, and we hope Letizia Guglielmo and Lynée Lewis Gaillet's "Academic Publication and Contingent Faculty: Establishing a Community of Scholars" will prompt reconsideration of this stance. Guglielmo and Gaillet reflect on how we might best support the research and publishing agendas of contingent faculty, who are often without departmental support but under the same pressure to publish as tenured and tenure stream faculty. Bringing recent scholarship on mentoring and professional development together with their own experiences, the experiences of other mentors, and the experiences of contingent faculty in a variety of academic situations, the authors offer suggestions for the creation of sustainable, ethical models of professional development and scholarship for all faculty.

Deepening these concepts and connecting writing to other aspects of faculty life, William P. Banks and Kerri B. Flinchbaugh suggest programming that focuses on introducing faculty writers to effective writing behaviors does not necessarily help faculty connect their research, teaching, and service lives. In "Experiencing Ourselves as Writers: An Exploration of How Faculty Writers Move from Dispositions to Identities" they take on the ethos and identity of the faculty writer and encourage us to help faculty rethink themselves as writers who teach and writers who research, which they say will then allow faculty to better embrace the practices and dispositions promoted in literature about supporting faculty writers.

While there are many disciplines that value collaborative writing and coauthorship, single authorship is still the norm in the humanities. William Duffy and John Pell ask us to stop thinking so much about the tactics and practices of coauthorship and ask us to think instead about the benefits of collaborative writing as an act. By defining "collaborative writing as an inventive process and reflexive relationship through which two or more writers synthesize their individual perspectives to create a new, shared voice to compose texts," in their chapter "Imagining CoAuthorship as Phased Collaboration," they argue collaborative writing offers an alternative model for imagining the production of texts.

Graduate writers—on the cusp of becoming faculty writers—span the space between faculty and students, so it is interesting to consider what there is to learn from the Michigan State University Writing Center, which hosts weekly, two-hour graduate writing groups facilitated by a writing center consultant, usually a doctoral student. In these groups, three to six cross-disciplinary doctoral students read and respond to one another's writing, sharing the process of becoming working scholars. Elena Marie-Adkins Garcia, Seung hee Eum, and Lorna Watt describe their Michigan State writing group experiences in "Experiencing the Benefits of Difference within Multidisciplinary Graduate Writing Groups" to argue that inter-disciplinary graduate writing groups provide space for graduate student scholars to practice being experts in their fields, which leads to gaining confidence for future writing and professional life. Garcia, Eum, and Watt also argue graduate writing groups provide space for future faculty to learn more about how to talk about writing and themselves as writers. Thus graduate writing groups contribute to the development of faculty across the disciplines who will be primed for later involvement with WAC/WID/CAC initiatives.

Finally, in "The Promise of Self-Authorship as an Integrative Framework for Supporting Faculty Writers," Carmen Werder proposes writers develop notions of *self-authorship*. In its cognitive, interpersonal, and intrapersonal dimensions, self-authorship situates faculty writers in more productive and healthier authorial identities. Werder also shows how moving from short-term production goals (used for job security and promotion) to goals that are more long-lasting is more fruitful for individual faculty and their institutions.

The afterword, written by my coeditor, Michele Eodice, extracts a sense of the future from what our forty-four authors have offered. Almost daily, news of how academic presses are adapting to survive and discussions of how faculty will respond to the demand for publication in electronic venues, for example, dominate our thoughts about scholarly work. Eodice proposes a turn toward each other as a way to find renewed energy and authentic value in our efforts to conduct research and participate in the dissemination of new knowledge.

As coeditors, we have worked with the authors of the chapters that follow to present solid writing, timely insights, emerging theories, and pragmatic case studies of authors in action. We hope that you will find this collection both useful and meaningful for your work with faculty writers.

REFERENCES

Belcher, Wendy Laura. 2009a. "Reflections on Ten Years of Teaching Writing for Publication to Graduate Students and Junior Faculty." *Journal of Scholarly Publishing* 40 (2): 184–200. http://dx.doi.org/10.3138/jsp.40.2.184.

Belcher, Wendy Laura. 2009b. *Writing Your Journal Article in Twelve Weeks: A Guide to Academic Publishing Success.* Thousand Oaks, CA: Sage Publications.

Boice, Robert. 1990. *Professors as Writers: A Self-Help Guide to Productive Writing.* Stillwater, OK: New Forums Press.

Bolker, Joan. 1998. *Writing Your Dissertation in Fifteen Minutes a Day: A Guide to Starting, Revising and Finishing Your Doctoral Thesis.* New York: Henry Holt and Co.

Bolter, David J. 2001. *Writing Space: Computers, Hypertext, and the Remediation of Print.* New York: Routledge.

Boquet, Elizabeth H. 1999. "'Our Little Secret': A History of Writing Centers, Pre- to Post-Open Admissions." *College Composition and Communication* 50 (3): 463–82. http://dx.doi.org/10.2307/358861.

Brown, Amy Benson. 2006. "Where Manuscript Development Meets Faculty Development." *Journal of Scholarly Publishing* 37 (2): 131–5. http://dx.doi.org/10.3138/jsp.37.2.131.

Carino, Peter. 1995. "Early Writing Centers: Toward a History." *Writing Center Journal* 15 (2): 103–15.

Carter, Michael. 2007. "Ways of Knowing, Doing, and Writing in the Disciplines." *College Composition and Communication* 58 (3): 385–418.

Day, Kami, and Michele Eodice. 2001. *(First Person)2: A Study of Co-Authoring in the Academy.* Logan: Utah State University Press.

Elbow, Peter, and Mary Deane Sorcinelli. 2006. "The Faculty Writing Place: A Room of Our Own." *Change Magazine* (November/December): 17–22.

Eodice, Michele, and Sharon Cramer. 2001. "Write On! A Model for Enhancing Faculty Publication." *Journal of Faculty Development* 18 (4): 113–21.

Farr, Cecilia Konchar, Joanne Cavallaro, Gabrielle Civil, and Susan Cochrane. 2009. "Taming the Publishing Beast: The College of St. Catherine Scholars' Retreat." *Change Magazine* (May/June). http://www.changemag.org/Archives/issue-lp/May-June-09.html.

Friend, Jennifer I., and Juan Carlos González. 2009. "Get Together to Write." *Academe Online.* American Association of University Professors. http://www.aaup.org/article/get-together-write.

Geller, Anne Ellen. 2011. "When in Rome." *Frontiers: The Interdisciplinary Journal of Study Abroad* 20 (April): 155–70.

Gere, Anne Ruggles. 1987. *Writing Groups: History, Theory, and Implications.* Carbondale: Southern Illinois University Press.

Germano, William. 2001. *Getting It Published: A Guide for Scholars and Anyone Else Serious About Serious Books.* Chicago: University of Chicago Press.

Grant, Barbara. 2006. "Writing in the Company of Other Women: Exceeding the Boundaries." *Studies in Higher Education* 31 (4): 483–95. http://dx.doi.org/10.1080/03075070600800624.

Gray, James. 2000. *Teachers at the Center: A Memoir of the Early Years of the National Writing Project.* Berkeley, CA: National Writing Project.

Lerner, Neal. 2003. "Punishment and Possibility: Representing Writing Centers, 1939–1970." *Composition Studies* 31 (Fall): 53–72.

McGrail, R.M., C.M. Rickard, and R. Jones. 2006. "Publish or Perish: A Systematic Review of Interventions to Increase Academic Publication Rates." *Higher Education Research & Development* 25 (1): 19–35. http://dx.doi.org/10.1080/07294360500453053.

Moore, Sarah. 2003. "Writers' Retreats for Academics: Exploring and Increasing the Motivation to Write." *Journal of Higher and Further Education* 27 (3): 333–42. http://dx.doi.org/10.1080/0309877032000098734.

Moss, Beverly J., Nels P. Highberg, and Melissa Nicolas, eds. 2004. *Writing Groups Inside and Outside the Classroom.* NJ: Earlbaum.

Moxley, Joseph M. 1992. *Publish, Don't Perish: The Scholar's Guide to Academic Writing & Publishing.* Westport, CT: Greenwood Publishing Group.

Moxley, Joseph M., and Todd Taylor. 1997. *Writing and Publishing for Academic Authors.* 2nd ed. Lanham, MD: Rowman and Littlefield.

Murray, Rowena, and Mary Newton. 2009. "Writing Retreat as Structured Intervention: Margin or Mainstream?" *Higher Education Research & Development* 28 (5): 541–53. http://dx.doi.org/10.1080/07294360903154126.

Rocco, Tonette S., and Tim Hatcher. 2011. *The Handbook of Scholarly Writing and Publishing.* San Francisco, CA: Jossey-Bass.

Savage, William W., Jr. 2003. "Scribble, Scribble, Toil and Trouble: Forced Productivity in the Modern University." *Journal of Scholarly Publishing* 35, no. 1 (October): 40–46.

Schroeder, Connie M. 2011. *Coming in from the Margins: Faculty Development's Emerging Organizational Development Role in Institutional Change.* Sterling, VA: Stylus.

Siegel, Donald, and Phillipe Baveye. 17 Sep, 2010. "Battling the paper glut." *Science* 329 (5998): 1466. http://dx.doi.org/10.1126/science.329.5998.1466-a. Medline:20847251.

Striphas, Ted. 2009. *The Late Age of Print: Everyday Book Culture from Consumerism to Control.* New York: Columbia University Press.

Thaiss, Chris, and Terry Meyers Zawacki. 2006. *Engaged Writers and Dynamic Disciplines: Research on the Academic Writing Life.* Portsmouth, NH: Heinemann.

Waters, Lindsay. 2004. *Enemies of Promise.* Chicago: Prickly Paradigm Press.

Weiner, Wendy. 2009. "Establishing a Culture of Assessment." http://www.aaup.org/article/establishing-culture-assessment#.UViCXsXA_Po.

PART 1

Leadership and Locations

1

BEYOND THE CURRICULUM
Supporting Faculty Writing Groups in WAC Programs

Chris Anson

An acquaintance, the director of a writing across the curriculum (WAC) program at a highly prestigious, research-obsessed university that sports a number of Nobel prize winners, once shared with me her frustrations attracting faculty to workshops and activities that focused on teaching. The program's heart beat to the rhythm of improving support for student writing. Outreach was its vascular system, circulating vital instructional reform throughout the campus. Participation was its lifeblood. But no matter how hard the program tried to draw faculty to its events, they shied away, almost embarrassed to be seen vacating their well-appointed labs and offices to attend a teaching-related event—even for the best box lunch in the state or a wine-and-hors d'oeuvres reception to rival an elegant fundraiser. Workshops, informal presentations, and colloquia on student writing drew scattered interest and uncomfortably few participants. What goals and interests, the director wondered, motivated her colleagues? Clearly, they feared wasting valuable time on something they were trying to do *less* of. How could she get them to that place where the hope of gain lines up, like a rare celestial phenomenon, with a willingness to engage?

After much thought, she decided to put on a session about faculty publication. Widely billed as an event focusing on how to improve the chances of getting into print, it featured three faculty members from different disciplines who each edited a prestigious journal and could provide advice and strategies about publication from well-informed positions. The session included testimonials by prolific scholar-writers about their own best practices, breakouts for small-group discussion, and presentations on campus resources.

DOI: 10.7330/9780874219029.c001

Faculty packed the room, giving up office hours, lab time, lunch dates, and even class sessions to attend. Realizing that they had a captive audience, the director and her colleagues drew attention to their program and urged faculty to become involved in some of its teaching-related activities. The faculty were there because, deep in their work ethic and reinforced through years of both explicit and tacit systems of rewards and punishments, they held sacred the goal of academic publication. But their need to understand and develop strategies for their own writing was potentially a way to begin thinking more deeply and productively about the role of writing in their courses.

Descriptions of WAC programs usually highlight their focus on instructional development and curricular improvement. Although today the approaches to this work vary considerably, shaped to specific institutional needs and cultures, it's still the exception to find activities and resources focusing on the faculty's own scholarly and professional writing. However, a number of WAC programs have mounted initiatives that draw on or support the writing experiences of faculty themselves. While these efforts are scattered, their success suggests that, on a national scale, we should pursue more opportunities to assist faculty with their own writing, in addition to helping them more richly understand, and tend to, the needs of their students. At the same time, we must continue to explore the assumption that focusing on the professional writing of faculty leads them inductively to improve their support for student writing. Although several chapters in this collection offer useful arguments for this relationship, it still remains largely unexplored and theoretically questionable.

This chapter will first briefly contextualize faculty writing in the history of the WAC movement. It will then turn to several types of writing-related activities that WAC programs are currently sponsoring as a way to extend their reach into supporting faculty members' own professional writing and making stronger connections between that writing, their teaching, and their students' writing. Finally, it will offer some cautions, particularly with respect to issues of agency, ownership, and disciplinarity, about how to encourage faculty writing in WAC programs even as this appears to define the next stage of program development and the creation of a culture of writing on college campuses.

THE LEGACY OF WRITING IN FACULTY WORKSHOPS

Engaging faculty in writing stretches back to the beginning of the WAC movement in the 1970s, when most workshops were organized at smaller liberal arts colleges that had strong teaching missions (Russell, 2002).

By the 1980s, WAC was rapidly taking hold at larger research-oriented universities, where writing continued to play an important role in teaching-oriented faculty development activities. Art Young, for example, describes the genesis of the workshops he and his colleagues founded at Michigan Technological University, one of the most self-studied WAC efforts at a larger institution:

> These workshops were hands-on-pen experiences that lasted two to four consecutive days and nights, and participants themselves spent much of the time writing . . . . Individual workshops were structured in such a way that teacher-writers experienced firsthand the pedagogical theories of James Britton, Peter Elbow, Janet Emig, Ken Macrorie, James Moffett, and others who advised teachers to consider the writing process in instruction and to emphasize writing as a learning activity as well as a means of communication. . . . Teachers who participated in the workshops experienced, in one way or another, collaborative writing exercises, small-group dynamics, oral and written peer feedback between successive drafts, writing anxiety, writer's block, writing for themselves, writing for others, writing for discovery, writing to communicate, and feeling good about writing. (Young 1986, 9)

Having faculty write and share that writing during workshops that focused mainly on teaching was said to mirror students' experiences in the classroom. Engaging in writing exercises could "reacquaint [participants] with the frustrations (and joys) of the composing process" (Fulwiler 1986b, 23). The struggle to write, and the humility of sharing half-baked drafts with colleagues who normally showcase the outcomes of their considerable disciplinary talents and expertise, yielded sympathies for students grappling with challenging course assignments; more important, those experiences could quite viscerally show faculty why instructional support for writing is so important.

Initially, the process movement's emphasis on experience ("What happens when I write?") was meant to show faculty how to support students' writing through various activities that made explicit what was needed for success—including revealing their own struggles. Integrating this sort of meta-awareness into coursework was also said to encourage students and teachers to recognize each other as writers. Starting in now-classic works such as Murray's (1968) *A Writer Teaches Writing* and continuing throughout the history of the National Writing Project, teachers have been urged to "write along with their students." As one NWP participant rhetorically asks, "When we write with our students and share with them our uncertainties about word-choice, a topic, or organization, won't they be much more willing to do the same?" (Alber 2012).

Over time, the extensive writing experiences included in early WAC workshops were replaced with a stronger focus on teaching (Thaiss, personal communication). The forces behind this evolution are not entirely clear, but may have come from recognition of certain tensions and contradictions between the domains of faculty and student writing, especially in higher-education institutions where scholarly publication carries such weight.

For example, while asking faculty to write helps to reform what Fulwiler calls "simplistic notions" about student writing (1986b, 23), it often serves no purpose beyond the workshop; the experience is context-bound and ephemeral. Workshop participants may come to understand the link between their own sharing of the workshop journal they are required to keep and their students' potential thinking and learning that the method fosters. But this and other tasks are, after all, usually nothing like what the participants do in their own professional circles. In the interests of connecting with faculty who hail from diverse disciplines and who write sophisticated material often impenetrable even to academics in other fields, workshop leaders usually choose disciplinarily neutral prompts, purposeful for the socially significant moment but useless once the participants leave the room. Faculty often do enjoy working with other colleagues in a "community of scholars" (Fulwiler 1986a, 243), but the disciplinary mix can't allow much, if any, serious sharing of scholarly writing. And faculty do gain insights, but they are often short-lived, soon dissipating into the other complexities of their professorial lives.

At the same time, the strategy of weaving general writing experiences into WAC workshops was meant to overcome the fact that faculty and students often write in mutually isolating domains. The genres of the academic professions are sometimes at such a distance from canonical college assignments or the kinds of pseudo-disciplinary writing that students must produce that it's difficult for faculty to imagine that it all exists along a developmental continuum. While faculty are reporting the results of complex biological experiments in food science or arguing sophisticated statistical projections in economics, students are trying their best to summarize articles, develop a thesis about two conflicting events, or put together accurate, concise lab reports. If there is any flaw in the principle that "our reflective interaction with our own writing efforts informs and animates our interactions with our student writers" (Gillespie 1985), it's that the processes and struggles of college-level faculty are most meaningful to them in the context of the most meaningful work they produce, which is the least often included in cross-disciplinary WAC workshops. The wall between faculty and student writing is a construction based on misunderstandings of the common processes and needs of writers at different ends of the sophistication continuum. But not directly appealing to the writing interests of faculty may simply strengthen that wall instead of breaking it down.

Teachers' perceptions of their own writing abilities also play a role in deciding how or whether to tap into their experiences (Young and Fulwiler 1990). When working with faculty across a range of disciplines, WAC leaders are often asked, "How can I help students to write if I'm not such a good writer myself?" The response, almost unanimous in the literature, argues that all faculty write within their disciplines, and that it's only their (mis)conceptions about "good writing" that make that fact invisible to them. The concern rises to even higher levels when it comes to grammar. Many faculty, whether English is their first language or not, confess to not knowing all the intricacies of grammar well enough to be of help. They are admonished to "focus on students' meaning." When faculty argue that they're not great writers because what they teach isn't even remotely about writing (dance, drawing, small engine repair), they're encouraged to see writing as a powerful medium for learning their subject, rather than as a skill to be mastered. Such a response suggests to faculty that there is no necessary relationship between being an accomplished writer as a teacher and supporting students' own writing. This strategy, wise for orienting faculty toward the uses of writing to learn, doesn't always clarify the differences between what students will write professionally after graduation and what they're writing in the classroom.

Another possible reason for the decline of heavily writing-focused WAC workshops was an eventual differentiation of K–12 and university interests. Early on, leaders of college-level WAC programs were inspired by the work of the National Writing Project, which focused primarily on teaching in the K–12 context (see Russell 1992; McLeod and Soven 2006). The aim of encouraging K–12 teachers to write grew from similar beliefs about the relationship between experiential self-awareness and the improvement of teaching. But the teachers had to be encouraged to write in the first place, and to do so "in front of . . . students, [so] they can see what a sloppy, difficult act writing is for all writers" (Gillespie 1985; see also Robbins 1992). This blurring of the needs of K–12 teachers with those of university faculty eventually gave way to sharper distinctions between the two groups. Books such as *Teacher as Writer: Entering the Professional Conversation* (Dahl 1992) inspired overworked K–12 teachers to write. Meanwhile, faculty in most colleges and universities needed no additional persuasion than their promotion and tenure codes, but few resources existed, alongside all the emphasis on student writing, to help them succeed.

Many teaching-oriented WAC workshops in colleges and universities still involve some vestigial writing, usually in brief episodes to demonstrate the principles of writing-to-learn. But the production of entire texts through cycles of drafting, sharing, and revising is now rare. Recognizing the loss of a focus on teachers' own writing, however, a number of WAC directors are rethinking ways they can bring faculty together to discuss and practice their own writing beyond the usual teaching workshop model. These opportunities appear to define the goals of faculty writing quite differently by avoiding the use of writing as a subterfuge for focusing directly on issues relating to students' own writing and learning, and enhancing opportunities for faculty to reflect on and learn strategies for their own professional publication. As we'll see in the next section, these more recent developments position faculty as writers in their disciplinary contexts and extend the role of the WAC program from student learning to faculty support. In this expansion of services, WAC programs rely on decades of instructional work helping faculty to think more deeply about the role of writing in their courses, but at the same time move into less charted territories where new dangers lurk beyond the edges of prior experience.

FACULTY WRITING WORKSHOPS AND RETREATS

The most direct expansion of WAC programs into the realm of faculty writing is through seminars or presentations that focus on strategies for writing and publishing, or on workshops or retreats where faculty work collaboratively to support the development of drafts in progress. Because they are brief, the former don't involve extensive work on individual projects, which will see progress at home or in the office as a result of the new insights and energy the sessions inspire. They typically include discussions of how to overcome self-defeating habits, how to target an article toward a specific journal, or how to create backward timelines or use online tools such as Timelinemaker to systematically move a project toward completion. Sessions sometimes include strategies for publishing a book and may feature invited editors from university and trade publishers or faculty with experience on editorial boards. Clearly, these sorts of events are especially helpful for early-career researchers and graduate students who recognize the importance of writing and publishing but have not yet developed tools for success.

The latter kind of direct experience may require a longer commitment from participants, who bring with them a writing project that they want to move toward completion. Typically, the sessions are at least a full day and more often take the form of multiple-day retreats. Participants write for long stretches of time, punctuated by occasional discussions and idea sharing. Faculty are often sent some articles to read before they meet, but the time is mostly devoted to writing. Some programs sponsor longer writing retreats when classes are not in session, such as week-long sanctuaries that often take place in a comfortable space, away from the distractions of home and office. Although the benefits of participating in writing workshops and retreats are intrinsic (moving a manuscript toward publication, developing new tools for productivity, meeting and working with colleagues from other disciplines), faculty at some institutions must apply competitively for admission and receive stipends for their participation. To earn these stipends, they are often required to set and achieve daily writing goals and engage in peer review.

Support for faculty writing also varies from directly-provided advice in briefer presentations, to the sort of hand-holding and collaboration common in longer workshops, to nothing but the requirement of engagement. The weeklong "boot camp" experience, for example, may include strict rules for participation, such as when participants must arrive, how long they must stay and write, what they may not bring (such as cell phones), and how much total time they must be in attendance. But as directed as these intensive experiences are, they also offer a high degree of camaraderie and often culminate in a party or happy hour. Interestingly, such retreats insist on the need for solitary immersion in one's work yet rely heavily on creating a sense of collective experience. As Elbow and Sorcinelli (2006, 18) put it in their description of running fifteen years of faculty writing retreats at Univerity of Massachusetts Amherst, success "is predicated on the notion that faculty will be more apt to do the solitary work of writing if they surround themselves with other writers pursuing the same goal." Such retreats represent a shift from "offering *workshops* to offering *space* to help faculty work on their scholarly writing" (18). Other varieties of workshop experiences include "courses" in which faculty meet once or twice a week for several months and may focus on specific topics such as improving academic style.

DISCIPLINARY AND CROSS-DISCIPLINARY WRITING GROUPS AND CIRCLES

General-advice sessions, the provision of "rooms of one's own" to write on campus, and the kinds of "lock-in" retreats described above avoid a vexing problem when faculty from different disciplines assemble to work together on writing projects: disciplinary specialization. Talking about how to avoid procrastination or hearing from journal editors about strategies for preparing articles can be useful across disciplinary contexts. But unless faculty from the same or closely allied disciplines can be grouped together, it's difficult or impossible for any member to get feedback of the kind they will face from manuscript reviewers in their field—feedback focusing on the complex, disciplinary content they're working with. At the highest reaches of work in their fields, writers need to move beyond general rhetorical concerns and into what they are saying about the sophisticated concepts, research findings, and phenomena they are writing about. Among all the processes that faculty can engage in to improve a piece of writing, none will be more effective than having other disciplinary professionals read and respond to it.

One solution to this problem is to create writing groups within departments or generalized disciplinary areas that produce closely allied kinds of scholarship (see Rankin 2001). Modeled on theories of "learning communities" or "communities of practice" (Lave and Wenger 1991), such groups or "circles" can be another extension of the service provided by a WAC program or office. Some programs, for example, help faculty to establish small, ongoing writing groups of two to five members each. Groups typically meet once a week but focus on one member's work during each meeting. To facilitate such discussions, WAC leaders need more than just good public relations skills and an ability to attract faculty from the same department or discipline. As Mullin (2008, 195) puts it, a WAC director "serves as a conduit who both facilitates and benefits from a continual evolution of strategies produced with faculty." This requires of WAC experts, Mullin argues, "a certain disciplinary neutrality, a meta-awareness of their own frames" (196). It also means cultivating knowledge of disciplinary discourses and their heteroglossic histories (Bazerman 1992, 243), which poses a challenge for the newer and less experienced WAC director.

Some WAC leaders' experiences running cross-disciplinary groups do point toward their benefits in spite of the problem of specialization. In one of the earliest faculty-writing efforts by WAC specialists, McLeod and Emery found that they could "give helpful suggestions to colleagues who were not in our disciplines, in spite of the fact that we might not always understand the more abstruse points being made" (McLeod and Emery 1988, 67). They also found that regardless of discipline, faculty brought shared problems to the workshops, such as the tendency to "clear the throat" in the first two pages of a draft before really getting to the point on the third (67). Similarly, Rankin reports that faculty in interdisciplinary writing groups felt that reading work in progress in other disciplines "stretches the mind," gets them out of their "normal routine," and provides one of the few places where faculty can hear about other disciplines (Rankin 2001, 105). More important, however, Rankin established working procedures that included a set of "writer's responsibilities" (such as providing explanations of drafts to orient readers), guidelines on how to read drafts in progress (such as starting not at the sentence level but at higher levels of content and purpose), and a requirement for progress reports. These processes focused entirely on creating a positive working climate for groups of scholar-teachers, but they obviously closely parallel best practices in supporting students' writing. In addition, the ground rules helped to overcome at least some of the challenges faculty face when reading the specialized work of their colleagues in other disciplines.

WRITING IN THE SCHOLARSHIP OF TEACHING AND LEARNING

The dominant model of faculty development in WAC programs assumes a strong focus on the principles of implementation with a relatively shallow emphasis on underlying theory and research. Teachers are often enjoined to use student revision groups, design evaluation rubrics with clear criteria, or integrate low-stakes writing-to-learn activities into their courses, but rarely are they encouraged to study, reflect on, or formally investigate the role of these strategies in their students' learning. It is in this context that WAC programs have taken an interest in a broader movement in higher education to encourage "reflective practice" among faculty (Schön 1983) and a more intentional focus on instructional problem-solving. Collectively known as the scholarship of teaching and learning (SoTL), these efforts can be seen in the number of recently published books and articles on subject; the founding of the *Journal of the Scholarship of Teaching and Learning*; shifts in focus from student achievement to teacher performance at various levels of assessment; the growth of teaching-focused programs such as Preparing Future Faculty; and the increase in organizational support for SoTL such as the Carnegie Academy for the Scholarship of Teaching and Learning, the Maricopa Institute, and the Visible Knowledge Project. This SoTL activity finds theoretical support from higher education reformers such as Ernest Boyer (1990), whose groundbreaking *Scholarship Reconsidered: Priorities of the Professoriate* (1990) led to widespread discussions about the false dichotomy of teaching and research.

Although activities focusing on SoTL have been more prominent in teaching and learning centers, some WAC leaders have asked how their programs can help faculty to engage in more systematic investigations of the role of writing in their instruction and whether their classroom strategies help students to improve as learners, thinkers, and writers. Faculty members' own writing plays a role in two kinds of SoTL-related activities: *teaching portfolios* and *classroom-based reflection and research* on writing that can be published in professional teaching journals and books on discipline-specific pedagogy.

The teaching portfolio drew considerable interest throughout the late 1980s and 1990s. Spurred on by activities sponsored by the American Association of Higher Education and a number of useful publications (e.g., Edgerton, Hutchings, and Quinlan 1991; Seldin 1991), the teaching portfolio encourages faculty to take control of how their work is displayed and provides richer descriptions of the contexts in which their teaching occurs. Like student writing portfolios, teaching portfolios are said to realize two assessment-related purposes. One is *formative*—creating, selecting, revising, and arranging the artifacts of teaching fosters deeper thinking about instruction and therefore indirectly leads to insights and improvements. The other is *summative*—the portfolio offers multiple perspectives on a teacher's work for purposes of evaluating strengths and weaknesses. Central to both functions is the role of reflection. In addition to "primary documents," or materials already required as a condition of the job (syllabi, assignments, student evaluations, etc.), teachers also write additional "secondary documents," such as educational philosophies, reflections on comments written on students' papers, annotations on syllabi explaining particular choices, analyses of student evaluation comments, and the like (see Anson 1994).

Most WAC programs have not yet extended their reach to help with teaching portfolios, which writing experts may be more comfortable supporting than those who coordinate general teaching and learning centers. In the late 1990s, I ran a number of faculty workshops at the University of Minnesota, on behalf of its teaching and learning center, that focused on writing strong portfolio entries. Participants raised complex questions about the style and voice of entries, how evaluation-minded readers might respond to specific details (particularly any disclosure of "failure moments" that led to new insights), what stance to take or ethos to convey, how to structure the portfolio, whether to cross-reference documents, and so on. These complexities suggested that WAC programs are excellent sites for sessions focusing on the preparation of teaching portfolios or other kinds of professional dossiers. However, WAC leaders must be prepared to help their colleagues—both faculty and administrators—to face "unique challenges in their responsibility to create fair, uniform practices in the creation and interpretation of portfolios" (Anson and Dannels 2002, 97). Facilitating such work requires WAC leaders who understand the ways that writing represents faculty members' instructional ideologies, which include whether they see themselves as "reflective practitioners" (Schön, 1983) who have a lifelong dedication to continuous improvement. Ideally, writing workshops sponsored by WAC programs can focus on the ethos faculty establish in their entries, their interpretation of teaching activities, and how the expression of their activities and beliefs can, in turn, continue to affect who they are as teachers. This professionally-oriented discourse stands somewhere between the purely discipline-based academic writing faculty must do and the direct artifacts of their teaching, such as syllabi and assignments, and the reflective demonstration of it to evaluators.

More formal versions of reflective practice involve classroom-based research, or "action research," designed to explore interesting dimensions of teaching and learning in a localized way but with potential generalizability. Using a process akin to Kolb's (1984) well-known experiential learning cycle, teachers go into their classrooms prepared not just to teach but to observe phenomena in their students' learning. The observations can easily turn into hypotheses involving various causal connections between, for example, instructional intervention and effects on students' behaviors or learning. The reflective practitioner experiments with new strategies and methods in an informal and student-centered way, both improving instructional delivery and, over time, developing higher levels of awareness and expertise. Regardless of their discipline, reflective practitioners ideally bring this expertise to public forums such as journals, electronic publications, and conferences that include a focus on teaching. Dozens of pedagogical journals exist for instructors on all levels, especially in higher education. In my work analyzing articles in fourteen of these journals (Anson 2010; Anson and Lyles 2011), many compelling descriptions of instructional approaches and strategies that might be considered "anecdotal" or based on teacher "lore" (North 1987) nevertheless had their genesis in careful, systematic observations and analyses with high levels of integrity. Meanwhile, collaborations between WAC specialists and faculty in the disciplines, which have a long if not robust tradition starting in the 1980s (e.g., Young and Fulwiler 1986), continue apace with the publication of entire edited volumes containing chapters by faculty at specific institutions (Monroe 2003; Rutz, 2004; Segall and Smart, 2005).

An interest in such experiments can lead to classroom-based projects that adhere to the principles of formal research and involve IRB approvals, careful data collection and analysis, and a grounding in existing knowledge about instructional method. The Campus Writing and Speaking Program at North Carolina State University, for example, offers faculty the opportunity to take part in an "assisted inquiry" program. This program provides faculty with support for carrying out classroom-based research studies that focus on writing and/or speaking in instruction. Typically, a teacher in a discipline is struck by some question relating to writing and/or speaking in their course instruction and becomes motivated to set up a research project to explore it. At that point, they can get assistance from the program in proportion to their needs. For some, help may include refining the question, deciding what kind of data will be best suited to exploring the question, collecting the data, choosing methods for analyzing it, and then collaboratively writing up the results of the project for publication in a teaching-related journal and/or for presentation at conferences. For others, it may involve getting some feedback on a project already informed by the teacher's expertise in researching writing- or speaking-related instructional questions. An extension of the assisted inquiry program involves collaboratively authoring grants focusing on communication in instruction and then, together, writing up the results for publication. In this way, the program involves reciprocity between *studying* writing-related instructional questions and then *writing and publishing* the results. Although assisted inquiry represents only a fraction of the services that the Campus Writing and Speaking Program provides to faculty, it adds an element of support for writing that emerges from the professional and academic interests of faculty while also contributing to the broader goals, through research, of improving undergraduate education. Working with colleagues in different disciplines on projects that move toward publication in professional journals also advances the career goals of the WAC directors and their graduate students, increases the visibility of the program as a place that promotes and assists in research, and furthers the program's interest in cross-disciplinary collaboration.

TREADING LIGHTLY

The preceding sketch of innovations, instantiated in several contributions to this collection, suggests that a growing number of WAC programs are reinventing themselves and extending their teaching-focused support to address the writing needs of faculty more directly. By all accounts, these innovations are being received positively if not enthusiastically. Although I have generalized them according to their goals, duration, and audiences, it is important for us to remember that each program has adapted to or developed from unique, local needs and cultures—a process that has characterized the development of WAC programs more broadly (see McLeod and Soven 2006, 5). Adapting *to* institutional cultures instead of adopting a "template" or "missionary" approach (Mullin 2008, 197) is crucial to the long-term success of any WAC program, which should brand itself not as a place that "talks to" faculty but where faculty can come together to explore and negotiate their professional identities and the way that writing shapes those identities. In WAC directors' eagerness to broaden our reach across our campuses and extend our programs' services, we ignore this principle of localizing practices to our disadvantage.

First, WAC leaders must position themselves and their programs carefully as they support the professional writing of faculty, and this will depend on an institution's mission, type, and culture. Tapping into the impressive base of knowledge that has accumulated in the field can be illuminating for colleagues who haven't thought much about writing and don't know what the research says about phenomena such as anxiety or self-efficacy. But it's also dangerous to tell faculty on some campuses about how writing works in their own disciplines, no matter how much discourse specialists have studied it and how little the faculty there have reflected on it. Deciding *what* to focus on in faculty workshops is perhaps less important than figuring out how to present it to experts who already know—if tacitly—about their field's genres and discourse practices. Walvoord (1992, 11), for example, has cautioned us about the instructional dimensions of WAC (not to adopt a "training" approach, not to assume a "conversion" model in which "faculty in other disciplines are heathen who must be converted to the Right Way," and not to simplify WAC into a "problem/solution" model). Likewise, in curricular consultations, WAC experts have learned to take on the ethos of an interested investigator, asking questions about how the discipline defines good communication, taking notes, and listening far more than talking (Anson et al. 2003; Carter 2003). Eventually, after days or weeks of study, the WAC expert can make some observations that the disciplinary faculty can consider and begin to implement—but the relationship is always asymmetrical, the authority for change clearly located among the "clients." Less examined but just as consequential is the question of role and authority in faculty writing workshops, where WAC leaders can take on the subject position of administrative functionaries, there purely to facilitate and organize, or of writing consultants who, like tutors in a writing center, may have quite varied expertise helping with the challenges of writing discipline-based and sometimes complex genres and dealing with content far beyond their own knowledge and expertise.

As WAC program continue to evolve, especially in providing more opportunities to focus on the professional writing of faculty, it will be important to return to the relationship between the professional contexts of that writing and the academic contexts in which students write. These relationships often surface during the faculty-centered opportunities surveyed here. But much depends on the perceived distance between students' writing and what their teachers write. While there is no question that faculty writing opportunities are also ideal venues to focus on teaching, how and when to "go meta" and explicitly address those linkages is a matter that deserves thoughtful planning and reflection. For example, encouraging teachers in the disciplines to design assignments and projects that help students to become "insiders" in their fields, as Eng (2002) does, may erase concerns about the disconnect between the kinds of discourse being practiced in the classroom and in the profession. Eng describes several ways he creates a continuum from classroom-based to publishable writing in his courses, strategies that could be profitably extended into teachers' work with student writing across the disciplines. Yet as empowering and instructionally useful as such practices appear on the surface, they remain largely untheorized. Sharing her own public genres of writing, a teacher's struggles to find the right tone or be persuasive can model certain kinds of composing strategies while also helping students to assume more accurate views of writing (e.g., that it doesn't get easier as it gets better). But such an apprenticeship approach must be adapted to the more specific context of instruction. A teacher who shows first-year composition students pages from the sixth chapter of his book in progress may do little to ease their writing apprehension or help them to see that all writers face the same challenges. Similarly, an engineering professor who shares her letter to the editor about gun control with a group of seniors in a capstone engineering course will do little to draw them into the professional world of engineering. And while the lore about writing alongside students includes powerful anecdotes about the success of this practice, it is confounded by too many variables to have produced much supporting research.

As the initiatives described in this volume demonstrate, expanding WAC programs to include support for faculty writing and publication is one way to broaden the program's influence. Many leaders of WAC programs have focused exclusively on the teaching mission—nobly so, but at some risk of losing a significant number of faculty who will not, under any circumstances, attend a teaching-related event. But this resistance is as true for faculty in the fast lane to academic stardom as it is for tenured idlers who have all but given up on the research mission (and may have convinced themselves on the basis of reasonably good student evaluations that "they already know how to teach"). No easy equation exists, then, between the amount of professional writing faculty members produce, or their passion for teaching, and the likelihood that they will engage in WAC-sponsored activities of any sort. Each program must find ways to balance the two sets of interests and, finally, be willing to give up on those who simply refuse to engage.

In thinking of ways that writing centers and WAC programs can extend their reach, Parks and Goldblatt (2000) suggest moving beyond discipline-based and academic contexts and into service-learning projects, community-based programs, and programs in business and industry. When a program's resources allow it, such support for writing in beyond-campus contexts is laudable. At the same time, we should not neglect areas on our campuses where additional support for writing can help to broaden the academic missions of WAC programs. And that certainly includes supporting the writing of faculty, staff, and graduate students alongside that of undergraduates. Healthy collaborations await— between WAC programs and centers for teaching and learning, offices of research development, certificate programs for graduate student development such as local Preparing Future Faculty efforts, professional writing programs housed within collegiate units (such as those in legal or business writing), and various extension programs that bring faculty together with business or agricultural leaders.

Perhaps more important, creating a "culture of writing" at an institution is not so much a matter of offering more and more workshops and retreats for different groups, but, as Herrington and Moran have suggested, viewing all participants on a campus—administrators, faculty, staff, and students—as part of an interrelated system (Herrington and Moran 1992, ix). Assuming such directions, the next stage in writing across the curriculum will need to include new and complex questions, many that are taken up in the other contributions to this collection: How can we coordinate resources effectively to meet the needs of these different participants while creating a sense of shared values? How can we position WAC programs neither as offices devoted to the logistics of arranging rooms and box lunches for open faculty discussions nor as centers of expertise that tell faculty what they ought to know or how best to write and teach writing? How can we raise the awareness of faculty about their own literate histories and current practices and *effectively* lead them to realize implications of that awareness for how they work with students? And how can WAC programs remain open to learning *from* faculty across the curriculum about the many specific genres, working conventions, and uses for writing that characterize and inform their disciplines? Such questions will require a new kind of inquisitiveness among WAC leaders and a willingness to relinquish some measure of authority in an effort to encourage the kinds of transformative experiences that lead to growth, self-awareness, and success.

REFERENCES

Alber, Rebecca. 2012. "Do You Write with Your Students?" *Edutopia* (blog). http://www.edutopia.org/blog/writing-students-literacy-rebecca-alber.

Anson, Chris M. 2010. "The Intradisciplinary Influence of Composition on Writing Across the Curriculum, 1967–1986." *WAC Journal* 21:5–20.

Anson, Chris M., and Karla Lyles. 2011. "The Intradisciplinary Influence of Composition on Writing Across the Curriculum, Part Two: 1986–2006." *WAC Journal* 22:7–19.

Anson, Chris M. 1994. "Portfolios for Teachers: Writing our Way to Reflective Practice." In *New Directions in Portfolio Assessment*, ed. Laurel Black, Donald A. Daiker, Jeffrey Sommers, and Gail Stygall, 185–200. Portsmouth, NH: Heinemann.

Anson, Chris M., and Deanna Dannels. 2002. "The Medium and the Message: Developing Responsible Methods for Assessing Teaching Portfolios." In *Composition Pedagogy and the Scholarship of Teaching*, ed. Deborah Minter and Amy M. Goodburn, 89–100. Portsmouth, NH: Heinemann.

Anson, Chris M., Michael Carter, Deanna Dannels, and Jon Rust. 2003. "Mutual Support: CAC Programs and Institutional Improvement in Undergraduate Education." *Journal of Language and Learning Across the Disciplines* 6:26–38.

Bazerman, Charles. 1992. "From Cultural Criticism to Disciplinary Participation: Living with Powerful Words." In *Writing, Teaching, and Learning in the Disciplines*, ed. Anne Herrington and Charles Moran, 61–68. New York: MLA.

Boyer, Ernest L. 1990. *Scholarship Reconsidered: Priorities of the Professoriate*. San Franscisco: Jossey-Bass and the Carnegie Foundation for the Advancement of Teaching. Carnegie Academy. http://www.carnegiefoundation.org/scholarship-teaching-learning.

Carter, Michael. 2003. "A Process for Establishing Outcomes-Based Assessment Plans for Writing and Speaking in the Disciplines." *Language and Learning Across the Disciplines* 6 (1): 4–29.

Dahl, Karyn, ed. 1992. *Teacher as Writer: Entering the Professional Conversation*. Urbana, IL: NCTE.

Edgerton, Russell, Pat Hutchings, and Kathleen Quinlan, eds. 1991. *The Teaching Portfolio: Capturing the Scholarship in Teaching*. Washington, D.C.: American Association of Higher Education.

Elbow, Peter, and Mary Deane Sorcinelli. 2006. "The Faculty Writing Place: A Room of One's Own." *Change* 38 (6): 17–22. http://dx.doi.org/10.3200/CHNG.38.6.17-22.

Eng, Joseph. 2002. "Teachers as Writers and Students as Writers: Writing, Publishing, and Monday-Morning Agendas." *Writing Instructor* 2 (5). http://www.writinginstructor.com/essays/eng.html.

Fulwiler, Toby. 1986a. "How Well Does Writing Across the Curriculum Work?" In *Writing Across the Disciplines: Theory Into Practice*, ed. Art Young and Toby Fulwiler, 235–246. Upper Montclair, NJ: Boynton/Cook.

Fulwiler, Toby. 1986b. "The Argument for Writing Across the Curriculum." In *Writing Across the Disciplines: Theory Into Practice*, ed. Art Young and Toby Fulwiler, 21–32. Upper Montclair, NJ: Boynton/Cook.

Gillespie, Tim. 1985. "Becoming Your Own Expert: Teachers as Writers." *The Quarterly* 8 (1): n.p. http://www.nwp.org/cs/public/print/resource/1708.

Herrington, Anne, and Charles Moran. 1992. *Writing, Teaching, and Learning in the Disciplines.* New York: Modern Language Association.

Kolb, David A. 1984. *Experiential Learning.* Englewood Cliffs, NJ: Prentice Hall.

Lave, Jean, and Etienne Wenger. 1991. *Situated Learning: Legitimate Peripheral Participation.* Cambridge: Cambridge University Press. http://dx.doi.org/10.1017/CBO9780511815355.

McLeod, Susan H., and Laura Emery. 1988. "When Faculty Write: A Workshop for Colleagues." *College Composition and Communication* 39 (1): 65–7. http://dx.doi.org/10.2307/357820.

McLeod, Susan H., and Margot Iris Soven, eds. 2006. *Composing a Community: A History of Writing across the Curriculum.* Anderson, SC: Parlor Press.

Monroe, Jonathan, ed. 2003. *Local Knowledges, Local Practices: Writing in the Disciplines at Cornell.* Pittsburgh: University of Pittsburgh Press.

Murray, Donald. 1968. *A Writer Teaches Writing: A Practical Method of Teaching Composition.* New York: Houghton Mifflin.

Mullin, Joan A. 2008. "Interdisciplinary Work as Professional Development: Changing the Culture of Teaching." *Pedagogy: Critical Approaches to Teaching Literature, Composition, and Culture* 8 (3): 495–508. http://dx.doi.org/10.1215/15314200-2008-008.

North, Stephen M. 1987. *The Making of Knowledge in Composition: Portrait of an Emerging Field.* Upper Montclair, NJ: Boynton/Cook.

Parks, Steve, and Eli Goldblatt. 2000. "Writing Beyond the Curriculum: Fostering New Collaborations in Literacy." *College English* 62 (5): 584–606. http://dx.doi.org/10.2307/378963.

Rankin, Elizabeth. 2001. *The Work of Writing: Insights and Strategies for Academics and Professionals.* San Francisco: Jossey-Bass.

Robbins, Bruce. 1992. "It's Not That Simple: Some Teachers as Writers." *English Journal* 81 (4): 72–74. http://dx.doi.org/10.2307/819936.

Russell, David. 2002. *Writing in the Academic Disciplines: A Curricular History.* Carbondale: Southern Illinois University Press.

Russell, David. 1992. "American Orgins of the Writing-Across-the-Curriculum Movement." In *Writing, Teaching and Learning in the Disciplines*, ed. Anne Herrington and Charles Moran, 22–42. New York: Modern Language Association.

Rutz, Carol. 2004. *Reflections on Learning as Teachers.* Northfield, MN: Carleton College.

Schön, Donald A. 1983. *The Reflective Practitioner: How Professionals Think in Action.* London: Temple Smith.

Segall, Mary T., and Robert A. Smart, eds. 2005. *Direct from the Disciplines: Writing Across the Curriculum.* Portsmouth, NH: Heinemann.

Seldin, Peter. 1991. *The Teaching Portfolio: A Practical Guide to Improved Performance and Promotion/Tenure Decisions.* Boston: Anker.

Walvoord, Barbara E. 1992. "Getting Started." In *Writing Across the Curriculum: A Guide to Developing Programs*, ed. Susan H. McLeod and Margaret Soven, 9–22. Newbury Park, CA: Sage.

Young, Art. 1986. "Rebuilding Community in the English Department." In *Writing Across the Disciplines: Theory into Practice*, ed. Art Young and Toby Fulwiler, 6–20. Upper Montclair, NJ: Boynton/Cook.

Young, Art, and Toby Fulwiler. 1990. "The Enemies of Writing Across the Curriculum." In *Programs that Work: Models and Methods for Writing Across the Curriculum*, ed. Toby Fulwiler and Art Young, 287–294. Portsmouth, NH: Heinemann Boynton/Cook.

Young, Art, and Toby Fulwiler. 1986. *Writing Across the Disciplines: Research into Practice.* Upper Montclair, NJ: Boynton/Cook.

2

THE SCHOLARLY WRITING CONTINUUM
A New Program Model for Teaching and Faculty Development Centers

Brian Baldi, Mary Deane Sorcinelli, and Jung H. Yun

INTRODUCTION

Since 2000, faculty roles and responsibilities have changed profoundly, with new patterns in faculty appointments, expanding workloads, and greater pressure to seek funding and publish scholarly work (Gappa, Austin, and Trice 2007). These new demands heighten the need for flexible professional development opportunities so that faculty with different needs can succeed in a more complex workplace.

A large-scale study of the field of faculty development indicates that most teaching and learning centers focus on supporting faculty in their role as teachers (Sorcinelli, Austin, et al. 2006). At the same time, research shows that faculty members encounter challenges beyond teaching that, if not overcome, can hurt their productivity and stall their careers. In particular, women faculty commonly report that a lack of support for scholarly writing is a key obstacle to a successful academic career (Grant and Knowles 2000).

In response, some centers for teaching and faculty development have created scholarly writing programs. Typically, these programs offer structured writing retreats or writing groups, both of which receive high ratings (Ambos, Wiley, and Allen 2009; Elbow and Sorcinelli 2006; Gray and Birch 2001; Sorcinelli, Gray, and Birch 2011). In fact, most of the literature on the benefits of academic writing programs focuses on intensive, highly structured interventions (Dickson-Swift et al. 2009; Grant and Knowles 2000; Gray and Birch 2001; Moore 2003; Murray and Newton 2009; Swaggerty et al. 2011). What is largely absent from

DOI: 10.7330/9780874219029.c002

the literature is a framework for scholarly writing programs that allows faculty to participate in their own development, according to their own needs, in a variety of times and formats.

At the University of Massachusetts Amherst's Center for Teaching and Faculty Development (CTFD), we have developed an innovative and comprehensive continuum of writing programs designed to accommodate the diverse needs of our faculty. In this chapter, we briefly discuss why supporting scholarly writing is important, why some teaching and/or faculty development centers are extending their programming into this arena, and how they are designing their offerings. We then describe the breadth of our faculty development programs for scholarly writing, which range from low-commitment, low-interaction spaces where faculty can work on their writing to personal consultations and intensive writing groups that help faculty better understand and improve their approach to writing. Our participation rates and ratings of overall effectiveness suggest that customized writing programs can better meet faculty members' unique needs and preferences for contact, structure, and commitment, and help them produce more scholarship.

THE CASE FOR SUPPORTING SCHOLARLY WRITING

The literature on faculty professional development offers compelling reasons to support faculty as writers. Many campuses are putting more emphasis on research, and reappointment, tenure, and promotion are increasingly linked to publications or successful grant writing (Mikhailova and Nilson 2007). At the same time, for many faculty, studies suggest that writing effectively and productively can be quite difficult. New faculty, for example, may have little experience with scholarly writing beyond their doctoral dissertations (Boice 2000). Publishing a book or article often requires technical as well as writing-related advice to navigate the publishing process (Dickson-Swift et al. 2009). For faculty at every career stage, finding time to write is a struggle. This is especially true for women faculty, who may have wider commitments at work and at home (Grant and Knowles 2000; Dickson-Swift et al. 2009; Misra et al. 2011; Moore 2003) Though faculty developers praise scholar-initiated writing interventions, they concur that faculty benefit from institutional support (e.g., time and space to write, formal structures and programs, access to peer mentoring and writing editors) that helps sustain scholarly writing habits (Elbow and Sorcinelli 2006; Gray and Birch 2001; Moore 2003; Sorcinelli, Gray, and Birch 2011).

Undoubtedly, strategic support for scholarly writing can enhance individual and institutional prestige. The extrinsic rewards for writing and publishing scholarly work are self-evident: reappointment, tenure and promotion, professional recognition, and salary or merit increases (Mikhailova and Nilson 2007). These rewards can extend to the institution because more and better publishing enhances institutional reputation. Studies, however, report that faculty members gain intrinsic rewards as well: greater career satisfaction, strengthened relationships with colleagues, and socialization into the larger academic culture (Boice 2000; Friend and Gonzalez 2009; Moore 2003; Washburn 2008). Ultimately, fostering a culture of support for scholarly writing can improve the academic workplace, ensuring a dynamic, supportive, and productive environment for faculty.

FACULTY DEVELOPMENT PROGRAMS FOR SCHOLARLY WRITING

A review of recent faculty development literature on scholarly writing shows that colleges and universities most frequently offer structured, intensive writing retreats and writing groups. Seven studies described writing retreats, four that were sponsored by teaching and faculty development programs (Ambos, Wiley, and Allen 2009; Dickson-Swift et al. 2009; Elbow and Sorcinelli 2006; Moore 2003) and three by faculty, academic departments, or colleges (Grant and Knowles 2000; Murray and Newton 2009; Swaggerty et al. 2011). The design and implementation of writing retreats varied. Some were off-campus and residential, and others took place on campus during working hours. The retreats ranged in length from one day to five days, and their formats included periods of individual writing only, group writing only, or individual writing mixed with group sharing and discussion of manuscripts. A few retreats also included facilitation by a writing expert, editing consultation, or panel discussions by prolific faculty writers. Faculty-initiated writing retreats were generally small, with four to twelve participants, while retreats sponsored by teaching and faculty development centers tended to be larger, with as many as fifty participants (Elbow and Sorcinelli 2006; Swaggerty et al. 2011). Meals or refreshments provided not only sustenance, but also networking time (Dickson-Swift et al. 2009). Interestingly, in five of the seven structured writing retreats reviewed, the majority or all of the participants were women (the other two studies did not report the gender of participants). Women participants were more likely to report that they struggled with heavier workloads and family commitments that stood in the way of writing; they expressed concern about their writing productivity and desired supportive networks of women (Dickson-Swift et al. 2009; Grant and Knowles 2000; Swaggerty et al. 2011).

Assessments of writers' retreats indicated that such dedicated forums can help jump-start writing projects, provide needed space and uninterrupted blocks of time for writing, create opportunities for networking with peers, and establish a community of writers (Elbow and Sorcinelli 2006; Moore 2003; Murray and Newton 2009). There was also evidence that faculty produced more and better scholarship. At the same time, participants' feedback suggested that their writing goals were often overly ambitious given the retreat timeframe, their needs as writers were too varied for a one-size-fits-all program, and they struggled to sustain the momentum of the retreat during the academic year (Ambos, Wiley, and Allen 2009; Moore 2003; Swaggerty et al. 2011).

Writing groups or "circles," sometimes linked to or preceded by a workshop on writing productivity, also figure prominently in the literature of faculty development. We examined five recent articles on writing groups, three sponsored by teaching and learning centers (Gray and Birch 2001; Sorcinelli, Gray, and Birch 2011; Washburn 2008) and two initiated by new and early-career faculty themselves (Franke 2001; Friend and Gonzalez 2009). Like writers' retreats, writers' groups vary in design and implementation, although most groups are small (three to six faculty), meet on campus, follow a regular schedule (meeting once each week to once each month), and typically use the time to share writing drafts and provide feedback on one another's manuscripts.

Perhaps the most successful model for structured writing groups originated at New Mexico State University's teaching center and has been emulated at the faculty development center at Brigham Young University, among other campuses. Both centers regularly host a writing expert to conduct a half-day, on-campus writing workshop that encourages daily writing, record-keeping, and sharing writing with peers. After the workshop, writing circles of three or four faculty meet for one hour weekly for the rest of the semester to support one another's efforts to write daily and to get feedback on what gets written each week (Gray and Birch 2001; Sorcinelli, Gray, and Birch 2011; Washburn 2008).

Evaluations of structured writers' groups show that they offer a safe, noncompetitive atmosphere for writing, a view of writing as a collaborative and developmental process, and individual and group accountability. Writing groups can also help with time management—encouraging faculty to schedule adequate time for writing amidst teaching and committee work (Franke 2001; Friend and Gonzalez 2009). Several studies also report significant increases in productivity—in the frequency of completion of writing projects, in accepted publications, and in progress made on larger works (Gray and Birch 2001; Washburn 2008). The chief limitation of structured writing groups appears to be the difficulty in sustaining them over time. Because of other work commitments, conference travel, and family vacations, attendance may be spotty, and writers may struggle to maintain the group's commitment to a regular writing and feedback cycle (Washburn 2008).

STARTING WITH ASSESSMENT

Needs assessments can help centers identify their greatest assets and challenges, as well as solicit new ideas for programming (Sorcinelli 2002). In 2006, the CTFD conducted a needs assessment to better understand the ways in which the Center could support faculty across disciplines and career stages. The assessment consisted of an online survey, focus groups with faculty at every rank, and interviews with deans, chairs, and administrators. In response to the feedback collected, we began to expand our scholarly writing offerings in 2007 with two new programs, each offered during the summer. "Publish and Thrive" was an in-person group of pre-tenure faculty that met bi-weekly with a local writing coach, while "Start Your Summer Write" was a wholly online month-long group, also comprised of pre-tenure faculty, led by a nationally-known writing coach. Originally, our intention was to compare summative feedback from both pilot groups to determine which one should continue the following year. However, we learned that faculty appreciated and benefitted from different aspects of the two programs due to their own unique work habits, writing challenges, career stages, and career advancement scenarios (e.g., plans for tenure, sabbatical, and promotion).

The data collected from our needs assessment and pilot programs drew our attention to the growing demand for not only more writing opportunities, but also a flexible range of opportunities that could accommodate the diversity of needs, interests, challenges, and preferences of faculty from our university's eighty-eight departments and nine schools and colleges. Some faculty, for example, wanted to improve their productivity by discussing their writing habits and progress on their projects in small accountability groups. Others simply wanted a quiet space where they could work on their manuscripts.

As a result, we expanded our offerings over time to create a continuum of scholarly writing programs that takes into consideration the three design features most often requested by faculty:

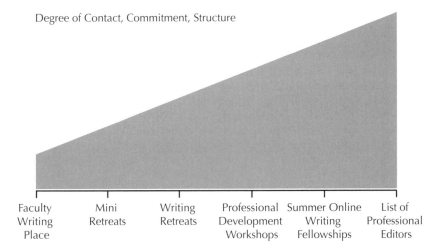

Degree of Contact, Commitment, Structure

Faculty	Mini	Writing	Professional	Summer Online	List of
Writing	Retreats	Retreats	Development	Writing	Professional
Place			Workshops	Fellowships	Editors

Figure 2.1

1. Preferences for contact (e.g., solo, one-on-one, writing group).

2. Preferences for commitment (e.g., one-time retreat, intensive, online writing fellowship).

3. Preferences for structure (e.g., unmediated writing space, highly structured writing groups).

Figure 2.1 shows the continuum of programs we have developed, and the varying degrees to which those programs offer personal contact, commitment, and structure.

Each opportunity on the continuum is carefully designed to address the varying programming preferences of our faculty while also maximizing faculty time and campus resources. Not every program is right for everyone, but somewhere along the continuum is a scholarly writing opportunity or combination of opportunities that can meet the needs of most interested faculty. What follows is a brief description of each offering, in order of degree of faculty contact, commitment, and structure, followed by an assessment of effectiveness through faculty participation rates and/or faculty's qualitative and quantitative evaluations.

CONTINUUM OF OPPORTUNITIES

- Faculty Writing Place (individual activity, low commitment, unstructured): Cosponsored by our Center and the campus library, the Faculty Writing Place is a quiet, comfortable, fully-wired common space for faculty, based on the notion that writing may be a solitary activity, but writers do not need to isolate themselves to get things done. Tucked away in a corner of the library, the room provides faculty with space to review research materials, sort through notes, start a new manuscript, or revise an existing one. It is equipped with comfortable tables and chairs, a computer and printer, a dry erase board, reference books, and writing supplies. Faculty members share the space with colleagues pursuing the same goals, and sometimes use it as a meeting place for team writing sessions. The most important aspect of the Faculty Writing Place—the focus provided by the room itself—can be replicated on many campuses at minimal cost simply by identifying a room that can be designated for faculty writing.

- Mini Writing Retreats (group activity, medium commitment, low structure): Our writing retreats have evolved over the years from offering formal writing workshops to offering time and space to help faculty work on their scholarly writing. Though the Faculty Writing Place is great for faculty who are self-motivated and require only a quiet location in which to work, some faculty find it more productive to attend scheduled writing sessions. For these writers, the CTFD offers three Mini Retreats each semester, each held in the Teaching Commons on the top floor of our campus library. Mini Retreats provide a more defined structure for writing and the shared sense of purpose afforded by a group of peers working together in proximity. Although a CTFD staff member and a Teaching Commons student worker are on site to make sure everything goes smoothly—e.g., greeting faculty, helping them get settled, passing out tickets redeemable for refreshments and light snacks at the ground floor café, and remaining available to address concerns over the course of the day—faculty frequently mention that the value of Mini Retreats is the structure they provide. A space with a regular, well-publicized schedule of dedicated writing days provides both consistency and momentum for faculty writers and their various projects.

- Writing Retreats (group activity, medium commitment, medium structure): For the past twenty years, the CTFD has hosted an Annual Faculty Writing Retreat at the end of the academic year. Originally codesigned with a noted writing professor who served as a faculty associate to our Center, the annual retreat encourages faculty to begin their summer with a full day of generative writing in an environment free from the pressures of their normal routines. As such, the annual retreat is held offsite at a proximate, affordable and quiet conference center overlooking a stream. The day begins with a brief ten-minute welcome, after which faculty set to work on their projects. A separate room is available for collaborative work. Participants gather at lunch to discuss their process, products, and plans. The CTFD also offers full-day writing retreats in August and January so faculty can make progress on their scholarly projects before the semester begins and their schedules become crowded. We advertise these retreats as opportunities to plan the semester, fine-tune syllabi, and put the finishing touches on writing projects worked on during the break. These events, which, like the Mini Retreats, are held on campus in the Teaching Commons, feature a bag lunch, an optional moderated lunchtime discussion about the craft of writing, and plenty of quiet time for working on projects. Although the details may vary from retreat to retreat and sometimes from year to year, these larger writing events during the winter and summer breaks are designed and scheduled to maximize our faculty's productivity patterns.

- Professional Development Workshops (group and individual activity, medium commitment, medium structure): In recent years, the CTFD has complemented our writing spaces and retreats with a range of professional development workshops that support the writing process in focused ways. For example, an author and editor has given presentations on the academic publishing market and converting a dissertation into a book, and she has held individual consultations about writing projects with pre-tenure faculty. A consultant on faculty diversity and development has led workshops for pre- and post-tenure faculty on writing productivity as it relates to career advancement and job satisfaction. Similarly, a productivity consultant has given campus presentations on time management, an extremely important topic to faculty writers. The CTFD typically brings in one external speaker per year and often shares sponsorship and expenses with other units.

- Summer Online Writing Fellowships (group activity, high commitment, high structure): Studies indicate that faculty produce more scholarly writing when they engage in brief, daily writing sessions, chart their progress, and share their work with others (Boice 2000). Taking this research into consideration, the CTFD has offered a month-long summer online writing program administered by two local writing coaches and experienced instructors. As part of the program, Fellows established concrete summer writing goals, tracked their writing progress online, received online guidance from a coach and peers in the program, and interacted with the writing coach and other participants through an in-person kick-off meeting and/or a mid-month consultation. The success of these online writing groups has led to the formation of smaller, self-directed groups that continue to operate online (at a minimal expense to faculty) after the end of the fellowships.

- List of Professional Editors (individual activity, high commitment, high structure): Finally, the CTFD maintains on its website a list of professional editors and coaches for faculty who want personalized scholarly writing assistance. Profiles for the editors include education credentials, relevant work experience, areas of expertise and interest, services offered, preferred work process, and rates. All editors submit three faculty references, which we check before adding them to the website. To further ensure productive work relationships, the CTFD refers writers to a helpful online tip sheet, authored by the University of Virginia's Teaching Resource Center, on how to choose an editor or coach. Faculty generally pay for editorial and coaching work using some combination of start-up funds, small research or faculty development grants, or their own personal resources. Faculty have successfully used the list of professional editors to fine-tune grant proposals, journal articles, book chapters, and full-length manuscripts. A list of editors requires occasional updating but otherwise is an inexpensive and valuable resource for faculty.

OUTCOMES AND IMPLICATIONS

Perhaps the most telling outcome of our scholarly writing continuum is that faculty show up in droves for every program we try, and they eagerly suggest more and more possible offerings. From 2007 to 2011, the programs across the continuum have drawn over 823 non-unique participants, 98 percent of whom were faculty, department chairs, or deans (the other 2 percent were professional staff or graduate students). As mentioned, the faculty development literature indicates that scholarly writing programs are particularly helpful for female faculty (Dickson-Swift et al. 2009; Grant and Knowles 2000), and our participation numbers certainly reflect this assertion. Notably, from 2007 to 2011, 68 percent of the participants in our scholarly writing programs have been women, whereas women as a whole constitute 41 percent of UMass Amherst's instructional faculty. In addition, faculty of color have comprised 28 percent of our program participants, whereas faculty of color as a whole constitute 19 percent of our instructional faculty (University of Massachusetts Amherst, Office of Institutional Research 2012). Interestingly, we have discovered that scholarly writing programs do not appeal only to pre-tenure faculty who need to establish productive writing habits to attain tenure. More than 36 percent of our participants have been associate and full professors, a strong indication that scholarly writing programs can engage, encourage, and support faculty across all ranks.

We designed the assessment of our programs to reflect the individual character of each offering and, in most cases, the position of the offering along our continuum. For low-commitment, low-structure programs, we collect comments informally or through suggestion boxes. For more structured events and programs—such as large writing retreats, professional development workshops, and online writing groups—we conduct a standard survey. Since 2007, the overall satisfaction rating of our annual faculty writing retreat has never dropped below 4.74 on a 5-point scale, and it has reached a high of 4.97, making it one of our Center's most popular programs. Participants in our "From Dissertation to Book" and "Mechanics of Publishing" workshops, when asked the degree to which the events were "informative and worthwhile," rated the programs as 4.28 and 4.78 on a 5-point scale, respectively. The overall satisfaction scores for our Summer Online Writing Fellowships have remained higher than 4.21 on a 5-point scale over the past three years and have reached a high of 4.76. Faculty survey data reveal that tangible outputs from these programs include significant progress on journal articles, conference proposals, grant submissions and reviews, reports, monographs, textbooks, and chapters.

The response to our scholarly writing programs has been exceedingly positive, but our effort to build a continuum of opportunities has presented some challenges. For one, the desire to create offerings that fit as many individual needs as possible can lead to some confusion about the nature and purpose of each program, both for the faculty participants and for the faculty developers. For every twenty people who are happy with a program, there is inevitably one who would prefer a different size room in which to write, on a different day of the week, and sometimes even with a different assortment of colleagues. Faculty developers can avoid confusion by having a clear conception of how a program fits into the continuum, and fully explaining the range of offerings to faculty so they can choose the program that best fits their needs. We have also observed that a multi-faceted scholarly writing program requires constant attention and administration to succeed. Retreat locations must be maintained against equipment failures and environmental inconveniences such as noise problems. A list of academic editors must be kept current, and editors must receive guidance on university reimbursement procedures. A calendar of events must be maintained and advertised to multiple audiences. In short, for a continuum of programs, there must be a continuum of work. As with everything, success lies in the details.

Finally, because we are not immune to the fiscal and staffing pressures now common at most colleges, universities, and teaching centers, we have had a particular interest in developing programs that are neither expensive nor labor intensive, that incorporate faculty volunteers and expertise, and that are cosponsored with campus partners. For many years, our annual writing retreats were co-hosted *pro bono* by an on-campus faculty member and writing expert. Currently, all writing retreats except for our annual retreat in May are held in the Teaching Commons of the library, a space that is adeptly managed by a librarian who heads our undergraduate teaching and learning services and for which we do not need to pay a fee. The local writing coaches who have managed our Summer Online Writing Fellowship program in recent years are personally familiar with our faculty and have offered in-person coaching opportunities as well as an inexpensive, faculty-initiated, self-directed online writing group option for those interested in extending their online writing experience at their own cost. To the degree that we are able, we have countered our limited resources with resourcefulness.

CONCLUSION

As the literature illustrates, faculty development support for scholarly writing can take different forms—each one potentially valuable, but none that alone can possibly satisfy the particular writing needs of all faculty. A scholarly writing continuum comprised of programs with varying degrees of contact, commitment, and structure, however, allows faculty to identify their own areas for professional growth and choose the intervention that best fits their needs. Maintaining a continuum of programs may require steady attention, but doing so allows centers for teaching and faculty development to better support the rising productivity demands on our campuses.

REFERENCES

Ambos, Elizabeth, Mark Wiley, and Terre Allen. 2009. "Romancing the Muse: Faculty Writing Institute as Professional Development." *To Improve the Academy: Resources for Faculty Instructional and Organizational Development* 27:135–49.

Boice, Robert. 2000. *Advice for New Faculty Members: Nihil Nimus*. Boston: Allyn and Bacon.

Dickson-Swift, Virginia, Erica L. James, Sandra Kippen, Lyn Talbot, Glenda Verrinder, and Bernadette Ward. 2009. "A Non-residential Alternative to Off Campus Writers' Retreats for Academics." *Journal of Further and Higher Education* 33 (3): 229–39. http://dx.doi.org/10.1080/03098770903026156.

Elbow, Peter, and Mary Deane Sorcinelli. 2006. "The Faculty Writing Place: A Room of Our Own." *Change: The Magazine of Higher Learning* 38 (6): 17-22. http://dx.doi.org/10.3200/CHNG.38.6.17-22.

Franke, David. 2001. "Completing the Circle: Faculty as Writers." Presentation at the 5th annual National Writing Across the Curriculum Conference, Bloomington, IN, May-June.

Friend, Jennifer I., and Juan Carlos Gonzalez. 2009. "Get Together to Write." *Academe* 95 (1): 31–3.

Gappa, Judith M., Ann E. Austin, and Andrea G. Trice. 2007. *Rethinking Faculty Work: Higher Education's Strategic Imperative*. San Francisco: Jossey-Bass.

Grant, Barbara, and And Sally Knowles. 2000. "Flights of Imagination: Academic Women Be(com)ing Writers." *International Journal for Academic Development* 5 (1): 6–19. http://dx.doi.org/10.1080/136014400410060.

Gray, Tara, and Jane Birch. 2001. "Publish, Don't Perish: A Program to Help Scholars Flourish." *To Improve the Academy: Resources for Faculty Instructional and Organizational Development* 19: 268–84.

Mikhailova, Elena A., and Linda B. Nilson. 2007. "Developing Prolific Scholars: The 'Fast Article Writing' Methodology." *Journal of Faculty Development* 21 (2): 93–100.

Misra, Joya, Jennifer H. Lundquist, Elissa D. Holmes, and Stephanie Agiomavritis. 2011. "The Ivory Ceiling of Service Work." *Academe* 97 (1): 22–6.

Moore, Sarah. 2003. "Writers' Retreats for Academics: Exploring and Increasing the Motivation to Write." *Journal of Further and Higher Education* 27 (3): 333–42. http://dx.doi.org/10.1080/0309877032000098734.

Murray, Rowena, and Mary Newton. 2009. "Writing Retreat as Structured Intervention: Margin or Mainstream?" *Higher Education Research & Development* 28 (5): 541–53. http://dx.doi.org/10.1080/07294360903154126.

Sorcinelli, Mary Deane. 2002. "Ten Principles of Good Practice in Creating and Sustaining Teaching and Learning Centers." In *A Guide to Faculty Development*, ed. Kay Herr Gillespie, 9–23. San Francisco: Jossey-Bass.

Sorcinelli, Mary Deane, Ann E. Austin, Pamela L. Eddy, and Andrea L. Beach. 2006. *Creating the Future of Faculty Development: Learning from the Past, Understanding the Present.* San Francisco: Jossey-Bass.

Sorcinelli, Mary Deane, Tara Gray, and A. Jane Birch. 2011. "Faculty Development Beyond Instructional Development: Ideas Centers Can Use." *To Improve the Academy: Resources for Faculty Instructional and Organizational Development* 30:247–61.

Swaggerty, Elizabeth, Terry S. Atkinson, Johna L. Faulconer, and Robin R. Griffith. 2011. "Academic Writing Retreat: A Time for Rejuvenated and Focused Writing." *Journal of Faculty Development* 25 (1): 5–10.

University of Massachusetts Amherst, Office of Institutional Research. 2012. *Factbook 2011–2012 Instructional Faculty by Gender and Minority Status by School/College, Fall 2010 and Fall 2011.* Amherst, MA. Accessed February 2012. http://www.umass.edu/oapa/publications/factbooks/facultystaff/FB_fs_07.pdf.

Washburn, Allyson. 2008. "Writing Circle Feedback: Creating a Vibrant Community of Scholars." *Journal of Faculty Development* 22 (1): 32–7.

3

THE IDEA OF A FACULTY WRITING CENTER

Moving from Troubling Deficiencies to Collaborative Engagement

Lori Salem and Jennifer Follett

In an open, sunny room with tables and comfortable chairs, people are writing and talking about writing. A small group of people is writing together; writers show up with questions (how to revise a section of their work, how to edit their prose, how to respond to feedback they've received) and peer writing advisors or writing coaches work with them to answer those questions. Special events in this space celebrate writers and writing; writers give presentations on what they are writing or about their own writing processes. Writing coaches eagerly describe how their work with other writers has led to reflection on their own writing processes or styles. To those of us in writing center administration, this scene is easy enough to imagine—in fact, it may be exactly how we see our own writing centers, or how we envision what we would like them to become. Now imagine that all of these people—writers, coaches, advisors, presenters—are not students, but university faculty. Imagine universities sponsoring and supporting faculty writers in ways that match the complexity and power of the writing they are producing, and that build upon what we have learned from student writing centers—that learning to write is an ongoing process; that mastery over particular writing practices takes time, practice, and feedback; and that the lived realities of writers' lives have a profound effect on their writing practices. Imagine the kinds of spaces that universities might create for faculty writing, spaces that would allow for rich conversations, for exploration, for critique, and for community building around the role of writing in academia. How do we advocate for this kind of a space?

DOI: 10.7330/9780874219029.c003

In the past fifty years, American universities have slowly but surely embraced writing centers for students. Writing centers were relatively unknown until the 1960s, but currently, nearly all four-year colleges and universities have them. It is interesting to consider how this came about. Previously, the existence of a writing center was troubling for a university, as it seemed to indicate that something was wrong. University faculty and administrators believed that university students should already have mastered writing skills before coming to the university, thus the need for a writing center suggested that the university was having trouble attracting well-qualified students. A recent history of the development of writing centers (Lerner 2009) suggests that when mid-twentieth century universities formed writing centers (which were usually called writing labs or writing clinics), they explained them by pointing to new and unusual educational needs among their student body, typically needs created by forces beyond the universities' control. For example, in the 1930s, the University of Minnesota General College articulated the need for its new writing laboratory in relation to a suddenly more diverse body of students (Lerner 2009, 76). In the same period, Dartmouth explained the creation of a writing clinic by saying that the new pedagogies of the Progressive movement had created a generation of students who were "ignor[ant] of civilized writing conventions" (Lerner 2009, 92).

In contemporary universities, many faculty and administrators still understand the purpose of a writing center as fixing students' "deficiencies," but the sense that students' struggles are new or unusual has diminished. And at the same time, there has been a shift in how universities understand their responsibilities toward their students. In earlier decades, it might have seemed reasonable for universities to allow students with writing problems to fail out, or simply to refuse to admit such students in the first place. However, those attitudes don't match the current academic climate, in which universities must compete for a declining number of students; in which retention rates are a closely watched index of a university's performance; and in which students and their parents are encouraged to feel a greater sense of choice, control, and entitlement over their educational experiences (Thelin 2004). These new realities are reflected in the standards of regional accreditation agencies, which now require universities to demonstrate that they provide adequate support for student learners (see, for example, MSCHE 2006). Thus, for universities, having students who struggle with writing is a normal condition, and creating a writing center to support them seems a responsible and logical thing to do.

Up to this point, most American universities have not extended this logic or sense of responsibility to faculty writers. It is well understood that the writing done by faculty is challenging, integral to their professional roles, and connected to high-stakes decision-making (e.g., getting tenure, winning grants). However, when faculty struggle to meet the writing-related challenges they face, the university generally does not assume responsibility for providing support to them. Indeed, the idea that faculty members would need support for writing is "troubling" in the same way that students' need for writing support used to be. Having a faculty writing center would seem to indicate that the university isn't able to attract well-qualified faculty.

However, there is strong evidence that attitudes toward support for faculty writing may be changing and that the conditions that would allow for the development of a faculty writing center movement may be developing. American colleges and universities are undergoing an unprecedented level of change in the nature and organization of faculty work (Schuster and Finkelstein 2006). The past thirty years have seen the diversification and stratification of faculty jobs. The typical faculty member of the 1970s was a full-time tenure-track professor whose work comprised a balance of teaching, research, and service. Faculty today are more likely to be part-time than full-time, and more likely than not to be off the tenure track. Many new faculty positions are "functionally specific" roles that require teaching, research, *or* service, rather than a mixture of the three.

Perhaps because of the changes in the professoriate, the past two decades have seen the rapid expansion of the Professional and Organizational Development Network (or the POD Network), a group that advocates for faculty development and support on a broad range of issues. Along with this has been the development of a large number of faculty support centers, often called Centers for Teaching and Learning (CTL). CTLs are often affiliated with the POD Network, and they provide development opportunities and support programs for faculty at a wide range of universities. Most CTLs focus primarily on helping university faculty develop as teachers, so they do not necessarily provide support for faculty *writers* per se. But supporting the development of faculty as scholars (including as "writers") is explicitly a part of the POD Network's mission statement, so to the extent that a CTL is affiliated with the POD Network, they are connected to the idea of supporting faculty writers. More generally, the broad development of CTLs, and the national professional organization that links and guides them, lays the groundwork for the large-scale development of faculty writing centers.

It is easy to imagine that faculty writing centers could follow the same path from "unusual and troubling" to "normal and expected" that student writing centers took.

We see the development of faculty support centers as cause for celebration. But based on our experience as directors of student writing centers, we want to insert a note of caution. There is no doubt that student writing centers do much good and that the appearance of such centers at universities across the country has helped many students succeed who might not otherwise have been able to do so. But writing centers' origins as places for fixing deficient students have never been erased, and that disquieting foundation continues to constrain the work of even the most well-funded and well-established writing centers. Student writing centers were founded on the belief that the "problem" they needed to address resided solely in individuals—namely, students who are "poor writers," so they have historically often left unexamined the role institutions, relationships, and cultural constructions played in producing and defining those poor writers in the first place. Grimm (1999) likened university writing centers to "missionaries" with good intentions: they want to make the world a better place, but because their energies are entirely directed toward helping (civilizing?) individuals, they don't or can't see the larger forces at play, or how they are implicated in those forces. Regardless of how much work such a writing center does, and regardless of how many individuals are helped, the inequalities, discontinuities, and contradictions of the education system that surrounds them never change (Grimm 1999). Of course, the professional field of writing center studies has made efforts to challenge these foundational beliefs, and to find ways to identify and influence the larger forces that shape the environment for student writing. Grimm's (1999) incisive critiques come out of that academic field, and her writings have had enormous influence on the writing center directors who participate in the field's professional venues. But at the institutional level, the foundational beliefs have proved resistant to change; the logic of providing support for individuals (while ignoring larger issues) seems to be hardwired into student writing centers and does not seem likely to change soon.

We are concerned, then, that faculty writing centers could develop along the same well-intended, but fundamentally limited and limiting ideological path. If faculty writing centers focus exclusively on supporting individual members of the faculty, they will undoubtedly help a lot of people. But the forces that are shaping the overall environment for faculty writing—from the large-scale shift toward part-time faculty, to the move toward English-language-only in academic journals in nearly all

fields, to the creation of controversial ranking systems for academic journals—are substantial and worrisome. If faculty writing centers do not, or
cannot, negotiate a larger role for themselves, they will have no voice in
the contexts for and expectations of faculty and writing.

But there is good reason to believe that a faculty writing center movement could be launched based on a more solid and less constraining
rationale than student writing centers were. For one thing, creators
of faculty writing centers will have the benefit of hindsight; we now
know much more about developing writing centers than we did when
the student writing center movement was being launched. But more
important, a faculty writing center movement can draw on the critical theoretical frameworks for understanding professional writing that
have developed in the last twenty-five years or so, frameworks that offer
a potential approach to side-stepping the "fixing-deficient-writers" trap.
These theoretical frameworks, particularly those associated with genre
studies and literacy studies, have explored how institutions, like universities, constrain and enable the writing practices of the individuals who
are affiliated with them.

Overall, these theories suggest that institutions shape the way their
employees use writing and understand themselves as writers, and that
institutions do this in ways that serve larger institutional goals, not necessarily in ways that serve employees. Thus, an institution seeking to establish itself as a leader in public policy would reward employees for writing
influential white papers, legal opinions, and the like, and it would work
to ensure that employees have access to resources (time, technology,
libraries, subscriptions, travel, etc.) that enable their work. But it would
not necessarily invest in programs to teach employees how to write
effective policy documents, if they did not know how to do so already.
By controlling access, rewards, and resources, institutions "sponsor" the
kinds of literate practices that serve their goals (Brandt 2001; Brandt
and Clinton 2002). This institutional sponsorship is sometimes difficult
to recognize: it is rarely stated explicitly, and in fact, what is stated explicitly is often misleading or idealized. Instead, institutional sponsorship of
writing tends to be quietly embedded in day-to-day practices and procedures—practices that often seem to be about something else other than
literacy. For example, when university faculty in the sciences are seeking
tenure and promotion, their publications are evaluated in part on the
basis of their "influence," that is gauged by how many other researchers
have cited their work. Such institutional practices typically don't seem to
be about "writing" nor do they seem to be driven by agendas specific to
our institution, since many other universities follow the same or similar

procedures. But in fact, this practice does influence the writing of faculty, especially in the sciences, and it does serve to assert one of our university's primary goals for faculty writing: namely, that it should contribute to the university's visibility and prestige as a research institution.

However, in complex institutions like universities, institutional sponsorship for writing is not monolithic. The university comprises different colleges, departments, centers, and other units, and those subunits often have specific missions that generate alternative ideas about writing. For example, units that are responsible for appointing and evaluating faculty may have different views about the practices related to faculty writing than do units charged with promoting the university's profile in terms of federal grant support. Thus, one can expect to find a variety of beliefs about literacy, including sharply contradictory ideas, sponsored at a single institution, though some of the beliefs may seem to apply only to certain people or situations (Dias et al. 1999, 117).

The hybridity of institutional literacy sponsorship represents a potential opportunity for faculty writing centers. If, among the various beliefs about faculty writing, we can uncover some that are conducive to faculty writing centers, we can look for ways to recruit those ideas to our cause. If we consciously build a rationale for a faculty writing center based on ideas that the university already sponsors, but selecting ideas that allow us to circumvent the idea of fixing poor writers, we can build a writing center on a solid foundation. In this chapter, then, we explore some of the ways that faculty writing is sponsored at our own university, and based on that we propose a possible rationale for a faculty writing center and a vision of what such a writing center would look like.

UNCOVERING INSTITUTIONAL SPONSORSHIP OF FACULTY WRITING

To explore our university's sponsorship of faculty writing, we reviewed a series of university documents that describe policies and procedures that relate, directly or indirectly, to faculty and their writing. We asked what the policies "do" for the institution, what effects they have on faculty, and what assumptions they make about faculty and writing. Analyzing institutional documents in this way allowed us to locate the implicit beliefs concerning faculty literacy that animate university policies, and to contextualize those beliefs in different aspects of the university's mission and history. It allowed us to see that "the university" is comprised of different units that hold contradictory views about faculty writing. Finally, it revealed the ways that our own views dovetail with and diverge from the university's views. It is a useful exercise, and one that we think might prove fruitful for others seeking to promote change at their institutions.

Our analysis focused on institutionally-authored documents—documents for which no particular individual author is named, or for which the author is presumed to be a university department or unit—and we focused particularly on documents that were intended to be relevant university-wide (i.e., we did not review documents aimed at faculty in particular colleges or academic departments.). The documents we reviewed included the "Faculty Handbook" (Temple University, n.d.), the "Organizational Outline for Promotion and Tenure Files" (Temple University 2011), and the "Guidelines for the Appointment and Promotion of Non-Tenure Track Faculty" (Temple University 2008b), all found on the website of the vice provost for faculty affairs. We also reviewed the collective bargaining agreement between the university and the faculty union (Temple University 2008a), available on the union's website, and linked to the website of the vice provost for faculty development and faculty affairs. Finally, we reviewed the websites of two units that are explicitly charged with providing support for faculty: the Teaching and Learning Center (TLC) and the Temple Research Administration office (TRA) (Teaching and Learning Center website; Temple Research Administration website).

There were other documents and websites that we could also have considered, but our goal here is not to present a complete map of all of the terms of university sponsorship of faculty writing, if that were even possible, but rather to uncover aspects of the university's sponsorship that might support the development of an effective, broadly-focused faculty writing center, as well as terms that might hinder it. In that regard, three significant ideas emerged from these documents and websites.

Faculty Do "Research" and Students "Write"

Temple University is a research institution, and as such, the tenure-track faculty are hired with the expectation that they will be publishing their research and scholarship in academic journals and books. "Writing" is certainly a part of publishing—one can't have published if one hasn't written anything—so in that sense, one could say that "writing" is understood to be an important part of faculty work. But the word "writing" does not appear in any of the documents that describe faculty job responsibilities, or policies and procedures. Instead, the documents refer to the overall project of getting published as "research" or "scholarship" or sometimes "publication." For example, the guidelines for tenure and promotion in the "Faculty Handbook" (Temple University, n.d., 2) state that "a decision to grant tenure shall be based on the judgment that an individual meets the accepted standards for (1) teaching; (2) scholarship, research, or creative work; and (3) service." The faculty collective bargaining agreement (Temple University 2008a) also uses these terms, as do the other texts linked to the vice provost for faculty affairs website.

The effects of this terminology are multiple. Using the word "research" to describe faculty work emphasizes the aspect of producing publications that faculty themselves often find most compelling. Faculty tend to think of themselves as "researchers" rather than "writers," and depending on their discipline, the aspects of "research" that faculty value most (e.g., scientific research at the bench) sometimes do not involve much "writing." In that sense, then, the university's use of the term indicates that it shares common values with faculty. But since publication is the ultimate goal of this knowledge-making activity, then writing is always a part of academic research—in fact, arguably, it is the one constant across all academic disciplines—so talking about faculty work without referring to writing says something about what the university is sponsoring. On the one hand, it creates a distinction between the work that faculty do and the work that students do. We regularly describe students' work as "writing," even when they are writing about "research" they have done. Writing is also commonly (and erroneously) understood as a basic skill, the mere transcription of thoughts into grammatically correct sentences. Thus, calling students' work "writing" and faculty work "research" may be appealing because it codes faculty work as more advanced or sophisticated than students' work. Or, to put this another way, it suggests that writing is a kind of pre-professional activity—something that learners do—and that faculty are, or should be, beyond that.

Eliminating the word "writing" from a discussion of faculty work also implies that the process one engages in to produce a published research manuscript is less meaningful than the fact of publication itself, eliding the hard work faculty do to achieve publication. The process of writing is extraordinarily challenging and time-consuming for some faculty, particularly those who are non-native speakers of English. Over the past two decades, English has emerged as the default language for academic publishing, and faculty who seek to publish must produce texts in English, regardless of their first language, or even of the countries in which they work. But producing a publishable academic text in one's second (or third or fourth) language is an enormous challenge. Reading source material and drafting text take longer when one is working in a second language. Moreover, producing texts in a second language typically requires support from what Lillis and Curry (2010, 93) have termed "language brokers"—that is, editors, translators, proofreaders, and English language teachers—and that support itself presents challenges. The costs can be prohibitive, and for speakers of less-widely-spoken languages (e.g., Hungarian, Kurdish) professional support may not be available at all. And unless the language broker is willing to engage with the writer—discussing and negotiating the right words to convey the meaning the writer intended—the writer may feel that she has lost control of her own text. For scholars in some disciplines, these challenges are compounded by larger cultural biases about the value and relevance of academic research published in languages other than English (143–5). For example, how does a writer situate his research in the literature of the field when that literature and the professional discourse related to his topic belong to another language?

"Meeting Accepted Standards": Faculty Writing as Individual Evaluation (for Some)

As part of the tenure and promotion process, faculty writing is utilized as a method of evaluating an individual faculty member's performance. In particular, their academic writing is used to evaluate their performance against an "accepted standard" for research/scholarship. The notion of an individual being measured against a standard, especially a standard that is understood to be "national" or at least trans-institutional, is a familiar trope in educational settings, as it comprises the underlying logic of standardized testing. The idea of a standardized test is to provide an objective measure of an individual's abilities that isn't influenced by personal relationships or histories, and that isn't based on local "norms," but instead is referenced to common standards.

The idea of tenure, and the processes of applying for tenure, are obviously not unique to our university, and neither has it developed purely in response to institutional needs, since faculty have also played a role in defining it. As a legal concept, tenure represents a negotiated compromise between faculty and university administrations that has played out at many universities over many years. However, it is still fair to say that tenure is part of how Temple sponsors faculty writing, since they could, after all, have chosen to opt out of tenure altogether, as some universities have done. The fact that tenure remains part of the university suggests that it "does" something that the university wants. For one thing, having tenure-eligible faculty lines at Temple ensures that the university will be competitive in hiring talented faculty; and once faculty are hired into tenure-eligible lines, it ensures that they will be productive as scholars. Having tenured and tenure-eligible faculty is prestigious: it marks Temple as a traditional research institution, and it signals that the institution considers research and academic freedom important enough to protect, in spite of the economic costs of tenure.

For faculty, earning tenure is the ultimate academic honor. It confers gravitas to the research and writing of a faculty member by signaling that her peers consider her work important enough to protect, and that her institution considers her research worthy of supporting with time away from the classroom. But the experience of bidding for tenure means submitting to a high-stakes, all-or-nothing examination of one's individual achievement, and to a process that is far less objective and impersonal than it appears. Candidates for tenure at Temple are directed to compile a dossier that includes all of the scholarly work they have published. These texts are supposed to serve as the basis for the evaluation. As with standardized tests in other educational settings, tenure strives to eliminate the candidate's personal life—health problems, children, financial issues, age, gender—or personal attributes from the decision. The candidate's dossier is read and evaluated by people from her field, who are familiar with the research literature in the field and are well-positioned to evaluate the quality of the candidate's work.

But the objectivity and impersonality of the process is belied by the fact that along with their publications, candidates must also submit "journal assessment reports" that are intended to measure the quality of the academic journals their work appeared in, and citation reports that indicate the "impact" of their work, even though theoretically the quality and impact of their work is precisely what the departmental colleagues and external evaluators should be able to determine. Indeed, it is hard to explain the need for these "objective" rating systems, except as a way to limit and check the biases and sympathies of the human evaluators. The evaluators' own intellectual commitments to methods, theories, topics, and texts from the field, as well as personal-academic facts about the candidate that can be often gleaned from the dossier (his alma mater, the timing of his academic degrees, languages spoken, age, ethnicity, sexual orientation, etc.) can and do shape their judgments of the textual evidence.

One of the most vexed situations in tenure reviews emerges when issues in a candidate's personal life clash with tenure requirements. If a colleague faced severe health issues that compromised her ability to write during the pre-tenure years, should that be taken into account when evaluating her work? What about a candidate who had children? Most tenure review policies are silent on this matter, leaving evaluators to wrestle with the fundamental problem. Namely, if we believe that the tenure requirements must be "the same" for everyone in order to ensure objectivity, then tenure will be attainable principally by those talented scholars who have excellent health, good financial resources, and who are willing and able to minimize all non-scholarly relationships and responsibilities. This is, of course, one of the reasons that women are still under-represented in the ranks of tenured faculty (Mason and Goulden, 2002). Many universities have implemented policies that allow candidates to stop the tenure clock under certain circumstances, but some faculty choose not to take advantage of them, fearing—correctly, as it turns out—that taking "extra" time could bias evaluators against them (Thornton, 2009). In other words, simply providing flexibility without changing the fundamental understanding of tenure as a purely objective evaluation does not solve the problem.

For faculty, then, the tenure process offers the possibility of achieving extraordinarily supportive sponsorship of their writing—a level of commitment that exists in almost no other profession and that imbues their work with a sense of meaning and importance. But, for a time, it also places them at the mercy of a process that has the potential to be very unfair and that treats their personal lives as irrelevant (and expects them to act accordingly.) Grimm (1999, 56) has noted that achieving success in such a situation can confer a sense of agency on writers; a newly-tenured faculty member may feel empowered because her academic work "passed the test." But at some level, this agency is false because the process itself isn't what it appears to be. Nevertheless, for faculty who have achieved tenure, the institutional sponsorship it confers, and the sense of agency it produces may serve to quiet any concerns about the fairness of the process.

Meanwhile, what goes almost entirely unstated in the university policies and procedures related to faculty writing is that relatively few members of the faculty are ever subject to this individual evaluation, because only a minority of the faculty are appointed to tenure-eligible lines. At Temple 30 percent of the faculty are tenured or tenure-eligible, while 27 percent are in full-time lines and 43 percent are in part-time lines that are not eligible for tenure. In this regard, our university is typical of other research institutions. Overall, in American four-year colleges and universities, the percentage of tenured and tenure-eligible faculty is around 36 percent ("Colleges" 2011). For the majority of faculty the tenure process, which is the primary framework within which the institution sponsors faculty writing, simply doesn't apply. And neither has the institution established any alternative way of making sense of the writing that faculty do off the tenure line. In fact, one might easily be led to assume that non-tenure-line faculty don't write for publication at all.

But evidence of writing-lives off the tenure track emerges in the "Guidelines for the Appointment and Promotion of Non-Tenure Track Faculty" (Temple University 2008b). The section related to non-tenure-eligible faculty on the "research track," indicates that research comprises their principle job requirement. Meanwhile, for non-tenure-eligible faculty on the "teaching/instructional" track, research *may* be included among an individual's job duties, at the discretion of their dean. For both positions, having a record of publications serves as a qualification for earning promotion. Similarly, the collective bargaining agreement reveals that non-tenure-line faculty are eligible for sabbaticals to support their research.

The national data of faculty experiences and satisfaction echo the persistent presence of writing lives among faculty whose jobs exclude them from tenure-related publication requirements. According to national data, non-tenure-track faculty in teaching-intensive positions publish less frequently than their tenure-track peers, but they do publish. Sixty percent had published at some point in their careers, while nearly half reported publishing in the last two years. Moreover, non-tenure-track faculty in research-intensive positions are among the most productive faculty in terms of publication; only a small minority do not publish, and most publish regularly (Schuster and Finkelstein 2006, 202). Data also suggest that publishing off the tenure track is associated with career mobility (200–221). Non-tenure-track faculty who publish are more likely than their non-publishing peers to transition to tenure-eligible lines. Similarly, part-time faculty who publish are more likely than non-publishers to transition to full-time faculty lines.

Thus what faculty *on* the tenure line do sometimes looks a lot like what faculty *off* the tenure line do: they write; the university supports and requires their writing; their writing counts toward promotion; and their writing supports their mobility. But writing off the tenure track still means something different because the terms of the university's sponsorship are different. Whereas the tenure process wraps the writing of tenured faculty in a grand narrative—this scholar produces work that is potentially important to the institution and to society, so for the good of all, the writer's freedom to pursue her work must be fully protected—the narrative surrounding non-tenure-line faculty is far more ambivalent. If a non-tenure-line faculty member is assigned to do research as part of her job, then a dean has decided that the research is important enough to devote salaried time to it. But this does not mean that the *individual researcher* is important enough to merit the protections that tenure provides.

Of course, this doesn't mean that the actual writing that is produced by non-tenure-line faculty is not potentially important to society, that non-tenure-line faculty are not in need of the protection that tenure proffers, or even that the university itself thinks less of the work that non-tenure-eligible faculty produce. The decision to create a category of fulltime non-tenure-eligible faculty was motivated by strategic budgetary concerns, not by an urge to undercut the validity of some scholars' work. Nevertheless, the creation of this multi-tiered faculty, where the university's contribution to knowledge-creation is ostensibly in the hands of a minority, does, in fact, change the terms of university sponsorship for most faculty writers.

The Mutual Benefits of Collaboration

Temple maintains two offices that are charged with providing direct support for faculty. The Teaching and Learning Center (TLC) provides support in the form of workshops, seminars, teaching circles, reading groups, and the like for faculty who want to develop their skills and abilities as teachers. The TLC programs center around introducing faculty to research-based teaching practices. The Temple Research Administration office (TRA), meanwhile, works with faculty who are trying to develop proposals for externally funded research. They provide general consultations for any faculty member who is working on such proposals—and in fact, proposals for funded research must be reviewed by them before they can be submitted. Their work is particularly directed toward helping faculty with certain technical aspects of proposals, such as developing realistic budgets, defining the university's "match" and overhead, and navigating the complex requirements of obtaining permissions and letters of support.

Taken together, these two websites indicate that under certain circumstances, the university does explicitly embrace a role in supporting faculty and in developing their skills in relation to their primary job duties. And significantly, they provide this support even though it potentially compromises the underlying logic of the tenure and promotion process: namely, that tenure and promotion are rewards given for strictly individual achievements. The support provided by the TLC and the TRA could easily have a direct influence on an individual's bid for tenure. If a faculty member earned a research grant because of the support of the TRA, and if the grant was a factor in that individual earning tenure then the tenure process would not be an evaluation of an individual's abilities, but rather an evaluation of the results of a collaboration between the university and the individual.

When they describe their work, both the TRA and the TLC highlight the fact that the support they provide is based on expert knowledge that faculty would be unlikely to have developed on their own or to have encountered in graduate school. Thus, these units provide an expertise that complements the expertise the faculty members themselves already possess. The support that the TRA provides would not produce a successful grant unless the faculty member had an idea for a fundable research program and the expertise to carry it through. By the same token, the TLC's support for teaching would not be useful if the faculty member did not already have the content knowledge of their discipline. Thus helping faculty in this way does not require thinking of faculty as "deficient" and in need of a fix; rather, it frames them as coexperts whose knowledge and potential can be unlocked with support.

Both units also carefully justify their work by articulating the relationship between helping an individual and achieving a larger institutional goal. The TLC website, for example, states that in helping faculty to become better teachers, ". . . our ultimate aim is to support the success of Temple's richly diverse student body and the development of our students as scholars and citizens." Meanwhile, by helping individual faculty with their proposals, the TRA's goal is to "support the research enterprise" at Temple, to improve Temple's standing and impact as a research institution, and to build "a strong research enterprise that benefits society, by creating and applying new knowledge."

LAYING THE FOUNDATION FOR A FACULTY WRITING CENTER

In our review of university documents, tenure emerges as the dominant way of understanding faculty writing. For this reason, it would be tempting to try to lay an ideological foundation for a faculty writing center on the grounds of tenure. In the short term, this would serve to connect the writing center to a high stakes issue that has enormous weight in the institution. The grief generated by a failed tenure bid, to say nothing of the potential for lawsuits that failed tenure decisions create, might also serve as incentives for a university to provide funding for a faculty writing center. The university and candidates' own departments have a strong interest in showing that faculty were not simply left to sink or swim during the tenure process, but instead that they were provided with guidance and support. Indeed, this argument would probably sound familiar and intuitively correct, since it is the argument that has supported student writing centers for many years.

It may be easy then to imagine a faculty writing center designed to assist faculty (on either a voluntary basis, or as required by a tenure committee) identified as being at risk of not producing an adequate tenure portfolio. Like student writing centers founded on a deficiency model, such a faculty writing center would certainly be in a position to "rescue" a number of faculty whose tenure-bids were in jeopardy, and, in so doing, would likely develop a grateful, relieved cadre of devotees. However, a center developed exclusively from and for this vision of a university's sponsorship of writing would be working at the point of failure, its existence justified by the presence of "problem writers" among the faculty in need of fixing. Likely, a writing center based on the idea of remediating struggling tenure-line faculty would likely have trouble attracting faculty to use its services, at least openly, since doing so would indicate that the user was "in trouble." Moreover, the writing center's work would probably also arouse the suspicion and anger of some faculty, and would place writing center users in a classic catch twenty-two. If a faculty member used the writing center and his tenure bid was ultimately unsuccessful, then the center's support would simply prove that he was the "problem" all along (since, after all, the university tried to help.) But if the faculty member's bid for tenure were successful, other faculty might feel that the writing center's support comprised an unfair advantage.

It seems natural to imagine that a writing center developed with the central mission of assisting with tenure bids would be staffed by writing advisors or coaches who have proven their own abilities: namely, faculty who themselves have already earned tenure. While the idea of the seasoned, institutionally-endorsed expert sharing the benefit of his or her experience to assist a struggling junior colleague might seem to make sense, it reinforces a false dichotomy between "good" writers and "bad." While it would foster conversation (at least at the one-to-one level) between faculty at different status levels in the university, that conversation seems likely to be limited and one sided, as this collaboration does not count on the junior faculty member's talents or expertise, as TRA collaborations above do. In fact, it assumes a lack of expertise. The center's "missionary" services would fail to raise any discussion of how writing is being used within the university and whether the expectations for tenure were fair and appropriate. And the services would also reify the idea that "faculty writing" is equivalent to "writing for tenure," thereby continuing to marginalize the majority of faculty for whom tenure is not a possibility.

A faculty writing center working from a tenure-centric version of university sponsorship may be endorsed across the disciplines because it would relieve departments of the responsibility of supporting faculty whose needs stymie potential mentors within the department. But this raises the issue of staffing—if not tenured faculty within the writer's discipline, who else would be in a position to offer the kind of help this version of a writing center would offer, and how would it fit into their official responsibilities to the university? And while many departments might be happy to refer faculty to generic "writing experts," from outside the department, the writing center, would then be in the position of reifying a notion of writing as a functional skill that is separate from content knowledge and disciplinary genre convention—a notion that has hampered university writing programs and student writing centers since their inception (Russell 2002, 241–46).

Meanwhile, however, the idea that the university and individual faculty members can and should productively collaborate on writing projects is a very fruitful one for writing centers. Right now, this idea is somewhat circumscribed at our university; it only applies when there is a specific and narrow expertise that it is "okay" for faculty to not have. But one can imagine that it would be possible to flex and expand this notion of collaboration. Moreover, it would be possible to link university-faculty collaborations to larger university goals. The university stands to gain visibility and prestige when faculty publish, and it stands to gain prestige and resources when faculty win grants and contracts. Moreover, if the university could demonstrate that faculty work is valued and supported, it would have an edge in competing for excellent faculty.

But perhaps the most fruitful idea that emerges from this review is the idea of expanding and complicating the university's sponsorship of faculty writing so that it accommodates the presence of non-tenure-eligible faculty. Non-tenure-line faculty positions are still relatively new in American universities, and the terms and conditions of the university's sponsorship of their work are clearly not settled. A faculty writing center could serve a powerful and useful role in this climate, helping the university uncover ways it could recognize and extend authority and support to the writing produced by non-tenure line faculty, even if the recognition and support does not include tenure.

IMAGINING A FACULTY WRITING CENTER

How, then, do we design a faculty writing center that both supports faculty's efforts to work within university discursive expectations, and yet can contribute to thoughtful evolution and revision of those expectations? We would begin by insisting that the central mission and message of a faculty writing center should echo that of student writing centers: that a place where writing can be transparently discussed and regularly practiced is good for everyone in the university. Through work with individual writers, writing groups, writing retreats, seminars, invited speakers, and sponsorship of publication—work many student writing centers do—a faculty writing center would foster a community discourse about faculty writing.

Indeed, the similarities between student and faculty writing centers suggest that creating an administrative connection between the two units would be a good idea. People who direct student writing centers would have the interest and the expertise required to direct faculty writing centers. Also, connecting the units might open up opportunities for collaboration and interaction among faculty writers and student writers, like "mixed" seminars and writers' groups, or invited speakers. Such programs model for students the idea that learning to write is a lifelong, ongoing process, and would probably give faculty strong insight into their practices of teaching writing. However, we would argue that a faculty writing center would need to have physical space and a staffing structure that is separate enough to allow both faculty and students writers to choose not to interact, should they prefer it. For students, having a space that is separate from faculty authority may be necessary to encourage productive risk-taking and critique of academic discourse, and to allow students to practice their emerging discourses on a non-evaluative audience (Kail and Trimbur 1987, Cooper 1994, Harris 1995). If students knew faculty—possibly even their own instructors—might be present during the students' writing center sessions, it might inhibit their use of the writing center, or at the very least, the way they talk about their writing and writing assignments. Similarly, separate space may be necessary to give faculty the freedom to grapple with the often messy process of writing, to talk about failures, frustrations and confusions, without risking their sense of authority in the classroom. This might be especially true of international faculty, who may sometimes feel they struggle to be understood when speaking English in the classroom already, and would prefer to avoid making the challenge of writing in a second language public, too.

We can't offer a universal blueprint for a center that would "work" at every institution, but our experiences in student writing centers and the findings of this investigation of our local context, suggest we needn't see our vision as necessarily in inevitable conflict with university expectations nor limited to the narrow model described above. Rather, they suggest that sponsorship of faculty writing at our university includes beliefs and practices that could be called on in service of a faculty writing center. We conclude this article by offering four broad principles that could serve as starting points for those designing faculty writing centers.

A Faculty Writing Center Should Support Individual Faculty Writers on Texts and Projects that Are Important to Them

Individual consultations with writers who have questions about their own writing are the backbone of student writing centers, where they serve as the principle way the centers reach out to and interact with their clients. Such consultations could also serve as a key element of a faculty writing center, giving individual faculty members an opportunity to ask questions and get help on a host of writerly concerns. They would also usefully complicate the notion that faculty "research" is fundamentally different from student "writing," and they would challenge the idea that learning to write is "pre-professional."

Similar to student writing centers, a faculty writing center could work on a near-peer model: it could be staffed by faculty from across the disciplines and from different positions and levels within the university who were chosen for their ability to coach other writers. Thus, success in winning tenure would be a less-important credential for a writing coach, than his or her ability to offer what we have found that faculty writers often need when they seek our support: awareness of and ability to discuss the writing process; facility for engaging in collaborative thinking, composing, and problem-solving; and a willingness to allow writers to test ideas and get lower stakes, peer feedback from a critical but supportive reader.

Our experiences working with faculty writers have shown us that many faculty members write in isolation. Away from the support of a peer cohort they may have enjoyed in graduate school, they may not have frequent conversation with other writers, know how other people write, or know whether their own practices are effective or problematic. We know that some faculty want types of support that are not available to them, including regular and ongoing feedback on their work, and conversations that help them develop ideas and concepts. And we know that many faculty have questions about the publication process (how to respond to revise-and-resubmit requests; how to write book proposals, etc.) and they don't have anyone they can ask. Helping faculty address these questions would provide a useful and needed service. Keeping detailed data about the kinds of questions and solutions that emerged in the consultations could serve as a foundation for the research and dialogue described below, and be the subject of frequent conversation between faculty writing coaches in the writing center and academic departments they may serve as formal or informal liaisons to.

For individual consultations to be effective, a faculty writing center would have to actively avoid any efforts to associate the services with "fixing" underperforming faculty. One way to do this would be to invoke the notion of "collaboration among experts" that the university has already embraced in other settings. This would involve uncovering and making visible the many aspects of professional writing and publishing that experience and expertise typically develop after graduate school. A faculty writing center could draw on external experts in those domains, including editors and publishers of academic presses, and professional grant writers; but local faculty with expertise in various research methodologies, research and design software, translation, supporting the work of international writers, coaching writers, and so forth, would also provide complementary expertise for faculty writers.

A Faculty Writing Center Should Sponsor Dialogue about the Practices and Goals of Faculty Writers, on and off the Tenure Track

Over the past two decades, American universities have responded to pressing and complex concerns about academic budgets and the need for flexibility by diversifying the kinds of faculty jobs they make available. Whatever we might think about that development, it seems unlikely that, having created this category of academic job, universities will return to models of all-tenured (or mostly tenured) faculty. But this does not mean that universities couldn't, or wouldn't want to design an environment that would support the writing that non-tenure-eligible faculty do. Indeed, as long as budget and flexibility concerns were unaffected, universities would have strong incentives to support such work. Non-tenure-eligible faculty could contribute to the university's efforts to build the visibility and strength of its research profile. Moreover, if the university could show that it valued and supported the research of non-tenure-eligible faculty, it would undoubtedly find the quality of the applicants for those positions would rise.

A writing center could play an important mediating role between the institution and non-tenure-eligible faculty. The center could offer direct support to non-tenure-eligible faculty by organizing opportunities for them to meet, network, and celebrate their work, as well as opportunities to strategize about gaining access to resources like research leave or funding. A well-established faculty writing center might even be in a position to sponsor its own writing or research grants to faculty across the disciplines, or acknowledge and raise awareness of non-tenure-track faculty members through annual writing awards. The center could also play a policy role, serving as a partner or consultant for the university in exploring how they might expand, clarify, and enhance their sponsorship of writing for non-tenure-eligible faculty.

A Faculty Writing Center Should Seek to Build Useful Knowledge about Professional Academic Writing and Writers

The past several decades have seen the publication of a substantial body of research into academic writing; however, most of this research has focused on student writing and writing processes, and, outside of composition studies programs or WID/WAC based writing-intensive programs, it is generally not regularly or purposefully discussed by faculty. Faculty writing centers could adopt a parallel agenda of producing serious and sustained research into faculty writing and research practices, shared with the university audience through seminars, invited speakers, and publication. Sustained research into faculty writing (especially if it were conducted at a wide variety of institutions) would undoubtedly have a lot to tell us about what, where, when, why, and how faculty write. And since both faculty and university administration potentially have an interest in and a use for such research, the writing center could collaborate with both groups to define the topics and methods of investigation. Qualitative studies might focus on such subjects as the material conditions under which faculty engage in writing and publication pursuits; the writing goals and practices of part-time faculty; the development of discursive authority over time; the daily literacy practices of international or multilingual faculty; and faculty approaches to collaboration/coauthorship in different settings. Quantitative studies might produce a more accurate accounting of how much faculty actually are writing; who among the faculty writes; how much of what faculty write gets published; and how published texts are used. Research of this kind would provide us with knowledge and insights that could, over time, promote healthy changes in the environment for writing at the university.

A Faculty Writing Center Should Make Visible the Kinds of Collaborations that Promote Strong Writing Practices

The university's notion of tenure as an objective evaluation of an individual has much in common with the romantic image of a writer who works alone in a garret creating his masterpiece. In both cases, the written text represents the work of a single mind, and in both cases, the individual writer is presumed to have what she needs to create the text on her own. (In fact, in both cases, interaction with others disrupts the individual's achievement.)

The goals of the tenure process aside, this notion of writing is a terrible fit for academia. Published academic writing nearly always begins by explicitly connecting the text to previously published research, and a scholar's research is typically framed by using methods, terminology, and theoretical constructs that were developed by prior researchers. Moreover, the normal practice for most academics is to seek feedback from peers in the field, and texts that are published without the benefit of formal peer review and professional editing usually suffer, both in quality and prestige. In the majority of academic disciplines, academic texts usually have multiple authors, and in many cases, the authors are presumed to have contributed different kinds of work and/or expertise to the text. Despite the necessity of writing collaboratively, though, there is little open discussion of the difficult process of collaborative research and writing, and how such projects are (or are not) rewarded within the academy. A faculty writing center could further the kind of research into faculty writing partnerships that Day and Eodice (2001), Lunsford and Ede (1990), and Ede and Lunsford (2001) have initiated, continuing an examination of how successful collaborations are formed and sustained, as well as how they are positioned within academia.

The ideal of academic discourse is an ongoing "conversation of mankind," as Bruffee (1984) puts it, in which knowledge is proposed, discussed, and reconstructed collaboratively across time. A faculty writing center, as we envision it, would respond to that dynamism and co-construction in ways that a model addressing only faculty "deficiencies" would not. Appointment as a writing coach in such a faculty writing center confers a chance for faculty to meet colleagues from other disciplines, to reflect on their own writing and pedagogy, and to engage in cross-disciplinary work with peers. Instead of a begrudged service begged of senior faculty, it would be seen as a prestigious opportunity to engage in collaborative knowledge-building that is compensated accordingly.

Perhaps the most key element of Bruffee's (1984) metaphor is that the academic conversation is a public one—hammered out in the pages of journals, at conferences, in classrooms, and in lecture halls. In order to develop from what we've learned from years of student writing center scholarship, a faculty writing center would need to be a highly visible, celebrated place for faculty to come together to talk openly about writing, rather than a shameful place where problematic faculty are privately referred for behind the scenes remediation. Such a writing center has the potential not only to support individual faculty members but also to make a significant contribution to knowledge-making in the academy.

REFERENCES

Brandt, Deborah. 2001. *Literacy in American Lives.* New York: Cambridge University Press. http://dx.doi.org/10.1017/CBO9780511810237.

Brandt, Deborah, and Katie Clinton. 2002. "Limits of the Local: Expanding Perspectives on Literacy as a Social Practice." *Journal of Literacy Research* 34 (3): 337–56. http://dx.doi.org/10.1207/s15548430jlr3403_4.

Bruffee, Kenneth. 1984. "Collaborative Learning and 'The Conversation of Mankind.'." *College English* 46 (7): 635–52. http://dx.doi.org/10.2307/376924.

Cooper, Marilyn. 1994. "Really Useful Knowledge: A Cultural Studies Agenda for Writing Centers." *Writing Center Journal* 14 (2): 97–111.

Day, Kami, and Michele Eodice. 2001. *(First Person)²: A Study of Co-Authoring in the Academy. Logan.* Utah State University Press.

Dias, Patrick, Aviva Freedman, Peter Medway, and Anthony Pare. 1999. *World's Apart: Acting and Writing in Academic and Workplace Contexts.* Mahwah, NJ: Lawrence Erlbaum Associates Publishers.

Ede, Lisa, and Andrea A. Lunsford. 2001. "Collaboration and Concepts of Authorship." *PMLA* 116: 354–69.

Grimm, Nancy. 1999. *Good Intentions: Writing Center Work for Postmodern Times. Portsmith.* Heinemann.

Harris, Muriel. 1995. "Talking in the Middle: Why Writers Need Writing Tutors." *College English* 57 (1): 27–42. http://dx.doi.org/10.2307/378348.

Kail, Harvey, and John Trimbur. 1987. "The Politics of Peer Tutoring." *Writing Center Journal* 11 (1): 5–12.

Lerner, Neal. 2009. *The Idea of a Writing Laboratory.* Carbondale: Southern Illinois University Press.

Lillis, Theresa, and Mary Jane Curry. 2010. *Academic Writing in a Global Context: The Politics and Practices of Publishing in English.* London: Routledge.

Lunsford, Andrea A., and Lisa Ede. 1990. *Singular Texts/Plural Authors: Perspectives on Collaborative Writing.* Carbondale: Southern Illinois University Press.

Mason, Mary Ann, and Marc Goulden. 2002. "Do Babies Matter? The effect of Family Formation on the Lifelong Careers of Academic Men and Women." *Academe Online* 88 (6): 21–27.

Middle States Commission on Higher Education (MSCHE). 2006. "Characteristics of Excellence in Higher Education: Requirements for Affiliation and Standards for Accreditation." http://www.msche.org/publications/CHX06_Aug08REVMarch09.pdf.

Professional and Organizational Development Network in Higher Education (POD Network). http://www.podnetwork.org/.

Russell, David R. 2002. *Writing in the Academic Disciplines: A Curricular History.* 2nd ed. Carbondale: Southern Illinois University Press.

Schuster, Jack H., and Martin J. Finkelstein. 2006. *The American Faculty: The Restructuring of Academic Work and Careers.* Baltimore: Johns Hopkins University Press.

Thelin, John R. 2004. *A History of American Higher Education.* Baltimore: Johns Hopkins University Press.

Thornton, Saranna R. 2009. "The Implementation and Utilization of Stop the Tenure Clock Policies in Canadian and U.S. Economics Departments." Paper presented at the American Economic Association Annual Meeting, San Francisco, CA, 2009. http://www.aeaweb.org/assa/2009/retrieve.php?pdfid=522.

WEBSITES AND DOCUMENTS AT TEMPLE UNIVERSITY

Teaching and Learning Center Website. http://www.temple.edu/tlc/.

Temple Research Administration Website. http://www.temple.edu/research/researchadmin/index.html.

Commonwealth System of Higher Education and Temple Association of University Professionals, American Federation of Teachers, AFL-CIO, Locals 4531." Temple University Vice Provost for Faculty Development and Faculty Affairs. http://www.temple.edu/hr/departments/employeerelations/documents/TAUP.pdf.

Temple University. 2008b."Guidelines for the Appointment and Promotion of Non-Tenure Track Faculty". Temple University Vice Provost for Faculty Development and Faculty Affairs. http://www.temple.edu/vpfaculty/docs/NTT_Promotion_Guidelines.pdf.

Temple University. 2011. "Organizational Outline for Tenure and Promotion Files." Temple University Vice Provost for Faculty Development and Faculty Affairs. http://www.temple.edu/vpfaculty/docs/TandP_Organizational_outline.pdf.

Temple University. n.d. "Faculty Handbook." Temple University Vice Provost for Faculty Development and Faculty Affairs. http://policies.temple.eduPDF/56.pdf.

4

TALKING ABOUT WRITING
Critical Dialogues on Supporting Faculty Writers

Gertrude Fraser and Deandra Little

In this chapter we briefly describe the University of Virginia's (UVa) Professors as Writers (PAW) program, established in 2005, and describe more fully our efforts to assess its impact on individual faculty and the institutional culture. We present this process as a critical dialogue between two complementary but distinct perspectives—that of an academic administrator and a faculty developer.[1] We chose this format because it models our efforts to be reflective practitioners as we create faculty programs, as well as our belief that faculty writing itself is a reflective practice (Schön 1983; Hillocks 1995; Raelin 2002; Bolton 2010). Through this dialogic approach, we think critically about program building as well as the converging and diverging views on the program's goals, focus, and measures of effectiveness that we found ourselves holding, based on our vantage points vis-à-vis the institution.

The PAW program began in response to discussions about faculty writing coming from two different directions—from promotion and tenure committees discussing writing quality and productivity with the Vice Provost (the faculty administrator noted above) and from individual faculty members expressing their concerns about writing and managing various, competing professional demands to the faculty developer and her colleagues at UVa's Teaching Resource Center (TRC). Responding to these concerns, the program has supported faculty writing in a number of ways, primarily through small grants, but also by connecting faculty interested in writing groups, providing web resources with

---

1. We gratefully acknowledge the essential work of Dawn Hunt, a colleague and former Professors as Writers (PAW) coach and editor, who served as an editor and coach for the piece, provided thoughtful and informed feedback, and nurtured our critical dialogue process.

DOI: 10.7330/9780874219029.c004

information on editorial or writing coaches, and sponsoring workshops on writing, publishing, and time management. The main focus of the program continues to be annual, one-time grants of $1,000 that faculty members can use to hire an editorial or writing coach for a manuscript or grant proposal or, more recently, $1,500 grants for a book manuscript conference to bring together a small group of scholars from inside and outside UVa. The grant process is competitive—we offer ten to fifteen annually—and open to all full time UVa faculty, both tenure-track and non-tenure track. Significantly, the focus of the grants is on writing and not research; the grants must be used to support some aspect of the writing process, and not for research assistance, conference travel, salary, or to pay for any of the technicalities of manuscript preparation, such as proofreading, subventions, or indexing.

Over the last six years, we have seen the program evolve in both predictable and unexpected ways. In this chapter we focus on how this evolution unfolded, as we discuss the process of developing the program using a set of questions that guided our inquiry. Our conversation here mirrors in many ways our continuing discussions about the program—a dialogue that has focused on the interplay of practice and theory and our underlying assumptions about each, as much as it has on the evolving structure of the program. What we model here is in one sense reflective practice (Schön 1983; Mezirow 1991) and in another what Carew, et al. (2008, 53) call Elastic Practice, or "an organic, responsive way of designing and evolving specific approaches to Academic [Faculty] Development." Reflection allows us to consider how and why we each bring alternately complementary and divergent perspectives, assumptions, and interpretations to the PAW program. Our shared conclusion is that successful faculty writers find a good balance between autonomy and interdependence. The PAW program intervenes at the individual and institutional levels so that diverse faculty members find the balance that works best for them.

THE DISCUSSANTS

How do our own backgrounds and experiences with academic writing influence our perspective on program design?

> *Gertrude:* Roberto Ibarra [2003], in his study of Latina/o graduate students, identifies the hidden cultural codes of the academy that privilege some forms of intellectual expression and inhibit others. He argues that modes of writing and argumentation are like the DNA through which these codes are communicated and expressed. Reflecting on my experi-

ence as an African American woman in graduate school in the 1980s, Ibarra's characterization resonates. I knew, without anyone actually telling me, that my worth as an emerging scholar was very much bound up in professors' assessment of my writing. Furthermore, the invisible language of race and competence fueled concern that the quality of my writing would be used to judge whether or not I belonged in the academy. I always felt secure about my commitment to anthropology as a field of study, however, I was uncertain about how I was doing as a writer in the discipline. Was I a person with important ideas, and how did I communicate that through my writing? These questions were rarely answered directly. My professors assumed that graduate students should just know how. A social hierarchy developed largely based on our perceptions of how well professors received fellow graduate students' written work. Often it felt like academic writing was a birthright available to some and not to others. This charged environment focused all our attention on writing and may have motivated some of us to write well and often. For others, it produced counterproductive responses such as procrastination, perfectionism, and anxiety that inhibited our sense of mastery and had a deleterious effect on writing productivity and quality. Writing was a fundamental aspect of our professionalization into the academy—visible, potent, an important part of our lived experience as graduate students— yet also operating below the surface with an embedded set of values that were rarely made explicit.

Deandra: My experience at Vanderbilt a decade later mirrored Gertrude's, but the elements that affected me most profoundly differed. In my graduate program, as in other humanities departments, scholarship and, even more so scholarly writing, was configured as a solitary activity. Research meant sitting alone, in an office or archive, poring over texts. Writing meant sitting alone, again, with a pad of paper or word processor. Because of their own immersion in the process, faculty members often assumed that graduate students had a greater knowledge of writing and publishing than we actually did, and offered well-meaning but vague advice. Raised in a rural, working class community, I was the first person I knew to enter a graduate program that was neither for a professional degree, nor particularly practical. I was conscious of the need to perform my identity as an academic to two distinct audiences: to "back home" skeptics, I found myself projecting a confidence I did not feel as a means to defend my choice to go to graduate school in literature; to faculty and graduate colleagues, I performed the role of competent future faculty member while internalizing my own imposter syndrome and trying to avoid asking questions that revealed insufficient understanding of the academic culture or mores. These dual performances left me feeling divided and motivated more by external factors, such as other people's perceptions of my work, than internal ones.

Though committed to the field, I had a fragmented sense of myself as an academic. This fragmentation was made more salient by the unspoken but implied dichotomy between writing and teaching, or between identifying as a scholar or as a teacher. I realize now that this relationship was less binary than it felt at the time, but my perception affected the way I understood my relation to writing and to my sense of a unified academic identity. Identifying as teacher first and writer second seemed to have real consequences for how faculty perceived us as graduate students and on the types of professional mentoring offered. Identifying as writer first and teacher second intensified my feelings of being alien to my home community. Ironically, I was simultaneously teaching about writing—in undergraduate courses that emphasized the importance of asking for feedback and of seeing writing as a series of learned behaviors improved through practice and dedication rather than a way of being.

As Wendy Belcher (2009, 190) writes, "some [of us] write consistently and well without having to talk about it; most of us need to admit our struggles if we are to move beyond them." Acknowledging and moving beyond my graduate experience, I find that scholarship and publishing look different from the vantage point of faculty developer, where collaboration is common, and writing and teaching (or writing about teaching) are intertwined rather than opposing efforts. My work as a developer is informed by my experiences in the academy, particularly when helping individual faculty and graduate students interpret, respond to, and navigate institutional cultures around teaching and learning, and in their academic writing through the PAW program.

DEVELOPING THE PROGRAM: OUR THEORETICAL FRAMEWORKS

How do we identify shared goals and clear outcomes while recognizing different points of agency and scope within the institutional structure? How do we arrive at satisfactory compromises when our perspectives or theoretical frameworks diverge?

Deandra: From my perspective as a developer, program design has to take into account both individual and institutional needs, but my primary focus is on the individual. Promoting organizational change remains an important backdrop, but one secondary to supporting individual faculty as they navigate the existing system. Coming from a teaching center, I have been most concerned with responding to individual needs within this broader context in ways that align with theories of adult learning (Knowles 1990 [1973]; Brookfield 1986) and motivation, specifically self-determination theory (Deci and Ryan 2000), which emphasize the importance of autonomy, choice, relatedness, and relevancy.

Given the current climate, where expectations for scholarly productivity have intensified even as the outlets for publishing and grants have dwindled, it was important that the program foster a mental shift away from viewing one's scholarship as a type of externally imposed or "forced productivity" (Savage 2003) that reified the "publish or perish" mentality. Lee and Boud (2003, 189) accurately describe the corollary effects of this climate on many faculty I work with: an "increase in self-questioning, by both individuals and institutions, concerning the nature and value of the academic enterprise and their place within it," and "fear and anxiety" caused by changing conditions, as well as the possibility for new opportunities in this rich and complex environment. In this climate, they conclude, educational development programs "must work with, and make visible, what is often left out of official accounts—the emotional dimensions of development and change" (189). Focusing on one-on-one work with an editorial or writing coach through the grants program helped address these emotional dimensions and seemed likely to increase grant winners' sense of autonomous motivation, so that they were writing because they felt intrinsically motivated to do so, because writing is an integral part of their academic identity, and because they felt a sense of volition and (yes) even joy in their writing and scholarship. Accordingly, focusing on grants rather than an established curriculum meant the program could provide choice and flexibility in a way responsive to promotion, tenure, and professional development contexts as well as emotional ones.

Promoting individual autonomy and relevance begins at the grant application stage, when applicants discuss their writing goals for the short and long term, along with how the grant will allow them to achieve these goals, and how these goals align with their professional development goals, the last of which is also discussed by the letter of support from a department chair or supervisor. Grant winners revisit and evaluate their progress toward their goals at several points during the grant cycle, individually and in discussion with other grant winners. They consult with me individually and in small groups to decide which aspects of their writing goals to focus on and to identify a short list of coaches to interview and then report on their progress or concerns in informal, mid-year reports and an extensive end-of-program report. At least twice a semester, they meet with other grant winners to discuss their progress and their work with their coaches. In these ways, the program is closely aligned with each individual's professional role and context.

Gertrude: As an anthropologist, I am always inclined to discern how culturally organized practices and approaches to knowledge can come to seem universal and preordained in the natural order. This disciplinary framework has influenced my approach to faculty development and specifically to the establishment of the PAW program. Writing in the academy can be described simultaneously as a social resource that is unequally distributed and accessed and as a cultural technology through which forms of disciplinary knowledge are communicated and evaluated. Academic writing is mediated by and through organizational forms, whether they are disciplines, evaluation or peer review panels, institutional policies on promotion and tenure, or editorial boards of publishing houses, with cultural insiders and outsiders who have greater or lesser knowledge about and access to the governing norms and rules. Perhaps this fact is integral to the development and dissemination of knowledge; however, it can also alienate and discourage. Unwritten rules and patterns of academic writing may be very transparent to some and hidden and mysterious to others. The inequities created by these cultural and political logics of writing in the academy predisposed me to envision a program that would not only offer faculty help with their own writing and encourage dialogue about writing processes and experiences but also be attentive to the ways that race, ethnicity, and social class could differently shape faculty members connections to and relationships with disciplinary traditions and the norms of writing associated with them (Sorcinelli 1994; Johnsrud and Sadao 1998; Ibarra 2000; Cooper and Stevens 2002; Sorcinelli et al. 2006; Stanley 2006). There is increasing consensus that universities can effectively encourage and provide resources to meet the range of challenges associated with academic writing at various stages of faculty careers, across race, gender, and class locations and in light of escalating organizational demands on faculty work and time (Sorcinelli 1994; Moody 2004; Sorcinelli et al. 2006). Against this broader conceptual framework, my initial thinking was that a centrally funded program would help to level the playing field to create more inclusive opportunities for faculty writing support and, at the same time, de-stigmatize help-seeking.

Faculty thrive or falter in their writing at the fault-line between the private and public, individual and organizational dimensions of academic and institutional life. These boundaries are normative expressions of organizational formations. Some individuals are more likely than others to experience alignment across these boundaries, others may primarily sense a lack of fit or distance between their sense of identity and organizational culture (Kreiner, Hollensbe and Sheep 2006). The program design addresses some of these concerns. We offer a menu of writing support and participants can tailor interventions to suit their specific needs—from private coaching to writing workshops. We position the program as a competitive grants program for junior and senior colleagues. Deandra creates a climate of trust and establishes joint agreements of confidentiality among participants as they share their writing stories. Word of mouth from PAW alumni about successes and positive outcomes encourages skeptical colleagues to apply.

Even as we highlight the positive dimensions of the program we developed, we recognize that a writing program can unintentionally stigmatize faculty members many of whom, by virtue of their identities or the kinds of scholarship they undertake, already feel themselves to be under a microscope. For example, a minority faculty member who is nominated for the PAW program might legitimately wonder whether they are perceived as less prepared or more in need of help. Someone who is concerned that their struggles with writing are unique and shameful may prefer to keep these thoughts private and might worry about exposure to peers or senior colleagues. These are legitimate fears and risks associated especially with a campus based writing program. During program design and as part of ongoing dialogue with participants and stakeholders, it is important to surface the issues of risk and help-seeking. Willingness to openly engage with issues of power, stigma, and identity that may be associated with supporting faculty writers not only helps to mitigate the actual or perceived barriers to participation, but also signals that the first-order priority is to serve faculty rather than institutional needs.

THE POLITICS OF PLACEMENT

In what ways does program placement matter? What are the implications of having a centrally funded faculty writing program administered from a teaching center?

Gertrude: Deandra and I have different points of entry about the decision to situate PAW within the TRC. My choice took into account the TRC's significant position within evaluation policies, politics, and practices that govern faculty career progression. Faculty and university leaders, such as department chairs, deans, and provost office administrators held the TRC in high regard for its previous success in other faculty development initiatives related to teaching awards, curriculum development, and onboarding of new, diverse faculty. A faculty member's participation in TRC career enhancement programs was often positively referenced in formal evaluation settings, such as third year review, and promotion and tenure committees. Further, my office had previously collaborated with the TRC on work-life topics that provided a model for initiating broader conversations on faculty writing. Thus the TRC's visibility and alignment with institutional goals, rather than its marginality, facilitated leadership buy-in and provided a mechanism through which, as a central administrator, I could establish a partnership to launch the faculty writing program. This constellation of reasons follows closely Schroeder's (2011) argument that programs that connect faculty and organizational development strategies are most successful when they are advocated for and funded by institutional leaders, align with institutional priorities, draw on the leadership and expertise of trusted faculty developers, and initiate or expand dialogue on critical institutional issues.

Deandra: A program supporting faculty writing can simultaneously be both a logical and awkward fit within a teaching center. Logical because our center takes a holistic approach to faculty work; my TRC colleagues and I have found that consultations with faculty frequently range beyond teaching into other aspects of academic careers, including writing productivity. We have also historically offered a range of programming for faculty and graduate instructors teaching undergraduate writing courses; taking a developmental approach to faculty writing seems a reasonable next step. And as Gertrude suggests, from an administrative perspective, other factors make the TRC seem a strategic choice for the program home.

From my vantage point, it is the marginal or liminal position of our center that makes it most appealing location for such a program. Located outside the promotion and tenure structure, the TRC is neither affiliated with any specific school or department nor involved with evaluation procedures at any level. In addition to legitimizing the program, the center offers a safe space for participants to talk about their writing concerns. The importance of this was expressed by a participant in the second year of the program: "It [the grant] has so many benefits, not the least of which is to provide very personal, safe help for the writing process."[2]

Ironically, the primary reasons why the TRC, situated outside the institutional evaluation structure, provides a good location for writing support also mean it is a less powerful agent in applying direct pressure to those structures. Absent direct access to promotion and tenure committee conversations, I have listened more to faculty voices when defining the "problem" the PAW program was responding to. Further, taking on a program focused on this aspect of academic life has meant rearticulating the TRC's mission and negotiating new collaborations with units that have a vested interest in faculty development, scholarship, or grant writing. Early conversations with the student writing center director, research office, and deans' offices helped us raise and allay questions of territory while identifying institutional allies, resistors, and those who were vaguely supportive or largely indifferent.

Reflections

A rising interest in support for faculty writing in recent years is evidenced by the growing body of literature on the topic. When we reviewed the literature about faculty writing programs published since 2006, we paid particular attention to the location of the sixteen different programs described in the fifteen articles or book chapters. Of these, nine originated from some centrally situated structure in the institution, usually a center for faculty development, sometimes a writing center or a dean's office (Elbow and Sorcinelli 2006; Grant 2006; McGowan 2006; Randall 2006; O'Malley and Lucey 2008; Steinert et al. 2008; Ambos, Wiley and Allen 2009; Burns and McCarthy 2010; Hoelscher 2011). The rest developed as a result of the efforts of one faculty member or a small group of faculty (Tysick and Babb 2006; Alonso 2007; Washburn 2008; Friend and González 2009; Burns and McCarthy 2010; Faulconer et al. 2010; Swaggerty et al. 2011). Interestingly, five of these faculty-initiated programs aroused the interest of someone more centrally situated, who then offered logistical and/or financial support. It is clear from this review that there is no one track for the development of a successful faculty writing program. Based on our experience, we would argue that

---

2. This and every other remark in this chapter from a faculty participant in the PAW Writing Grant program is an excerpt from an end-of-grant report. Each remark represents a different faculty member; program year is usually indicated in parentheses following the quote.

a combination of faculty investment, trust, and central support contributes to the success and sustainability of such programs. For anyone considering the creation of a new program, or evaluation of an existing one, we recommend an open and vigorous dialogue with all concerned parties as to how and where to situate their program.

EXPLORING THE TERRAIN: WHICH FACULTY?

Who should the program support? How have our answers to this question changed over time?

> *Deandra:* We initially assumed that the program would attract tenure-track junior faculty, particularly those from underrepresented groups, and that it would address the diminished mentoring around writing that these faculty members were reporting. We did not, however, limit the program to this group. In the interests of equity, we left the program open to faculty across the university, at all career stages and to all full-time faculty, on and off the tenure-track. Our initial assumptions about who the program would support have been both challenged and affirmed in the succeeding years.
>
> We have met our initial goal of serving the needs of a diverse group of faculty. Grant winners come from all disciplines and career stages, from both tenure and non-tenure tracks, and from various racial, ethnic, and cultural groups; additionally, women are very well represented. This diversity becomes especially apparent when we compare the demographics of the group of seventy-six PAW participants with the larger group of teaching faculty at UVa. Between 2005 and 2011, 75 percent of PAW grantees (and an even larger percentage of applicants) were women. As a point of contrast, in 2011, university-wide, only 26 percent of tenured/tenure-track and 48 percent of non-tenure track faculty were female. The program has successfully supported faculty from other underrepresented groups as well; slightly over half (53%) of grant winners identified as white, slightly less (47%) from an underrepresented group (including "non-resident aliens"). These percentages become even more striking when viewed in the context of UVa's broader faculty population: 86 percent of both tenured/tenure-track and non-tenure-track faculty are white. An unexpectedly high number of mid-career faculty have applied for and been awarded a grant. This number has increased over time; in 2005, three out of ten participants were mid-career or senior faculty, by fall 2010, eight out of seventeen were.
>
> *Gertrude:* My initial concerns that underrepresented faculty would be reluctant to apply because of heightened visibility or negative associations with writing remediation have been substantially allayed by the evidence of participant diversity. Having diverse participants and shared learning reaches the intended faculty members and accomplishes our programmatic and institutional goals. Implementation of the PAW program

overlaps with a period from 2005–2008 of increased faculty hiring and with concerted and successful efforts to recruit diverse faculty (Fraser and Hunt 2011), many of whom are new assistant professors. The PAW program fits within these institutional efforts to develop and retain these colleagues, and new hires are alerted early on about the program. Following on Boice (1989, 1990) and Moody (2010), the program gets pre-tenured faculty off to a good start; the involvement of department chairs and deans in the nomination and recommendation process is intended to connect this central program to the local context as well as to ensure their endorsement of the participant's overall plan of work. In a faculty development environment that invests largely in new and pre-tenured faculty, associate professors often fall through the cracks. Extending PAW grants to include this demographic shows our commitment to the ideals of lifelong faculty learning and engagement by allowing mid-career participants to complete longstanding work or initiate new interdisciplinary collaborations with colleagues. Our expectation is that their experience in the program will also influence more active and informed involvement in mentoring pre-tenured colleagues. Since 2008, the university has experienced a hiring slowdown for new faculty, which means that we were able to increase the number of grants to mid-career faculty. Unless there are significant additional programming funds, we may need to revisit allocations and priorities once significant hiring begins again. For now, I am satisfied that the program has substantially achieved its goals of de-stigmatizing help-seeking and created access to resources, expertise, and dialogue about academic writing by a broad cross-section of the faculty.

Reflections

Analyzing the trends in the applicant pool has forced us to reexamine our program goals as we notice the divergent needs and experiences different groups bring. Considering how and whether to target the grants to faculty from particular disciplines or writing in particular formats remains an ongoing discussion with no easy solution. One example: having more mid-career or senior faculty in the program offers more opportunities for short-term mentoring across career stages, as when a scholar who has published extensively but wants to focus on time management talks informally during a program meeting with a junior colleague working on her first book manuscript. Conversely, it has occasionally led to more problematic exchanges, when it has shifted away from collegial comentoring into unidirectional advice-giving sessions, or when junior colleagues have taken what was perhaps unfair advantage of senior colleagues' time and good will. Determining who the program should support, in what proportion, and how this support best fosters the professional growth of the wide ranging goals of any given cohort of program participants remains a lingering question we are still trying to address.

EXPLORING THE TERRAIN: WHAT KIND OF SUPPORT?

What kinds of writing support do faculty want or need given the current state of publishing and grant-giving? According to whom?

Gertrude: Following my years as a faculty member I became an academic administrator in the provost's office and cochair of the provost's promotion and tenure committee. The committee was composed of senior faculty members who, after reading a number of dossiers, expressed concern that more could be done to improve mentoring about writing and publishing for the pre-tenured, to better prepare them for promotion and tenure. Committee members also noted that as their obligations to mentor graduate student writing increased, less time remained to read and comment on the work of junior colleagues. They expressed a sense of divided time and commitments. It would be hard to underestimate the value of having white women and women of color on the promotion and tenure committee who spoke directly to the difficulty of meeting their own writing and scholarship goals, while supporting those of their junior colleagues and graduate students. These reflective comments led to the conclusion that there was room for an extra-departmental initiative to address directly the need for a faculty development program focused on academic writing. The committee members' conversation also nudged me towards the idea that such a program should create an environment for active and robust discussions of successful writing—talk about academic writing as an ongoing dialogue among colleagues, as an institutional resource—rather than as a remedial activity for less successful individuals. Further, such a program could contribute to overall institutional goals to recruit and retain under-represented and women faculty. My submission of a funding proposal for a pilot faculty writing program was well received and approved. By the time we approached faculty at the focus groups, the general framework for the PAW program had begun to emerge.

Deandra: Preliminary planning was based on conversations with individual faculty who perceived the greatest challenge to their writing productivity as the tension between their conflicting job responsibilities (teaching, administrative work, research, and publishing), particularly as institutional expectations in all these areas increased. To test this anecdotal understanding of writing needs and concerns, we held two focus groups—one targeted to humanities and social science faculty and one to faculty in science, technology, engineering, and math (STEM). During each session, we asked participants to generate and rank a list of challenges to academic writing and publishing or to writing grant proposals. After discussing these, a panel of experienced faculty offered strategies they used to address many of them successfully.

The focus groups confirmed my hypothesis: 80 percent of the faculty attending the Humanities and Social Science session indicated that finding time to write, including dealing with seemingly "incompatible priorities" was their major concern. Other challenges expressed were those common to academic writers (Boice 1990; Rankin 2001), including, among others, psychological barriers, a perceived lack of community around writing, and ambiguity about institutional expectations for scholarly productivity. During the second, smaller focus group, STEM faculty revealed similar challenges, namely perfectionism and difficulty finding senior faculty writing mentors; however, their primary concerns differed, and included working with graduate student coauthors and on grant proposals: how to develop coherent proposals, keep up with deadlines, and develop relationships with program managers at granting agencies, and so on—concerns that were less relevant to humanities faculty in 2005, but have become increasingly so.

Reflections

A tension between enhancing individual or organizational capacity surfaced in the focus groups, on the promotion and tenure committee, and in the coauthors' discussions, and is an ongoing theme in program implementation, delivery, and evaluation. The lesson we offer here on early planning, assessing perceived needs for writing support, and program launching is the importance of recognizing the complexities inherent in creating faculty writing programs: be as alert as possible to the range of issues and stakeholders, resist the urge to oversimplify, be prepared to change strategies as new contingencies emerge, create safe spaces for dialogue and help-seeking, but do not allow this complexity to stall implementation.

MEASURING OUTCOMES AND IMPACT

What does success look like for this program? How do we measure program outcomes and impacts, both at individual and organizational levels?

> *Deandra:* Overall, the PAW program has been successful in reaching individual—and program-level—goals. For the past six years, faculty report the program supported them in ways that positively affected the productivity, quality, and ease of their writing, as well as promoted affective and attitudinal changes such as increased confidence, feelings of connection, and enjoyment of the writing process. As in other programs discussed in this book, participants report an improved ability to prioritize writing and manage time in ways that transferred beyond the specific writing projects they focused on during the grant cycle. All indications suggest that the PAW program has not only enabled grant winners to achieve their specific writing goals, but also engaged them in reflection about the writing process as well as their professional goals around writing, publishing, and balance.

Some of these successes were ones we anticipated. Convinced by the research, we predicted that grant winners' work with an editorial or writing coach would help address the psychosocial dimensions of writing that Boice (1989, 1990) and others (Rankin 2001; Belcher 2009) discuss, and found these predictions were well founded. Grant winners indicated they had learned productive ways to deal with such challenges as perfectionism and procrastination. One, for example, confessed she had begun the year approaching writing with feelings of dread, but ended, "now writing with confidence and joy" (2008–09); another wrote that the grant got "me started writing again at a time I had pretty much given up on writing" (2009–10).

Other outcomes suggested we exceeded our goals for the program. In the aggregate, the grant winners' reports indicated they felt less isolated in their writing, that help-seeking for their writing was de-stigmatized, and that the program also positively affected both their motivation to write and their understanding of their own academic identity, as both a scholar and a mentor. One participant wrote, *"this will be my greatest outcome from the grant* . . . envisioning myself as a writer—not just as a professor with a variety of responsibilities" (2008–09). Another grantee described her increased awareness of teaching and mentoring other writers by saying she had developed a "diagnostic eye" that would help her take a more process-oriented approach to her students' writing. Others came up with specific interventions, such as adding a process-oriented assignment to an introductory graduate course.

Analyzing the qualitative feedback from former grant winners also helped correct an initial assumption I held regarding how our goals for community building would be realized. Knowing that formal and informal faculty writing support frequently builds on the community of practice model (Lee and Boud 2003; Pasternak et al. 2009), often as an explicit antidote to the isolationism in academic life surrounding writing (Herard 2005; Grant 2006), I assumed our program would create specific types of community (or pre-defined "products"). At first, I tried to foster community within the program in one or two predetermined ways, organizing either an interdisciplinary learning community of grantees or writing groups that were interdisciplinary or discipline- or genre-based. Though each of these efforts found small-scale success, none worked across an entire cohort or were sustained beyond the year of the program. At first, I was convinced this meant we were not meeting our goals.

Instead, I found that participants' perceptions of community ran counter to mine, because they focused (rightly so) on community as a process-oriented outcome, in which community building around writing took various forms. In fact, they described many opportunities for meaningful community building that the program provided as they moved away from a solo model of writing. For most, this sense of community came from their relationship with an editorial or writing coach, which helped them begin to see writing as a collaborative process because it "meant that you are not writing in a vacuum; rather that someone is actually interacting with you about your own writing" (2006–07). Others found the infrequent meetings with fellow grant winners "supportive and heartening" (2008–09) and even that coming "in contact with scholars whose main goal is to be productive in an intellectual way," was "the main benefit" of the program (2009–10). And still others began to build community outside the program, forming their own writing groups or helping colleagues who were undertaking similar writing projects. A grant winner revising a book introduction, for example, passed along her "new philosophy of introduction writing" (2008–09) to two colleagues outside the program who were working on the same; another invited his editor to work with his entire research team.

Gertrude: There have been a number of positive institutional level changes as a result of the PAW program and the broader conversations about support for faculty writing. There is an expanded approach to faculty writing mentorship that incorporates not only internal and external colleagues, but also the recognition of professional coaches and other points of access to help. As previously noted, third-year reviews and annual reports in the past five years have positively referenced faculty who have utilized the PAW program or other resources in their manuscript preparation. We have reached our intended audience as measured by the diversity of the participating fellows and their creativity in using modest program resources to initiate or complete projects or scaffold larger projects. Faculty, departmental leadership, and deans are increasingly aware of the program and its successes; this is reflected in the number of multiple nominations from departments and schools. We have incorporated PAW annual reports into the central level critical functions document that identifies core areas of responsibility for provost level staff and is submitted to the provost and president. Within the past three years, a number of PAW fellows have garnered national attention for scholarship that crosses the boundary between academic and public. Whenever PAW fellows publish, a quick note of praise and thanks to the provost is one way that we communicate about the program to central leadership. In what is an unintended consequence, we are finding that previous PAW fellows have recently taken on school level leadership positions as department chairs and associate deans. Through the accumulation of their experiences in PAW, we envision the incorporation of organizational support for faculty writers into their leadership tool kits.

REFLECTIONS: CONTINUING THE CONVERSATION

The PAW program is successful in part because it aligns well with other types of structures and routines that combine peer-driven interactions and evaluative processes. In her ethnography of interdisciplinary peer review panels for prestigious fellowships, Lamont (2009) suggests that in certain evaluative contexts, academic cultural norms may encourage meta-level discourse across disciplines about knowledge claims, including how they are communicated in academic writing, lead to solution-driven talk routines, and connect to common values such as fairness and equity. She observes that reviewers are not only motivated by "the opportunity to maximize their position, but also by their pragmatic involvement in collective problem-solving" (Lamont 2009, 20). In the case of fellowships panel review, commitment to the fairness of the process entailed commitment to improving it (37). Gillespie et al. (2005) describe a similar dynamic when they participated in interdisciplinary research circles, noting among other benefits, a sense that engagement in feedback on peer writing reinforced their commitment to the ideal of collegiality and institutional building in what could have been otherwise a highly alienating and demanding experience of being junior faculty on a newly established campus. Earlier reference in this paper to dialogue about writing among our university's promotion and tenure committee is another example. These examples suggest that the PAW program that brings faculty together in reflexive dialogue about writing is synergistic with established academic norms. It connects with the more transformative, rather than conservative, potential embedded in what Austin (1990, 65) refers to as a core central value in American higher education "a commitment to collegiality coupled with autonomy as the appropriate organizational context within which faculty should work." Rowland's (2000) model, later adapted by Bolton (2010), posits three main areas in which knowledge is conveyed and actively learned by university professors and then taught: knowledge from disciplines existing as a public resource, personal experiential knowledge through which professional expertise is filtered, and the shared context of new knowledge being created in the present. The work of the PAW program is most visible institutionally in the personal dimension of this reflexive process as it is articulated by individual faculty when they describe their previous and current approaches to writing, and the emergence of new writing identities filtered through their professional and academic lives. The shared context of their work is a communal process that involves them not only with editors or coaches, but also in the broader community of learners, including graduate students, fellow colleagues, and in interactions with other PAW participants. For our work going forward, it would be important to deepen our call for participants to describe the ways that they actively engage in this dimension of critique and reflection, since it is at this level that they can begin to change the scripts of how academic culture is inculcated. There is an organizational dimension to the engagement with learning about one's writing that is represented in the idea of moving individual voices from the margins to the center. To the extent that faculty who would otherwise feel isolated or struggle to register their contributions now take ownership of their work in disciplinary or counter-disciplinary traditions, we have gained an institutional impact and an individual who is more likely to claim his or her place in the academy.

As we consider the next phase of program development, one emphasis will be on the communal nature of the writing process, both at UVa and beyond. We have recently begun offering a new set of small grants faculty members can use to bring outside scholars and UVa colleagues together to workshop a book manuscript, which enables faculty to build short-term communities while gaining constructive writing feedback. Finding ways to make this type of opportunity available to faculty outside of book-oriented disciplines is an important next step, as is supporting a range of short- and long-term writing communities depending on faculty interest. A possible model, for example, are affinity-based interdisciplinary groups such as Sisters of the Academy and Brothers of the Academy, which organize peer-to-peer writing and scholarship mentorship around the shared experience of being minorities in higher education. However configured, bringing together diverse underrepresented and majority faculty across disciplines with the explicit purpose of talking about and working on writing stimulates systemic thinking about the nature of disciplines, of taxonomies, and how knowledge is constituted and voiced through written expression (Kingston-Mann and Sieber 2001; Lamont 2009; Young 2011). We would claim that participation in PAW offers a space of freedom where participants are encouraged to bring the complexity of their writing identities to the foreground, not as solo agents but as interacting members of a writing cohort and community. A window into the liberatory outcomes of this sustained engagement with self and other in the writing process is offered by feminist sociologist Laurel Richardson, who documents her especially painful navigation of what she terms the "normalizing process" of the academy and then discerns that "writing is both a theoretical and practical process through which we can (a) reveal epistemological assumptions, (b) discover grounds for questioning received scripts and hegemonic ideals—both those within the academy and those incorporated within ourselves, (c) finds ways to change those scripts, (d) connect to others and form community, and (e) nurture our emergent selves" (Richardson 2000, 153).

Although faculty participants in the program do not explicitly describe their experience in these political terms, focusing rather on the practical resource dimensions of time, work demands, or writing for institutional reasons of promotion and tenure, our call to action is to respond to these tangible issues and at the same time listen for and encourage activities that would imagine and enact transformative approaches to academic life and academic writing so that future members of the professorate can have a better experience than we have had.

REFERENCES

Alonso, Anne. Apr 2007. "Reflections on the writing group." *International Journal of Group Psychotherapy* 57 (2): 219–23. http://dx.doi.org/10.1521/ijgp.2007.57.2.219. Medline:17419671.

Ambos, Elizabeth, Mark Wiley, and Terre H. Allen. 2009. "Romancing the Muse: Faculty Writing Institutes as Professional Development." In *To Improve the Academy: Resources for Faculty, Instructional, and Organizational Development*, edited by L. Nelson and J. E. Miller, 27: 135–49. San Francisco: Jossey-Bass.

Austin, Anne E. 1990. "Faculty Culture, Faculty Values." *New Directions for Institutional Research* 1990 (68): 61–74. http://dx.doi.org/10.1002/ir.37019906807.

Belcher, Wendy. 2009. "Reflections on Ten Years of Teaching Writing for Publication to Graduate Students and Junior Faculty." *Journal of Scholarly Publishing* 40 (2): 184–200. http://dx.doi.org/10.3138/jsp.40.2.184.

Boice, Robert. 1989. "Procrastination, busyness and bingeing." *Behaviour Research and Therapy* 27 (6): 605–11. http://dx.doi.org/10.1016/0005-7967(89)90144-7. Medline:2610657.

Boice, Robert. 1990. *Professors as Writers: A Self-Help Guide to Productive Writing*. Stillwater, OK: New Forums Press.

Bolton, Gille. 2010. *Reflective Practice: Writing and Professional Development*. Los Angeles: Sage Publications.

Brookfield, Stephen D. 1986. *Understanding and Facilitating Adult Learning*. San Francisco: Jossey-Bass.

Burns, Barbara, and Dianne S. McCarthy. 2010. "Working Together to Ease the Pressure to Publish in Higher Education." *Academic Leadership* 8 (4): 22–6.

Carew, Anna L., Geraldine Lefoe, Maureen Bell, and Lenore Armour. 2008. "Elastic Practice in Academic Developers." *International Journal for Academic Development* 13 (1): 51–66. http://dx.doi.org/10.1080/13601440701860250.

Cooper, Joanne E., and Danelle D. Stevens, eds. 2002. *Tenure in the Sacred Grove: Issues and Strategies for Women and Minority Faculty*. Albany: State University of New York Press.

Deci, Edward L., and Richard M. Ryan. 2000. "The 'What' and 'Why' of Goal Pursuits: Human Needs and the Self-Determination of Behavior." *Psychological Inquiry* 11 (4): 227–68. http://dx.doi.org/10.1207/S15327965PLI1104_01.

Elbow, Peter, and Mary D. Sorcinelli. 2006. "The Faculty Writing Place: A Room of Our Own." *Change: The Magazine for Higher Learning* 38: 1–7.

Faulconer, Johna L., Terry Atkinson, Robert Griffith, Melissa Matusevich, and Elizabeth Swaggerty. 2010. "The Power of Living the Writerly Life: A Group Model for Women Writers." *NASPA Journal about Women in Higher Education* 3 (1): 207–35. http://dx.doi.org/10.2202/1940-7890.1047.

Fraser, Gertrude J., and Dawn E. Hunt. 2011. "Faculty Diversity and Search Committee Training: Learning From a Critical Incident." *Journal of Diversity in Higher Education* 4 (3): 185–98. http://dx.doi.org/10.1037/a0022248.

Friend, Jennifer I., and Juan C. González. 2009. "Get Together to Write." *Academe Online*. January–February.

Gillespie, Dianne, Nives Dolšak, Bruce Kochis, Ron Krabill, Karli Lerum, Anne Peterson, and Elizabeth Thomas. 2005. "Research Circles: Supporting the Scholarship of Junior Faculty." *Innovative Higher Education* 30 (3): 149–62. http://dx.doi.org/10.1007/s10755-005-6300-9.

Grant, Barbara M. 2006. "Writing in the Company of Other Women: Exceeding the Boundaries." *Studies in Higher Education* 31 (4): 483–95. http://dx.doi.org/10.1080/03075070600800624.

Herard, Tiffany. 2005. "Writing in Solidarity: The New Generation." *Race & Class* 47 (2): 88–99. http://dx.doi.org/10.1177/0306396805058089.

Hillocks, George. 1995. *Teaching Reflective Writing as Reflective Practice.* New York: Teachers College Press.

Hoelscher, Karen. 2011. "Revising a Writing Group." *Inside Higher Ed,* January 28, 2011. http://www.insidehighered.com/advice/hoelscher/one_university_re_envisions_how_it_supports_faculty_writing.

Ibarra, Robert A. 2000. *Beyond Affirmative Action: Reframing the Context of Higher Education.* Madison: University of Wisconsin Press.

Ibarra, Robert A. 2003. "The Latina/o Faculty and the Tenure Process in Cultural Context." In *Majority in the Minority: Expanding the Representation of Latina/o Faculty, Administrators, and Students in Higher Education,* ed. J. Castellanos and L. Jones, 207–219. Alexandria, VA: Stylus.

Johnsrud, L.inda K., and Kathleen C. Sadao. 1998. "The Common Experience of 'Otherness': Ethnic and Racial Minority Faculty." *Review of Higher Education* 21 (4): 315–42. http://dx.doi.org/10.1353/rhe.1998.0010.

Kingston-Mann, Esther, and Timothy Sieber, eds. 2001. *Achieving Against the Odds: How Academics Become Teachers of Diverse Students.* Philadelphia: Temple University Press.

Kreiner, Glen E., Elaine C. Hollensbe, and Mathew L. Sheep. 2006. "On the Edge of Identity: Boundary Dynamics at the Interface of Individual and Organizational Identities." *Human Relations* 59 (10): 1315–41. http://dx.doi.org/10.1177/0018726706071525.

Knowles, Malcolm S. 1990 [1973]. *The Adult Learner: A Neglected Species.* Houston: Gulf Publishing.

Lamont, Michele. 2009. *How Professors Think.* Cambridge, MA: Harvard University Press.

Lee, Alison, and David Boud. 2003. "Writing Groups, Change and Academic Identity: Research Development as Local Practice." *Studies in Higher Education* 28 (2): 187–200. http://dx.doi.org/10.1080/0307507032000058109.

McGowan, Susannah. 2006. ""The Visible Writing Project's Writing Residency," sidebar in "The Faculty Writing Place: A Room of Our Own" by P. Elbow and M. D. Sorcinelli." *Change: The Magazine for Higher Learning* 38: 22.

Merriam, Sharan B., and Rosemary S. Cafferella. 1999. *Learning in Adulthood,* 2nd ed. San Francisco: Jossey-Bass.

Mezirow, Jack. 1991. *Transformative Dimensions of Adult Learning.* San Francisco: Jossey-Bass.

Moody, JoAnn. 2004. "Supporting Women and Minority Faculty." *Academe* 90 (1): 47–52. http://dx.doi.org/10.2307/40252590.

Moody, JoAnn. (Original work published 1997) 2010. *Demystifying the Profession: Helping Junior Faculty Succeed.* New Haven, CT: University of New Haven Press.

O'Malley, Gary S., and Thomas A. Lucey. 2008. "Promise and Possibility: Building Collegial Opportunities for Scholarship." *Academic Leadership* 6 (3): 66–68.

Pasternak, Donna L., Hope Longwell-Grice, Kelly A. Shea, and Linda K. Hanson. 2009. "Alien Environments or Supportive Writing Communities? Pursuing Writing Groups in Academe." *Arts and Humanities in Higher Education* 8 (3): 355–67. http://dx.doi.org/10.1177/1474022209339958.

Raelin, Joseph A. 2002. "'I Don't Have Time to Think' versus the Art of Reflective Practice." *Reflections: The SoL Journal* 4 (1): 66–79. http://dx.doi. org/10.1162/152417302320467571.

Randall, Nancy. 2006. "Blue Pencil Retreats at Malaspina University-College, Nanaimo, BC [sidebar in "The Faculty Writing Place: A Room of Our Own" by P. Elbow and M.D. Sorcinelli]." *Change: The Magazine for Higher Learning* 38: 20.

Rankin, Elizabeth. 2001. *The Work of Writing: Insights and Strategies for Academics and Professionals.* San Francisco: Jossey-Bass.

Richardson, Laurel. 2000. "Skirting a Pleated Text: De-Disciplining an Academic Life." In *Working the Ruins: Feminist Poststructural Theory and Methods in Education,* ed. E.A. St. Pierre and W.S. Pillow, 153–163. New York: Routledge.

Rowland, Stephen. 2000. *The Enquiring University Teacher.* Philadelphia: Open University Press, with the Society for Research into Higher Education.

Savage, William W., Jr. 2003. "Scribble, Scribble, Toil and Trouble: Forced Productivity in the Modern University." *Journal of Scholarly Publishing* 35 (1): 40–6.http://dx.doi.org/10.3138/jsp.35.1.40.

Schön, Donald A. 1983. *The Reflective Practitioner: How Professionals Think in Action.* New York: Basic Books.

Schroeder, Connie M. 2011. *Coming In from the Margins: Faculty Development's Emerging Organizational Development Role in Institutional Change.* Sterling, VA: Stylus.

Sorcinelli, Mary D. 1994. "Effective Approaches to New Faculty Development." *Journal of Counseling and Development* 72 (5): 474–9. http://dx.doi. org/10.1002/j.1556-6676.1994.tb00976.x.

Sorcinelli, Mary D., Ann E. Austin, Pamela L. Eddy, and Andrea L. Beach. 2006. *Creating the Future of Faculty Development: Learning from the Past, Understanding the Present.* Bolton, MA: Anker Publishing Company.

Stanley, Christine A. 2006. *Faculty of Color: Teaching in Predominantly White Colleges and Universities.* San Francisco: Jossey-Bass.

Steinert, Yvonne, Peter J. McLeod, Stephen Liben, and Linda Snell. 2008. "Writing for Publication in Medical Education: The Benefits of a Faculty Development Workshop and Peer Writing Group." *Medical Teacher* 30 (8): 280–85. http:// dx.doi.org/10.1080/01421590802337120. Medline:18484455.

Swaggerty, Elizabeth A., Terry S. Atkinson, Johna L. Faulconer, and Robin R. Griffith. 2011. "Academic Writing Retreat: A Time for Rejuvenated and Focused Writing." *Journal of Faculty Development* 25 (1): 5–11.

Tysick, Cynthia, and Nancy Babb. 2006. "Writing Support for Junior Faculty Librarians: A Case Study." *Journal of Academic Librarianship* 32 (1): 94–100. http://dx.doi. org/10.1016/j.acalib.2005.10.005.

Washburn, Allyson. 2008. "Writing Circle Feedback: Creating a Vibrant Community of Scholars." *Journal of Faculty Development* 22 (1): 32–8.

Young, James B. 2011. "Cross-Domain Collaborative Learning and the Transformation of Faculty Identity." In *To Improve the Academy: Resources for Faculty, Instructional and Organizational Development,* edited by J. E. Miller and J. E. Groccia, 29: 89–101. San Francisco: Jossey-Bass.

PART 2

Writing Groups/Retreats/Residencies

DOI: 10.7330/9780874219029.c0??

5

HOW TEACHING CENTERS CAN SUPPORT FACULTY AS WRITERS

Tara Gray, A. Jane Birch, and Laura Madson

At first blush, it may seem that teaching centers need not support scholarly writing.[1] This is especially true of centers with narrowly defined missions, e.g., instructional development only. However, writing and publishing are essential to faculty success at many institutions of higher education. Scholarly productivity is increasingly valued even at teaching-oriented institutions (Massy 2003) and is the single best predictor of faculty salaries regardless of institution type (Fairweather 2005). Even excellent teachers can fail to achieve the level of success they desire if they are not also successful scholars. In short, most faculty members need to write and publish.

Nonetheless, for many scholars writing remains a struggle and writing interventions can help. Among faculty at four-year institutions, 28 percent have not published a manuscript in the last two years (Hurtado et al. 2012, 23). In addition, 13 percent of professors spend zero hours per week on scholarship and writing, and 43 percent spend four hours or fewer (Hurtado et al. 2012, 49).Many books bemoan the quality of academic writing (Sword 2012; Williams 1990) and for those who write poorly, scholarly productivity will also be a problem. Writing interventions offer faculty the skills and support they need to become better, more productive scholars. For faculty who are hampered by anxiety about writing and publishing, who struggle to make time to write, or who simply feel too exhausted to write, writing programs can make the difference between a *promising* and a *successful* career.

Besides helping struggling faculty writers achieve their potential, there are other reasons for teaching centers to support faculty in their

---

1. The authors thank Robert Boice, Jean Conway, Rene Hajigeorgalis, Mary Deane Sorcinelli, and Lynn Sorenson for their helpful comments on the chapter.

DOI: 10.7330/9780874219029.c005

scholarly work. First, writing interventions generate a big bang for the buck; that is, relatively simple and inexpensive interventions can dramatically increase faculty publishing (Boice 1989; Boice 2000; McGrail, Rickard, and Jones 2006). Second, writing interventions help build a community of scholars among participants (Gray and Conway 2007). Third, writing interventions can motivate faculty to return to teaching centers for other programs, including teaching programs (Gray and Shadle 2009; Sorcinelli, Gray, and Birch, 2011). Fourth, writing interventions can help faculty teach writing better (Finkelmeyer 2011; Gillespie 1985; Hairston 1986; National Writing Project Research Brief 2008). For all these reasons, we believe that teaching centers *should* support scholarly writing. Here we discuss *how* teaching centers can support scholars in their efforts to increase the quantity of scholarly writing and improve the quality. We base our discussion on fifteen years of experience directing such interventions at Brigham Young University (BYU) and New Mexico State University (NMSU).[2]

HOW TEACHING CENTERS CAN SUPPORT SCHOLARLY WRITING

We direct a number of scholarly writing interventions on our campuses (Gray 2010; Gray and Birch 2000; Sorcinelli, Gray, and Birch, 2011). These interventions include writing support groups, workshops followed by writing support groups, general writing retreats, and retreats aimed at writing teaching portfolios or promotion and tenure portfolios. In this chapter we share information about administering each of these programs. We begin by discussing Publish & Flourish, the program we've directed the longest and with the most success. It involves an opening workshop followed by writing support groups. At several points in the discussion, we will highlight differences in how Publish & Flourish is conducted at our two institutions to emphasize the flexibility of the program.

Publish & Flourish

Publish & Flourish is a semester-long program designed to help participants improve the quality and quantity of their scholarly writing. The program begins with a half-day workshop at the beginning of the summer or an academic semester. During the opening workshop, participants are

---

2. Although we focus this chapter on how teaching centers can support faculty, these ideas can be useful to support graduate student writers as well. In addition, writing centers can also support writers as well (or better) than teaching centers.

introduced to the twelve steps of the program, which are described in the book, *Publish & Flourish: Become a Prolific Scholar* by Tara Gray:

MANAGE TIME
- Differentiate between the urgent and the important.
- Write fifteen to thirty minutes daily.
- Keep records of writing daily; share your records weekly.

WRITE
- Write from the first day of your research project.
- Post your thesis on the wall and write to it.

REVISE
- Organize around key sentences.
- Use your key sentences as an after-the-fact outline.

GET HELP
- Share early drafts with non-experts and later drafts with experts.
- Learn how to listen.
- Respond to each specific comment.

POLISH AND PUBLISH
- Read your prose out loud.
- Kick it out the door, and make 'em say, "No."

The opening workshop is followed by weekly meetings of writing teams during which teammates exchange feedback on their writing. Together, the opening workshop and the weekly meetings assist participants in achieving the twin pillars of the program: improving the quality and quantity of their writing.

The first pillar of the program is increasing writing quantity. This is done primarily by encouraging faculty to write daily (Boice 1989; Boice 2000; Gray 2010; Gray and Birch 2000). Participants are held accountable for writing daily in three ways. First, participants record their minutes spent writing and share their records with others.[3] Similarly,

---

3. Although NMSU and BYU both use writing logs, we handle the logistics differently. At NMSU, participants record their minutes of daily writing on a shared Google spreadsheet, which is accessible to all participants. At BYU, participants record their minutes on paper writing logs, which they can then pass around at team meetings for discussion and mutual encouragement. Participants submit these logs to the BYU Faculty Center weekly. The center then sends them a yummy treat and a short motivational article about writing through campus mail. (Note that all the materials mentioned in this chapter are available upon request.)

participants report their minutes of daily writing in the subject line of a daily e-mail message sent to their teammates. Finally, participants are held accountable for writing or revising three or four pages of prose weekly because they bring their pages of writing to the writing group each week. One study of the program showed that if participants continued writing at the rate they wrote during the program, they would each produce seventy-five pages of prose per year (Gray and Birch 2000). *Many scholars report, in the strongest possible terms, that the program greatly increases their writing productivity:*

> Your methods changed my writing life. For the four years before the workshop, I wrote or revised forty-four pages a year, but in the four years after, I wrote or revised 220 pages per year—five times as much!
>
> I decided to try these steps on a paper I had been trying to put together for five years. Four weeks later, the paper is out for review.
>
> I participated in Publish & Flourish as a junior faculty member. I earned tenure and promotion by following the program's principles, particularly writing daily.

The second pillar of the program is writing quality. In Publish & Flourish participants use key or topic sentences to organize their own prose and to give feedback to each other. In the opening workshop, participants learn how to organize manuscripts around key or topic sentences (Booth, Colomb, and Williams 2008). This revision system teaches participants to focus on organization within and between paragraphs instead of the easier but less effective task of improving manuscripts at the sentence level (Belcher, 2009). In our experience, focusing on within- and between-paragraph writing is the fastest way to improve scholarly writing. Participants bring copies of their own writing to the workshop so they can practice identifying key sentences and using these sentences to discuss their writing. This exercise serves as a model for how participants will conduct the weekly one-hour meetings of their writing teams after the workshop.

The weekly meetings use the following system. Each participant brings three or four pages of prose to share with teammates. The session opens with a short round of sharing about how the writing process is going. This sharing helps build community and give participants a chance to reach out to each other in support and encouragement. Next, participants spend fifteen to twenty minutes discussing each paper, one at a time. That is, the writer reads his or her own paper at the same time others read it. Reading one's own paper as others read it is as effective as watching oneself on video tape: the writer begins to see the paper as a reader would. As all members of the team read, they search each paragraph for a key or topic sentence. Team members then compare which sentences they have identified as the key sentences. If there is disagreement about which sentence is key, discussion ensues. If there is agreement, the team moves on. Next, discussion focuses on any other aspect of the draft that may need attention (e.g., a confusing or possibly irrelevant idea that is detracting from the paper). The final round for each paper is a positive one in which participants shower the writer with praise for all the good things in the paper. This is arguably the most important round because it motivates the writer to want to write another day. Finally, the team moves on to the next participant's paper.

Looking for key sentences and exchanging feedback improves the quality of writing. Many participants comment on how key sentences affect their writing:

> It has been a drastic improvement. I am constantly thinking about key sentences, and checking whether the paragraph is about that key sentence or not. It helped me write in an organized way.
>
> My writing benefited in several ways. I learned the key sentence routine that really clarified the structure of my paragraphs.

Other participants comment more generally on the feedback they receive from team members:

> My writing is clearer and better organized. When I make revisions based on my team members' input, the result is always better than the original and much closer to my final version, i.e., the program gets my work ready to go out the door.
>
> The feedback I received from my colleagues was invaluable. When I would read my original writing v. the revised paper using their feedback, my writing improvement was like night and day.

There is a third benefit to helping faculty members improve their writing: their teaching of writing also improves. Participants in *Publish & Flourish* report that the program helps them make changes in their teaching of writing. For example, participants report inviting students to give feedback on each other's papers in much the same way they have done in *Publish & Flourish*.

> I switched my writing class to a peer review workshop and the students (after getting used to it) seemed to respond. I think they write more now than before and they proofread their work before bringing it in.

In addition, participants report that *Publish & Flourish* improves their ability to comment on student prose:

This program helped me look at student writing analytically instead of critically. It made it easier to make constructive comments.

This [program] helped in my teaching of writing in that I could pick out topic sentences better.

I feel more capable of giving students more assistance and better feedback.

Clearly, helping instructors become better writers also helps them become better teachers of writing. Therefore, offering writing interventions for scholars is consistent with the mission of teaching centers, even those that focus on instructional development.

Publish & Flourish is our most successful writing intervention based on impact and numbers served. At both BYU and NMSU, we have offered *Publish & Flourish* to many participants over fifteen years. At BYU, we offer *Publish & Flourish* every year with about one hundred participants. Over the course of the years, 30 percent of the approximately 1,500 full-time faculty members at BYU have participated. Almost half of the 576 people who have participated during this time have participated more than once (42 people have participated five times or more). Because NMSU has about half as many faculty members as BYU, we offer *Publish & Flourish* every other year. At NMSU, between 60 and 90 scholars participate in the opening workshop and 40 to 60 scholars complete the semester-long program.[4]

One reason *Publish & Flourish* has been so successful is that it is easy to customize the program to fit the needs and resources of one's institution. For example, *Publish & Flourish* can either be administered centrally or run by participants. At NMSU and BYU, we administer the program centrally using the techniques described above (i.e., holding participants accountable for meeting with their groups and writing daily). We find that the more structured the program is in requiring writing minutes to be shared in a public way, the more participants commit to the program, and the more they write. Although this approach has been very successful, it does require more resources. Most schools that host *Publish & Flourish* let the participants run the program once the workshop is over. Over the years, the opening workshop of *Publish & Flourish* has been given at institutions in more than thirty states and several foreign countries. At virtually all of these schools, *Publish & Flourish* has been run by participants after the opening workshop. That is, the participants who join writing

---

4. At NMSU, participants are invited to attend the opening workshop only or to join a team and participate all semester. At BYU, participants are expected to participate in both the opening workshop and the semester-long program, though a few attend just the workshop.

teams during the opening workshop are left to their own devices. There is no centralized way of holding them accountable for meeting with their groups or for writing daily. Thus, hosting a program like *Publish & Flourish* can be as easy as inviting a presenter and reserving a room.

TEAMS AND TEAM LEADERS IN *PUBLISH & FLOURISH*

Teams and team leaders are both critical to the effectiveness of *Publish & Flourish*. Writing teams give participants a stable community of fellow writers with whom to share their writing. Team leaders help each team function effectively. In the participant-run version of *Publish & Flourish,* the workshop presenter can handle team formation. In the centrally-administered version of *Publish & Flourish,* the teaching center staff will want to decide how to establish teams and team leaders.

Although both NMSU and BYU offer a centrally-administered version of *Publish & Flourish*, we take different approaches to forming the writing teams. At NMSU, participants enroll through the teaching center for one of two available times they can meet weekly throughout the semester. The director then places everyone into teams by first separating graduate students from faculty, and then technical writers from non-technical writers.[5] Because of the way teams are formed at NMSU, they include participants from very different disciplines (e.g., faculty from biology and engineering can end up on the same writing team).

At BYU, team leaders form their own teams and determine the time and location of their weekly meetings.[6] This strategy was developed in the hope that (1) team leaders would recruit their colleagues to participate with them, and (2) the teams would be more likely to persist beyond the semester-long program. Both goals have been achieved. Team leaders recruit many participants and a handful of teams meet throughout the entire year. These teams often re-enroll in the program the following year, and we encourage such teams to welcome new faculty into their team.

Asking team leaders to form their own teams also results in teams that are often composed of participants in the same or closely related disciplines. Participants seem to prefer writing teams that are more nearly

---

5. At NMSU, we have not found it a problem to work with both faculty and graduate students in one large program except for the year in which we had to mix faculty and graduate students in one writing team. That year, the faculty complained that they "did not want to advise another thesis student." In general, we think it is wonderful to open the program to both grads and faculty because both groups need help with their writing.

6. When participants enroll without forming a team, the program director then helps these participants find a team to join, or combines several such participants into one team.

intra-disciplinary than inter-disciplinary because the program at BYU, which uses intra-disciplinary teams, is bigger with far better year-to-year retention than the NMSU program. As a result, in 2013, NMSU plans to try the BYU system for creating teams for faculty, but not for graduate students.[7]

Team leaders are also recruited and trained differently at NMSU and BYU. At BYU, faculty members volunteer to be team leaders; when faculty members sign up to participate in the program, they also indicate whether or not they are willing to serve as a team leader. Most, though not all, team leaders are former participants. Before the opening workshop, the program director meets with all the team leaders over lunch to discuss the duties of team leaders and how to create productive teams. At this meeting, past participants are invited to talk about their experience, and this helps motivate everyone to commit to a successful semester.

At NMSU, we recruit only former participants who wrote nearly every day to be team leaders. The invitation to serve as a team leader includes a detailed description of the duties. For example, each team leader helps build a community of scholars. Team leaders have the same responsibility to their teams that a teacher has to a class. Team leaders are "super-participants" in that they practice the principles espoused by the program (i.e., writing daily, keeping track of writing time, organizing text around key sentences). Team leaders must also be evangelistic: they help sell the program. Although participants are told these things about being team leaders, they do not come together to discuss it. Their "training," if you will, is having been a super-participant in the past. When first starting a program, there will be no such participants from the past. In this case, we recommend that you recruit composition instructors or other excellent writers to serve as team leaders. At NMSU, team leaders are paid $250.

GETTING BUY-IN FROM ADMINISTRATORS AND FACULTY

Any type of writing intervention will be more successful if it has the support of the administration and faculty. Ideally, other units on campus will cosponsor the intervention with the teaching center (e.g., college deans, the research unit, the writing center). These cosponsors can help defray the cost of conducting the program (e.g., paying team leaders and/or outside speakers, providing books for participants). When

---

7. We mention the NMSU model because it may be a better model for dealing with graduate students who do not return to the program year after year or for a new program that does not yet have established team leaders.

approaching administrators, prepare for some resistance. At NMSU, our first attempt at raising money took two years. After the deans saw the value of the program, subsequent fund raising goals were met in a few hours. Eventually, the money they gave was permanently added to our operating budget.

At BYU, *Publish & Flourish* has always been cosponsored by the university's research unit, but it did not immediately garner support from other administrators. Some administrators questioned whether faculty could get anything done in fifteen to thirty minutes of daily writing. Perhaps they themselves learned to write in "big blocks of time" and were therefore not open to alternative writing approaches, despite what the literature says about productive writing. Our own center director, a very productive scholar, did not initially rate *Publish & Flourish* as being one of the more important services provided to faculty. We persisted, however, because we knew how important writing is to our faculty, and we were convinced by the literature that the intervention is based on sound principles.

It took three to four years before the attitude about *Publish & Flourish* at BYU began to change. With time, our center director began to hear excellent reports about the program from college deans and department chairs. They shared stories of how *Publish & Flourish* was making a difference in the productivity of faculty in their units. Our director became an avid supporter and promoter. Now campus administrators often help us by encouraging their faculty to participate. Some administrators even form their own writing teams. Thirty percent of our current department chairs are past participants.

What about faculty buy-in? Do faculty members need stipends or other rewards to fully commit to a writing program? At NMSU, we have experimented with and without stipends for participants. By trying it both ways, we have found that small stipends of $100 (amounting to about $6.60 an hour) do not improve retention. BYU did not experiment with giving participants stipends, believing it would not be necessary. Based on our experience, this has been a good decision for our campus; participation rates are high, and we've had no indication from faculty that they need further incentives to join.

Team leaders may or may not need a stipend. As mentioned above, team leaders at NMSU are rewarded with a $250 stipend. Accordingly, BYU also did so during the first three years of the intervention. Over time, it became apparent that BYU team leaders were not participating for the money. We decided the dollars would be better spent by providing small incentives for all participants to reach three stated benchmarks by the end of the intervention: turning in all the writing logs, attending all the team meetings, and writing every day. At the end of the intervention, eligible participants now choose among a variety of prizes for each benchmark they reach (e.g., books on productive writing and other fun or useful items more or less related to writing such as book lights, book or pen holders, fancy staplers, magnetic poetry, stress balls, and chocolate!). Each prize averages $13 in value. Participants enjoy these rewards and are quite happy to receive them, but they are neither the primary focus nor participant's primary motivation. However, rewards do help some faculty take more care in keeping records and submitting logs. We also reward team leaders with a $25 campus-wide gift certificate at the end of the intervention, but this comes as a bonus gift and not something promised at the beginning of the semester.

In short, monetary stipends are not necessary to motivate faculty members to participate in writing interventions, but team leaders may require some sort of compensation depending on the campus. For participants, token fun rewards can increase enthusiasm and enjoyment. Token rewards also reduce the need to approach reluctant administrators hat-in-hand. Regardless of an intervention's budget or structure, the enthusiastic reviews from early participants will overcome any initial resistance from administrators or from other faculty.

OTHER SCHOLARSHIP INTERVENTIONS

Although BYU and NMSU offer versions of *Publish & Flourish* regularly, both institutions also offer additional support for faculty scholarship. One or more of these interventions might be the right intervention for some centers. At BYU, our center supports faculty scholarship in three additional ways. First, the center offers a variety of short (i.e., forty five minutes to two-hour) workshops led by successful on-campus faculty scholars. Example topics include the following:

- developing a coherent program of research
- getting published
- building a strong scholarly reputation
- securing grants
- using student assistance
- doing interdisciplinary research
- developing effective strategies for scholarly reading
- using library tools to support scholarly productivity

In addition to the workshops, BYU sponsors faculty to attend regional conferences on grant writing. And finally, the center maintains an excellent library of quality books on scholarly productivity that we actively encourage faculty to borrow. Although the number of faculty who borrow books is not high, faculty who do borrow books report that the reading is very useful to them. At BYU, we also give away books on scholarly productivity to faculty in conjunction with other seminars. For example, every new tenure-track faculty participant chooses one such book from an excellent set of options. Faculty love getting free books, but we have little data on how effectively they use them. According to the feedback we have received at BYU, all these activities serve important groups of faculty at critical times, and we plan to continue providing them.

At NMSU, we direct four other interventions to support faculty writing: *Scholarly Writing Retreat, Writing Groups, Teaching Portfolio Workshop* and *Promotion & Tenure Portfolio Workshop. The Scholarly Writing Retreat* emphasizes scholarly productivity by encouraging participants to jumpstart a project or finish one during the retreat. The other three programs emphasize improving writing quality through peer feedback. To that end, participants in these interventions are given guidelines on how to give effective feedback and then placed in small groups to exchange feedback. These interventions also enlist a group leader or mentor to facilitate the group.

Scholarly Writing Retreat. In summer 2011, NMSU started a week-long *Scholarly Writing Retreat* (Elbow and Sorcinelli 2006; Farr et al. 2009). The retreat promised a quiet, comfortable place to write free of distractions, with the synergy of writing while others write. It also promised brief goal-setting sessions at the beginning of each daily three-hour writing session and a chance for writers to exchange feedback on their writing at any time (in another room). In the first two years, an average of eight faculty and graduate students participated in the retreat. Participants rated the workshop a perfect seven on a seven-point scale on the statements, "This workshop was a good investment of my time" and "I would recommend this workshop to my colleagues." At the end of the retreat, the participants made significant resolutions about their writing habits:

> I will keep my e-mail closed during my writing time. I will turn off my cell phone. I will do nothing but write, leaving the literature review for later. And I will try to write in a location other than my office where competing tasks are always calling to me.

Writing Groups. In 2004, NMSU began an intervention called *Writing Groups,* which is based on the work of Libby Rankin (2001) as well as

Wayne Booth, Gregory Colomb, and Joseph Williams (2008). This intervention is designed to give participants feedback on an entire manuscript rather than shorter excerpts of a paper. Participants meet for a mandatory orientation followed by three or four meetings of their own writing group. Each group reviews one full manuscript at each group meeting.

The mandatory orientation has two parts. To begin the first part, the facilitator acts as the author and provides a manuscript of his or her own for review.[8] All the participants sit in a big circle and act as a mock writing group, (i.e., participants practice providing useful feedback, while the author models non-defensive listening by asking lots of questions and taking good notes).

For the second part of the orientation, the facilitator forms groups of three or four scholars and each group selects a group leader. Groups are formed using two criteria: (a) scholars are placed in faculty or graduate student groups; and (b) scholars are sorted into groups for technical and non-technical fields. Once the groups are formed, each group selects a group leader who is responsible for sending an e-mail reminder to the group before each meeting and keeping records of attendance. The small groups also decide when and where to meet. To facilitate this, participants are advised before the orientation to bring their calendars to schedule group meetings.

Once scheduled, each group meeting follows the same procedure. Because the group reviews an entire manuscript at each meeting, these meetings require advance preparation. Before each meeting, participants are asked to spend one hour reading and commenting on that week's manuscript. During each meeting, participants give structured feedback on the manuscript to the author. Comments are shared in rounds in which readers (1) share positive comments about something specific they liked; (2) respond to the title, thesis, abstract, introduction, and conclusion; (3) respond to the writer's stated questions; and (4) address other issues. Groups meet three or four times (depending on the number of members) and then disband.

Smaller and shorter interventions like *Writing Groups* have some unique advantages. *Writing Groups* offer faculty members an opportunity to exchange feedback on full manuscripts rather than smaller writing samples. It keeps the focus on big picture issues such as purpose and audience, rather than focusing on organization within and between

---

8. If the program director does not wish to act as the author during the orientation, a participant could be asked to do so instead.

paragraphs. It provides peer feedback to participants who have a draft of a manuscript ready and want feedback on it. About ten or fifteen faculty members and graduate students join *Writing Groups* each fall, spring, and summer term. Thank you e-mails from participants have included comments like these:

> I found the writing groups to be a wonderful experience . . . It was somewhat intimidating, but it didn't take long to recognize that everyone was intimidated, and we grew comfortable with the process together.
>
> I appreciated my group's comments and having more pairs of eyes to find ways to improve my writing before I submitted it.

Teaching Portfolio Workshop and *Promotion & Tenure Portfolio Workshop.* Since 2009, NMSU has offered two different weeklong workshops aimed at writing specific institutional documents: *Teaching Portfolio Workshop* and *Promotion & Tenure Portfolio Workshop.* Each workshop is conducted during the summer when participants have a better chance of being able to devote a whole week to a workshop. The workshops are based on the following books:

> *The Teaching Portfolio: A Practical Guide to Improved Performance and Promotion/Tenure Decisions.* (Peter Seldin, J. Elizabeth Miller, and Clement A. Seldin 2011).
>
> *The Academic Portfolio: A Practical Guide to Documenting Teaching, Research, and Service.* (Peter Seldin and J. Elizabeth Miller 2008).

Before each workshop begins, all participants and mentors are asked to read the first part of the corresponding book and some sample portfolios from the book. The first part of each book discusses the what, why, and how of portfolios as well as specific steps to creating, improving, and evaluating portfolios. Having participants pre-read this part of the book gives a jump-start to the workshop rather than burning a day going over the basics.

As in other interventions at NMSU, participants are separated into groups of three or four scholars with a group mentor. In the *Teaching Portfolio Workshop*, graduate students are first separated from faculty and then participants are divided into groups based, very loosely, on discipline (e.g., sciences and engineering vs. everyone else). In the *Promotion & Tenure Portfolios Workshop*, there are no graduate students, so faculty participants are divided by broad disciplines.

Each day of both workshops, participants exchange feedback for two hours with their group and spend the rest of the day revising their portfolios. To exchange feedback, participants bring copies of their drafts for every participant in their group. Under the guidance of the mentor, participants review and comment on each portfolio in turn. To guide their discussion, participants are given a rubric that emphasizes conveying a singular theme or thesis, communicating the purpose clearly to the audience, providing evidence for each claim, and being organized and persuasive.

Mentors for both portfolio workshops are paid $250 and are chosen from participants who have successfully completed the workshop before. Stipends are very important here because unlike *Publish & Flourish,* where faculty members quickly agree to be team leaders, it is hard to find mentors for these programs. We think this is because the mentors do not get their own work read and responded to as in *Publish & Flourish.* Instead, they are helping others.

When offering a portfolio workshop for the first time, there are no past participants to serve as mentors. We invite seasoned faculty to serve as teaching portfolio mentors, perhaps including those who have submitted something like a teaching portfolio to win a teaching award or to gain tenure. For the promotion and tenure portfolio workshop, it is important to have team leaders who have the greatest knowledge of P&T. At NMSU, we typically ask members of the college P&T committees. (Note that our college P&T committees do not judge the portfolios for their quality, only for whether or not the process was followed; on a campus where college P&T committees do judge portfolios for their quality, past members of the committees could serve as mentors.) In addition, department heads make excellent mentors because they, too, have experience reviewing portfolios. Another possibility is to hire experts like Peter Seldin, Elizabeth Miller, and Clement Seldin to serve as mentors for the first round of portfolios and specifically recruit participants who would make excellent mentors for subsequent years.

In the end, both these workshops are small, with between ten and twenty participants, but participants are most appreciative. Each time, participants give nearly perfect marks on a Likert scale to the statements, "This workshop was a good investment of my time" and "I would recommend this workshop to my colleagues." Open-ended comments from participants include:

> Phenomenal help preparing for P&T. Everyone in the tenure track should do this.
>
> This was the single most significant activity I've ever engaged in for improving and evaluating my teaching.
>
> The combination of self-reflection and peer review was extremely effective.
>
> Superb. Never miss it! Never!

Clearly, writing interventions that focus on specific documents, like *Teaching Portfolio Workshop* and *Promotion & Tenure Portfolio Workshop*, help faculty construct these very important and difficult institutional documents.

CONCLUSION

We believe that writing interventions for faculty should be customized to meet the needs of the faculty and the resources of the center; they should also help faculty improve the quality and/or the quantity of their writing. To improve the quantity of writing, interventions should encourage faculty to write every day and provide as much structure as possible to help build and support that habit (Boice 1989; Boice 2000; Gray 2010; Gray and Birch 2000). To improve quality of writing, interventions should arrange for participants to give and receive regular feedback on drafts with other scholars (Becker and Richards 2007; Gray 2010; Rankin 2001). To improve both of these simultaneously to the greatest possible extent, a program like *Publish & Flourish*, administered centrally, may be the best choice. However, many schools have chosen to host such a program without administering it centrally, which certainly reduces the staff resources required.

If your school does not have the financial resources for an outside presenter, you might consider several other options. You might invite excellent scholarly writers from your own campus to speak. Or, you might host a *Scholarly Writing Retreat* to improve scholarly productivity or *Writing Groups* to improve the quality of academic writing. If you are trying to improve the quality of teaching or promotion and tenure portfolios, we would suggest programs aimed just at those documents as described earlier: *Teaching Portfolio Workshop* or *Promotion & Tenure Portfolio Workshop*. The important point is to start supporting faculty writing in whatever way is appropriate given the needs of the faculty and the resources of the center.

REFERENCES

Becker, Howard S., and Pamela Richards. 2007. *Writing for Social Scientists.* Chicago: University of Chicago Press.

Belcher, Wendy L. 2009. "Reflections on Ten Years of Teaching Writing for Publication to Graduate Students and Junior Faculty." *Journal of Scholarly Publishing* 40 (2): 184–200. http://dx.doi.org/10.3138/jsp.40.2.184.

Boice, Robert. 1989. "Procrastination, Busyness and Bingeing." *Behaviour Research and Therapy* 27 (6): 605–11. http://dx.doi.org/10.1016/0005-7967(89)90144-7. Medline:2610657.

Boice, Robert. 2000. *Advice for New Faculty Members: Nihil Nimus.* Boston: Allyn and Bacon.

Booth, Wayne C., Gregory C. Colomb, and Joseph M. Williams. 2008. *The Craft of Research.* Chicago: University of Chicago Press.

Elbow, Peter, and Mary D. Sorcinelli. 2006. "The Faculty Writing Place: A Room of our Own." *Change: The Magazine of Higher Learning* 38 (6): 17–22. http://dx.doi. org/10.3200/CHNG.38.6.17-22.

Fairweather, James S. 2005. "Beyond the Rhetoric: Trends in the Relative Value of Teaching and Research in Faculty Salaries." *Journal of Higher Education* 76 (4): 401–22. http://dx.doi.org/10.1353/jhe.2005.0027.

Farr, Cecilia K., Joanne Cavallaro, Gabrielle Civil, and Susan Cochrane. 2009. "Taming the Publishing Beast: College of St. Catherine Scholars' Retreat." *Change* 41 (3): 14–9. http://dx.doi.org/10.3200/CHNG.41.3.14-19.

Finkelmeyer, Todd. 2011. New UW Project Helps Teachers become Better Writers. *The Capital Times.* http://host.madison.com/ct/news/local/education/university/ article_8ad49f08-274f-11e0-acb6-001cc4c002e0.html. Accessed January 24, 2011.

Gillespie, Tim. 1985. "Becoming Your Own Expert: Teachers as Writers." *National Writing Project Network Newsletter* 8 (1): 1–2.

Gray, Tara. 2010. *Publish & Flourish: Become a Prolific Scholar.* Las Cruces, NM: Teaching Academy, New Mexico State University.

Gray, Tara, and Jane Birch. 2000. "Publish, Don't Perish: A Program to Help Scholars Flourish." *To Improve the Academy* 19: 268–84.

Gray, Tara, and Jean Conway. 2007. "Build it [Right] and They Will Come: Boost Attendance at Your Teaching Center by Building Community." *Journal of Faculty Development* 21 (3): 179–84.

Gray, Tara, and Susan Shadle. 2009. "Launching or Revitalizing a Teaching Center: Portraits of Practice." *Journal of Faculty Development* 23 (2): 5–12.

Hairston, Maxine. 1986. "When Writing Teachers Don't Write: Speculations about Probable Causes and Possible Cures." *Rhetoric Review* 5 (1): 62–70. http://dx.doi. org/10.1080/07350198609359136.

Hurtado, Sylvia, Kevin Eagan, John H. Pryor, Hannah Whang, and Serge Tran. 2012. *Undergraduate Teaching Faculty: The 2010-2011 HERI Faculty Survey.* Los Angeles: UCLA Higher Education Research Institute.

Massy, William F. 2003. *Honoring the Trust: Quality and Cost Containment in Higher Education.* Bolton, MA: Anker.

McGrail, Matthew R., Claire M. Rickard, and Rebecca Jones. 2006. "Publish or Perish: A Systematic Review of Interventions to Increase Academic Publication Rates." *Higher Education Research & Development* 25 (1): 19–35. http://dx.doi. org/10.1080/07294360500453053.

National Writing Project Research Brief. 2008. *NWP 2008 Research Brief: Writing Project Professional Development for Teachers Yields Gains in Student Writing Achievement.* http:// www.nwp.org/cs/public/print/resource/2668. Accessed August 27, 2008.

Rankin, Elizabeth. 2001. *The Work of Writing: Insights and Strategies for Academics and Professionals.* San Francisco: Jossey-Bass.

Seldin, Peter J., and J. Elizabeth Miller. 2008. *The Academic Portfolio: A Practical Guide to Documenting Teaching, Research, and Service.* San Francisco: Jossey-Bass.

Seldin, Peter J., J. Elizabeth Miller, and Clement A. Seldin. 2011. *The Teaching Portfolio: A Practical Guide to Improved Performance and Promotion/Tenure Decisions.* San Francisco: Jossey-Bass.

Sorcinelli, Mary D., Tara Gray, and A. Jane Birch. 2011. "Faculty Development Beyond Instructional Development: Ideas Centers Can Use." *To Improve the Academy* 30: 247–61.

Sword, Helen. 2012. *Stylish Academic Writing.* Cambridge, MA: Harvard University Press.

Williams, Joseph. 1990. *Style: Toward Clarity and Grace.* Chicago: University of Chicago Press.

6
FACULTY WRITING GROUPS
Writing Centers and Third Space Collaborations

Angela Clark-Oates and Lisa Cahill

This chapter explores the question of why university and college writing centers are well-positioned institutionally to facilitate and support faculty writers as they navigate the expected literacy events (Heath 1982; Barton and Hamilton 2000) of the academy, including the promotion and tenure process, publishing demands, discipline-specific writing pedagogies, and curriculum design. In contrast to some understandings of writing centers only as places that students are sent for remediation, writing centers more often serve as hubs for a variety of writing discussions on their campuses—as places where talk that evaluates writing and where dialogue that moves revision forward are common refrains; where books about writing and resources for writing are available to writers and readers from a variety of disciplines or experiences; where instructors visit to get feedback on assignments and student writing; and where the physical space is designed and organized to facilitate discussions and interactions between readers and writers. In other words, writing centers provide spaces and enact practices that construct literacy events in very particular ways.

Drawing from Shirley Brice Heath's (1983, 96) definition of literacy event as "any occasion in which a piece of writing is integral to the nature of participants' interactions and their interpretations of meaning," and from Barton and Hamilton (2000, 8) who describe a literacy event as an observable activity where texts and talk around texts are shaped by the situated practices of a social context, this chapter focuses on the ways that writing centers can serve the needs of faculty writers as they refine their participation in the valued literacy events of the academy. Adding to an understanding of literacy events is Elmborg (2006, 195) who explains

DOI: 10.7330/9780874219029.c006

the central function that texts play in literacy events: "the text provides an occasion for shared reading and interpretation. Literacy events allow community members to develop regular, recurring interpretive patterns over time. Being an insider to a community means recognizing and participating in literacy events—knowing the codes used by the community and the customs and conventions in play." Much like literacy events elsewhere, we argue that the literacy events in two-year college and four-year university environments put many demands on faculty to communicate in specific ways that mark their membership in a postsecondary environment and that more specifically mark their membership in a particular community, a particular field of study or discipline. And although faculty typically are expected to meet the demands of their profession through more solitary means, we believe, like many (Elbow and Sorcinelli 2006; Schendel 2010), that faculty need opportunities to refine their literacy practices beyond the physical and discursive spaces of their departments and disciplines. To this end, we argue that regardless of where faculty are positioned—as senior or junior faculty, as tenured or clinical, or in the humanities or sciences—they can benefit from a more pan-institutional network that puts them in contact with other colleagues who are writing, a network that can be provided and facilitated by their campus writing centers. In fact, many of the literacy practices and events that faculty experience and develop within their discipline are commonly shared by other faculty colleagues: finding time to research and write, constructing an argument, finding disciplinarily appropriate sources to support an argument, analyzing and critiquing others' writing, analyzing and revising one's own writing, adjusting to a discipline's style, and learning to take risks (Houfek et al. 2010).

By expanding their disciplinary literacy practices to include the writing center, faculty have the opportunity to co-construct a new space for engaging in literacy events within the academy and, in these new spaces, can be reinvigorated by varied approaches to reading, writing, and teaching; interdisciplinary ideas; and opportunities to discuss writing-in-progress. Therefore, writing centers have a unique opportunity to expand their support to faculty by providing faculty with a social and collaborative practice of reading, writing, and teaching. By providing such opportunities to write with others, writing center expertise and faculty disciplinary expertise can converge to create opportunities that can disrupt the epistemological binaries that limit creativity and productivity in all intellectual spaces: writer/reader; expert/novice; faculty/student; producer/consumer. Furthermore, when a writing center illustrates its capacity to address the needs of a variety of writers, a unique discursive opportunity presents itself to address the alternative and competing discourses of the university, turning a seemingly conflicted space between expert/novice into "rich zones of collaboration and learning" (Gutiérrez, Baquedano-López, and Tejeda 1999, 286–87). In short, a third space is created.

CONSTRUCTING A THIRD SPACE: WRITING CENTERS AND FACULTY WRITERS

When deans and departments encourage faculty to cross the boundaries defined by their disciplinary affiliations, they are offering faculty a unique professional development opportunity, one that has the potential to disrupt what may appear as static and deterministic ways of being a writer. This movement could also be interpreted as an acknowledgment that academic literacy events are constructed, negotiated, defined, and redefined in a variety of spaces on campus through lived experiences that are brimming with "issues of contestation, ambiguity, and contradiction" (González 2001, 170). By seeking participation in these spaces across campus, faculty will also have the opportunity to commit to expanding their understanding of literacy events in their own disciplines and to recognizing that literacy events in different contexts have the potential to change how they and their students participate in the culturally valued practices of academic writing (Gutiérrez and Larson 2007).

Through collaborations, writing centers can work with faculty to address the ambiguities and contradictions of producing academic writing; both parties can learn more about their institution's construction and expectations of writing by committing to participation in a hybrid space where ownership of writing is tenuous and negotiated and where expertise can be shared and combined. Through writing center support of faculty writing, we argue that writing centers have the potential to not only support faculty in finding time to write while also receiving and processing feedback effectively and in meaningful ways, but also in expanding their repertoires of writing and teaching practices (Gutiérrez and Larson 2007). To provide this kind of support, both faculty and professional writing center staff have to be open to participation beyond their institutional residencies and beyond their regular writing routines in order to try something new. Both physical and pedagogical travel can be a challenge, especially when faculty and writing centers acknowledge that different academic spaces dictate varied forms of expertise that sometimes require negotiation and compromise. Yet, in the context of faculty-writing center collaborations, the benefit of this physical and pedagogical travel is that movement from one space to another creates the potential for knowledge, values, and motives to collide, thus challenging members to choose *if* or *how* to read, write, and work through those collisions to reach an agreed upon understanding about a particular text or about a writing group practice. We accept that, when working with faculty writers, tensions are bound to arise around disciplinary differences—ways of being and habits of knowing that characterize faculty's perspectives and writing center staff's perspectives—because these differences may or may not be visible (Bazerman 2011) to all participants. Consequently, for writing center and faculty collaborations to be productive, both groups have to commit to co-constructing solutions to writing tensions by recognizing one another as fellow writers—albeit writers with different types and years of experience but, nevertheless, fellow members who slide along the continuum of novice and expert.

Ultimately, our argument is that faculty writers have largely participated in cultures of writing as individuals navigating the terrain alone or with minimal support. When professional writing center staff, such as directors, assistant directors, and coordinators, work with faculty writers in writing groups to discuss the production of texts, such as research articles, syllabi, and tenure and review packages, an institutional space opens up that enables both parties, using their respective disciplinary knowledge, to negotiate practices and texts that can influence the larger theoretical and pedagogical knowledge of writing at the university. In short, we believe that a writing center's conceptualization of literacy as a socially situated practice and its theoretical allies of talk and time (Geller et al. 2007) can benefit faculty as they write to meet the demands of their disciplines. In this way, faculty and writing centers can join together to co-construct a third space, one that has the potential to shape and define academic writing—literacy events in the academy—in ways that alone would be impossible.

THEORIZING A PRACTICE: WRITING GROUPS AS THIRD SPACE

A third space is only likely if a shared activity can bring groups together, especially groups who may have similar agendas but differing methodologies, such as the seemingly disparate spaces of writing centers (that have traditionally been positioned to serve student writers' needs) and faculty's departmental homes (that have traditionally served as the locus for faculty support). Therefore, in this section we conceptualize writing groups and their respective methodologies as having the greatest potential for allowing for the construction of a third space. Writing groups offer writing centers the greatest potential for working with faculty writers (Moss, Highberg, and Nicolas 2004) because writing group methodologies provide a common ground for writing centers and faculty to engage in more collaborative and shared writing practices that still honor their disciplinary conventions. In the same manner, faculty can collaborate with writing centers to form a writing group and develop practices that at once provide an alternative to their solitary writing practices by giving them access to the expertise, experiences, and networks of their colleagues while also allowing them to integrate new habits of mind into their repertoire of strategies for publishing, creating curriculum, and understanding their students' literacy practices. Moreover, writing groups allow for the contact zone between writer and reader to be addressed—positional identities that exist within and across social spaces and within or across individuals. Because this zone exists, we see value in writing group methodologies that do not try to shut down the contestation and ambiguity between individual writers. Instead, writing groups create a dialectical space, a third space (Grego and Thompson 2008; Gutiérrez, Rymes, and Larson 1995; Moje et al. 2004; Rowe and Leander 2005), that offers participants opportunities to work through disagreements about texts and to make informed choices about their purpose and the discursive risks they are willing to take or would rather avoid. In doing so, this third space that writing centers construct with faculty in the form of writing groups becomes a space where tensions can give way to more hybrid writing practices—hybrid because approaches to time and scheduling, understanding of genres of publications, and strategies for writing efficiently and effectively can be shared, discussed, renegotiated, synthesized, and appropriated either individually or as a group so that the writing practices fit the needs and goals of each member of the writing group.

Similarly, Gere (1987, 123) acknowledges that writing groups can merge the social and individual dimensions of writing by "reminding participants that literacy does not function in isolation." Like Gere, we believe that a key value of a writing group is its ability to bring people together for the purpose of active revision and commentary on writing. Participation in writing groups can also foster interactions between individuals who come from varied backgrounds, histories, and languages and whose participation in socially situated sets of literacy practices enables them to construct common discourse stories (Barton and Hamilton 2000; Gee 2000; Prior 1998). The benefit of constructing common discourse stories is that doing so creates openings for others—junior faculty, clinical faculty, graduate and undergraduate students—to contribute to the growth of a discipline and to the way that individuals within postsecondary environments understand the act and process of writing as well as the importance of communicating ideas in meaningful ways that incorporate their voices instead of co-opting them. While literacy practices within a larger literacy event are often unique to a discipline, (Casanave and Vandrick 2003) and to an individual, faculty writers can benefit from writing group participation because participants can find common ground in their engagement with the processes of generating, revising, reacting to, and sharing academic writing, creative writing, or community-based writing. And by facilitating writing groups for faculty, writing centers have an opportunity to co-construct new writing spaces for themselves and for faculty—in other words, a third space—where the writing center and the faculty are challenged to engage in practices that reflect a different kind of epistemology that allows time and space for the negotiation of issues of textual ownership, authorship, and collaboration (Spigelman 2000). Moreover, the writing group functions as another discursive option or space in addition to the classroom, the writing center, faculty college homes, and centers for teaching and learning because it allows for the lived experience of the writer (Rowe and Leander 2005). Interactions between writing center professionals and faculty—through the third space of writing group work—make it possible for both groups to better understand each other in terms of writing practices, styles, preferences, habits, and knowledge. As a result, a hybrid practice of writing emerges with the potential to reconceptualize literacy as a socially situated practice that can benefit many populations in postsecondary environments. For example, through increased understandings about how faculty write in their disciplines, writing centers can better support the disciplinary writing practices of not only faculty but also graduate students as they are socialized into their disciplines, as well as undergraduate students as they write to learn and learn to write; faculty can increase their productivity as writers while also expanding their pedagogies as teachers of disciplinary writing practices; and administrators can create and sponsor opportunities designed to support the learning and production of literacy practices across the university. Ultimately, through the hybrid practice of writing that emerges from faculty participation in writing center facilitated writing groups, these institutional groups can partner to better meet the institutional expectations of co-creating scholars and practitioners.

In addition, when writing centers aspire to support the lived writing experiences of faculty by co-constructing a third space through writing groups, they acknowledge how "different spatial arrangements indicate changes in social relationships" (Grego and Thompson 2008, 78) and begin to foster a new lived experience for faculty. From a writing center perspective, this lived experience for faculty would include the social, collaborative nature of group writing discussions that are routinely available to their students who engage in conferences with writing center tutors. When writing centers extend their support to faculty writers through writing groups, they commit to sharing the social benefits of writing with others just as faculty commit to sharing their disciplinary literacy practices, knowledge of disciplinary conventions, and habits of being a writer with their peers in the groups and with the writing center. Therefore, if academic disciplines and departments recognize that faculty often need support as they pursue their research and writing agendas in order to earn tenure and can consequently benefit from being actively and explicitly socialized into their institutional and disciplinary cultures of expectation (Eodice and Cramer 2002; Gillespie et al. 2005), then we pose the question: In what ways can faculty writing practices benefit from writing group participation? We offer some possibilities below:

- Provide faculty with increased incentives for writing through the availability of a committed writing group with regular meetings and agreed upon practices
- Have writing group participants regularly receive feedback on their writing as well as regularly share feedback about peers' writing
- Further hone faculty writers' facility at evaluating and revising their own writing and developing their style
- Facilitate faculty developing more empathy toward their colleagues' and students' lived writing experiences
- Support faculty in more explicitly mentoring their colleagues and students in the critical reading processes needed to evaluate their own writing, other scholars' writing, and their peers' writing
- Highlight the discourse structures that disciplines require their members to illustrate in their writing
- Provide support to faculty throughout the writing process—from conceptualization of an idea to drafting to revising—as they work to meet the expectations of journal submission policies, conferences, and department needs

As writing centers move forward to support the scholarly writing lives of faculty, they have the potential to positively impact writing practices through a writing group model, making the construction of a third space possible.

CO-CONSTRUCTING A PRACTICE: FACULTY WRITING GROUPS

This section grounds our theoretical understanding of third space within our lived experience as a Writing Center Coordinator and an Assistant Director of University Academic Success Programs at Arizona State University's Downtown Phoenix campus. To participate more fully in the disciplinary cultures of writing at our campus, we accepted an invitation to travel out of the physical space of our writing center to partner with faculty in colleges to engage in discussions about their own writing processes, time constraints, goals, and expectations. In doing so, we began to develop a third space approach to writing center practice, one that went beyond communities of practice and one that acknowledged the risk of taking one's message on the road (Pemberton 2009). We saw this as an opportunity for our writing center to expand its practice by demonstrating the ways that we could support faculty writing. Furthermore, by being responsive to faculty writing needs, we engaged in an opportunity to do what Boquet (2002) argues for in her book—to amplify the noise of our center to resound in the walled spaces of the colleges and faculty offices on campus. Our intention was to effect change in the cultures of *and* attitudes about writing to which students and faculty often subscribe by being responsive to faculty writing needs.

Based on scholarship and research on writing groups (Gere 1987; Moss, Highberg, and Nicolas 2004), we believed faculty writing groups were the best vehicle for responding to faculty writing practices and needs. To provide meaningful writing group experiences, we drew from writing center theories and pedagogies about writing processes, revision, and reader response and designed a faculty writing group model based on the following premises: the groups would (1) mirror the collaborative discussions taking place between tutors and students in the writing center by providing faculty with access to peers and feedback on writing-in-progress, (2) provide social support to faculty as they engaged in discipline-specific literacy practices, (3) provide a faculty writing group facilitator—trained by the writing center—for each group, (4) develop their own norms, including routines about how often and where to meet; procedures about who would share writing and at what times; and guidelines about how readers would provide feedback, and (5) be supplemented by writing seminars designed and facilitated by the writing center professional staff to help faculty connect their writing group experience to the writing pedagogies practiced in their classrooms. By adding the writing seminars, we would be able to address the ambiguous space that students are asked to travel, the space between their disciplinary/departmental homes and the writing center. By advocating for the inclusion of writing seminars at the onset of our partnership, we ensured there would be an opportunity to co-construct a third space.

These seminars gave us sustained opportunities to address the unspoken tensions about student writing that sometimes existed between faculty and the writing center. In doing so, we risked our tenuous position with individual departments, but we also opened up moments for them to learn from us and for us to learn from them. One faculty member even said that at first she had not even thought about how her students could benefit from her own writing group participation; however, when asked directly, she shared that her students might now find her more empathetic to their experience as novice writers in the discipline and in her courses. For us the writing group became a third space by providing faculty participants with opportunities to consider not only the practices of writing for publication, grant funding, and professional promotion but also "the social structures in which they are embedded and which they help shape" (Barton et al. 2007, 14) within their disciplines. Moreover, the writing groups also provided a third space by generating the interest of faculty in their institutional roles as teachers to seek writing center expertise about writing pedagogies, methods of evaluating student writing, and strategies for designing writing assignments. This opening of a third space allowed us to renegotiate the terms of our collaboration with faculty across our campus, thus working to hybridize a variety of disciplinary perspectives (Gutiérrez, Baquedano-López, and Tejeda 1999) and needs. This hybridization meant that knowledge construction about academic writing was not uni-directional, flowing from the departments into the writing center or even from the writing center into the departments. Instead, we were working together to redefine how literacy practices were enacted at our institution. By garnering invitations to participate in conversations about how faculty were apprenticing students into disciplinary practices of writing—opportunities we had never had prior to the formation of the faculty writing groups—these groups opened a space where participants from a variety of disciplinary perspectives could find new ways to approach their own writing. In finding new ways to approach their own writing and in seeing the benefits of receiving support from a writing group, participating faculty could also find ways to address student writing. In doing so, a hybrid approach (Grego and Thompson 2008; Gutiérrez, Baquedano-López, and Turner 1997; Gutiérrez, Rymes, and Larson 1995) emerged, allowing for what Gutiérrez, Rymes, and Larson (1995) posit as a redefinition of what counts in effective classroom practice. The faculty writing groups allowed the participating faculty and the writing center staff to co-create a mutually beneficial third space where we could participate in a rethinking of the institutional script about academic writing for both faculty writers and student writers.

This revised institutional script depicts writing as a complicated, contextual, situated practice specific to discourse communities. Without this revised script or understanding, traditional scripts depict writing as being decontextualized and arhetorical—as an activity that is not tied to and defined by context, community, and convention (Bazerman and Russell 2003; Russell 1997; Russell 2000). In other words, what counts as "good" or "effective" writing does not transcend all contexts or genres for all readers—what may count as effective in one context may not count as effective style, purpose, or content for another context. Such a script not only impacts students' writing experiences and faculty perceptions of student writing but also faculty's own writing experiences as this script. This view can frustrate faculty as they read student work that does not seem to meet their course writing expectations. Similarly, it can also frustrate faculty as they engage in their own writing processes and find their articles assigned to the "revise and resubmit" category with extensive required revisions or find that their grant proposals are denied (Myers, 1990). Faculty writing groups as a third space create moments for writing center staff to engage with faculty in conversations about academic writing. Moreover, these conversations can lead to discussions about the novice/expert continuum. When faculty realize that writing centers' disciplinary expertise can help them negotiate this continuum, they can begin to make a connection between the work writing centers do and the issues they face as writers. These types of interactions present social, collaborative moments where a writing center and its campus faculty can meet to renegotiate perspectives about academic writing, thus making improvised, off-script interactions and conversations possible (Gutiérrez, Baquedano-López, and Tejeda 1999). A lack of third space, which plagues much of the cross-disciplinary work of writing centers, reinforces a power differential between writing centers and institutions in terms of expertise and knowledge construction where one side can be deemed expert while the other is not. This power differential uncritically and inaccurately constructs writing as anything *but* learning with others, and faculty are not immune to the impact of this binary, which can cause fissures in departments, limit faculty's ability to publish in the revered journals in their fields, and create false dichotomies between administrators and faculty. These dichotomies can foster an untenable expectation on the part of the administration about how much faculty should be producing and can perhaps lead to a false sense of failure on the part of the faculty. Without moments (as provided in writing group interactions) to counter the traditional scripts about academic writing, binaries persist, and can be detrimental to the intellectual, creative, and social life of a faculty member and ultimately of a discipline.

As a result, without opportunities where third spaces can be co-constructed through productive and critical dialogue, faculty writers may have few opportunities to ask themselves or their colleagues to engage in a process of reconsidering to what degree they may or may not adopt new writing habits or to what degree they agree with their field's and college's ideological ways of thinking about how writing gets done (Bazerman and Prior 2004). Instead, we advocate—for the life of the department, the intellectual health of the faculty, and the engagement of the students—that faculty engage more socially in literacy events that allow for unscripted discourses to interact, "where two scripts or normative patterns of interactions intersect, creating the potential for authentic interaction and learning to occur" (Gutiérrez, Baquedano-López, and Turner 1997, 369). By engaging in conversations about writing outside of classrooms and writing center spaces, faculty are able to receive feedback from and provide feedback to colleagues on work-in-progress. This makes writing centers' engagement in faculty writing groups as foundational to affecting a postsecondary culture of writing as offering one-to-one and small group writing support to students. When faculty interact in writing groups and see the disciplinary expertise of writing centers in helping them to achieve their own scholarly writing goals and address their own writing process dilemmas, they have an opportunity to connect these processes to the instructional needs of their students in the classroom and to see a different value in the writing center's disciplinary expertise, thus merging the two halves of most faculty's lives: that of the researcher who writes for publication and that of the teacher who socializes students into disciplinary ways of reading, writing, and revising.

IMPLICATIONS

A third space approach to supporting faculty writing allows a writing center to adapt its use of a peer-to-peer model to address the needs of faculty writers in ways that acknowledge the complexity of faculty literacy events of publishing, writing grants, and applying for promotion and tenure—literacy events in which faculty do not have to engage alone. Invariably, this challenges a writing center to expand its practice to other spaces and challenges faculty to understand that academic success does not have to be achieved in the solitary moments of analyzing data or rewriting a purpose statement for a grant application. If faculty reach out to or accept the support of their campus writing center, they create a possibility of benefiting from a shared expertise, a hybridization of the practices and discourses of academic writing.

In this chapter, we explained one type of literacy event that holds much potential for a mutually beneficial relationship between faculty and writing centers: writing groups. Writing groups can provide moments for participating members to co-construct a third space, where knowledge construction, literacy practices, and literacy events hinge not just upon how well something is written but also upon a deeper understanding of how context, audience, and genre influence a piece. Through dialogue and reflection with others, participants in writing groups can be empowered to be at once the reader and the writer because one is never just reading and evaluating a piece. This was evident in our campus partnership. We noticed that because our writing groups allowed faculty and professional writing center staff to disrupt the binaries of reader/writer and novice/expert, a more social and collaborative space for engaging in academic writing for faculty and students emerged.

Another important consequence of the emerging third space of our faculty writing groups was that it allowed for the critique of another compartmentalizing binary: faculty as teacher/faculty as writer. When faculty interact with writing centers only in their role as teacher, they limit the possibilities of both groups' eventual participation in the larger construction of literacy events in postsecondary cultures of writing. Because these cultures are predicated on the disciplinary habits and practices that inform various micro-cultures of writing across college and university campuses, faculty can work with writing centers to contribute as a writer and a teacher to the micro-culture and to the larger disciplinary habits and practices. In recognizing the subtleties of literacy events, practices, and texts, all of which are imbued with unexamined assumptions, faculty and writing centers can work together in third spaces outside of classrooms, faculty offices, and the physical space of writing centers to illuminate the power dynamic inherent in literacy practices and texts. For disciplines to thrive and innovate, they must be willing to integrate the novice's voice and style alongside that of the experts. A third space allows for more than critique of codified genres and language structures; it allows for a rebuilding of cultures.

Faculty writing groups, then, provide a third space that can foster cultures of writing on two-year college and four-year university campuses by allowing faculty writers to be supported in their pursuit of contributing to their discipline through writing. Moreover, these writing groups encourage faculty to live Donald Murray's (2004, 4) metaphor of going "backstage to watch the pigeons being tucked up the magician's sleeve," meaning that, through writing group discussions, faculty can uncover and reflect on the work that goes into producing and revising scholarly writing. Therefore, the writing group experience can also provide a guide for helping faculty to integrate writing discussions into the classroom that will illuminate the mystery that students often experience in terms of meeting expectations.

By choosing to address the needs of faculty writers and by engaging with faculty writers, writing centers can support faculty as they engage in explicit conversations about how their writing is influenced by disciplinary writing expectations, genres, and rhetorical choices. By committing to support faculty as writers, writing centers can also begin to ask faculty to consider a more empathetic position toward their students, one that may encourage faculty to connect their own writing experiences to that of their students' writing experiences, resulting in more generous readings of student writing (Spence 2010). To be a generous reader, one's feedback must be critical and framed by a mentoring perspective—much like faculty would expect to be read by a fellow writing group member. Monroe (2002, 7-8) articulates the need for this empathy or this generous read by drawing parallels between the experiences of undergraduates, graduate students, and faculty:

> [W]riting is clearly an area of profound concern to virtually all fields, which are themselves constantly rewriting and revising what it is we understand by writing in, with, against, outside of, across, and beyond the disciplines as they currently understand themselves. The writing issues our students confront, from entering students to advanced undergraduates, to graduate students, to the most distinguished scholars, remain in fundamental respects the same issues, including especially the process of socialization or acculturation into a particular field that may have recognizable beginnings—though beginnings can be notoriously difficult to pin down and tend toward the mythical—but has no end in sight for as long as one continues to be committed to the production of knowledge in that field.

Consequently, writing groups provide third spaces that allow for the recognition of the multiple processes and many factors that all writers—student and faculty alike—must negotiate in order to be deemed an effective writer by the academic discourse community. It becomes useful then for faculty to apply their own academic writing journeys as legitimated members of their discourse communities to not only supporting their colleagues' production of writing but also to the teaching of writing. In addition, empathy is imperative when constructing viable postsecondary cultures of writing, cultures that will only be sustainable if they are enacted on the ideas of reciprocity and hybridization in third spaces—spaces that exist outside of traditional teaching and learning spaces and that allow for innovation in writing. Therefore, by supporting faculty writing groups, writing centers can provide a third institutional space. This approach allows writing centers to engage in a multitude of discursive stories, stories that are constructed in a space that can offer faculty and student writers the opportunity to dialogue with interested and invested readers, provide access to individuals who can serve as an approximation of an audience and as a testing ground for the development and organization of ideas, and construct moments to experiment with and discuss their writing as well as the writing of their peers. When this happens, faculty begin to build their own vehicles for third space dialogues, where a vibrant, diverse, and hybrid definition of academic writing begins to emerge.

REFERENCES

Barton, David, and Mary Hamilton. 2000. "Literacy Practices." In *Situated Literacies: Reading and Writing in Context*, ed. David Barton, Mary Hamilton, and Roz Ivani , 7–15. New York: Routledge.

Barton, David, Roz Ivani , Yvon Appleby, Rachel Hodge, and Karin Tusting. 2007. *Literacy, Lives, and Learning*. New York: Routledge.

Bazerman, Charles. 2011. "The Disciplined Interdisciplinarity of Writing Studies." *Research in the Teaching of English* 46:8–21.

Bazerman, Charles, and Paul Prior, eds. 2004. *What Writing Does and How It Does It: An Introduction to Analyzing Texts and Textual Practices*. Mahwah, NJ: Lawrence Erlbaum Associates, Publishers.

Bazerman, Charles, and David R. Russell, eds. 2003. *Writing Selves/Writing Societies: Research from Activity Perspectives*. Fort Collins, CO: The WAC Clearinghouse and Mind, Culture and Activity.

Boquet, Elizabeth H. 2002. *Noise from the Writing Center*. Logan, UT: Utah State University Press.

Casanave, Christine P., and Stephanie Vandrick, eds. 2003. *Writing for Scholarly Publication: Behind the Scenes in Language Education*. Mahwah, NJ: Lawrence Erlbaum Associates, Publishers.

Elbow, Peter, and Mary D. Sorcinelli. 2006. "A Faculty Writing Space: A Room of Our Own." *Change* 38 (6): 17–22. http://dx.doi.org/10.3200/CHNG.38.6.17-22.

Elmborg, James. 2006. "Critical Information Literacy: Implications for Instructional Practice." *Journal of Academic Librarianship* 32 (2): 192–9. http://dx.doi.org/10.1016/j.acalib.2005.12.004.

Eodice, Michele, and Sharon Cramer. 2002. "Write On! A Model for Enhancing Faculty Publication." *Journal of Faculty Development* 18:113–21.

Gee, James P. 2000. "The New Literacy Studies: From 'Socially Situated' to the Work of the Social." In *Situated Literacies: Reading and Writing in Context*, ed. David Barton, Mary Hamilton, and Roz Ivani , 180–196. New York, NY: Routledge.

Geller, Anne Ellen, Michele Eodice, Frankie Condon, Meg Carroll, and Elizabeth H. Boquet. 2007. "Introduction." In *The Everyday Writing Center: A Community of Practice*, 5-14. Logan: Utah State University Press.

Gere, Anne R. 1987. *Writing Groups: History, Theory, Implications.* Carbonale, IL: Southern Illinois Press.

Gillespie, Diane, Nives Dolšak, Bruce Kochis, Ron Krabill, Kari Lerum, Anne Peterson, and Elizabeth Thomas. 2005. "Research Circles: Supporting the Scholarship of Junior Faculty." *Innovative Higher Education* 30 (3): 149–62. http://dx.doi.org/10.1007/s10755-005-6300-9.

González, Norma. 2001. *I Am My Language: Discourses of Women and Children in the Borderlands.* Tucson, AZ: The University of Arizona Press.

Grego, Rhonda C., and Nancy S. Thompson. 2008. *Teaching/Writing in Thirdspaces: The Studio Approach.* Carbondale: Southern Illinois University Press.

Gutiérrez, Kris D., Patricia Baquedano-López, and Carlos Tejeda. 1999. "Rethinking Diversity: Hybridity and Hybrid Language Practices in the Third Space." *Mind, Culture, and Activity* 6 (4): 286–303. http://dx.doi.org/10.1080/10749039909524733.

Gutiérrez, Kris D., Patricia Baquedano-López, and Myrna G. Turner. 1997. "Putting Language Back into Language Arts: When the Radical Middle Meets the Third Space." *Language Arts* 74:368–78.

Gutiérrez, Kris D., and Joanne Larson. 2007. "Discussing Expanded Spaces for Learning." *Language Arts* 85:69–77.

Gutiérrez, Kris D., Betsy Rymes, and Joanne Larson. 1995. "Script, Counterscript, and Underlife in the Classroom: James Brown versus Brown v. Board Education." *Harvard Educational Review* 65:445–71.

Heath, Shirley Brice. 1982. "Protean Shapes in Literacy Events: Ever-Shifting Oral and Literate Traditions." In *Spoken and Written Language: Exploring Orality and Literacy*, ed. Deborah Tannen, 91–117. Norwood, NJ: Ablex.

Heath, Shirley Brice. 1983. *Ways with Words: Language, Life, and Work in Communities and Classrooms.* New York, NY: Cambridge University Press.

Houfek, Julia F., K. L. Kaiser, C. Visovsky, T. L. Barry, A. E. Nelson, M. M. Kaiser, and C. L. Miller. Jan-Feb 2010. "Using a Writing Group to Promote Faculty Scholarship." *Nurse Educator* 35 (1): 41–5. http://dx.doi.org/10.1097/NNE.0b013e3181c42133. Medline:20010271.

Moje, Elizabeth B., Kathryn McIntosh Ciechanowski, Katherine Kramer, Lindsay Ellis, Rosario Carrillo, and Tehani Collazo. 2004. "Working toward Third Space in Content Area Literacy: An Examination of Everyday Funds of Knowledge and Discourse." *Reading Research Quarterly* 39 (1): 38–70. http://dx.doi.org/10.1598/RRQ.39.1.4.

Monroe, Jonathan. 2002. "Introduction: The Shape of Fields." In *Writing and Revising the Disciplines*, ed. Jonathan Monroe, 1–12. Ithaca, NY: Cornell University Press.

Moss, Beverly J., Nels P. Highberg, and Melissa Nicolas. 2004. "Introduction: Writing Groups as Literacy Events." In *Writing Groups Inside and Outside the Classroom*, ed. Beverly J. Moss, Nels P. Highberg, and Melissa Nicolas, 1–10. Mahwah, NJ: Lawrence Erlbaum Associates, Publishers.

Murray, Donald M. 2004. *A Writer Teaches Writing.* 2nd ed. Boston: Thomson Heinle.

Myers, Greg. 1990. *Writing Biology: Texts in the Social Construction of Scientific Knowledge.* Madison, WI: The University of Wisconsin Press.

Pemberton, Michael A. 2009. "A Finger in Every Pie: The Expanding Role of Writing Centers in Writing Instruction." *Writing & Pedagogy* 1, no. 1: 89–100.

Prior, Paul A. 1998. *Writing/Disciplinarity: A Sociohistoric Account of Literate Activity in the Academy.* Mahwah, New Jersey: Lawrence Erlbaum Associates.

Rowe, Diana, and Kevin M. Leander. 2005. "Analyzing the Production of Thirdspace in Classroom Literacy Events." *54th Yearbook of the National Reading Conference.*

Russell, David R. 1997. "Rethinking Genre in School and Society: An Activity Theory Analysis." *Written Communication* 14 (4): 504–54. http://dx.doi.org/10.1177/0741088397014004004.

Russell, David R. 2000. *Writing in the Academic Disciplines: A Curricular History*. 2nd ed. Carbondale: Southern Illinois University Press.

Schendel, Ellen. 2010. "Retreating into the Center: Supporting Faculty and Staff as Writers." *Writing Lab Newsletter* 34 (6):1–6.

Spence, Lucy K. 2010. "Generous Reading: Seeing Students Through Their Writing." *Reading Teacher* 63 (8): 634–42. http://dx.doi.org/10.1598/RT.63.8.2.

Spigelman, Candace. 2000. *Across Property Lines: Textual Ownership in Writing Groups*. Carbondale: Southern Illinois University Press.

7

SUPPORTING A CULTURE OF WRITING
Faculty Writing Residencies as a WAC Initiative

Jessie L. Moore, Peter Felten, and Michael Strickland

In a recent analysis of teaching and learning in US higher education, Hutchings, Huber, and Ciccone argue that "Educational innovation today invites, even requires, levels of preparation, imagination, collaboration, and support that are not always a good fit (to say the least) with the inherited routines of academic life" (Hutchings, Huber, and Ciccone 2011, 6). As we have worked to enhance and deepen faculty writing at Elon University, this statement has resonated with us. With increasing expectations for scholarship at our institution, as well as our own goal of growing the Scholarship of Teaching and Learning (SoTL) at Elon, we often find ourselves helping faculty work against the flow of their inherited teaching and service routines to make space for innovative writing projects. Faculty writing residencies offer a break from these routines so that faculty can jumpstart their writing—*with* imagination, collaboration, and support.

Elon University is a 6,000 student private (primarily undergraduate) university in central North Carolina. Teaching traditionally has been the main criteria for faculty promotion and tenure, but expectations for scholarly activity have increased over the past decade. Elon follows Boyer's (1997) definition of scholarship, making space for faculty to have SoTL as a component, or even the central focus, of their research agendas. However, in the 1990s and early 2000s, faculty SoTL projects usually existed in isolation on campus, and many did not result in peer reviewed publications or off-campus scholarly presentations.

In 2005–2006, when the authors of this chapter assessed the gap between the number of SoTL inquiry projects at Elon and the number

DOI: 10.7330/9780874219029.c007

of SoTL publications being produced by our colleagues, we identified two common problems faculty encountered related to SoTL writing. First, while faculty receive some training in writing for a particular discipline (although Ambos, Wiley, and Allen, 2009 note that training's limitations), SoTL writing requires faculty to consider, often for the first time, how to write about classroom practice and evidence of student learning, raising sometimes troubling questions about genre, voice, and expertise (Cambridge 2004). Without such support, faculty may not successfully publish even otherwise high-quality SoTL work (Gale 2008; Peters, Schodt and Walczak 2008). Second, many Elon faculty felt relatively isolated in their SoTL work—particularly in what Lee Shulman (2004) calls the "going public" portion of the scholarly process. Since research suggests that feeling part of a supportive community of writing peers is important to productivity (Eodice and Cramer 2003; Lee and Boud 2003; Belcher 2009), the silos that separated faculty and their projects represented a real barrier to SoTL writing in our context. Faculty struggled to identify viable publication venues for SoTL projects (particularly if the main journals in their discipline did not regularly publish SoTL work) and for strategies and feedback on how to write about SoTL. Throughout their graduate educations and professional careers, faculty develop strategies for writing in their disciplines, but most do not encounter professional development on learning to write for other audiences or how to describe research methods and results that are outside of their narrow disciplinary training (Hutchings, Huber, and Ciccone 2011).

To fill those gaps, the authors created a "faculty writing residency." This approach represented a new kind of faculty development on our campus. Our well-established Writing Across the Curriculum (WAC) program traditionally offered practical workshops for faculty using writing in their courses, while our new Center for the Advancement of Teaching and Learning (CATL) focused on other pedagogical concerns. Neither had a record of supporting faculty doing their own scholarly writing, and they had only begun to work together during CATL's first year of existence. The writing residency, then, represented just the kind of new collaboration that Hutchings, Huber, and Ciccone identify as necessary in academia. While we do not claim to have created an ideal model, our experience over the past six years demonstrates the power and potential for faculty development partnerships to promote faculty writing and to enhance writing pedagogy.

CREATING AND REFINING ELON'S FACULTY WRITING RESIDENCY

Typically, the professional writing of faculty is not considered within the domain of WAC. Nor do teaching centers, such as Elon's CATL, support the scholarly writing of faculty (Sorcinelli et al. 2005). However, when we first started conversations about how the work of WAC and CATL could connect, we decided to broaden our horizons to look beyond the conventional (and effective) workshops and consultations we already offered. Our observations about the gaps in SoTL practice on campus suggested the promise of working with faculty on their own writing.

We initially considered several formats for our faculty writing program, such as monthly day-long writing sessions or bi-weekly half-days (Elbow and Sorcinelli 2006), but we decided to model our first (June 2006) writing residency on a program offered by the Visible Knowledge Project, a five-year project hosted by Georgetown University with the goal of integrating technology into discussions about student learning and faculty development (McGowan 2006). That project featured three-day immersive writing residencies for faculty participants from across the country, including one of this chapter's coauthors. Writers circulated a draft SoTL article to fellow participants before the residency began, and then the group met for days of writing and small group feedback that was facilitated by experienced SoTL scholars. At the time, few models were available in the published literature, and this approach seemed to offer us the highest potential for building faculty community around writing. Other comparable programs, like the Writers' Retreat at the University of Limerick (Moore 2003) and the Scholarly Writing Institute at California State University, Long Beach (Ambos, Wiley, and Allen 2009), promoted similar community building around faculty writing but lacked the ongoing, facilitated small group component. Even more recent models, like Murray and Newton's (2009) structured writing retreat, which prompts participants to complete focused writing process activities like free-writing and to write in fixed time slots, lack the small-group facilitation that we sought in order to mentor faculty on writing strategies for "going public" in SoTL. Similarly, many excellent SoTL initiatives, like the University of Wisconsin's Lesson Study Project support collaborative inquiry into student learning (see Chick, Hassel, and Haynie 2009, for instance), but they often do not provide comparable attention to producing scholarly writing about that inquiry.

The immersive nature of the Visible Knowledge Project schedule also seemed to offer a shield against the many other obligations (with students, service responsibilities, etc.) that make it difficult for some faculty on our busy campus to focus on their writing. While we encourage participants to write each day when and where they are most productive, we offered a space where faculty could escape distractions. In a nod to the life realities that contribute to those distractions, we made one significant change to our model program, eliminating the overnight stays of the original Visible Knowledge Project structure to make our program attractive to our campus's many faculty with young children or other obligations at home. Yet, as the name "residency" implies, faculty participants still are in-residence during the day for four consecutive days, joining a learning community of writers.

Every year, the residency runs for four days, beginning approximately one week after our university's spring commencement. This timing allows faculty to enjoy a few days break from the spring semester but also is early enough that summer's distractions are not in full swing. In addition, the local school districts are still in session, so faculty with school age children do not have to make special childcare plans. The timing also allows the residency to serve as a springboard for summer writing projects; faculty can leave the residency with significant progress already made on one writing project and a summer plan for next steps on that (and perhaps other) manuscripts.

We chose an off-campus location for our residency, Timberlake Farms. This local environmental education foundation offers a nature preserve with walking trails, a "treehouse" with three comfortable small-group spaces spread across two levels, porches, and a picturesque view of a pond. We also initially valued Timberlake Farms' lack of Internet access, which kept e-mail from encroaching on faculty writing time. The facility now has Internet access, but as our library has moved to more online access to journals—and even e-books—we have come to consider it a helpful resource. In addition, the Internet access enables participants to exchange drafts with group members on site, without a printer. While this setting is deep in the woods, it is only ten miles from campus and easy to reach on local highways. There are modern bathroom facilities and a full kitchen. Timberlake works with a local caterer to provide coffee, tea and pastries for the morning and lunches at mid-day.

In our first year, worried that such a new concept might intrude on sacred summer research and recharge time and thus not attract a critical mass of participants, we invited faculty to apply to work on any type of writing project that was at any stage of the writing process. We emphasized the residency as an opportunity for intensive focus on writing and for communing with and eliciting feedback from interested peers. Indeed, we hosted a wide variety of projects, ranging from book manuscripts to conference proposals, from individual to team projects, and from stages of readiness that varied from a barely scribbled blue-sky idea to an already developed rough draft that had somehow stalled out.

From the perspective of most participants, and judging from their achievement rates, that first year succeeded. Half of our year one participants have published the projects they brought to the residency. But, from our perspective, the diversity of project goals, disciplinary foci, and intended audiences created problems for small groups' peer response and support—a critical element to learning to "go public" in an unfamiliar discourse community. While participants reported that discussing writing problems in their groups was quite helpful, we observed that insightful responses on the disciplinary content of the various pieces were uneven at best. An English faculty member, for instance, might feel comfortable offering line editing advice to a Religious Studies faculty member, but when the Religious Studies faculty member sought feedback on how well she framed a nuanced argument for a disciplinary audience, the disconnect could spark frustration—for both the writer and the reader.

For the second year of our residency, therefore, we sought to find common ground for faculty members' writing projects. Emboldened by the strong faculty interest in the first year of the residency, and building on a growing set of SoTL programs sponsored by CATL, we decided that the faculty writing residencies would be a good vehicle for supporting faculty efforts to go public with the outcomes of their SoTL research. Our next (2007) call for applications specifically targeted faculty working on SoTL projects. We also specified that we preferred projects that were well positioned to benefit from the residency, rather than preliminary ideas or near-finished manuscripts. This focus worked. Not only have we always had more applications than we can accommodate, but also we have found that the feedback and engagement within the groups has been much deeper and more consistent than in our first year. We have continued this SoTL emphasis ever since, enabling us to better support faculty who are learning how to go public with their SoTL research.

STRUCTURING AND ORGANIZING THE RESIDENCY

We typically accept nine to twelve projects, including coauthored manuscripts if all the authors can participate in the residency. Although some writing institute models are able to accommodate more participants (Ambos, Wiley, and Allen 2009), a critical component of our residency is facilitated feedback groups, which we have found to be most effective when they have no more than five members. Once we have selected our participants from the applicant pool, we create three small writing groups, and each of us facilitates one group throughout the residency. Our sorting strategies vary based on the types of projects, but we look for groupings around similar SoTL questions, potential resource exchanges, or shared research methods. We avoid grouping writers from the same department, in part to help participants meet and establish professional relationships with colleagues from other parts of campus. Again, one of our goals is to facilitate a campus-wide community of SoTL scholars, not to reinforce existing silos. We also intentionally keep our overall residency participation small—rather than adding an additional facilitator and group—in order to foster meaningful interaction among faculty who might not have opportunities to visit during the regular rhythms of the academic year. Finally, each year brings a few repeat participants, so we distribute them among the groups, allowing facilitators to rely on these veterans to help model the writing residency process.

About two weeks before the residency starts we introduce the writers to their teams and ask them to do some pre-writing. In this assignment we ask each participant to e-mail her group members a brief description of her writing project, the intended audience, and her goals for the residency. We also ask participants to send brief samples of draft writing from their projects. These pieces are due the Thursday before the residency so that group members can read them before the first meeting the next week.

We begin the first day with a large group meeting with another pre-write activity (described in more detail below) and brief group introductions—to each other and to our writing projects. We then break into the small working groups to plan group schedules for the week. Each group meets once each day to offer feedback on the writing in progress and to establish goals for the next twenty-four hours, but groups vary their meeting times (e.g., early morning, late morning, lunch, early afternoon) based on group members' peak writing times. Outside of these 90–120 minute daily group meetings, and corresponding time reading group members' drafts each day, the rest of the time is devoted to writing. As facilitators, we are available for one-on-one consultations as needed, but we emphasize making use of the extended daily time with minimal distractions to make significant progress toward writers' daily goals.

During writing time, participants arrive at the treehouse on their own timetable, find a conducive spot, and write. A few opt to use the time to write at coffee shops, or even in rare cases, on campus. We emphasize that this time should be seen as residency time and participants should avoid their usual distractions. Our priorities are productivity and focus over the need to be physically present during the residency, except during group times, but the vast majority of participants opt to write at the residency site.

As hinted above, goal setting has become a critical piece of our writing residency structure. We ask participants to set goals for the week, establish daily goals that help them work toward their residency goals, and report out to their small groups on a daily basis. Goals are usually specific, even though they may range from a hoped for number of pages generated to a specific concept fleshed out. We encourage writers to be as detailed as possible and urge readers to add their suggestions to the goals, especially in the daily work of the groups. While additional reading and research sometimes are an outcome of a feedback session, we make it clear that this should not subsume the writing task at hand. We have found over the years that many faculty writers encounter the *must-read-everything-before-I-can-write syndrome*, so we emphasize setting daily writing goals, even while participants are continuing to read and brainstorm. Not only do the daily goals help participants break down their projects into more manageable pieces, but they also provide a friendly peer pressure, as participants strive to meet the goals they shared with their groups.

Lunch breaks offer participants an opportunity to mingle outside their own groups and to talk not only about their projects but other issues. Participants who might not cross paths on campus get to know each other, providing a significant bonding experience that allows faculty from disparate disciplines to become acquainted with each other's teaching and scholarship.

When groups meet to intensively workshop participants' latest drafts, each session begins in a similar fashion. One writer revisits her goals from the previous day, evaluates how well she thinks she has accomplished them, explains any changes in the new draft, and clarifies her call for the kinds of feedback she would most appreciate. At that point each group member gives his or her response to the latest draft, beginning by answering the primary questions the writer has asked, and then flowing into a more global response, which may include suggestions for new sources, positing new questions for the writer to consider, and engaging other members of the group in discussing a particular point of interest or contention. As facilitators, we help the group stay on task and focus on the writer's goals. After each member has had an opportunity to respond in kind, the discussion concludes with the writer summing up her new writing goals for the next day. The process is then repeated for the next writer in the group. These facilitated small group sessions provide timely feedback on participants' efforts to adapt their disciplinary writing processes and styles for SoTL, helping faculty "go public" with a new avenue of scholarship, and in the company of colleagues who are encountering similar challenges learning to write for new audiences and purposes. Even for groups meeting in the afternoon, the workshopping process for the group ends in time for the individual writers to return to a quiet place and continue some end-of-the-day writing, in hopes of capturing the energy of the previous discussion and channeling it into new pathways and pages generated.

On day four, the final day, the large group reconvenes for a brief post-write and reflective discussion. While we encourage participants to share how they have met their goals, we also facilitate discussion about participants' writing processes. We attempt to help participants identify writing strategies that they can continue throughout the rest of the summer and into the future. We also prompt reflection on how participants' experiences might carry over into their teaching. What new writing strategies did they try that they could use with students? What did they learn about the variety of writing processes within their group, and how might they share that recognition with their students? What did they learn about helpful feedback that they would like to reproduce in their feedback—and peer feedback—to students? Talking through the applicability of the experience to their teaching also gives us an opportunity to remind participants about Writing Across the Curriculum (WAC) workshops and other faculty development initiatives relevant to the teaching of writing across the disciplines. As a result, the faculty writing residencies have a significant secondary role as an informal WAC initiative.

ASSESSING THE RESIDENCY

To examine the outcomes of the faculty writing residencies, we implemented multiple forms of assessment: pre-writes, post-writes, informal progress reports, a survey, and interviews. Pre-writes, administered on the first day of each residency, prompt participants to briefly summarize their writing projects and intended audiences, identify their timelines for their projects, and articulate goals for the week. Additional questions ask faculty to indicate what type of feedback they hope to receive and what else would make the week productive for them. In 2009, we also began asking participants about the role of writing in the courses they teach so that we could better assess any changes in how faculty approach the teaching of writing after they participate in the writing residencies.

The post-write, administered at the end of the week, asks participants to explain how and why significant aspects of their writing projects (i.e., focus, audience, timeline, etc.) changed during the week and how they will continue to make time for writing during the rest of the summer. We also ask faculty to assess whether they achieved their personal goals for the week (as articulated in the pre-write), how the writing residency helped them work toward those goals, and what the facilitators could have done to better support their work. These questions both help us plan revisions to the structure of the residency and reinforce the goal setting practices we establish on the first day. Finally, we ask how participants' writing experiences during the week might influence their future work with student writers.

About every six months, we follow-up with previous writing residency participants to ask for updates on their writing projects. We emphasize that we love to celebrate publications, but we also are interested in any types of progress participants have made toward their goals for their projects, or even if they have decided to abandon a manuscript. We track responses over time, enabling us to report on publication and presentation outcomes, and to examine how many projects are still in progress. These frequent contacts also pave the way for follow-up conversations with participants about the impact of the writing residencies.

In spring 2011, we extended these ongoing assessment measures with an online survey of former participants. The eight question survey (approved by the Elon University Institutional Review Board) asked participants about the writing assignments and activities they use in their classes and the impact the residency had on their teaching of writing, their teaching more generally, and their understanding of the Scholarship of Teaching and Learning. Our survey had a 54 percent response rate, and of the participants who took the survey, 88 percent completed all the questions.

The following discussion of the writing residency outcomes draws from our survey data, post-write data, and ongoing requests for updates.

FACULTY SCHOLARSHIP OUTCOMES

The residencies have helped faculty go public with their SoTL work. To date, 57 percent of all residency participants met their identified goals, with 95 percent of those success stories resulting in peer-reviewed publications. Other participants have presented their writing residency projects at national conferences. An additional 37 percent are still working

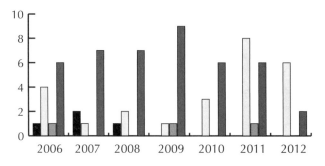

Figure 7.1. Faculty writing residency outcomes by year.

on their projects, and only four projects have been abandoned. Figure 7.1 provides a further break-down of the in-progress category, showing that some of these projects are under-review. Beyond publication outcomes, the residencies also have a positive impact on the campus SoTL initiatives. Sixty-five percent of the survey respondents indicated that the writing residences had informed or changed their understanding of SoTL. Participants specifically identified: introductions to new coding strategies or other data analysis approaches, heightened awareness of the interdisciplinary nature of SoTL, greater appreciation for the importance of SoTL to the local institution and to academia more broadly, and renewed motivation to pursue a SoTL research agenda.

The residency provides a safe space to learn about publishing, particularly in SoTL, and faculty comments highlight the learning curve that the writing residencies help faculty navigate as they embark on SoTL:

- It has shown me that I don't have any training in this field. I know how to do scholarship in cultural and literary criticism and it is so different. When I participated in the Writing Residency for the first time I didn't even know where to start. I think through my teaching experience I had interesting points to make, but I didn't know what format/structure to follow, how things were done in the field of the SoTL. (Foreign Language Faculty, survey response)
- Time spent at the writing residency helped me to better understand

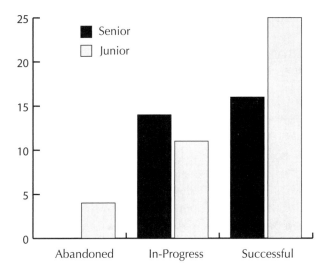

Figure 7.2. Faculty Writing Residency Outcomes by Career Stage

the differences among educational practitioner writing, research reporting, and SoTL. (anonymous survey response)

As a result, the Faculty Writing Residencies have played a key role in helping faculty across career stages learn to write SoTL pieces, and in turn, prepare for tenure and/or promotion applications that incorporate SoTL research agendas. Junior faculty account for 53 percent of the residency participants, and to date, 63 percent of these faculty have achieved successful outcomes (publication or presentation) with their projects. An additional 28 percent of the junior faculty participants still have projects in-progress. Figure 7.2 shows faculty outcomes by career stage, using the raw numbers of participants. These faculty outcomes also have implications for the institution. The steady stream of SoTL publications emerging from the writing residencies reinforces the institution's commitment to SoTL and highlights for new (and *all*) faculty that SoTL can be a viable component of their research agendas. While we have not formally tracked the numbers, we also know that several residency groups have continued to meet to support each other's additional writing projects during the year, suggesting that the writing residencies (1) built motivation, and (2) established the groundwork for ongoing writing groups, meeting two of Davis, Provost, and Major's

(2011) recommendations for supporting faculty writing groups. Further, the residencies have fostered programmatic publications and projects, including a publication for the school's honors program and a reexamination of foreign language instruction.

WRITING ACROSS THE CURRICULUM OUTCOMES AND FACULTY TEACHING OUTCOMES

While the residency was not designed to change writing instruction on campus, the program has had that affect for some participants. Several faculty have noted, in surveys or interviews, that the residency had fundamentally changed how they think about teaching and assessing student writing. For example, a Human Service Studies faculty member recreated a version of the writing residency in a junior-year seminar for social sciences majors in the honors program, and the experience also shaped her teaching of writing in other classes. In her survey response, she writes, "I talk about the writing residency when I teach disciplinary writing. I let students know that all writers struggle with the process of writing and that writing is just that, a process. I frequently bring in the multiple drafts I have written for a single article to help students see the process of writing. I have also shared feedback from reviewers on manuscripts to illustrate how two reviewers may offer the writer contradictory feedback. I explain that it is up to the writer to come to a decision about how to move forward." She also integrates peer review into every class. Collectively, her takeaways from the writing residency illustrate her conviction that "It is critical that faculty be able to teach writing in their discipline, as that is one way to assess student comprehension on student learning."

While this type of transformation is impressive, it also is relatively rare. We have found more generally that the residency has had modest but positive effects on participants' teaching of writing. Some faculty, for example, simply gained new appreciation for students' struggles with writing, as one participant shares, "Watching others' work develop showed me that both faculty and students struggle with seeing their own work with new eyes" (First-year Writing Faculty 2009). Half of the survey respondents indicated that the writing residency had informed their teaching of writing, leading them to refine and/or offer additional opportunities for peer review and multiple drafts in their classes. Typical post-write faculty responses and large-group conversations at the end of each residency include comments like:

- I always thought I gave "enough" time & "enough" feedback on their (students') writing, but I am beginning to seriously rethink that. I haven't fully developed my thoughts on this, but, off the top of my head I probably will ask for drafts first, give comments (both mine and peer) & then ask for final. (Dance Faculty 2009)

- I plan to allow student writers to set their own goals more often, as this was a useful feature of our workshop group. Also, I plan to allow workshop groups in my comp classes to generate more of their own review criteria. I can certainly empathize with student writers more closely, since research writing on academic topics isn't easy! (First-year Writing Faculty 2009)

- I think I realized how much it helps to comment on the content of writing. Even small comments such as "Why would you say this? Explain"; "This is vague, more description/clarification"; "Make your own voice be heard" etc. are very helpful. It was very valuable to have three to four readers who saw different strong or weak aspects of my writing and helped me improve it. I will also consider peer reviewing more seriously in my classes. But this would require guiding them through the review process. They would have to be good readers, and it isn't easy, it requires knowledge and experience. (Foreign Language Faculty 2009)

These changes also led faculty to yearn for policy changes that would facilitate more writing instruction in their classes. As one participant writes, "I wish I had fewer students in my writing intensive classes to be able to dedicate more time to writing and offer everyone my comments on the content of their papers/essays."

These faculty comments and experiences suggest that even though most faculty do not explicitly associate changes in their perceptions of WAC and their practices teaching writing with their writing residency experiences, the residencies clearly do impact their teaching. Regardless of whether the modifications are attributed to the writing residency itself or to group members talking about their teaching, many participants change peer review or assessment practices or implement a multiple draft process in their classes.

PROGRAM COLLABORATIONS

Finally, our partnership to organize and facilitate the residencies every year also has strengthened collaborations between our Center for the Advancement of Teaching and Learning (which Peter directs) and the Elon Writing Program Administrators Committee (which both Michael and Jessie have served on as previous writing program administrators). As a result, we have pursued other partnerships in support of writing, including a grant to study digital literacies in first-year writing courses and a multi-year research seminar on writing transfer. Although not the intent of the Writing Residency program, this collaboration has taken us out of our own silos, and lessened the isolation that writing program administrators and teaching center directors sometimes experience on campus.

CONCLUSION

Our primary goal with the faculty writing residencies has been to support faculty writers, and our participants' publication record suggests that we are meeting that goal. Our emphasis on SoTL has extended and deepened the campus community around this type of scholarship, which more and more regularly manifests itself as a continuation of residency writing groups throughout the summer and into subsequent academic years. Furthermore, a deliberate side-effect of this initiative for many of our participants has been a renewed focus on teaching writing across the curriculum; we look forward to seeing additional integration of peer review and multiple drafts in campus classrooms as more participants take what they have experienced at the residency into their own classrooms. Finally, our faculty development work is more collaborative and integrated; our programs intentionally complement each other, supporting both our separate programs and a community of scholarly teachers on campus. For a one-week residency, these are exciting outcomes.

We attribute our success to several key features of our residency model. The facilitated small groups are essential to supporting faculty efforts to learn how to write about SoTL projects so that faculty can "go public" with their results; facilitators reinforce daily goal setting, provide immediate feedback on writing and strategies for strengthening faculty writing processes, and help group members learn how to offer the most helpful types of feedback in relation to writers' goals. Designing groups with members from multiple disciplines also helps writers develop an effective voice for many SoTL journals that publish articles from diverse disciplines. If faculty can describe their projects and outcomes in ways that their interdisciplinary group members comprehend, SoTL journal readers likely will follow the writing, too. A relaxing, retreat environment with flexible work spaces helps writers find physical writing locations that work for them and enables them to move among different spaces throughout the day. Last but not least, the mix of faculty at different career stages and from different academic programs facilitates community building and extends faculty's mentoring networks for SoTL writing projects and other aspects of faculty's professional lives. In combination, these essential elements sustain the success of the faculty writing residency.

REFERENCES

Ambos, Elizabeth, Mark Wiley, and Terre H. Allen. 2009. "Romancing the Muse: Faculty Writing Institutes as Professional Development." In *To Improve the Academy*, ed. Linda B. Nilson and Judith E. Miller, 135–149. San Francisco: Jossey-Bass.

Belcher, Wendy L. 2009. "Reflection on Ten Years of Teaching Writing for Publication to Graduate Students and Junior Faculty." *Journal of Scholarly Publishing* 40 (2): 184–200. http://dx.doi.org/10.3138/jsp.40.2.184.

Boyer, Ernest L. 1997. *Scholarship Reconsidered.* San Francisco: Jossey-Bass.

Cambridge, Barbara L., ed. 2004. *Campus Progress: Supporting the Scholarship of Teaching and Learning.* Sterling, VA: Stylus.

Chick, Nancy L., Holly Hassel, and Aeron Haynie. 2009. "'Pressing an Ear Against the Hive': Reading Literature for Complexity." *Pedagogy* 9 (3): 399–422.

Davis, Dannielle Joy, Kara Provost, and Amanda E. Major. 2011. "Writing Groups for Work-Life Balance: Faculty Writing Group Leaders Share Their Stories." In *To Improve the Academy*, ed. Judith E. Miller and James E. Groccia, 31–42. San Francisco: Jossey-Bass.

Elbow, Peter, and Mary Deane Sorcinelli. 2006. "The Faculty Writing Place: A Room of Our Own." *Change* 38 (6): 17–22. http://dx.doi.org/10.3200/CHNG.38.6.17-22.

Eodice, Michele, and Sharon F. Cramer. 2003. "Dynamic Leadership Solutions." *Journal of Faculty Development* 18 (4): 113–21.

Gale, Richard. 2008. "Points Without Limits." In *To Improve the Academy*, ed. Douglas Reimondo Robertson and Linda B. Nilson, 39–52. San Francisco: Jossey-Bass.

Hutchings, Pat, Mary Taylor Huber, and Anthony Ciccone. 2011. *The Scholarship of Teaching and Learning Reconsidered.* San Francisco: Jossey-Bass.

Lee, Alison, and David Boud. 2003. Writing Groups, Change and Academic Identity: Research Development as Local Practice." *Studies in Higher Education* 28 (2): 187–200. http://dx.doi.org/10.1080/0307507032000058109.

McGowan, Susannah. 2006. "The Visible Knowledge Project's Writing Residency." *Change* 38 (6): 22.

Moore, Sarah. 2003. "Writers' Retreats for Academics: Exploring and Increasing the Motivation to Write." *Journal of Further and Higher Education* 27 (3): 333–42. http://dx.doi.org/10.1080/0309877032000098734.

Murray, Rowena, and Mary Newton. 2009. "Writing Retreat as Structured Intervention: Margin or Mainstream?" *Higher Education Research & Development* 28 (5): 541–53. http://dx.doi.org/10.1080/07294360903154126.

Peters, Dolores, David Schodt, and Mary Walczak. 2008. "Supporting the Scholarship of Teaching and Learning in Liberal Arts Colleges." In *To Improve the Academy*, ed. Douglas Reimondo Robertson and Linda B. Nilson, 68–86. San Francisco: Jossey-Bass.

Shulman, Lee. 2004. *Teaching as Community Property: Essays on Higher Education.* San Francisco: Jossey-Bass.

Sorcinelli, Mary Deane, Ann E. Austin, Pamela L. Eddy, and Andrea L. Beach. 2005. *Creating the Future of Faculty Development: Learning from the Past, Understanding the Present.* San Francisco: Anker/Jossey-Bass.

8
ASSESSING THE EFFECTS OF FACULTY AND STAFF WRITING RETREATS
Four Institutional Perspectives

Ellen Schendel, Susan Callaway, Violet
Dutcher, and Claudine Griggs

The writing retreats at our institutions—Grand Valley State University (GVSU) in Grand Rapids, Michigan, the University of St. Thomas (UST) in St. Paul, Minnesota, Eastern Mennonite University (EMU) in Harrisonburg, Virginia, and Rhode Island College (RIC) in Providence, Rhode Island—share several basic but critical characteristics. In fact, after Ellen published an article in the *Writing Lab Newsletter* about the retreats at GVSU, Claudine, Susan, and Violet all contacted her to learn more. Despite diverse institutional settings, our common goals in conducting writing retreats gave us an opportunity to talk with each other about assessing and modifying the retreats.

In this chapter, we describe what our assessments reveal about week-long writing retreats as specific opportunities for faculty and staff to immerse themselves in a space and time to engage with writing as a messy, demanding, and social process. Just as we want student writers to leave our writing centers with better understandings of themselves as writers and with specific plans for revision, faculty leave our retreats more productive and in tune with their writerly selves, and more receptive to practices that sustain them as writers throughout the academic year. They seek feedback for their writing and offer feedback to colleagues; find and commit themselves to a community of writers; and set aside and protect time in their lives for writing. We know that program assessment should be "regular, systemic, and coherent . . . ongoing . . . counted on to provide information to the institution . . . and whose development over time reflects the emerging concerns of [the people at the institution]"

DOI: 10.7330/9780874219029.c008

(Yancey and Huot 1997, 11). We have used assessment to improve our retreats, generate ideas for additional writing support programming, and enhance our knowledge about writing at our institutions.

Our assessments are fourfold. We first pay attention to the preparatory work that we ask each participant to do and to the communications—face-to-face and by e-mail—that participants undertake in the weeks before the retreats. Then throughout the retreats, we are participant-observers, trying to ensure that writers are getting what they need at that moment and looking for opportunities to discuss what might sustain an individual's writing beyond the retreat. On the last day of the retreat, we then gather feedback about the participants' productivity, attitudes, and feelings of accomplishment during the week. Finally, we follow up with surveys to learn what happened to the projects participants were working on during the retreat—were they finished and/or published?— as well as what happened to them as writers since the retreat.

Although we collaborated on the designs and goals of our assessments, each campus context required slightly different approaches. Also, because the writing retreat concept was well-established at GVSU and relatively new at UST, EMU, and RIC, we had differing opportunities to test and compare data-gathering strategies. In all cases, however, the assessments have helped us, as writing center directors, to shape our faculty-as-writers programming. In the end, our assessments have shown us that the key ingredients for these retreats to have lasting impact on the writers who participate include: prompting faculty to set goals and prepare to write during the retreat; focusing the week on providing extended time to write rather than activities or workshops; having the flexibility to change programming throughout the week in order to meet the individualized needs of writers; and building a sense of community throughout the week so that writers feel empowered to continue writing and sharing drafts with colleagues beyond the retreat.

GETTING STARTED: ASSESSING THE FIRST RETREATS
Claudine Griggs, Rhode Island College

Meg Carroll retired as Director of the RIC Writing Center in May 2009 after twenty years of service. And when I assumed that position, I understood that she was well known among the writing center community, had gained recognition of our peer tutoring center in the Northeast, and had coauthored the recently released *Everyday Writing Center*. Believing that only a fool would disrupt an already effective operating system, I left the basic organizational structure intact while looking for ways to build on Carroll's success. Yet I also wanted to emerge from under a significant professional shadow, and I began searching for something new, something distinctly Griggsian, and something that would expand the writing center's service to faculty. So when I read Ellen's article "Retreating into the Center: Supporting Faculty and Staff as Writers" (Schendel 2010) in March 2010, followed by several e-mails and a twenty-minute telephone conference with Ellen, I decided to hold at least one writing retreat even if I had to pay for it. This wasn't required. Within twenty-four hours of sending my proposal to four possible sources of support, I received a commitment to fund the event.

Our first two faculty writing retreats were held August 16–20, 2010 (with eight participants) and August 15–19, 2011 (with nine). My greatest concern as I organized the inaugural event—coordinating food service, purchasing snacks, reserving extra space for peer review or conferencing, drafting information and registration forms, advertising the retreat, and even cleaning the writing center beforehand—was: If I build it, will they come? As a writer myself, I wondered, Why would anyone need a retreat? I write regularly without one; so can other faculty. But I put my faith in the concept and moved ahead.

The participants came; they wrote; they wrote some more. In fact, the RIC retreats have been so productive that, in September 2011, I received a commitment from the Office of Academic Support and Information Services to fund two separate events in 2012. Our faculty not only worked hard, they seemed to value the retreat "process." For example, at our second retreat, faculty attended from seven departments—Economics and Finance; History; Anthropology; Psychology; Counseling, Educational Leadership, and School Psychology; English; Management and Marketing; along with an engineer from the Rhode Island State Highway Department who heard about our retreat, e-mailed me, and was invited to attend. Regarding the week, Debra Skaradizinski, Assistant Professor of Economics and Finance, wrote: "What struck me about the experience is how 'social' it seems even though writing is considered a solitary pursuit. It reminds me a little bit of the old-fashioned sewing circles . . . So I'm beginning to consider ways that [our] business professors could get together for an evening a week to work on their research. I'm amazed at how much less painful it is to sit at a computer when other people around me are doing the same!" (Debra Skaradizinski, e-mail message to author, August 19, 2011).

Other comments from the 2011 exit surveys, conferences, and/or post-retreat questionnaires (collected August 19 through September 7) include:

- The retreat framed a solid, focused time block with no distractions—that is golden.

- It was congenial but work-like, and the "scheduled" attitude toward writing was reinforced. Great! Do it twice a year!

- [The retreat was] tremendously helpful. It kept me dedicated and disciplined . . . Offer another in January if possible.

- I did more writing [this week] than I have done in the last year . . . People were very accommodating. The room was perfect for writing. You should offer this retreat forever.

Praveena Gullapalli, Assistant Professor of Anthropology, attended both retreats, insisting that the structure got her "on track" with her project but that she loses momentum at the end of summer because she must think about fall classes. She asked if the retreat could be held in May or June. And for 2011, we also included optional conferences with Carla Weiss, one of our campus research librarians. Four participants met with her, reporting that the appointments "should be offered in the future" and "with the research resources constantly changing, it was a very valuable conference."

The overall productivity among participants surprised me. During the 2010 retreat, eight faculty reported completing or making significant progress on the following projects (along with related research and readings): four academic articles, one book chapter, two conference papers, two book manuscripts, three short stories, and two academic PowerPoint presentations. In 2011, nine participants worked on five academic articles, a dissertation, book chapter, conference proposal, book review, grant application, book manuscript, two short stories, and a pilot-study proposal; three participants also conducted literature reviews related to their projects (one of whom reported reading fourteen journal articles as part of that process); and another said that in preparing for the retreat, she became so energized that she finished one of the papers she had planned to work on during the week.

Perhaps we should not be surprised that faculty who voluntarily sign up for a writing retreat will produce written work; but according to Sarah Moore (citing Grant and Knowles [2000]; Cohen [1986]; Kagan [1988]; Slavin [1986]), "People writing as part of a community of writers are more likely to learn faster about the conventions and challenges of writing, to support each other at times of blockage, and to demystify the process of writing by sharing each others' successes and failures" (Moore 2003, 334). Inadvertently acknowledging such benefits, almost every RIC participant in 2010 and 2011 suggested that we offer two retreats per year. Some requested a week at the beginning and end of summer, some during winter break and summer, and others over spring break and summer. Two people suggested a single two-week event. I also received comments from half a dozen other faculty in 2011 who wanted to attend the retreat but could not because of the August time slot; most asked me to consider another month.

I was also surprised during the initial planning stages by the speedy and enthusiastic support from administration. Funding for our first two retreats (August 2010 and 2011) came from the Office of Academic Support and Information Services (OASIS), which primarily assists students. When asked why "student services" would fund a faculty writing retreat, Dolores Passarelli, the OASIS Director, said, "Collegiality. This event brings junior and senior faculty from across the campus to work together for one week, getting to know each other in the process. It should also provide participants with a better understanding of the ongoing writing issues students encounter in their classrooms. And by holding the retreat in our writing center, it demonstrates that this is a good place for faculty to refer their students" (Dolores Passarelli, July 6, 2001).[1] Ron Pitt, the Vice President for Academic Affairs, has also offered funding assistance (if needed), and I asked Dr. Pitt, "Why should it matter to the college whether we hold a writing retreat? After all, faculty are expected to write anyway." His reply: "Faculty life is demanding, the college's teaching standards are high, and scholarly expectations are important to teaching. The retreat helps each faculty member to focus on a specific writing project and make a commitment to developing that project. And, essentially, anytime we support faculty and scholarship, we are helping students" (Ronald Pitt, June 28, 2011).[2]

Rhode Island College is a public master's institution with a twelve-unit teaching requirement per semester, yet faculty are expected to produce scholarship. I wanted to support faculty as writers, and as we prepare for our fourth retreat in August 2012, I am pleased that our writing center has become a place where they can gather among peers from all disciplines and ranks, publicly underpinning their efforts to teach, write, and publish.

---

1. Dolores Passarelli (Director, Office of Academic Support and Information Services, Rhode Island College) in discussion with Claudine Griggs, July 6, 2011.
2. Ronald Pitt (Vice President of Academic Affairs, Rhode Island College), paraphrased from an interview with Claudine Griggs on June 28, 2011.

CREATING AND ASSESSING A SCHOLARLY WRITING CULTURE
Violet Dutcher, Eastern Mennonite University

Eastern Mennonite University is a teaching university and has its roots in the Mennonite Church. What this means for the university is that service to others and departments that graduate students into the professions of teaching, nursing, and peace-building are highly valued. At the time I initiated the writing retreat on our campus, I had been at EMU nearly four years. I had observed that our faculty engaged in conversations about student writing, but we had not discussed faculty writing. As writing program director, I read Ellen's article in the March 2010 issue of *The Writing Lab Newsletter* about holding writing retreats for faculty. I was struck by the simplicity of Grand Valley's retreats. I also saw the labor intensive aspects of this retreat, but I was willing to work hard in order to help shape our EMU culture as one with faculty at work on their writing with a heightened awareness of their own practices. I immediately contacted Ellen, and her advice was invaluable to our efforts.

Our provost gave this idea immediate and strong support, and I began making plans, creating a name for the retreat, and talking to faculty, spreading the word. I met with the Anabaptist Center for Religion and Society (ACRS), an organization formed by EMU retirees to continue their own work and to support current faculty, to gain their support. As a result, the ACRS endorsed the retreat, and the Provost's office underwrote it through the Writing Program.

We named our retreat Kairos Place, wanting to emphasize the idea of a timely space for faculty in which to do their scholarly work. While most of the faculty who participate in the retreat are doing so in order to write, we talk, now, intentionally about "scholarly work" because some of the faculty who take part in this retreat are artists, and their scholarly work is judged upon their painting, drawing, and art shows.

Our library director, who supports the collaborative nature of library space, offered the university library for the retreat space. The librarians and staff are highly supportive, providing resources for us. The library director offered to welcome Kairos Place participants during the first day welcome session. Two librarians offered to meet with the participants during our first lunch period to review the library resources for faculty scholarly work.

In May, four months after reading Ellen's article, EMU's Writing Program hosted its first Kairos Place, a timely place in which to do faculty scholarly work. Seventeen faculty participated. Fourteen faculty, representing nine departments/programs (undergraduate and graduate);

one staff member from Marketing; one retired faculty member; and one recent graduate from our undergraduate history department joined us. The recent graduate wanted to revise his capstone project for a history writing contest at another university. The retired professor from the ACRS joined us as both writer and support for our faculty. He provided this by engaging us in rigorous discussion and by reading our work and giving comments.

The goal of this retreat was two-pronged. We wanted to create quiet space for faculty in which to do their writing. Another goal was to develop a writing community, a sense that we write together in communal space, that we are all engaged in scholarly work together, not in isolation. Each morning, before the participants went to their library space to work, we gathered together in a large circle, and we took turns telling the group about that day's work. By the second morning, and thereafter, participants gave each other tips and shared resources for their work. In addition, coffee breaks became longer as faculty lingered to discuss their projects with each other and, specifically, to explore ways to collaborate with their projects. In the context of this retreat, this activity was testimony to the sense of connectedness shared by our faculty. I observed high morale and a sense of anticipation each time we met. Again, in the context of this event, this shared experience seemed to be spurring us onward as a working community.

At the beginning and end of each day, I briefly shared thoughts and led guided exercises from several writing publications. These had to do with observing the ritual of making a space in which to work, listening, reading aloud, writing a title, breathing, eliminating words, and revising. One article to which I referred the participants was Anne Lamott's (1995) chapter, "Shitty First Drafts," which is how we began to refer to our writing. In this way, a shared vocabulary for writing began to emerge and evolve throughout the retreat time resulting in a shared meaning concerning our various projects.

The first two days, we ended our day by meeting for fifteen minutes, ending at 5:00 p.m., to report to each other what we had accomplished, how this might change what we had planned for the following day, and what we hoped to accomplish the next day. At the end of the second day, one of the faculty participants requested that we meet for thirty minutes, giving us a lengthier time to be together and report to each other. Earlier in the day, at 10:00 a.m. and at 2:30 p.m., homemade snacks and coffee/tea/soda were provided in the library's kitchen on the third floor. These junctures were intended originally to be times of providing snacks to faculty who would come to take what they needed and return to their workspace. However, these times quickly became gathering times for conversation, sharing work and ideas, making connections with each other around their work, and planning collaborative ventures. The request for more time for sharing at the end of the day and more time for lingering over the coffee pot were data I collected as evidence that we were building a community.

From noon–1:00 p.m., the participants met in a previously-reserved dining room to share lunch together. Meal tickets were provided. (On the one day the cafeteria was closed, our lunch was brought in from Bowl of Good, a nearby café serving local food.) On several days, other faculty joined us to discuss various topics of relevance: Librarians met with faculty the first day and gave an orientation to research and scholarly databases. A chemistry professor discussed the process of publishing a peer-reviewed article, an art professor discussed the process of showing a juried art piece, a member of ACRS described this organization and explained the ways it will support current EMU faculty, math professors discussed the process of publishing a book, and the provost met with us during a lunch period to hear our stories and to discuss EMU's scholarly work culture.

The first writing retreat caught on. Faculty left this retreat energized for their summer work. They completed a very short evaluation form asking two questions about what they accomplished and asking whether or not the retreat was conducive to their productivity. Their responses were overwhelmingly positive. They stayed in touch with each other throughout the summer, letting us know that a proposal was accepted for a conference, a revised book chapter was accepted, an article was accepted in a scholarly journal, a painting was accepted to a juried art show. We celebrated these events via e-mail. When a Kairos Place participant sent an e-mail to me about his/her accomplishment, I sent an e-mail to the entire list of participants in celebration. Often my e-mails caused a flurry of e-mails from the participants expressing again how much their productivity had increased along with their own self-confidence and sense of being part of a community. In August, I invited Kairos Place participants to my home for conversation and snacks, and we celebrated our scholarly accomplishments and discussed changes we wanted to see in the next year's Kairos Place. This was an important event for gathering data together as we assessed the previous Kairos Place and planned ahead for the next one.

The most resounding accomplishment of the first-year's retreat was to develop a sense of scholarly community within EMU culture. This assessment was not only seen in anecdotal evidence as faculty talked throughout the week's event, but it was described in their reviews of the retreat.

That retreat became part of faculty discussions within departments and other venues. Something was happening. At last, faculty could talk about their fears, their writing blocks, their angst. And when they did articulate this, they found other faculty who felt the same way or who had faced this particular demon successfully.

In February 2011, Kairos Place participants from Kairos Place 2010 hosted a faculty luncheon, forming a panel to tell their writing stories. As a backdrop to the panel, we displayed a 36" x 48" oil and acrylic painting that one of our faculty artists had created during Kairos Place. When she had presented it to the faculty participants at the end of the 2010 Kairos Place, faculty unanimously decided to title it "Kairos." "Kairos" was used to create a colorful postcard with the painting on one side and information about the 2011 retreat on the other. This postcard was available at the luncheon and was placed, subsequently, in every faculty member's campus mailbox.

In May 2011, twenty-two faculty participated in Kairos Place, representing thirteen departments, two graduate programs, two staff offices, two administrative VPs, and one member of ACRS. Many of the faculty who took part the year before were the first to sign up. I followed the suggestion of Kairos Place 2010 participants and offered the retreat for two weeks instead of one. Faculty could be in retreat either of the two weeks or for a two week stretch. Another faculty member offered to help with leadership for the second week. Six of the faculty worked collaboratively on projects in three groups of two, representing the Education, Nursing, and Math departments. During the first week, eighteen participants met, and during the second week, four new participants joined, with five participants from the previous week remaining for a second week of writing work and community building, making a total of nine participants for the second week. "Kairos," composed last year during our retreat, dominated our retreat space propped high on a shelf. We also constructed a sacred space with roadmap, journal, ink pot, container of water, peace lamp. The peace lamp was lit and extinguished at the beginning and end of each day as a symbolic way to start and finish the writing day and our time together as a community of scholars at work.

I knew for certain that Kairos Place was catching on at our campus when the director of our undergraduate Honors Program and another faculty member extended the Kairos Place 2011 invitation to seven honors students. They adapted the hours for students, meeting at noon and into the evening, sharing an evening meal. Students and the two faculty members met at a cabin in the nearby Shenandoah Mountains, writing, talking about writing, reading their writing, listening to others' writing, and writing some more. Mid-week, they met with us, sharing their stories and listening to faculty talk about their writing. The faculty leading the Kairos Place for Students received positive feedback from the students who participated. Word of mouth news about the student retreat spread rapidly across campus, and the faculty leading the student retreat antici-pate double or triple attendance in Spring 2012. These students will have the option of enrolling in a Kairos Place summer course, earning credit for this time. In addition, at our latest Writing Committee meet-ing, graduate faculty representatives reported that graduate faculty are discussing ways to offer this in Spring 2012 to their graduate students who are completing theses and capstone projects. These are unexpected ways that Kairos Place is spreading across the university campus.

At the end of the second annual Kairos Place, participants completed an exit survey with the same two questions from the previous year about what they accomplished and whether or not the retreat was condu-cive to their productivity. In addition, I added two questions: Do you plan to attend future retreats? Would you recommend participation in Kairos Place to your colleagues? Without exception, both answers were a resounding "yes." At least half of the participants added their ideas about their future projects for future retreats. Moreover, as our new year began in August, three months after Kairos Place ended its second year, I met with new in-coming faculty during their orientation to discuss our writing program and initiatives. One new faculty member said that she wanted to hear about our writing retreat because she wanted to attend. After explaining Kairos Place to them, several expressed interest in sign-ing up for the retreat. In a variety of venues across campus, this new fac-ulty member's enthusiasm is echoed by many faculty and students, both graduate and undergraduate.

Faculty, alert to the provost's emphasis on scholarly work, view the retreat as welcome support from the provost for their work and for uni-versity expectations. Accustomed to the solitary aspect of scholarly work, faculty welcome the collegiality they experience during the retreats and the relationships continued with other faculty long after the retreat is over. At EMU, professors mentoring students is strongly emphasized, and Kairos Place for Students is one more way to implement professor and student interaction. Students "catch" faculty and staff enthusiasm, and they seem to thrive in this atmosphere. EMU is a small school where faculty are invested in its mission and values. Thus, faculty and staff work hard together on various committees and task forces where the focus is usually upon some aspect of teaching, and the service expecta-tion of the threefold expectation upon professors–research, teaching, and service–is high. Kairos Place brings a welcome complement. The retreat comes in May, after faculty contracts are finished, and focuses upon one's own work, reminds faculty and staff of their scholarly selves, brings faculty and staff together in common goals (although different projects), and treats them well by giving input from others, giving feedback on their work, and by feeding them. Those who work hard to support students at EMU and the institution of EMU, in turn, receive support for themselves. At the end of an academic year, this support goes a long way toward helping faculty and staff meet their goals for scholarly work while fostering community among them.

ASSESSING FACULTY WRITING RETREAT CONVERSATIONS
Susan Callaway, University of St. Thomas

Assessment can and should capture the impact faculty retreats have on the productivity of the participants. From the very first retreat I provided on our campus, faculty writers have been enthusiastically responsive to the opportunities to write during the week, and then asked for more. My various assessments have also revealed the deeper issues faculty face in sustaining their productivity, and thus have directed me toward further initiatives to support my colleagues' writing and to encourage another facet of a growing culture of writing at my university. While these assessments seem at first only anecdotal, I see them as "contextualized," to borrow Cynthia Selfe's (1999) concept, and potent methods for plumbing the effects of our retreats at UST.

My conversations with faculty reveal predictable yet critical obstacles they encounter in establishing and maintaining their productivity, namely the distraction of cell phones, social media, interruption by family members and issues at home, and interruption by students and colleagues in the office. Faculty report how engrossing preparing for and teaching itself can be, and how demanding service to their department and university is. Also prevalent are reports on procrastination, lack of confidence in their scholarly writing, writing blocks, and isolation. My assessment of what impedes my colleagues' productivity supports the following crucial features of the retreats:

- Ample time and quiet space for writers to individually immerse themselves in their writing projects to reignite their interest in it, to make substantial headway on it, or to complete it.
- Freeing writers from the research process, or helping them focus their research to support the advancement of a particular writing project,

and thus enabling writers to work through difficult parts that they would otherwise avoid and lead to blocking.

- Shielding writers for one week from daily distractions and environments not conducive to writing, making them aware of their individual needs as writers.

- Writers writing in the presence of others and interacting formally and socially to gain perspective, draw support from colleagues, and strategize with and for others on how to establish or maintain productivity during and beyond the retreat.

Underneath the initial assessments that clearly support the general design of the retreats are several stories of faculty writers that provide a deeper picture of the challenges of scholarly writing. These stories as part of an assessment should fuel future retreats and other support systems we can provide for our colleagues through our writing centers.

One colleague's story speaks to the isolation faculty experience as they work, and yet the depth of commitment we can have in our research agendas and as scholars. My colleague had e-mailed me before the retreat to make sure that she was, in fact, some way qualified to participate as an adjunct. She also chose to talk to me privately the first day to describe her vast yet fascinating project she had been working on for several years. But she was "paralyzed," she said, and suspected that she needed to just walk away from the piles of notes and stacks of research she had amassed on her desk at home and come in to "just write." In the days of the retreat, she discovered how right she was. She reported to the group how freeing it was to not be able to search for just the right quotation or to not tell herself that she needs to do more reading before she can write. The retreat had freed her from the process of continually researching and scholarly reading and unleashed her as a writer.

Other participants also noted an awareness that they were locked in a rigid writing process, taking precious time, for example, to search for just the right quotation, or to read yet another article. One participant reported: "It probably would have taken me three–four weeks to accomplish what I did in this one week, simply because I was forced to sit down and work through the difficult parts." The stories of being "paralyzed" or "blocked" may be revealing a vicious-cycle writing process borne sometimes at the graduate level where we're led to believe that we are not good enough, or our research might not be thorough enough, to begin to write. This self-doubt might manifest itself in a never-ending need to justify and validate one's own ideas through yet more extensive research, and such attitudes toward one's own writing can surface before and during a retreat.

The story of one participant speaks to the obstacles faculty face just finding time to write. Soon after I sent out an e-mail to the retreat participants this past semester, I received a reply from a colleague who asked if the retreat would be offering a workshop or time to write. I had met with him months before—he is an adjunct instructor just beginning his dissertation at an out-of-state university where he is earning his PhD. His aim for the retreat was to finish his dissertation proposal, a project that he had been struggling with for several months. His questions to me were: How much time during the week will he spend being instructed, and how much time will he be writing? That is, how much of the retreat is a workshop, and how much will he be able to just write? Since the first retreat, faculty have reported they appreciate this time to write, as one participant commented: "I just needed space—'a place of my own'—to actually sit down and write, away from the maddening crowd." During the week of the retreat, my colleague worked as if on fire. He explained to the group the first day that he has two small children at home and that he had taken a week off from his full time job for the retreat. At midweek, he asked to see me in my office, and after a brief discussion on a topic I have little memory of, I do vividly recall he suddenly said, "I'm sorry to cut you off, but I know now what I need to do—," and he bolted out of my office, ran across the hall to his work station, and resumed his position at the computer and started typing way. Toward the end of the week, he admitted to the group that he almost cried the first day when he heard one participant describe her goal for the week of finishing the final editing on her dissertation.

Participants' reports to the group during the end of the day reflections revealed to all of us the challenges writers face—the stress, the isolation, the stages of the process that seem to take forever, the battles with reviewers, coauthors, and for dissertators a committee, the number of pages that still need to be written. One participant echoed this in an evaluation: "I felt so isolated from my subject and those who would be interested in it that I let my project stagnate for two years. Being surrounded by other writers who unequivocally support my work was immeasurably helpful." This could have been written by any of us at the retreat, myself included.

While the retreats' final evaluation form is short, it enables the writers to describe what worked in the retreat for them, what didn't, and to give me some quotable quotes. It does not capture, however, the conversation that occurs in that last hour of celebration at the end of the long week together. Combined with the "check-in" survey I send by e-mail a month or so later, these post-retreat assessments document the participants' descriptions of the need for continuing support given the challenges that they'll return to shortly. One theme leaps off the pages: retreats simply provide time to write, as in "I never realized what a significant difference it would make to have this non-interrupted time for my writing." Our retreats emphasize writing rather than reading and research, on pulling from good habits faculty already have rather than on guiding faculty through strategies to write. So designed, the retreats enable faculty to break writing blocks and focus more productively on other challenges they face, like creating more junctures to be productive over the academic year, or working more consciously to create space for themselves to write.

The retreats have given rise to spin-off initiatives. The first are the Friday "Hide and Writes" where I open the Center's doors on Friday afternoons (when we're typically closed) so faculty can come, hide, and write. The second initiative has been to help faculty form writing groups just to write. These groups of three to four colleagues have been cross-disciplinary and many are thriving because of the writers' commitment to the act of establishing the habit of writing throughout the academic year. The group members meet deliberately to hide somewhere on campus during the week to write, give each other personal and professional support as needed, and share strategies for maintaining scholarly agendas. Because of their clear commitment to continuing to be productive, I am providing individual support to writers as needed during the year.

Certainly I will turn what I learn from my conversations with faculty into more traditional and formal assessment in the future. Meanwhile, I am paying particular attention to more immediate opportunities for faculty to establish their writing lives and maintain their productivity. One of my colleagues wrote in her evaluation of the retreat: "I never realized how important a physically and aesthetically comfortable working environment is to me. Ever since the retreat, I write six days a week in the mornings." Such comments have already led me to a more extensive collaboration with our Office of Faculty Development. We have established the Faculty Writers Program that I direct. The program includes a series of workshops offered during the year on publishing. These were already in place before the retreats but are now connected to other writing support initiatives specifically for faculty, adjunct faculty, and staff. The program also offers the retreats three times a year, the Friday mini-retreat "Hide and Write," a clearinghouse for those wanting to start or join a writing group, and personal consultations. The retreats have, in other words, spawned more ways for writers on campus to be supported.

I am keeping data to justify my re-assigned time devoted to this. Yet the "loop" that is most critical to close is the one that helps articulate what faculty writing is like and how challenging it is for all writers—from undergraduate to graduate to faculty, staff and alumni, to write and maintain a writing life. Our writing center benefits from this knowledge, and faculty themselves benefit. And the knowledge about the realities of writing needs to be shared with students, so I am also devising ways for participants to connect their experiences with their students' and to measure the ways they are achieving this.

Besides making sure I turn the achievements of the retreats into supporting faculty productivity, essential to my assessment is a cost-benefit analysis that examines how the writing center, the director, the university, and of course the faculty benefit but also at what cost. Certainly there are prices to be paid, and each institution needs to consider the real costs to having retreats, from individuals needing to arrange for child care to providing compensation for the facilitator. There is much to be gained by all stakeholders.

Conversations before, during, and following the faculty retreats provide important junctures to assess the effectiveness of time away to write for faculty writers and unearth assumptions about writing on campus. Certainly there is much to be gained through traditional assessment methods. But in this early stage of our faculty retreats—and our faculty writers program—noticing and at times purposefully prompting conversations about writing and productivity gives a deeper, contextualized picture of faculty lives as writers.

ASSESSING A WELL-ESTABLISHED WRITING RETREAT PROGRAM
Ellen Schendel, Grand Valley State University

Grand Valley State University is a comprehensive liberal arts institution with an enrollment of twenty-five thousand students. Though the university has a tradition of focusing on providing a high-quality undergraduate experience, the graduate programs (mainly in the professional schools) have experienced growth in recent years. Faculty typically teach a nine-credit load each semester, with the expectation that they will publish and present at conferences on a regular basis. The university values a wide range of scholarly and creative activity and is inclusive of the scholarship of teaching.

Faculty Writing Retreats were originally conceived as "dissertation boot camps" over a decade ago that included instructional programming to help participants become more efficient and effective writers.

At that time, the campus was growing rapidly—both in terms of enrollment and faculty hires; some of these hires were ABD. In their earliest incarnation, the retreats were funded in part by registration fees paid by participants—the idea being that by paying a fee, one will be more focused and deliberate about attendance. Too, those early retreats were mainly about helping the faculty to complete their dissertations. By the time I became the writing center director in 2004, there were many fewer ABD faculty on our campus, and the expectations for scholarly output had risen. The retreats' focus has subsequently changed from supporting ABD faculty to supporting anyone—faculty or staff—working on scholarly and creative projects.

The overarching goal behind the retreat is for staff and faculty to have the time and space in which to write among supportive colleagues. Aside from brief kickoff meetings in the mornings and sharing at the close of day, the group simply writes—there are no lectures or workshops or demonstrations—and this is the model preferred by participants. Therefore, the typical writing retreat offers a quiet working space for participants, Monday through Friday, from 9:00 a.m. to 5:00 p.m. As sponsor, the writing center provides laptops, research and style guides, coffee, tea, sodas, snacks, and/or lunches. As facilitator, my main role is to be available to talk about immediate issues writers face or read and comment on the participants' drafts. Participants generally spend six to seven hours per day on writing or writing-related activities, may work in individual cubicles or community space as they prefer, and come together for lunch each day. Over the years, the retreats have attracted anywhere between fifteen to twenty-five participants who are adjunct or full-time faculty or staff. To meet rising demand, our center has begun offering two of the week-long retreats each summer.

Much of the writing retreat has become rather rote and routine. When I was first contacted by Susan, Claudine, and Violet, I was interested to hear about the ways they adapted the retreats to their campus cultures, adding and removing elements that had become rather routine at Grand Valley. It was invigorating to think about how I could start incorporating their ideas into our retreat. But even more than that, I became energized at the idea of constructing assessment processes that would allow us to learn about the impacts of the retreats on our individual campuses, as well as more generally. Was there research we could engage in together?

After sharing with each other the kinds of ways we gauged the success of the retreats, we worked together to create a survey that we could offer to retreat participants well after the retreat had ended. We were interested in knowing what happened to the projects they worked on, as well as whether they wrote more frequently, or exhibited different kinds of writing behaviors, as a result of participating in the retreat. For example, were they more likely to share their writing with others? To carve out time to write despite their busy teaching schedules? To read and respond to the writing of their colleagues?

I was able to offer this survey online to 101 writers who had participated in retreats held between 2006 and 2011. In all, the survey received thirty-seven responses, for a satisfactory return rate of 37 percent. Survey results show that in addition to helping writers produce tangible results—articles and dissertation chapters and creative works, among other genres—retreats helped faculty and staff to build capacities for writing that indicate they're building sustainable writing practices. They immersed themselves in a writing community; offered and received feedback from colleagues; thought metacognitively and strategically about their writing processes and the genres in which they write; opened themselves to the writing-related resources on campus; got into the habit of writing more frequently, and over a sustained period of time; set and met specific goals for the writing time they had each day.

Three things seem clear about these survey responses. First, it appears that we shouldn't underestimate the one-time effects of the retreat on writers. When asked to rate various statements about the retreat on a scale of one to five (with one being "strongly disagree" and five being "strongly agree"), respondents assessed in positive ways the capacities that we had hoped they'd build upon as writers. However, the greatest levels of agreement came regarding the statements:

- The retreat helped me to become (re)energized about my project.
- The retreat helped me to accomplish a quantity of work that satisfied me.
- The retreat helped me to accomplish the quality of work that satisfied me.

Second, although fewer survey respondents agreed with statements focused on engaging with colleagues as writers—sharing their own writing, or offering feedback to colleagues' drafts—the survey responses indicate that over 50 percent of retreat participants have engaged in these activities after leaving the retreat. Seeking out collegial, supportive readers and giving feedback to others' writing is important to a scholar's or artist's productivity as Botshon and Raimon (2009) suggest, and retreat participants seem to have strengthened this capacity; however, writing centers can provide further opportunities for faculty to find others with whom to share their writing and to whom they can lend support via faculty/staff writing groups. In addition, since ten of the thirty-seven respondents (or a total of 27%) have attended multiple week-long retreats, the retreats themselves can be seen as a long-term commitment by some respondents to maintaining a level of productivity, quality, and enthusiasm for writing.

Too, there is evidence that the retreats did achieve the objective of helping faculty to make progress on a major writing project—and even considering that many writers did not complete the project during the retreat, they still made substantive progress after the retreat on that same writing project. In almost all cases, writers continued forward momentum on their projects, with most culminating in publication/presentation (Yancey and Huot 1997, 11). The surveys also indicate that faculty and staff are more productive since the retreat. Three respondents who had not completed their terminal degree had made more progress—either moving from coursework to dissertation or from dissertation to degree completion—since their retreats. In addition, many faculty and staff indicate their post-retreat writing habits are more productive than their pre-retreat writing habits. Though a few respondents indicated that their productivity slumped after attending the retreat, most reported that their productivity was maintained or improved—slightly or greatly—with the greatest improvement seen among respondents who indicated being very unproductive, somewhat productive, or "average" in productivity before attending the retreat. We take this to mean that while there are many factors in a writer's productivity that cannot be explained or accounted for by participation in a retreat, the week-long experience seems to enhance writers' motivation and commitment to write.

Respondents had the opportunity to suggest programming or support they would benefit from. We are already implementing those ideas across campus: this year, we are hiring a professional writing consultant to work one-to-one with faculty writers targeting publication in academic journals and presses. We will continue to open the writing center on Friday afternoons as a faculty and staff-only writing space, relocating our undergraduate and graduate consultations to other venues. We will begin to offer weekend retreats in the near future; strategically placed throughout the regular academic year, these mini-retreats—as well as Faculty Fridays—will be opportunities for faculty to dedicate shorter bursts of writing energy to continue their progress throughout the busy semester. The open-ended answers to the survey I report on in this chapter once again affirm what the post-evaluation forms overwhelming say: faculty and staff value having a university-sanctioned retreat, away from their colleagues and students and families, which allows them to say "no" to other obligations and "yes" to writing.

But there are opportunities to dig deeper, continuing to evolve our assessment of Grand Valley's writing retreats. We will begin having writers submit a "writing inventory" ahead of their writing retreat, which reports on their level of satisfaction with their productivity, as well as the time they spend writing during an average semester. This data, compared to that generated by the survey I reported on here, will give us a better sense of the "value addedness" of the writing retreats. Other units on campus, such as our Teaching and Learning Center, and our Center for Scholarly and Creative Excellence, are always surveying the needs of faculty and providing programming to support their professional, scholarly, and creative development. These assessments, too, provide the basis for our three units' collaboration in growing the writing-related programming available to faculty and staff. Writing, after all, is an area in which faculty and staff can build multiple important capacities: integrating writing effectively into their teaching, and producing scholarship regularly are the two that most immediately come to mind. But becoming a more reflective, more practiced, more engaged writer is key to thinking creatively about the integration of writing into a course and becoming a more productive scholar or artist.

CONCLUSION

If there is a lesson to be learned from our assessments, it is this: our writing retreats have immediate impact on participants, and a great potential for lasting impact. Participants report they are more productive, more engaged in their work, more receptive to feedback, happy that they've met colleagues from other departments, more supportive of their colleagues' writing, and feel more supported by their institutions. The retreats also have a great potential for lasting impact through new initiatives on our campuses to further support faculty writing, including: individual consultations throughout the academic year; weekend retreats; professional writing consultants who work with faculty during the retreat or between retreats; consultations with research librarians; specialized retreats for staff or retired faculty; retreats focusing on grading student writing and reading scholarly articles; a faculty writers program.

Despite the great potential of the retreats, there are still issues that concern us. Retreats add to someone's workload to advertise, organize, coordinate the preparation and maintenance of the retreats, as well as assess. Who will step up to compensate them for their time and effort?

Some faculty, particularly senior colleagues, believe they should not need any sort of support for their scholarly work, and so may remain in isolation. What might challenge their beliefs? The needs of new faculty and those coming up for tenure are very sensitive, and it takes a knowledgeable and experienced individual to support the more vulnerable participants. Who can and should take on this responsibility? Women in particular can be challenged in their hopes to balance life and work. How can retreats be scheduled so that they don't present even more childcare issues for potential participants?

Ultimately, the challenge for faculty as writers remains-time. Faculty struggle to meet the demands of teaching and service to their departments and the university, while they want and need to devote time to their lives off campus. Retreats provide so much more than time to write. They provide perspective and insight in how to balance—if this is possible—lives within and away from campus. They prompt crosstalk between colleagues across disciplines and across stages of careers. Retreats are simple yet powerful ways that administration, writing centers, and faculty development offices can support productivity, enabling faculty to sustain—and sometimes reignite—the love for research and scholarship that inspired them in graduate school. Retreats empower faculty by affirming their identities as writers. The four of us are proud of our work with writers at our institutions. We're glad to be seen by our administrations and our peers as actively supporting a culture of writing on our campuses. And we're especially gratified that our assessments have continually provided insight into the lives of ourselves and our colleagues as writers. The retreats are well worth our efforts.

REFERENCES

Botshon, Lisa, and Eve Raimon. 2009. "Writing Group as Sanctuary." *Chronicle of Higher Education*, last modified May 1, 2009, http://chronicle.com/article/Writing-Group-as-Sanctuary/44815.

Cohen, Elizabeth G. 1986. *Designing Group Work for the Heterogeneous Classroom.* New York: Teachers College Press.

Grant, Barbara, and Sally Knowles. 2000. "Flights of Imagination: Academic Women Becoming Writers." *International Journal of Academic Development* 5, no. 1: 6–19.

Kagan, Spencer. 1988. *Co-operative Learning: Resources for Teachers.* Riverside: University of California.

Moore, Sarah. 2003. "Writers' Retreats for Academics: Exploring and Increasing the Motivation to Write." *Journal of Further and Higher Education* 27 (3): 333–42. http://dx.doi.org/10.1080/0309877032000098734.

Schendel, Ellen. 2010. "Retreating into the Center: Supporting Faculty and Staff as Writers." *Writing Lab Newsletter* 34 (6): 1–6.

Selfe, Cynthia. 1999. "Contextual Evaluation in WAC Programs: Theory, Issues, and

Strategies for Teachers." In *Assessing Writing Across the Curriculum: Diverse Approaches and Practices*, ed. Kathleen Blake Yancey and Brian Huot, 51–67. Greenwich, CT: Ablex.

Slavin, Robert E. 1986. *Student Team Learning: An Overview and Practical Guide.* Washington, DC: National Education Association.

Yancey, Kathleen Blake, and Brian Huot. 1997. "Assumptions about Assessing WAC Programs." In *Assessing Writing Across the Curriculum: Diverse Approaches and Practices*, ed. Kathleen Blake Yancey, and Brian Huot. 7-14. Greenwich, CT: Ablex.

9

FEEDBACK AND FELLOWSHIP
Stories from a Successful Writing Group

Virginia Fajt, Fran I. Gelwick, Verónica Loureiro-
Rodríguez, Prudence Merton, Georgianne Moore,
María Irene Moyna, and Jill Zarestky

How can academics from diverse disciplines create a productive and enduring writing group? In this chapter we tell the story of a writing group initially created to boost writing productivity but that evolved into supporting much broader collaboration and professional growth for its members. Founded in 2005 at Texas A&M University (TAMU), and going strong since that time, our writing group has provided a safe haven to several developing scholars, who credit it with increased productivity and creating the conditions for successful professional integration into the university community.

Our writing group's equitable environment is the foundation of its success. By bringing together members based on their commonalities, most notably gender (all current members are women), while also respecting and cherishing their differences as a strength, we have developed into a productive writing group and built a community of support in which we are able to construct our academic identities.

By sharing our story, we hope to inspire the creation of similarly successful writing groups on other university campuses. We believe our experience can serve as a positive example for campus leaders and administrators who wish to invest in effective faculty development opportunities, as well as for faculty and graduate students who would like to form their own groups.

HISTORY OF THE GROUP

In 2005 at TAMU, the Dean of Faculty's office hosted Dr. Tara Gray's popular workshop "Publish and Flourish," in which she championed a

DOI: 10.7330/9780874219029.c009

systematic approach to increase both writing productivity and quality. She encouraged attendees to form writing groups whose mission was to meet regularly (preferably weekly) and use the process learned during the workshop to support each other's writing. At the end of that workshop, four people came together to take up Tara's charge—two fairly new assistant professors, one lecturer/graduate student, and one staff member/graduate student from the Center for Teaching Excellence (CTE), TAMU's office that supports faculty development.

The CTE staff member with expertise in adult learning and faculty professional development served as a catalyst for motivating the three other group members to commit to the task, because, while all academics write or should be writing, reserving space and time for writing is a formidable challenge for most. Her leadership legitimized the academic importance of dedicating time from our busy schedules to participate.

Group composition has varied, but historically has included both graduate students and faculty from a diverse array of backgrounds and disciplines. Graduate students are typically in the writing stage of their dissertation and are treated as equals. Faculty members typically join as assistant professors but, since the group's inception, two members have earned tenure. Some faculty members have been speakers of English as a second language, in which case the other members helped them to negotiate the nuances of writing in English, beyond grammar and vocabulary.

While always open to new members, expansion was not promoted, such as through explicit publicizing. Rather, members could propose to include others who had expressed a desire to be more productive writers. As current members invite new members, pairs of faculty from the same department or related disciplines may result, but that has not necessarily homogenized group membership.

Our membership now spans six of the ten colleges at Texas A&M University – Education, Science, Liberal Arts, Veterinary Medicine, Agriculture and Life Sciences, and Engineering – and consists of two linguists, a pharmacologist, a mathematician specializing in education, a microbiologist, a civil engineer, and two ecologists. Of the eight current members, most have participated for multiple years, and one is a veteran from the original cast.

As new members join, and skills of all members grow (e.g., in editing and feedback), our process has evolved and stabilized. With group maturation, the kinds of support have expanded to suit the objectives of individual members, and grown into mutual trust and recognition of both singular and collective accomplishments. Veterans mentor new members who more quickly establish their footing, and all provide relentless encouragement to one another to write frequently and share their writing at each meeting.

REFLECTING ON OUR PROCESS AND PROGRESS

For our now seasoned group, collaborating on this chapter seemed like a perfect opportunity to demonstrate our cohesion. Considering our diverse academic fields, certainly no other such occasion would present itself. In addition, this collective writing format precipitated reflection upon the process (i.e., to write about writing) and exploration of factors contributing to group longevity and success.

To begin the process, and because our original volunteer organizer was no longer at TAMU, we needed ways to collaborate over time and across space. We used both GoogleDocs and a Blackboard learning site as repositories for group members' reflective writing, for published articles about writing and community, and to host our conversations about the group. To spark the discussion, we posted questions designed to elicit reflection on our writing group, inquiring about, to name just a few, the group's interdisciplinary nature, academic resilience, and motivation. Members responded to the initial questions and commented on one another's responses, all of which became our data set for analysis.

After we identified the major themes in our reflections, one member volunteered to ground our findings in the literature and to write a first draft of the chapter. Then, in round-robin style, group members reviewed and edited the draft. We chose to include some reflections verbatim so as to preserve eloquent expressions that resonated among us and yet represented our individuality.

In the final analysis, the following three themes characterized the success of our writing group: becoming productive writers, finding a safe haven, and creating an academic identity that acknowledges our shared lens of gender. These are expanded in the following sections.

BECOMING PRODUCTIVE WRITERS

The original four members ranked academic writing as a high priority because they were in the process of completing dissertations and building tenure review packages leading to two of the most critical milestones in academic careers—earning a PhD and gaining tenure. The pressure on academics to write and publish comes from all sides and the subsequent publication output by members is evidence that we achieved the group's goal to support both quality and quantity of academic writing.

Current members credit the group for reviewing the following memorable products, many of which were submitted and accepted through a peer-review process: one book, two book chapters, seventeen journal articles, two book reviews, ten grant proposals, one tenure and two annual review packages. Other products were doubtless reviewed, but escaped enumeration.

Upon reflection, we determined much of our productivity came out of the shared process of group feedback, but we did not begin with this in mind. As outlined in the aforementioned Tara Gray workshop, in the beginning, individuals wrote at least fifteen minutes daily and met weekly to review two or three pages of members' writing and share writing logs. By verbalizing to the group how many minutes per week were spent writing, members were more conscious of their steady progress. As part of Gray's recommendations, our primary task was to underline key sentences in each paragraph of the work under review. If they were difficult to recognize, or if discrepancies arose within the group as to what constituted a "key" sentence, this indicated to the author that the purpose was not communicated clearly, or that the writing lacked internal cohesiveness.

We quickly realized that the key sentence exercise was not the best use of the group's diverse editing skills, nor did it necessarily meet the needs of the author. Each of us naturally differs in her approach to reading and critiquing, and together we offered diverse feedback on many aspects of the focal writing sample. One member was good at grammar and sentence structure, another saw redundancies and excessive wordiness, and still another found more efficient and powerful ways to craft the author's argument. We talked about content, structure, readability, voice, and audience; key sentences were no longer the focus of our group process.

Now, our weekly session starts with an inventory of who brought writing. Typically, if multiple people seek feedback, writing is sorted by priority or urgency. The author then describes the context and history of the excerpt she brought. Important background information might include the intended journal for submission and its priorities, perhaps also the coauthors and their roles, or the project from which the research originated, current status of the work, and most important, what the author specifically needs from the group (e.g., "Is the argument logical?" or "I'm struggling with this section."). Based on the author's expressed needs, feedback might target the big picture or minor details, organization and flow, argument strength, length, and so forth. Any of these could be the task in a given session.

Copies of the one-to-five page excerpt are then distributed to every-one and we read quietly, scribbling notes and editorial marks, before beginning a discussion. As the reading winds down, members provide verbal feedback, which often leads to discussion, finding common ground, and consensus building. For example, if one of us identifies a sentence that is confusing perhaps others did too, so we brainstorm to arrive at a provisional resolution. We might pause to discuss alternatives in wording, or even "decide" that whole passages are misplaced or super-fluous. One member described the process this way:

> When we first write something, we might get attached to the way we com-municate a point. Then, when we show up to the meeting, something transformative happens. When I read over my writing again in the pres-ence of the group, it instantly changes the way I view it. I can imagine what it might sound like to others. This feels, at first, quite naked and exposing (even before anyone utters a word!). I can't recreate that perspective any other way. Next, my peers begin to speak up about what might not make sense or what I didn't make quite clear, which typically reinforces my realization that my writing could be improved AND gives me a window into how to do it. The next step is to verbalize what it means, what it really means, what it probably did not say, in a way I probably didn't say it! Voila! That's when the magic happens. This iterative process is key to improvement of writing and this is, to me, what a "community of practice" does best.

In addition to our customized reviewing strategy, we find that a weekly meeting cultivates writing as a "good" habit, which echoes the benefits of participation in writing groups as reported in the literature. One member of our group verifies "[Meeting] keeps my writing on the fast track. Writing can be a very lonely process. It is extremely helpful to have fresh eyes on your writing. I always take away something valuable, whether we work on my writing or someone else's." The continuing feedback increases our writing output by keeping each of us energized and preventing the hurdles of self-doubt and frustration from impeding our writing progress.

We have attempted several times to create a common log to record and track our writing. For example, one member created a Google group web-site where three members uploaded Excel files documenting the status of their writing projects. However, like several previous attempts, the moni-toring effort was not sustained, and logs were not updated. Although not successful at the group level, these efforts did work for individuals. Our one remaining founding member, who has used her participation in the group to support her publication goal for tenure, profited from a log to help track and manage the status of multiple projects:

I keep a spreadsheet of all the papers I have "in the works." In it I track dates when each manuscript is submitted: reviews come back, I submit rebuttals, etc. It helps me see how long the process takes, but it also reminds me of all the papers I need to finalize and submit! It also shows when a manuscript is rejected how I respond, whether submitting elsewhere or back to the same journal. When they are in review, I mark them yellow. When they are accepted, I change the color to green. Rejected manuscripts are, of course, red.

While Tara Gray's workshop provided the impetus for creating our writing group, not all of her strategies and recommendations have worked for us collectively. Yet, by taking her ideas and reshaping them to our own purpose, particularly the feedback process, we have built a system by which we are accountable, motivated, and productive.

FINDING A SAFE HAVEN

Reflecting on the process of how we became more productive writers and the accomplishments our members have achieved to date helped us visualize the stages of our academic writing progress. These stages have become topics of discussion and strategy development, leading to dialogues focused less on individual writing issues and more on negotiating institutional or cultural barriers to professional growth. Such informal, but intentional, conversations about professional development are centrally important to what we see as a shared benefit of participating in the writing group.

From the very beginning, we have been atypical of academics brought together to accomplish a task. We work collaboratively, making decisions as a group rather than designating a chair or leader. In meetings we regularly check in with each member and recalibrate to find a balance between individual and group needs, rather than being driven by a goal or deadline. We feel accountable to ourselves and to each other rather than to an external authority. In fact, we occasionally meet even if there is no writing to share, just to talk, and organize social events to mark milestones, such as the end of the semester or a promotion.

Because we value our time with the group, we tend to protect it. For example, a request from a potential new member sparked a lengthy discussion about increasing our membership to ten. Was that too big? Would we need to change our process or add alternative meetings? All favored admitting new members, but recognized the potential drawbacks of larger attendance. One member suggested splitting the group on days when more than five showed up or having two meetings per week to add some "useful flexibility." One member countered that "part of the reason I come is to see everyone, so I would hate to have to miss part of the group by picking one time or other." Another agreed, "Meeting with the whole group is one of the incentives to attend." This demonstrates a shared commitment to the group in face of hectic schedules.

As a second example of our consensus-building practices, each semester the group negotiates a meeting time that accommodates as many members' calendars as possible. We often are willing to move the meeting day and time to accommodate individual schedules, especially when a member wants group feedback on her writing as she approaches an important deadline. Of course, not all of us can attend every meeting and there have been some weeks when meetings did not occur. Members share various reasons when unable to attend, including, in one case, ironically, writing itself conflicting with group attendance. Sharing and reflecting on our attendance patterns produced some insights. One member said: "My worst hurdles have been my students and last minute service requirements relating to [course] coordination. Looking back, I realize that often I was the one bending over backwards to fit into students' schedules when it should have been the other way around. I have become more protective of my time, though, and it feels pretty good."

Thus, key contributions to this group's longevity are its support and encouragement. These are not accomplished via the typical kind of academic peer pressure, such as "Where were you last week?" or "I thought you were planning to finish that manuscript by now." Instead, we endeavor to send the messages "We understand you are busy" and "Let us know how we can help."

Because our focus was research writing and publication, we would often strategize on how to deal with what Deborah Tannen (2002) has called "agonism in academic discourse" or "ritualized adversativeness." In our experience, this agonism manifested as uncooperative coauthors, confusing or rude reviewer comments, and generally unsupportive behaviors in our respective academic environments.

Throughout all challenges, the writing group provided support and encouragement and a space for empathy. We helped each other to not take criticism personally. One member commented: "Knowing that others in the group are always dealing with the criticism of reviewers . . . takes the sting out some . . . It is easier to bear when someone you know, who you respect, but who you also can see processing writing on a weekly basis, has gone through the same thing."

Tannen (2002, 1652) suggests that an assumption underlying the agonistic model of academic discourse is the illusion that the "personal has no place in scholarship," and we challenge that illusion at every meeting. Tannen also noted that agonism encourages disrespect for other disciplines. In contrast, our group's multidisciplinary nature is a major contribution to its effectiveness and support function:

> The impact of being a member of the group has been significant to me in terms of providing an outlet for professional yet friendly, noncompetitive input on writing as well as other aspects of academic life. We have had conversations about teaching, advising, interacting with colleagues, and promotion and tenure that have been useful and helpful, but also energizing and healing . . . The undertone of the group is always supportive and friendly. I think this is one of the advantages of being from multiple disciplines: there is no need for competition or one-upmanship, because we are in different departments or colleges.

Another described it as "the safest environment to share setbacks, obstacles, and defeat because we are equals and far-separated from those who could "hurt" us with this information."

The benefits of safe haven extend beyond the sense of belonging that supports faculty well-being and productivity. At a departmental and institutional level, such support systems may increase the likelihood of retaining faculty and reduce the time and resources spent on new faculty searches. From a departmental perspective, increased faculty research output in the form of publications increases visibility, perhaps attracting new funding sources, and aiding recruitment of students and new faculty.

Frequently, we dealt with (and sometimes struggled with) honoring the norms of other members' disciplinary discourses, which often starkly contrasted with our own. Imagine a liberal arts professor helping a computer engineer write about circuitry—amazing breakthroughs in rhetoric can happen. Rather than complicate or impede our process, the multidisciplinary aspect of our group has enhanced our experience. Our diverse group offered a welcomed alternative to the traditional, department-centered (and sometimes competitive) "collegiality" and also provided unique opportunities for feedback. A social science researcher revealed, "For me to be able to run my writing by actual hard scientists is a great bonus. I couldn't get this type of feedback from my departmental colleagues." As another member described, the group creates "a level field, outside the pecking order that structures departments." A third member explained,

> I feel more rounded as a professional because of this group. Being part of something university-wide (small but diverse) helps me feel connected to the whole of academia. It reminds me of why I like being in academia. Coming to meetings of this group is not a chore because the amount

of giving and taking is equal, and it happens on a university-wide plat-
form . . . In the traditional "silos" of our departments, I never feel there is
an equal amount of give and take. Why is that? Perhaps because we do not
offer any support for one another. Instead, it is a system of trading favors,
which feels fundamentally different than our group.

Given the supportive and egalitarian nature of the group described
above, it should come as no surprise that over time its members started
to use it as a forum for much more than just writing and revising. We
have gradually started bringing other kinds of academic writing to the
meetings for feedback. Teaching philosophy statements, letters of recommendation, book and grant proposals, and conference keynote
speeches were not only critiqued and improved, but a welcomed change
of pace. Reviewing these led to conversations about other facets of our
academic work, such as teaching, mentoring graduate students, navigating the promotion and tenure system, and our respective departmental
politics. Thus, while still maintaining writing and productivity at its core,
the group has become a safe haven for frank discussion and reflection
upon our roles in academia, as well as personal and professional development and growth.

CREATING AN ACADEMIC IDENTITY

As a result of the safety we felt in the writing group, and the varied conversations it produced, we came to see how, as women in academia,
our shared identity has been a key to the group's success and longevity.
Many of our common experiences and challenges are attributable to
women's struggle with what Aisenberg and Harrington (1988) in their
book *Women of Academe* called "rules of the game." Unwritten but highly
ingrained, these rules emanate from a culture that values competition
and independence, and encourages self-promotion—ways of being that
are not native to many women.

Six years before *Women of Academe* (1988) was published, Sandler
(Sandler, 1993, 1) coined the term "chilly climate" to label the "many
small behaviors that together make up an inhospitable climate for
women" in academia. Since Aisenberg and Harrington's landmark
study, change in that "chilly climate" has come slowly to higher education. Women's advancement and parity in pay still lag behind those of
men (Jaschik 2011). While more women than men are awarded undergraduate degrees (King 2010), their numbers dwindle as they move up
the academic hierarchy. Only one-third of full-time faculty members
are women, and that ratio is even less favorable in the sciences and

engineering. It appears that gender bias is a consistent factor impeding women's success in academic institutions (Bingham and Nix 2010).

The meaning and impact of our gender on our professional lives and
identity surfaced in our meetings. Being an all-woman group was never
intentional but our group composition reflects the observation by our
faculty developer member that women take advantage of professional
and faculty development activities more frequently and in greater numbers than do their male colleagues. Our all-female group may also be
explained by women's relational orientation, and the view that women,
as they develop, grow toward connections and interdependence with
others (Gilligan 1982). In our preparatory reflections on this chapter,
our common gender was specifically identified as a positive aspect of
the group. One member described why she continues to be a member:

> . . . to interact with faculty women from outside my own department. I enjoy
> and learn from the supportive and open conversations we have as women
> in academia and I think that dynamic is unique to our writing group, at
> least in my experience. I learn about subject areas that are not my own. It
> is an intellectually enriching experience . . . Interactions with this group
> of bright, independent, ambitious women have been fantastic. The women
> in academia who have previously been visible to me were either getting
> pushed down or were so high up that it was difficult to imagine they ever
> struggled. Our group includes women from all over the academic spec-
> trum (tenured, preparing to go up for tenure, non-tenure track, staff) and
> we often have to face similar challenges. As a result, I think the group has
> a sense of team spirit that is often missing in other aspects of academic life.

Another reason to value our shared identity appeared in how the
group provided support for balancing work and family:

> I think that really the most prominent feature of the group, which has
> made me come back time and time again, is the fact that I am surrounded
> by talented women, with whom it is very easy for me to identify myself even
> if they are in different fields. The fact that other women, who are as busy
> as me with their family and work obligations, come to the group regularly
> and get their writing done is a great incentive. I know that they face the
> same kind of pressures that I do, on and off the job. And this makes it
> much easier for me to say: if they can, so can I. If there were males in the
> group, I'd think "sure, he's got a bunch of writing done, but he's got a
> wife at home making him dinner" and I would find a perfect excuse to
> not expect the same of myself. Here, there is no competition among us,
> but there are also no excuses.

While reflecting on our group experiences, we discussed using the
word "support." We did not want to communicate to readers that joining the group meant that we viewed ourselves somehow deficient in
our writing ability or needy in negotiating academia. We noted that the

culture of academia does not look kindly on academics appearing to need help, especially women academics. Despite the advancement of women in the academy, their position is still precarious. As Aisenberg and Harrington (1988, 50) noted. "[Women] enter competitive professional worlds from different starting points and with heavier burdens than their male peers . . . They carry the same sorts of individual disadvantage as men—matters of class, race, education, health, appearance—but in addition they carry the weight of the old norms that foster suspicion, in themselves and in others, about their professional capacities." As a result, women have had to provide each other with practical advice, moral support, and intellectual guidance at all career stages. Our group has been successful in this by providing a safe place for empathy, understanding, and exchanging strategies that work.

CONCLUSION

When looking at our group structure, we originally thought the literature on learning communities, particularly faculty learning communities, (Cox and Richlin 2004) would help us understand and ground our experience in the existing research. Yet, it was not until we considered for the purpose of this chapter how to describe ourselves as something other than a "writing group," that we discovered the kinds of learning our group fostered.

We learned how to better structure our writing and both give and receive quality feedback, increasing motivation and productivity. We learned how collaboration helps us resist becoming needlessly isolated in our specialized academic disciplines. And finally, we learned how our shared identity as women in academia was important common ground from which we could relate and support one another.

Like any new collaboration, ours needed time to build trust and community. While always a highly functional group, we learned that our sense of belonging, dedication, and commitment to the group and each other have grown into a deep solidarity over time. As one member remarked, "we all implicitly agreed to work in an environment of trust," and fortunately for us, building trust among members and learning to attain consensus came naturally.

On the surface this chapter is the story of a group of faculty and staff supporting each other to improve the quality and quantity of their writing. But it is also about change, at both the personal and institutional level. Institutions of higher education are notorious for their resistance to educational reform or efforts to change the academic culture.

However, as Hall (2007, 4) writes about academics' complicity with forces that impede change, we need ways to "denaturalize our attitudes about work and professional values" in order to identify ways we can effect change, both individually and as members of a community. By exploring our roles as women in academia within the safe haven of our writing group, we have brought to light the complexity of our interactions, both positive and negative, within the system of higher education institutions. While our diverse interdisciplinary composition clearly led to improved writing, our commonalities as women affirmed our academic identity.

We hope the voices in this chapter will activate the process of change in your institution. Our participation in the writers group improved our writing and productivity but, perhaps most significantly, it provided all of us with moments of enlightenment like those shared in this chapter. Perhaps, ultimately, it is our willingness to be open, flexible, and welcoming to change that has made our "fellowship" so rewarding.

As academics, our primary goal is to produce and disseminate knowledge. We participate in the writing group to further that goal. However, in the process, we have constructed and refined our professional identities through dialogue. Over time, each of us has tested and adapted her professional voice, and used the inclusive and affirming qualities of the group to validate our emergence as productive, confident, and authoritative academics.

REFERENCES

Aisenberg, Nadya, and Mona Harrington. 1988. *Women of Academe: Outsiders in the Sacred Grove*. Amherst: University of Massachusetts Press.

Bingham, Teri, and Susan J. Nix. 2010. "Women Faculty in Higher Education: A Case Study on Gender Bias." *Forum on Public Policy: A Journal of the Oxford Roundtable* 2. http://forumonpublicpolicy.com/spring2010.vol2010/womencareers2010.html.

Cox, Milton D., and Laurie Richlin. 2004. *Building Faculty Learning Communities: New Directions for Teaching and Learning*. San Francisco: Jossey-Bass Publications.

Gilligan, Carol. 1982. *In a Different Voice: Psychological Theory and Women's Development*. Cambridge, MA: Harvard University Press.

Hall, Donald. 2007. *The Academic Community: A Manual for Change*. Columbus: Ohio State University Press.

Jaschik, Scott. "The Enduring Gender Gap in Pay," *Inside Higher Ed* April 5, 2011. http://www.insidehighered.com/news/2011/04/052/the_enduring_gender_gap_in_faculty_pay.

King, Jacqueline. 2010. *Gender Equity in Higher Education: 2010*. Washington, DC: American Council on Education.

Sandler, Bernice R. 1993. *Women Faculty at Work in the Classroom: Or, Why It Still Hurts to Be a Woman in Labor*. Washington, DC: Center for Women Policy Studies.

Tannen, Deborah. 2002. "Agonism in Academic Discourse." *Journal of Pragmatics* 34 (10-11): 1651–69. http://dx.doi.org/10.1016/S0378-2166(02)00079-6.

10

DEVELOPING A HEURISTIC FOR MULTIDISCIPLINARY FACULTY WRITING GROUPS
A Case Study

Trixie G. Smith, Janice C. Molloy, Eva Kassens-Noor, Wen Li, and Manuel Colunga-Garcia

From its inception, The Writing Center at Michigan State University has operated on a peer-to-peer consultancy model. In "Reforming Education in the Land-Grant University: Contributions From a Writing Center," Patti Stock, founding director of the center at MSU, explains that "in these consultancies, less-experienced, less-practiced writers benefit from the greater experience and greater expertise of their peers; at the same time, consultants expand and enrich their general education as they read and discuss articles their peers are composing in a wide variety of fields and disciplines" (Stock 1997, 13). This approach helps develop a genuine community of writers and learners. Our faculty writing groups (FWG) are very much a piece of this model, providing space for small groups of faculty to build their own communities of support and inquiry for improving writing and thus publication and grant success. Not all center-made groups of faculty work, especially on a long-term basis; however, this is a success story—the case study of a multidisciplinary group of five (including the facilitator) that is viable and productive as it enters its third year. Consequently, we wanted to examine what makes this particular group work in hopes that such an examination would help with other groups in the future.

The group originally formed in 2009 with four members, each with distinct specialties, including invasion ecology (Manuel), transportation and urban planning (Eva), human resource management (Janice), and rhetoric and writing (Trixie). In the middle of the

DOI: 10.7330/9780874219029.c010

first year, an additional member joined the group; however, she only remained with the group for a few months. Later that same year a second group was formed, which, unfortunately, quickly fell apart due to conflicting time schedules and individual priorities. The one member who was committed to the process was folded into our group; thus, biomedical and materials engineering (Wen) was added to this case study group.

The group meets in person on a weekly basis. The agenda rotates so that each writer is the focus of one meeting a month; Trixie, the Writing Center director acts as group facilitator and typically does not insert her own writing into the schedule. Meetings are held for two hours, and begin with the writer talking about the status of the project, the specific challenge(s) she/he is facing, and the help wanted from writing group members. This discussion typically lasts about fifteen minutes and is followed by thirty minutes of reading, during which members focus on the assigned task. Over time this process has moved to e-mail, so that individual authors can more clearly articulate what kind of feedback they need and group members have more time to do focused reading before the dialogue starts. Discussion is the mainstay of the meeting and includes each person's impression of the writing and task at hand. Often this discussion fine-tunes the specific challenge or refocuses the writer's attention on equally pressing issues. The weekly meetings close with members giving the writer their handwritten comments (which typically include more detailed edits than those discussed) and general conversation about how members' writing is going (submissions, revise and resubmits, rejections, etc.).

The questions we asked ourselves for this study include: Why is this group working? What has helped this particular group, these group members, work together to achieve both individual and group success? What caused other members to leave or not commit to the group? We turned to a number of different theories from the various fields represented in the group, but found a theory in organizational psychology the most relevant. Using a case study methodology, we combined this theoretical framework with individuals' narratives to reason out the factors contributing to the group's success. We offer this self-reflective case study on how shared values foster the vital outcomes members view as success: learning and growth. We present a broad heuristic to guide others who want to form similar FWGs, hoping that theorizing our own experiences will help you achieve success as well.

UNDERSTANDING ATTRACTION, SELECTION, ATTRITION THEORY

Attraction, Selection, Attrition (ASA) theory explains the formation and composition of groups and organizations (Schneider 1987) and is applicable to writing groups in general, and this case study, in particular. Simply put, ASA theory explains that groups (or organizations) that survive the initial pressures of formation do so because members share one or more deeply-held values. More specifically, a group initially attracts into it individuals with common interests. In time, the group will narrow its focus from general interest in a topic to more specific values pertaining to the interest. In turn, people will be attracted to and self-select into the group who share the value(s), and people will leave the group (either voluntarily or involuntarily) who either do not hold the value(s) or hold the value(s) to a different extent than other group members.

Consider, how ASA theory can be applied to the value of goal orientations (Dweck 1986) within writing groups. Goal orientations are individual differences in how people see problems or challenges encountered in their performance. As applied to writing groups, individuals would see sharing their writing as a performance and have different needs to demonstrate their ability (performance goal orientation) or develop their ability (learning goal orientation). Writers with a performance orientation are characterized by a need to demonstrate their mastery, a desire for public recognition, and a need to avoid looking incompetent (Vandewalle 1997). Given that writing groups shine a light on improvement opportunities, both in a specific piece of writing and in one's writing style and processes overall, those with strong performance goal orientation would not likely be attracted to, self-select into or remain in a writing group. Moreover, a multidisciplinary writing group would be especially unappealing because members are not able to provide assurances that the writer wrote in precisely the expected disciplinary style. Indeed, those with strong performance orientations are likely to feel vulnerable in a setting involving critique of their writing. This vulnerability may be exacerbated in early-career faculty who, through the pressures of the tenure track and the rejections of the publication process, may already have their self-efficacy for writing and publishing threatened.

Alternatively, those with a learning orientation value are attracted to situations that help them acquire new skills, master new situations, and improve their competencies (Vandewalle 1997). As such, those with learning orientations are likely to find multidisciplinary writing groups appealing. These writers would value the development of new skills, creating a more complete understanding of their topic by triangulating related theories and thinking from other fields, and exposing their writing to the critique of others. Whereas those with a performance goal orientation would leave writing group sessions during which their writing was 'torn apart' feeling devastated and demotivated, the exact opposite is predicted for those with a learning goal orientation. Although those with a learning orientation might feel temporarily disheartened about the amount of work that remains post session, overall, they would value the opportunity to improve their work and grow as a writer.

Returning to Schneider, it is "the attributes of people" that are the determinants of behavior in groups or organizational settings. In fact, Schneider goes so far as to claim that "people *are* the setting [the organization] because it is they who make the setting" (1987, 450). Furthermore, Schneider explains that it is similar values that attract people to a group and that if someone joins a group but finds that she doesn't fit or share the same values, she will leave (attrition). As a group, we believe that ASA theory can help us and others understand how our group is functioning; therefore, in our case study, we question how and when the principles of Attraction, Selection, and Attrition manifest themselves. Questions we ask include: Do members share similar goals/ values? If so, what are these values? Did those who left have different values? Do the actions of the group reflect shared values?

IDENTIFYING SHARED VALUES

After multiple open discussions, thinking through, applying, then rejecting various theories from our respective fields, we found that ASA theory helped us most clearly reflect on the actions and outcomes of our group. Simultaneously, we asked each individual to write/tell his or her own story of the group. Through these individual reflections and narratives, we found that indeed the members do have many shared values that reveal themselves in the actions of individuals and the group. These shared values hold the group together and allow for continuous learning and writing growth. Since it is through individual's stories of the group that these shared beliefs and values are revealed and theorized, it is individual stories and reflections we will now share. In this case study, common values of the FWG include the importance of multidisciplinarity, consistency within the group, mutual support of and respect for group members, and space for social networking.

Multidisciplinarity

One core value that attracts members to the group, as explained by Manuel, is the importance of and value in being a multidisciplinary FWG:

> Being involved in multidisciplinary or interdisciplinary groups has always fascinated me as a learning and productive experience. Perhaps the most challenging part for the participants in these groups is attempting to understand each other's perspective. In fact, through such group inter-actions, I have been able to experience firsthand two of Churchman's aphorisms regarding the systems approach - originally published in Churchman (1968) and recently revised by Khisty (2006, 4): (a) "systems approach begins when first you see the world through the eyes of another," and (b) "every world view is terribly restricted."

> "Multidisciplinary" and "interdisciplinary" are two terms used to indicate the degree of integration among participants' disciplines on a given project or problem (Miller et al. 2008). In a multidisciplinary activity, participants work primarily "within their own disciplinary setting" whereas an interdisciplinary activity implies a greater integration of disciplines. Unless the members of a FWG are collaborating on the same research projects (an interdisciplinary activity), a FWG can be best served if each member maintains their own disciplinary perspective (i.e., being multidisciplinary) while making an effort to appreciate other members' perspectives.

> What is the main advantage of a multidisciplinary FWG? Well, this type of FWG provides a friendly environment for members to test their initial presentation of ideas on a paper or a research grant at a very early phase of the writing process. Often authors discover, during the review sessions, that there are several hidden assumptions in their papers. Those hidden assumptions are the result of many years of experience working in their field of expertise. However, what may seem obvious from an author's disciplinary perspective may not be so to other members in the group. The same is true for concepts and jargon used in the paper. The fact that I come from a different discipline makes me comfortable saying to an author "I don't get it" as many times as necessary during the discussion of her paper. This is important because, in general, the intended audience of our papers is narrower than the disciplinary gamut we face in our FWG. This is not in relation to the number of disciplines but in relation to the breadth of perspectives in the group. Thus, if our group members understand our paper, then we can be confident that our audience is very likely to understand it too.

Consistency

Another attraction and shared benefit is the consistency in writing the group fosters. As Eva puts it, sharing once a month encourages her to "write continuously" especially since it is one of her goals to always be prepared for our meetings. Wen makes the same claim, "The weekly meeting schedule motivates me to write continuously and manage my time more efficiently." Similarly, Janice explains, "We've all seen the cartoon where a graduate student's productivity spikes immediately before a meeting with an advisor. I have a parallel graph for writing group! I plan my writing around when it is my week, and my research has definitely come along faster because of the forced writing." Having a group of people hold you accountable for writing and sharing on a regular basis definitely keeps you brainstorming, planning, drafting, and revising. In fact, often group members close out our weekly meetings by sharing snippets of projects in progress or letting us know what to look forward to in the weeks to come. In addition, Manuel explains that keeping a regular schedule also helps members understand each other's disciplines and ways of making meaning. "It is important to allow group members to meet often, at least at the beginning, to facilitate the building of the necessary chemistry for a multidisciplinary FWG to work. It may take several meetings before members internalize each other's disciplinary perspective." Consistency becomes a characteristic of the successful group because it is a value shared by all the group members.

Mutual Support

Another shared expectation or value from our group members is support. Janice mentions the group meeting her high expectations for social, process, and technical support and insights to help her grow as a writer and scholar. Eva puts it in terms of positive support and encouragement with her writing as well as mentorship from more experienced colleagues in order to become the "excellent writer" she feels her discipline expects. Likewise, Wen came to the group seeking help, especially non-competitive feedback on her work: "Compared with professional peer reviews, I have less pressure and really enjoy this relaxing atmosphere. In fact, when I heard other group members also complained about writing manuscripts, revising papers, and declined proposals, I felt that I was not writing in isolation or struggling alone." Manuel explains the group this way: "Our goal has been primarily (a) to support each other through all phases of writing a paper or a research grant (from its conception to its submission), and (b) to provide feedback to enhance the clarity of our writing thus making papers/research grants understandable to broader audiences."

Respect

Group members also share similar work ethics and habits that include respect for each other and the goals each member is working to attain.

As previously mentioned, members are diligent about being prepared for their week to share. They are just as diligent about reading each other's writing and offering productive, respectful feedback. In fact, we see it as a sign of respect to be prepared and to give as much help as you receive. The one member who left our group or was pushed out (the attrition piece of the ASA model) was consistently unprepared when showing up for weekly meetings. She expected group members to read her writing but did not act in a reciprocal manner. Furthermore, she gave inappropriate or stereotypically disciplinary comments that favored her disciplinary view and were dismissive of the disciplines of other writing group members.

Equally important for group viability is a shared openness to learn from the feedback offered. As Janice explains,

> When I leave writing group after it is my week, I always feel energized. I feel like skipping back to my office (but instead walk) and cannot wait to dig into the document. This is good because typically I'm sick of a paper by the time it comes to writing group. The difference is that the writing group helps me to see the paper in new ways—both the problems of the paper and the untapped potential. I like that I have a plan of attack in the form of "I'll fix, X, Y, and Z" and interestingly taking the physical copies that writing group members have written on means a great deal to me. After I fix the "big things," I go through each person's comments. I see little fixes they didn't mention and think ("oooohh, good catch").

Wen tells a similar story:

> Multidisciplinarity adds to the value of the group, and particularly, works well for my proposal writing since I need opinions and constructive criticism from different viewpoints to improve the readability and quality of my proposals. In fact, I shared my NSF CAREER proposal with the group last summer. The group brainstorming provided comments on the title, grammar, logical flow, and overall structure of the proposal. Combining these comments with the expert technical suggestions from my colleagues, I reshaped my proposal and submitted it. I was happy to learn recently that this proposal received very positive feedback from the NSF review committee and was recommended for award.

Members are attracted to the respect and support they receive from group members and in turn offer this back to each other, sustaining each other as well as the group.

Social Networking

Group members may not have come to the group seeking friendships, but they all mention finding camaraderie and a support system that goes beyond the writing. As mentioned previously those who remain in a group help narrow its scope and values; Schneider's (1987) explanation of ASA calls this restricting the group. Wen explains that over time, the members of the group have developed friendships, which create a strong bond within the group. We share not only writing pieces but also our stories, successes, joys, and frustrations with each other. Eva claims that she would never want to leave the group unless it was just impossible to stay: "Besides all the wonderful help I have received from my team members throughout the past two years, I have found friendship among the group members, and some of us are thinking about cross-disciplinary ways to integrate, expand, and move our research agendas jointly forward." For Janice the community of the group works to keep her from feeling like an isolated writer, alone in the academic tower.

> Sometimes when I don't feel like writing I think "oh, but this week is Eva's week and I'm sure she's working on writing today . . ." So in some ways my writing when I know she, Wen, and Manuel are writing makes the effort feel communal. It is as if my writing "virtually helps" Eva, Wen, or Manuel as positive writing vibes get spread. As a different example, I find that when I am under a tough deadline, implementing the advice I have received in writing group is such a technical help—but also comfort. For example, I had a deadline in fourteen days and the draft was dreadful. Eva said "no problem, here's what you do . . ." And she laid out a fourteen-day plan. I put her plan (in her handwriting) on a clipboard and followed her plan to a T! The paper was done on time, made it through a few tough R&R's, and is now in press.

As the ASA model helps us understand, shared values are integral to the group. However, we believe the model is positively complicated by the fact that one of our values is a healthy respect for each others' differences, as well as an eagerness to learn from each other. Schneider (1987) warns that groups that become too narrow are often resistant to change and can suffer what he calls "dry rot." Our group continues to thrive because we have come to not only appreciate but count on the various strengths of our members and value the fact that members bring their personality and individuality to the group. Members have different ways of seeing the work of the group based on their own disciplinary paradigms and values, as well as their own personalities and experiences. As Manuel explains, "A FWG provides me with the opportunity to actively learn a completely different subject matter (in relation to my field of expertise). The fact that I can learn something new at the same time I am supposed to provide constructive criticism on a paper for that subject makes every session very interesting." Such reciprocity is essential for maintaining the group and limiting attrition.

LEARNING AND GROWING THROUGH THE GROUP

As mentioned previously, members of this FWG appear to share a learning orientation, which attracted them to the group in the first place. Not surprisingly then, group members' reports of the group's success related to their lessons in three areas: writing, broader scholarly interests, and professional development. Relative to writing, common outcomes relate to both the macro writing process and micro editing and polishing. More broadly, members expressed gratification for a range of results, from expanding one's horizon to exposure to literatures beyond their specialty, and further mastering English as a second language; and what they learned from writing group positively spilling over into their own teaching. Finally, members reported that the group supported their professional development.

Writing

Beginning with the macro writing process, a common focus is the overall structure of the writing and argument construction. Janice has learned from her fellow members much about structuring an article, and specifically distilling ideas. The fact that the group sees the same manuscript multiple times has been instrumental in her learning. Janice had the group review one specific manuscript six times over its development and expressed surprise at how "less was more" in the writing. That is, as the writing progresses, the points to be made become fewer, the argument simpler, and the outcome exponentially better. Janice comments that Eva's visualizations and Manuel's synthesis ("okay, so what you are trying to say is . . .") as instrumental to her growth, the sharpening of the paper's logic, and ultimately the publication of her paper. Moreover, although all members contribute to learning relative to structure and argumentation, Trixie's insights, mentoring, and instruction about writing processes more generally are highly appreciated by all.

Turning to more micro lessons regarding editing and polishing manuscripts, members expressed much growth in these domains. Wen notes that she learned that editing "is a process not only to correct errors, but also to make a writing piece more concise and stronger." As an example, Janice became aware of—and has corrected—an unusual and problematic approach to defining terms. The group coined the term "reverse definition" for how Janice would define terms first by what they were not, and then (after several paragraphs) by what they were. More technically, Wen and Eva noted interest and value in a color-coding process Janice introduced to identify improvement opportunities (cf. Belcher

2009). For example, one member has a tendency to use the same word too much (e.g., the word "because" might appear six times on the same page). By using the find feature in Word, and using the replace function to change the font color for a targeted word, problematic repetition can be identified with a simple glance at the page.

Broader Scholarly Learnings

Shifting to broad learning outcomes, participation in the group expands members' awareness of interesting research at MSU and the diversity of expectations for scholars by outlet. Group members consistently reported Wen's research as a source of inspiration. One example is scholarship pertaining to glaucoma and implanted sensors that replace uncomfortable assessments of eye pressure with automated reporting from sensors. This improves human and animal health and comfort in many ways, including the more regular reporting of eye pressure by humans, who often do not follow expected eye pressure reporting protocols because of discomfort. Similarly, Manuel's research regarding pest infestations and strategies to identify infestations at ports (before ships dock and unload) and track potential infestations were raised as interesting and broadening. Indeed, members often found and would share with Manuel stories in the news pertaining to pests.

Writing difficulties related to English as a second language is an interest of three of the five group members. Wen explains,

> In the past, I learned English writing primarily from articles and proposals, but didn't realize [I had developed] some bad writing habits from them. For example, I often used passive voice in most of my manuscripts. From the writing group, I learned that passive voice should be avoided whenever possible. I also learned how to avoid repeating words and substitute them with stronger or similar words.

All of the group members recall asking questions about appropriate word choice and vocabulary, as well as sentence arrangement—skills that many non-native speakers of English question in their own writing.

Participation in the writing group has influenced many members teaching of writing as well. As group meetings begin and close, a common topic is student writing. During this time, Trixie's knowledge is tapped regarding common patterns in undergraduate writing and ways to integrate writing into their own teaching. Janice now teaches about writing to learn vs. writing to communicate—and she is now most interested in having students writing to communicate (previously, they submitted writing to learn, which she now views as pre-writing or rough drafts). With the assistance of writing center consultants, her classes now more comprehensively discuss the writing process and the importance of writing to learn as a precursor to writing to communicate. Eva now teaches memo writing explicitly, requiring two drafts and peer feedback. Similarly, Wen shares how learning to quickly read a paper (i.e., during the half-hour of writing group time allocated to reading) has helped her become more efficient when grading student assignments. Moreover, Janice, Wen, and Eva have encouraged (or required) graduate students to use the writing center and have explained its value from their own personal experience. And, given his expertise, Manuel has partnered with Trixie on roundtables regarding grant-writing to disseminate their expertise to faculty and graduate students. In addition, meeting in the Writing Center every week gives members easy access to and reminders of the services offered by the center, whether it's in-class workshops or special faculty workshops and brown bags, designed to support faculty as they teach, or teach with, writing.

Professional Development

Members expected to learn about writing, but were surprised by other areas of growth. Members acknowledge the group supported their professional development and adjustment to Michigan State. Such positive spillovers were made possible by the fluid agenda that allowed time and "space" for members to bring up pressing issues. These discussions typically took place while members were arriving and getting settled or when disbanding; we mention this here because although unanticipated, such positive spillovers had important implications for members, and ultimately the growth and development of faculty. Eva and Wen, for example, sought counsel from the group relative to managing students on their research teams (e.g., addressing performance problems, raising awareness of a potential violence in the workplace liability with a disgruntled graduate student). Similarly, the group discussed challenges relating to tenure and promotion. Review of Janice's reappointment essay prepared Eva and Wen for the work they would need to do the next year, and sharing of electronic documents eased preparation of the dossier.

Returning to the ASA framework, we see that the members of this particular FWG have been attracted to the group because of the people who make up the group and because of the shared values and the methods whereby individuals' strengths and work habits support their mutual goals. Mutual support and respect as well as a willingness to learn from and about each other and our various disciplines makes it possible for members to develop, most important, as writers, but also as teachers and professionals in the academy. While we may have been saddened by the attrition of some (potential) group members, the ongoing viability of the group requires that members be willing to actively participate in the groups' processes and share the groups' values.

We have heard many deans and provosts claim that it is in the university's best interest to retain faculty and staff once they are recruited, given the churn and costs caused by turnover. From the individual's perspective, staying at a school can make for better social, professional, and emotional investments. Writing groups that help faculty be successful—with their writing, their grants and research, their teaching—are an investment in faculty growth and retention, thus an investment in the well being of the university as a whole. As we continue to invest in FWGs and as we continue to ask other campus leaders to invest in FWGs, we wanted to showcase a well-developed plan for fostering success for FWG members, FWGs themselves and ultimately, success for the colleges and universities supporting FWG.

THINKING ABOUT GROUP FORMATION: A HEURISTIC

There is much to think about as faculty members, graduate students, writing center directors, teaching and learning facilitators, and others form and sustain FWGs because if, as Schneider says, the people are the group, each group will be different. What will attract members? What will help them select to stay in a group? How will the group progress as it develops its own shared values and goals? What basic values are being determined through recruitment strategies and advertisements? By way of summary and based on our case study group's learning experiences, we offer these tips to help group organizers and participants think about the formation of their own FWG.

1. Constitute groups with members having similar goals. For example, one type of successful group might come from the junior faculty ranks, preferably faculty in the earlier phase of their tenure track process. Since publications are one of the requirements for tenure, being with colleagues who share a similar goal (tenure) and pressure to publish helps to unify the group.

2. Invite a group facilitator with expertise about writing in general.

3. Offer an orientation session in which the purpose and function of writing groups is discussed and some ground rules are established.

Moreover, during the initial rotations, know that some coaching is required to help members become accustomed to determining and clearly sharing what it is, specifically, that they seek assistance with and establishing a task scope that fits the time allotted.

4. Recruit learning-oriented members for multidisciplinary groups.

5. Build in weekly reading time at the start of meetings. Some members may choose to schedule their initial reading time before the group discussion begins, whereas others will take this time to refresh their thoughts and comments.

6. Schedule in-person meetings that allow for more interaction and are thus more effective.

7. Try meeting even if the member in turn has "nothing to present to the group." Many times a simple discussion on the subject can stimulate ideas that the member needs to continue the writing process and avoid problematic procrastination.

8. Allow some fluidity in each weekly session to provide time for informal interactions pertaining to teaching, professional development, and the writing process. Indeed, members have mentioned learning that writing is a social process. Similarly, allow some fluidity in the weekly schedule for members facing pressing deadlines to "switch weeks" with other writers.

9. Respect writing as a craft, and honor variations in writing and research processes across disciplines.

10. Come with an open mind because you never know when opportunities will present themselves within and through the group.

11. Stress that members should put into the group what they expect or want to get out of the group.

12. Pay attention to growth in all areas. Members will be pleasantly surprised when they learn about more than just micro-writing techniques.

REFERENCES

Belcher, Wendy. 2009. *Writing Your Journal Article in Twelve Weeks: A Guide to Academic Publishing Success.* Thousand Oaks, CA: Sage.

Churchman, Charles W. 1968. *The Systems Approach.* New York: Dell Publishing Co.

Dweck, Carol S. 1986. "Motivational Processes Affecting Learning." *American Psychologist* 41 (10): 1040–8. http://dx.doi.org/10.1037/0003-066X.41.10.1040.

Khisty, C. Jotin. 2006. "A Fresh Look at the Systems Approach and an Agenda for Action: Peeking Through the Lens of Churchman's Aphorisms." *Systemic Practice and Action Research* 19 (1): 3–25. http://dx.doi.org/10.1007/s11213-005-9001-5.

Miller, T.R., T.D. Baird, C.M. Littlefield, G. Kofinas, F.S. Chapin, III, and C.L. Redman. 2008. "Epistemological Pluralism: Reorganizing Interdisciplinary Research." *Ecology and Society* 13 (2): 46. Accessed May 2, 2011. http://www.ecologyandsociety.org/vol13/iss2/art46/.

Schneider, Benjamin. 1987. "The People Make the Place." *Personnel Psychology* 40 (3): 437–53. http://dx.doi.org/10.1111/j.1744-6570.1987.tb00609.x.

Stock, Patti. 1997. "Reforming Education in the Land-Grant University: Contributions from a Writing Center." *Writing Center Journal* 18 (1): 7–29.

Vandewalle, Don. 1997. "Development and Validation of a Work Domain Goal Orientation Instrument." *Educational and Psychological Measurement* 57 (6): 995–1015. http://dx.doi.org/10.1177/0013164497057006009.

PART 3

Issues and Authors

11

GUIDING PRINCIPLES FOR SUPPORTING FACULTY AS WRITERS AT A TEACHING-MISSION INSTITUTION

Michelle Cox and Ann Brunjes

At many universities, support for faculty writing is motivated by the need for faculty to publish in order to attain reappointment, tenure, and promotion. In fact, at some institutions, access to such support as faculty writing retreats is made most available to junior faculty, the faculty in most need of securing publications. In this chapter, we argue for the importance of support for faculty writing at teaching-mission community colleges and universities, where the tenure process privileges teaching and service over publication. This support is particularly important at institutions that emphasize student writing across the curriculum, ask faculty to teach writing-intensive courses, and promote engaging approaches to teaching and learning. In this chapter, the directors of a Writing Across the Curriculum (WAC) program and an Office of Teaching and Learning (OTL) draw from a faculty writing retreat initiative at Bridgewater State University (BSU) to argue that support for faculty writing fits the missions of WAC and OTL programs at teaching-mission universities, but that writing retreats at such institutions should be distinct from programs at research-intensive universities in several key ways. First, we discuss why it makes sense for faculty at teaching-mission universities to write, drawing from literature on teacher-writer identity. Next we describe the distinct aspects of faculty writing retreats at teaching-mission institutions. We then shift focus to the BSU Writing Retreat as a case study, drawing on the program evaluation, participant final reports, and an IRB-approved anonymous survey conducted ten months after the retreat.

DOI: 10.7330/9780874219029.c011

WHY WRITING MAKES SENSE FOR TEACHING-MISSION COLLEGE AND UNIVERSITY FACULTY

Despite a long scholarly emphasis by rhetoric-composition scholars on the linkage between teachers' experience as writers and teaching effectiveness, in recent years WAC programs tend not to focus on support for faculty writing. The reigning assumption may be that faculty are already writing, as publication is necessary at many institutions for tenure and promotion. At teaching-mission colleges and universities, though, faculty may become distanced from their writing, thus missing an opportunity to keep their knowledge and practice around the teaching of writing invigorated and effective.

Tim Gillespie, a long-time National Writing Project affiliate, has argued that the experience of writing and the teaching of writing are strongly connected. In "Becoming Our Own Expert—Teachers as Writers," Gillespie (1985) outlines three reasons why teachers should also write:

- "When teachers write, we help demystify the act of writing. . . . If we share our projects or write in front of our students, they can see what a sloppy, difficult act writing is for all writers."
- "When teachers write, we learn empathy for our students."
- "When teachers write, we become partners in a community of writers, full participants in our classroom writing workshop."

At WAC workshops, leaders regularly advise faculty to share their own writing-in-process with students, and yet we don't ask faculty if they are currently writing or offer support for this writing. We try to create empathy for student writers by sharing information about the student writing experience, yet we don't place faculty into the shoes of a writer. We attempt to create a community of teachers through WAC programming, but we rarely extend this into a community of writers. By including support for writing in WAC programs at teaching-mission universities, WAC program leaders are able to harness some of the success and energy that has fueled the National Writing Project for decades, drawing on the strengths teachers gain from expertise in writing.

Support for faculty writing also makes sense for Offices of Teaching and Learning at teaching-mission universities. One of the primary goals of Teaching and Learning Centers is reinforcing the importance of reflection on one's own practice as teacher, scholar, and writer, in the belief that this reflection leads to more effective teaching practice and richer learning experiences for our students. Once we accept a clear linkage between the depth of a faculty member's writing practice, his or her reflection upon that practice, and the effectiveness of that faculty member as a writing teacher, the necessity for providing writing opportunities is clear. And, as Elbow and Sorcinelli (2006, 20) attest, faculty writing support that includes writing-process approaches "support the natural and positive connections between scholarship and teaching." Incorporating writing-process methods, such as peer review, supportive writing groups, and time to reflect on the writing process can lead faculty retreat participants to insights about the writing process of student writers, an outcome described by Felten, Moore, and Strickland (2009) in their study of the faculty writing retreat at Elon. While it is becoming more common for teaching and learning centers to offer faculty writing retreats and other kinds of support for faculty writing, the support is usually focused on producing publications tied to the Scholarship of Teaching and Learning (SoTL), as it is at Elon. By opening faculty writing retreats to a range of topics, Teaching and Learning Centers support faculty members *as writers*, scholars, and teachers.

WHAT IS DISTINCT ABOUT A WRITING RETREAT AT A TEACHING-MISSION INSTITUTION?

Faculty writing retreats developed for teaching-mission colleges and universities need to be developed with sensitivity to the goals and professional identities of faculty committed primarily to teaching. In this section, we describe aspects of the faculty writing retreats developed for teaching-intensive colleges and universities that differ from those developed for research-intensive universities.

Embrace the Teacher-Scholar Identity

Many faculty at teaching-mission institutions ground their identities in their work as teachers and members of the college community rather than in their scholarly output. Successful teaching-mission writing retreats recognize and celebrate the faculty member as teacher, writer, and scholar.

The separation of teacher-identity and scholar-identity is common at many institutions. As Anne Ellen Geller (2011, 161) writes, support for teaching and for scholarship are often distinct, enforcing the separation of these identities:

> Faculty attend [a] writing retreat or boot camp . . . to work on their own writing among their scholar colleagues, and they attend writing or communication across the curriculum workshops or institutes to consider their teaching of writing among their teacher colleagues. Thus the two

types of learning—learning to be a more successful academic writing oneself and learning to be a more successful teacher of writing—are separated. And faculty find the roles they inhabit—scholar and teacher—split, even as they are told these roles are and should be intertwined.

Emphasizing connections among teaching and scholarship is especially important since at many teaching-mission institutions, faculty fear that their institution will increase expectations for scholarly publications without decreasing teaching or service responsibilities. WAC and OTL programs need to be aware of campus perceptions of institutional pressure to publish, and make sure that advertisements for faculty writing retreats emphasize the links between teaching, writing, and scholarship.

Compensate Participants

While at some research-intensive universities faculty have to pay to participate in writing retreats, at teaching-intensive colleges and universities it is important that faculty are well compensated for participation. At many teaching-mission universities, faculty teach a 4–4 load, and faculty at many community colleges teach 5–5 loads; many also take on additional courses in summer, on weekends, and during the academic year. Faculty at research institutions view publications resulting from a writing retreat as sufficient compensation, as publications are the currency of their careers. At teaching-mission institutions, scholarship may be seen as peripheral to a faculty member's career.

Emphasize the Experience of Writing over Publication for Career Advancement

Faculty writing retreats at teaching-mission institutions should place emphasis on the experience of writing and the writing process over publication, in keeping with the retreat's goals of supporting faculty as writers and teachers. Applicants should be encouraged to see the retreat as an opportunity for growth and risk-taking in their writerly identities and practices, rather than solely as a venue for completion of current scholarly projects.

A focus on the experience of writing rather than on publication for career advancement affects the type of projects welcomed and the way applicants are evaluated. Retreats addressed career issues, particularly those of junior faculty, evaluating applicants based on where the applicant is in his/her career, the scholarly merit of the project for advancing his/her career, and the prospects for the project's publication. Retreats at teaching-mission institutions can welcome faculty from different stages in their careers (as well as welcome some part-time and non-tenure track faculty), projects not linked to the applicant's discipline (such as fiction or memoir), and genres not typically valued during tenure review (such as conference papers, book proposals, and textbooks). Evaluation of applicants can then be based on how the retreat would enhance the participant's writerly, teacherly and scholarly identities. In addition, the following criteria can be considered:

- Experience. Striking a balance between group members experienced with writing groups and peer review and novices is crucial to success.
- Project status. Projects must be feedback-ready, with completed data sets and realistic research and writing plans.
- Potential benefit. Applicants with existing support for their writing receive less priority than those without support already in place.
- Openness to format/process. Successful participants are amenable to the process of giving and receiving feedback, generally supportive to colleagues, and open to working in this way with and receiving feedback from colleagues from other disciplines.

Emphasize the Writing Process over Product

At research-intensive universities, faculty writing retreats are often advertised as a writing "boot camp"—an intensive experience leading to completed publications. In fact, such writing retreats often assess their own success based on the number of publications resulting from the retreat. At teaching-mission institutions, the writing process itself takes precedence over the resulting product, since the writing process will have more impact on the participants' identities as writers and practices as teachers. Further, once the retreat ends, faculty at teaching-mission institutions return to the reality of intensive teaching and service commitments, with little, if any, time reserved for writing. Placing too much focus on completed products can lead retreat participants to feel like failures. It is important, then, that participants of writing retreats at teaching-mission institutions be allowed to make their own goals for the retreat, and that the goals not only focus on publishable scholarly texts, but can include such things as completing a first draft, completing a conference presentation, and completing part of a scholarly article, such as the literature review.

Emphasize Community over Individual Scholarly Pursuit

The writing retreat creates important space and time for building community. At teaching-intensive institutions, there can be few opportunities for faculty to form relationships with other faculty. This is especially true for the increasing numbers of part-time faculty, many of whom migrate between institutions with few or no opportunities to build professional relationships. The writing retreat enhances community for full- and part-time faculty in several ways. While many faculty are accustomed to only sharing completed writing, the act of sharing writing-in-process makes people feel vulnerable. This shared vulnerability shifts the playing field, and creates more open relationships among retreat participants. Second, the retreat creates meaningful cross-disciplinary relationships, relationships that can be difficult to otherwise foster at teaching-mission institutions. Third, the retreat introduces faculty to their colleagues' scholarly identities. At teaching-mission institutions, faculty tend to only know each other as teachers and through their service, not through their scholarship. Learning about each other's scholarly projects enhances community and opens possibilities for cross-disciplinary collaboration.

THE FACULTY WRITING RETREAT AT BSU

BSU, a regional university enrolling about eleven thousand students, is located forty-minutes south of Boston, MA. As we worked together to develop the BSU Writing Retreat, we drew from materials developed for faculty writing retreats at Grand State Valley University, St. John's University (Queens), Elon University, and University of Massachusetts, Amherst, that were generously shared during personal correspondence with program directors or through the programs' websites. As recommended by Felten, Moore, and Strickland (2009), we kept the program small, and limited participation to fifteen faculty. To highlight connections between teaching, writing, and scholarship, we proposed the retreat be held in conjunction with a pedagogy retreat (referred to within BSU and in all our advertising materials as the "pedagogy track") during which faculty would engage in workshops and discussions on incorporating sustainability, cultural inclusion, and undergraduate research into our teaching practice. (These "themes" or foci for the pedagogy retreat would change each year depending on institutional priorities and faculty interest.) These two retreats would be offered jointly under the title, "The Teacher-Scholar Institute," to emphasize the ideal of the teacher-scholar-that at BSU we define as a faculty member whose teaching is energized by inquiry and whose inquiry is energized by teaching.

The proposal was written collaboratively by the OTL director, the WAC director, the faculty fellow in the Office of Institutional Diversity, and the faculty research fellow in the Center for the Advancement of Research and Teaching (CART). This collaboration among diverse faculty development initiatives further underscored the writing retreat's emphasis on the ideal of the teacher-scholar and kept us focused on the goals of supporting the scholarly and teacherly identities of the faculty participants throughout the organization and implementation of the Institute.

The budget for this proposal was substantial, as each of the Institute participants received $2000 for participation in the week and $1000 when the goals as stated on their applications were met; each of the six institute leaders also received $3000. Other significant costs were for hospitality (breakfast, lunch, and refreshments) and some supplies (primarily books). The pilot year (2010) was funded internally by the President's Office and Academic Affairs, with additional funding from an existing Project Compass grant from the Nellie Mae Foundation. For 2011 and 2012, we were awarded a Davis Educational Foundation Grant. Continuing institutional support also funds the Institute. Such generous institutional and grant support during difficult fiscal times speaks to how such programming at a teaching-mission regional university is valued. The 2012 Institute budget, with costs for the writing retreat broken out, are as follows:

Item	Cost
Faculty-participants, Writing Retreat (19 @ $3,000 each)	$57,000
Faculty-participants, Pedagogy Track (32 @ $3,000 each)	$96,000
Facilitators, Writing Retreat (3 @ $3,000 each	$9,000
Facilitators, Pedagogy Track (6 @ $3,000 each)	$18,000
Hospitality (total)	$7,600
Supplies	$1,000
Total Writing Retreat Cost per Retreat (excluding supplies)	$69,344
Total Project Cost	$257,000

The Teacher-Scholar Institute is held over five full days in late summer when no classes are in session. During the pilot year, two faculty directed the writing retreat—the WAC director and the CART Research Fellow, who is responsible for developing programming that supports faculty research. For the second iteration of the retreat, a third director (an enthusiastic participant in the 2010 retreat) was added, as we expanded the program to nineteen participants. These directors were responsible for meeting daily with writing groups and providing feedback and support to individual faculty writers throughout the retreat. Participants were organized in three- to four-member writing groups that were cross-disciplinary and focused around genre and point in the writing process (when possible). For instance, one writing group was composed of faculty from the fields of literature, linguistics, history, and sociology, who were each focused on experimental writing projects that included narrative writing. Two of the participants were attempting to bring together narrative and academic writing; a third was writing creative non-fiction; and the fourth, the sociologist, was writing a collection of short stories. Another group, composed of faculty from communication studies, counselor education, and sociology, were all writing book proposals (one for a textbook, another for a monograph, and a third for a popular book based on academic research), with two at the beginning stages and the third revamping a book proposal after it received review.

When creating a schedule for the retreat, we took care to create extended periods of time for writing, time for peer review and goal setting, and time for the writing retreat participants to interact with those participating in the pedagogy retreat (see Appendix A). The three hours between breakfast and lunch were set aside for uninterrupted writing. During individual writing time, the retreat directors sat in visible spaces in the library (where all groups met and meals were shared), serving almost as a drop-in faculty writing center. Writing groups swapped drafts for peer review by lunch, and then met for ninety minutes at the end of the day to report on work accomplished, set goals for the next day, conduct peer review, and plan the next day's peer review.

During the pilot year, it became apparent that, despite the retreat's general success, faculty needed guidance in how to work in a writing group, specifically on the peer review process. Many of the participants expressed discomfort with the idea of sharing unfinished writing and had only experienced peer review after submitting journal articles. For the second year, we developed a one-hour writing retreat orientation on day one of the retreat. The orientation started with guidelines for peer review, with emphasis on the supportive feedback; letting the writer steer the discussion; and giving feedback that is appropriate for different points in the writing process (see Appendix B). Writing groups then held their initial meeting during the orientation. Participants had been asked to complete a "Project Inventory and Goals" form prior to the retreat that they used during the orientation to introduce each other to their projects and daily goals. Each group then made plans for which pieces would be peer reviewed each day. The orientation emphasized the retreat's focus on the writing experience, the writing process, and community, three important goals for the program.

RESULTS

Overall, the BSU Writing Retreat was successful beyond the directors' expectations. In this section, we discuss the participants' experience of the writing retreat as well as lasting effects, drawing from the 2010 and 2011 program evaluations that summarized surveys taken on the last day of the Institute; 2010 and 2011 participant final reports that were written when the participants met their writing goals and submitted materials for the last part of the stipend; and a follow-up survey conducted almost a year after the 2010 Institute that focused on lasting effects of the writing retreat on the participants' writing, scholarship, and teaching.

The program evaluation collected both quantitative and qualitative data. Overall, participants from both years of the retreat reported high rates of satisfaction. The Table 11.1 compares data from the 2010 and 2011 evaluations on how well the writing retreat met specific goals:

Table 11.1 Percentage of participants reporting "well" or "very well" to the following question: "How well did the Institute meet its goals of . . . ?:

	2010	*2011*
Building a community of writers	71%	90%
Helping you feel energized about your work	93%	100%
Building your interest in faculty development opportunities	57%	100%
Helping you to meet goals that you set for yourself	79%	94%
Taking your teaching to the next stage	93%	100%

While results from both years show high satisfaction, it's clear that the writing retreat more successfully met its goals in its second year. This increased satisfaction may be due to changes we made to the structure of the program in response to feedback. Demands for more writing time were met by increasing the morning writing block to ninety minutes; a directive and detailed writing group orientation (see above) addressed participants' reported lack of facility in the process of peer review; and a reorganized schedule clearly delineated the time dedicated to peer review.

In addition, we made changes to the opening and closing sessions of the Institute. Rather than highlighting the connections between teaching, writing, and scholarship in joint-sessions, we created a brief informational opening session and replaced the joint closing session with separate closing reflections for the teaching and writing retreat participants. The week ended in a celebratory joint reception. As shown in Table 11.2, both changes brought higher satisfaction rates, but we need to continue to think about ways to structure the opening joint session.

Table 11.2 Percentage of participants responding "useful" or "very useful" to the following question: "How useful was the following to your writing?"

	2010	2011
Goal setting with my writing group	79%	79%
Peer feedback from my writing group	93%	95%
Reporting to my writing group	86%	95%
Time for individual writing	100%	100%
Opening joint session with teaching track	42%	61%
Closing joint session with teaching track (2010) / Closing Reflection (2011)	57%	82%
Writing group orientation (added in 2011)		79%
Support from our group's facilitator (question added in 2011)		89%

The program evaluation also gave participants opportunities to write open responses to the above questions, to discuss their accomplishments for the week, and to provide suggestions for the structure of the program for future years. Overall, faculty reported that they accomplished more in relation to their writing goals than they had anticipated. The following comment is representative: "I must say that I am happily surprised that I was able to accomplish so much in a week. It was truly a worthwhile experience for me. I was able to meet the goals that I set for myself at Monday's breakfast within the time frame of a week." Most faculty also commented positively on the structure of the retreat, especially the use of cross-disciplinary writing groups. One participant explained: "By explaining my unique profession and project I found clarity. Their questions and suggestions were fresh. They helped me find appropriate ways to express my concept to potential editors because they accurately represented them—people who won't know the ins and outs of my profession's thoughts and lingo." Another commented, in the program evaluation, that "It was nice to be free of discipline-specific politics and focus on the work—rather than the ongoing debates."

Comments in the evaluation and final reports also revealed how the retreat shaped participants' identities as writers, scholars, and BSU community members, as well as their perspectives on teaching writing.

On Writer Identity

At teaching-mission institutions, faculty can become distanced from their identities as writers. At the beginning of the retreat, some faculty confessed that they hadn't written since finishing their dissertations. The retreat then had a pivotal role in reconnecting faculty to their identities as writers. As one faculty member commented:

> Participating in the writing group has greatly changed my thoughts about myself as a writer and a member of a community of scholars. I have a greater level of confidence in my ability. Stimulated by my work during the Institute week I produced a manuscript that . . . was [not only] published but I received an award for "Outstanding Contribution" at the national conference . . . This is an incredibly far cry from the hyper anxious, unconfident, and perceived incompetent writer that I saw myself to be.

Another described how the retreat removed barriers to writing created by lack of confidence:

> I have been aware for a long time that my lack of confidence in my work has been holding me back from writing. This week I learned the value of "professionalizing" the writing process. That is, when I treat research/writing as part of my professional identity by making time for it and by seeing it as a process (rather than focusing solely on an outcome), I am better able to engage with the material, which in turn develops my confidence in my own ideas and writing ability.

A part-time faculty member reported:

> Writing has always been a difficult task for me. I tend to see the world as divided into writers and non-writers. During this week I realized that this is a false dichotomy I created somewhere early on in my academic career. I explored different types of voice as I considered whether to focus on an academic audience or a broader, more mainstream market. As a result I found that I enjoy writing and look forward to finding new ways to use my writing in my scholarship.

Faculty also reported new identification with the term "writer." In a final report, one participant stated, "I believe that I can now make a stronger identification as a writer in the BSU community, and that the Institute has been most helpful. I have produced a fair amount of scholarly writing, but the week at the Institute has helped center this activity on my identity."

One participant observed that the generous stipend helped to foster this identity: "The retreat was great because I was being paid to be a writer, and so I felt that I was being valued by the institution as a writer."

On Scholarly Identity

Many participants experienced a reconnection to their identities as scholars through the retreat. One faculty member wrote, "I feel more ready for my own research and writing than I have in a long time. It has renewed my desire to continue my own interests and reminded me of what I love about scholarship." Others commented that the retreat helped them connect with other BSU community members as scholars, as in this statement from a final report: "This [writing] group helped me to feel there is a community of scholars at BSU who resonate with my work (content, theory, methods, writing goals). I feel more a part of BSU . . . than I did before." Another made this powerful claim: "The writer's retreat worked exceptionally well for fostering a sense of a scholarly community and for energizing the participants about their research. I think this was probably the most fulfilling week I have experienced at BSU. It's made me feel excited about my life as a scholar and a teacher."

On Identity as a BSU Community Member

Many participants commented on how the retreat helped them feel more a part of the BSU community. One participant commented, "One of the best things I will walk away with is new friends/colleagues/collaborators on campus. I networked more this week than the last two years!" Another echoed this sentiment: "I feel more comfortable that others in the school will understand what I do and why, share some theoretical orientations, etc. I love multi/interdisciplinary dialogue but have had very little opportunity since I got here." Other participants emphasized the emotional side of these new connections: "I realized that the campus-wide community of BSU is not as compartmentalized as I believed. I have networked with writers across our campus that are genuinely invested in me, my process, my work, and my achievements. When I run into these people, we ask about each other's progress, share hugs, and walk away feeling connected to each other and our campus environment."

Part-time faculty, in particular, highlighted this outcome of the retreat. One commented, "Working with colleagues from other disciplines gave me a new sense of being part of the larger BSU community." Another wrote: "It was a rich, rewarding opportunity to be with faculty from other disciplines who obviously love their teaching and their scholarship. I am grateful to be a part of it. I also want to report how I appreciated the Institute being open to part-time faculty as many opportunities are not. I felt respected and appreciated. I truly felt I was a member of a community of scholars."

On Teaching Writing

The retreat did not include workshops explicitly focused on teaching writing, but the experience of reconnecting with writing, being part of a writing group, giving and receiving peer review, and reflecting on the writing process led participants to insights on teaching writing. Several participants commented on this:

I use writing groups [in my teaching], but after this experience I will try to give more time for those groups. Our first day [at the writing group orientation] was really a trust-building time, and I heard this echoed by other groups. You can't rush this process, but it is tempting to do so when it appears that some students aren't focusing much.

I think what I really need to help my students focus on is keeping the writer's needs/goals in mind and also making sure students have enough time to really talk to each other about their writing. I realized this week how much time is needed to do peer review and I don't give enough of it during the semester.

The experience will also change my teaching since I found much value in a writing group. I realize that when I work with students I focus almost solely on the mechanics of the writing. I plan to provide more feedback about the ideas expressed. I am wondering how I might provide verbal feedback in addition to written comments through a tool such as podcasts . . . I will use the guidelines for writing groups [the retreat leaders] shared to work with students so they can grow as writers . . . I have a deeper appreciation for the collaborative process.

One participant emphasized the importance of creating opportunities for reflection and creating a community of writers in the classroom: "I think I can incorporate part of the goal setting and peer evaluation exercises into my classes. In the past, rather than create a community of writers, I have focused more on feedback and critique. The institute provided me with some concrete ideas about how to revise this in the future so that students are less fearful about sharing their writing."

LASTING EFFECTS OF THE RETREAT ON TEACHING AND WRITING

From responses to our follow-up survey, it became clear that the retreat had lasting impact on writing pedagogy and the ways that participants related to student writers. One person wrote that, over the academic year, "I was more open to [students'] writing style. I didn't correct as much punctuation and grammar, but focused more on the central idea of the sentence or paragraph. Each person develops a style of writing." Another emphasized the writing process when talking to student writers: "I reminded students that regardless of our ability to write effectively, all of us as writers can benefit from support and feedback." Another said that they had always supported student writing, but noted, "[the retreat] remind[ed] me of the artificial constraints our students face—good writing takes some time and investment." One respondent reported that the retreat helped them become a better mentor to student writing outside of the classroom: "[The retreat] helped me feel more competent to take on my first graduate research assistant (already applied before the institute), and later to take on two undergrad students for a semester. As I helped these three students very closely with both presentations and finished papers, I was able to translate much of my own experience with writing into teaching them how to think about the writing process."

One of most prominent themes to emerge from the different evaluations was participants' new confidence in their writing. As one participant reported, "The retreat did change the way I think of myself as a writer. The simple fact that I could complete the project was in itself a great confidence building exercise. The retreat also challenged me to move beyond my assumptions that I am not a 'writer' and to try to make more room for writing in my life. Finally, the retreat gave validation to the idea that writing is an important aspect of my professional work and should be given time just as I do for my teaching."

But responses to a question on whether the retreat had lasting results for the practice of writing were mixed. One participant reported that it had: "The retreat time allowed me to get moving on my writing and then to make changes in my schedule so that I could devote a few hours each week to writing. I have continued to write a few hours each week since last August." Another stated: "It did affect my writing process to some extent, making me more immediately aware of audience issues and of the need to revise my outline as needed. These changes have lasted beyond the retreat, I think, largely because I have been in touch with the writing mentor for our group and participated in a follow-up writing day last month."

But other participants reported that they had difficulty sustaining their writing after the retreat ended. One stated, "Writing daily was a revelation—I wish I could say that I kept it up." Another stated that while the changes to their writing practice will last, "I had already over-committed before the retreat, they were hard to implement immediately after. But I believe I was more productive (presentations and a manuscript draft) this past year than I would have been without the retreat."

SUPPORT FOR FACULTY WRITING AT BSU: A GOOD IDEA THAT CONTINUES TO GROW

The BSU Writing Retreat highlighted a need for additional support for faculty writing. During a final discussion at the end of the retreat, the participants expressed interest in support for faculty writing during the semester. Participants offered specific ideas in the final reports, e-mails to us after the retreat, and in the follow-up survey. Here are a few of them:

- "I would love a drop-in writing space/time that mimicked the institute (quiet, computer access, a facilitator to talk through, possibly a group to check in with at the start), once or twice a month. Then I could structure my own work around preparing for those designated times."
- "I would be interested in participating in a writing group at BSU. For me, this might be a once per month meeting where members exchange written work for feedback and engage in thoughtful discussion."
- "I would also like to see workshops on writing including sessions on how to craft a book proposal."

WAC has collaborated with the CART Research Fellow to put these ideas into action. In Fall 2010, WAC and CART launched the BSU Community of Writers (COW) Colloquia, and have since offered monthly sixty-minute workshops led by BSU faculty from across the curriculum on different aspects of writing and publishing, which have included such topics as writing memoir, editing and publishing an edited collection, writing and publishing a textbook, and researching and writing about pedagogy. In Spring 2011, WAC, CART and OTL partnered to reconnect with faculty from the summer 2010 writing retreat, some of whom had yet to meet their stated writing goals. To support these faculty and to foster the nascent "culture of writing" at BSU, we held a one-day writing retreat called simply "Writing Day." The planning was simple and the funding minimal. In the morning, faculty gathered to enjoy a hot breakfast and talk about their writing projects and goals for the day. Faculty gathered again at lunch to discuss progress over sandwiches and brownies. The rest of the time was dedicated to writing. Michelle was available to give feedback from morning to late afternoon, but no one took her up on this offer, as they wanted to use the time to write. All who participated in this event completed their writing projects from summer 2010, reinforcing our belief that small-scale, targeted writing events can yield real benefits for the participants.

In fall 2011, CART and WAC launched two additional initiatives. The first picked up on the success of the one-day writing retreat, by offering designated time and space for writing across the semester, and open to all BSU part- and full-time faculty. During the one-day writing retreat organized by WAC and OTL, we learned from faculty that having scheduled time for writing allows them to clear their schedule for these times as well as prepare for writing on these days. During our morning conversation at Writing Day, several faculty joked that they turned down meetings and excused themselves from family chores because they had committed to participating in Writing Day. They also told us, because they knew Writing Day was coming, they used the days ahead to get their notes in order, organized necessary books and articles, and generally reacquainted themselves with their draft and research. Starting in Fall 2011, we have held two writing days a month. As faculty schedules wouldn't allow for a full-day writing retreat, these writing days offer four-hour blocks of time in a reserved conference room, with light refreshments available. These writing days offer faculty scheduled and uninterrupted time for writing. The second new initiative is COW writing groups. In September 2011, CART and WAC put out a call for people interested in joining writing groups, and matched groups according to schedules and interest areas. We co-hosted a writing group reception that discussed effective writing group strategies and organized five cross-disciplinary writing groups, matching people according to schedule and type of writing project. We emphasized that effective writing groups are those that set realistic goals, ones that can be accomplished in spite of heavy teaching and service commitments. We will hold another reception at the end of spring semester, to learn how things went and share accomplishments.

These multiple initiatives and annual writing retreat make support for faculty writing available to a larger group of faculty, and make support available throughout the year. One of the BSU WAC program's key missions is to "foster a culture of writing" at BSU. Now, faculty writing will be part of this campus culture. This network of support for faculty writing at BSU also fosters a sense of community among faculty writers, thus meeting OTL's mission to "build communities of teaching and learning among departments, programs and schools." We end with the words of one of our faculty participants, from the retreat survey:

> I am truly grateful for the opportunity to spend so much time on my writing. It was an energizing and community building experience. I heard from . . . many colleagues throughout the week and know that everyone felt that the institute not only advanced their work but allowed them the opportunity to meet people from other disciplines and share ideas with them. I STRONGLY believe that holding an annual institute would be a key part of professional development and creating a community of scholars at BSU.

APPENDIX 11.A

Daily Schedule: Writing Retreat 2011

Coffee and water are available throughout each day in the second-floor lobby of Maxwell Library.

Additional light refreshments served at 2:30 p.m. in second-floor lobby of Maxwell Library.

	8:15–9:55	*10:00– 11:00*	*11:00– 12:15*	*12:15– 1:15*	*1:30–4:00*	*3:00–4:30*
Monday 8/22	Introduction to Institute, to Participants and to Facilitators (with breakfast). Heritage Room	Writing Retreat Orientation	Individual writing Michelle, Theresa, and Tom are available for providing support.	LunchTime to swap drafts for peer review. Heritage Room	Read and comment on peer writing; time for individual writing; Michelle, Theresa, and Tom are available for providing support.	Meet with writing group: Report on work and set goals for the next day; peer review; plan next day's peer review.

	8:30–9:00	*9:00– 10:00*	*10:00– 12:15*	*12:15– 1:15*	*1:30–3:00*	*3:00–4:30*
Tuesday 8/23	Arrival, Breakfast and Announcements. Heritage Room	Individual writing	Individual writing- Michelle, Theresa, and Tom are available for providing support.	LunchTime to swap drafts for peer review. Heritage Room	Read and comment on peer writing; time for individual writing; Michelle, Theresa, and Tom are available for providing support.	Meet with writing group: Report on work and set goals for the next day; peer review; plan next day's peer review.
Wednesday 8/24	Arrival, Breakfast and Announcements. Heritage Room	Individual writing	Individual writing Michelle, Theresa, and Tom are available for providing support.	LunchTime to swap drafts for peer review. Heritage Room	Read and comment on peer writing; time for individual writing; Michelle, Theresa, and Tom are available for providing support.	Meet with writing group: Report on work and set goals for the next day; peer review; plan next day's peer review.

	8:30–9:00	9:00–10:00	10:00–12:15	12:15–1:15	1:30–3:00	3:00–4:30
Thursday 8/25	Arrival, Breakfast, and Announcements. Heritage Room	Individual writing	Individual writing- Michelle, Theresa, and Tom are available for providing support.	Lunch- Time to swap drafts for peer review. Heritage Room	Read and comment on peer writing; time for individual writing; Michelle, Theresa, and Tom are available for providing support.	Meet with writing group: Report on work and set goals for the next day; peer review; plan next day's peer review.

	8:30–9:00	9:00–10:00	10:00–12:15	12:15–1:15	1:20–2:20	2:30–3:30	3:30–5:30
Friday 8/26	Arrival, Breakfast, and Announcements. Heritage Room	Individual writing	Individual writing- Michelle, Theresa, and Tom are available for providing support.	Lunch- Heritage Room	Writing Retreat closing reflection (you will meet with the Retreat facilitators and other writing groups to discuss the Final Report and reflect on the experience of the Retreat)	Evaluation of Summer Institute (please bring your laptop computer; a computer lab will also be available)	Closing Reception with teaching track and emeritus faculty.

APPENDIX 11.B

Peer Review Guidelines for Writing Groups

As a group, you will find your own rhythm for peer review suggestions. Here are a few guidelines to help you get started:

- Generally, it is best to start the peer review session with a statement by the writer on where she/he is in the writing process, how she/he feels about the draft at present, the writer's plans for continuing drafting, and what type of feedback would be most useful at this point.
- When giving feedback, readers should start their comments with positive feedback before moving on to critical feedback.
- Try to keep the overall mood of the peer review session positive, with attention paid to feedback that will keep the writer motivated and excited to continue the writing process, and ending the session with clear steps for the writer to take next in their writing.
- Peer review in writing groups is very different from peer review that happens during the publication process, when writers send manuscripts

to journals or publishers. In the latter situation, peer review is evaluative, as reviewers are making a judgment on whether the manuscript is appropriate for that venue and ready for publication. In writing groups, peer review is supportive, meant to help the writer move through the writing process.

- The writing process is messy, for everyone. In writing groups, writers see each other's messes—the incomplete drafts, the tangents, the sentences that stop in the middle of nowhere, the insights that bubble to the surface during the act of writing. It takes trust to show people writing-in-progress. When it is your turn to present a draft to the group, try not to worry about "cleaning up the draft" for the readers. Let them see that "messiness."

- Writing-in-progress typically displays many "surface-level" or editorial issues. This is a natural occurrence during the writing process, as the mind is busy creating ideas, new connections, organizational structures, and prose—focusing on "global issues." The part of the mind that creates isn't the same part of the mind that critiques and edits. In fact, if you see an early draft from a colleague (or a student) that is "clean," it may mean that the writer wasn't able to quiet the inner critic and just plain write. Since surface-level issues are typical of early drafts, it doesn't make sense for a writing group to spend time focusing on these issues during peer review sessions. If the writer is toward the end of the writing process, simply circle or highlight editorial concerns on the draft. There is no need to correct errors or mention or explain them during the peer review session. If the writer is early in the writing process, there's no need to point out editorial concerns at all. The draft may change so much by the end of the process that pointing out these errors may only serve to embarrass the writer.

- Remember: the writer owns their draft. We all get excited by our own visions for other people's writing, but we need to honor the writer's vision, goals, and direction. During peer review sessions, try to keep control in the writer's hands. When you are unsure about a writer's intention, ask them before guessing. If the writer is in the midst of making a decision, ask the writer questions until the writer comes to see a path to try.

REFERENCES

Elbow, Peter, and Mary Deane Sorcinelli. 2006. "The Faculty Writing Place: A Room of Our Own." *Change: The Magazine of Higher Learning* 38 (6): 17–22. http://dx.doi.org/10.3200/CHNG.38.6.17-22.

Felten, Peter, Jessie Moore, and Michael Strickland. 2009. "Faculty Writing Residencies: Supporting Scholarly Writing and Teaching." *The Journal for Centers of Teaching and Learning* 1. http://celt.muohio.edu/jctl/.

Geller, Anne Ellen. 2011. "When in Rome." *Frontiers: The Interdisciplinary Journal of Study Abroad* 20:155–70.

Gillespie, Tim. 1985. "Becoming Our Own Expert—Teachers as Writers." *The Quarterly* 8 (1). http://www.nwp.org/cs/public/print/resource/1708.

12

ACADEMIC PUBLICATION AND CONTINGENT FACULTY
Establishing a Community of Scholars

Letizia Guglielmo and Lynée Lewis Gaillet

There should not be a cumulative disadvantage to being employed in a contingent position, which permits academics to gain experience and demonstrate competence.

—Gary Rhoades

The American Association of University Professors (AAUP) reports, "Today, over 50 percent of faculty serve in part-time appointments, and non-tenure-track positions of all types account for 68 percent of all faculty appointments in American higher education. Both part- and full-time non-tenure-track appointments are continuing to increase" (AAUP 2009). Nontraditional, hybrid, contingent faculty positions proliferate the academic landscape in the wake of economic downturn—with no resolution or plans for returning to "status quo" in sight. Although publication manuals and writing guides targeted to graduate students and junior faculty permeate the market, particularly given the media attention focused on the ubiquitous "crisis is scholarly publication," current publications neither fully account for the range of academic positions often characterized as "other" nor offer comprehensive discussions of publishing scenarios coupled with practical advice. Although the nature and look of publishing is shifting, we recognize that the admonishment to "publish or perish" is still relevant; publications still equal cultural currency in academia and provide the means for purchasing advancement—even in contingent positions, which we define as teachers in positions, both full- and part-time, that are dependent on yearly or semester-to-semester contract renewals, who are not eligible for tenure, and who most often are not supported with funding or release time for scholarship and professional

DOI: 10.7330/9780874219029.c012

development. As Deirdre McMahon and Ann Green (2008) explain in an issue of *Academe Online* devoted to contingency faculty issues, "Because the primary means to be recognized as a scholar remains publication, adjuncts and other contingent faculty face the same pressures to publish to secure a tenure-track job as those on the track do to advance."

Publishing opportunities and "research agendas" often emerge out of professional development and mentoring initiatives offered to tenure-track faculty and newly-hired assistant professors; however, contingent faculty find few opportunities to take advantage of this kind of training/mentoring and rarely find allies and peers within their departments. Furthermore, contingent faculty members are often isolated from and sometimes ignored within the traditional structure of academic departments. As Gary Rhoades (2008) explains, "We must imagine new ways to strengthen the academic profession that validate the work, expertise, and qualifications of colleagues in contingent positions." With all that has been written on the subject of academic publication, we still see a significant need not only to redefine our current conceptions of both mentoring and scholarship, but also to draw other teacher-scholars into these important discussions in order to adequately address broader missions of "the scholarship of teaching and learning," prepare all faculty members for full participation in the academy, and discover ways for mentors to document their important work.

PRESSURE TO PUBLISH

Although at one time a division existed between teaching and research universities, today, more often than not, nearly all faculty members are expected to publish and engage in research. The problem with the system as it stands is that "[research] has become the measure of individuals. Faculty may be paid to teach, but they are judged on their research" (Dalton 2006, 256). And, although it is becoming more difficult to publish books, monographs are still the gold standard when it comes to promotion and tenure decisions (and increasingly hiring decisions as well), despite claims made to the contrary by position statements such as the report of the MLA Task Force on Evaluating Scholarship for Tenure and Promotion, published in *Profession* in 2007 ("Report of the MLA Task Force" 2007). Equally troubling is the impact of the ongoing crisis in scholarly publishing both on scholars' access to research resources given tight university library budgets and, more important, on the competition for book contracts when presses themselves are facing a financial crisis, particularly within the humanities. At its core, this crisis in scholarly publishing results from competing goals and agendas among many stakeholders including faculty, publishers, and libraries. William W. Savage, Jr. argues that this current system of "forced productivity" not only results in too much scholarship to be read but also in a devaluing of instruction when teaching loads are increased for those who do not publish enough: "Teaching-as-punishment is certainly a remarkable concept, when you think about it. And when you think about it, you begin to understand just how seriously the academy takes the matter of productivity" (Savage 2003, 45).

Within the field of Rhetoric and Composition in particular, the larger problem is one of voice and representation:

> Despite the fact that there are over 11,000 members of the Conference on College Composition and Communication and that there are several thousand more instructors of composition throughout the nation who are not members of CCCC, only a relatively small number of these compositionists regularly produce scholarly books and articles. Part of the reason why many professionals do not attempt to author their own scholarship or fail to get their scholarship published is a lack of familiarity with the politics, conventions, and procedures of publishing scholarship. (Olson and Taylor 1997, 1)

Considering the pedagogical overreliance on contingent faculty in composition studies who are generally not supported and often not encouraged to publish as well as the heavy administrative loads of composition specialists, especially women, practical advice and tested strategies guided by a new vision of scholarly publication certainly are needed within the academy. If current hiring practices continue and those in rhetoric and composition will be engaged in more teaching, the expertise of seasoned, contingent faculty becomes essential for new graduates just entering writing classrooms.

Without graduate seminars in publication and often without the time to devote to creating a research agenda prompted by "going on the market," contingent faculty voices are notably absent in much of the scholarship on the teaching of writing. Yet for adjunct teachers and non-tenure-track academics who are not expected and often not encouraged to publish, "publishing credits may provide. . . some career maneuverability" (Moxley 1997, 4); more important, we argue, opportunities to share expertise and validate teaching, to grow as teachers, and to connect with colleagues become essential to a thriving network of teaching professionals.

> I hold a tenure-track position at a state institution with a number of contingent faculty members. To get to my office, I wait on the slowest

elevator in the universe to arrive, and I spend this time staring at the departmental bookcase, located in the same hallway. For years, I have noticed the same thing: the books within the case are usually written by the same few members of our department, members who are full-time tenured or tenure-track professors, typically at the full or associate level. While our department is justifiably proud of our colleagues' literary achievements, I wish people would notice that our bookcase is equally notable for its empty spaces and what those spaces represent—important scholarship from other wonderful scholars, scholarship that could come from our talented and diverse group of contingent faculty. Often I have heard people say that our contingent faculty members would never be interested in publishing because that would be another unfair "burden" to place on them. While this sentiment is well-intentioned, I think it is an incomplete assumption. Maybe we should also consider the possibility that being encouraged to participate in the department's publishing activities as a valuable scholarly peer might actually make the burden of contingent labor more bearable. If this perspective was true for even half of our contingent faculty, and we encouraged and supported their scholarship in a systemic and intentional way, I'd really love to see the size of the new bookcase I bet we'd have to order.

Laura Davis, Kennesaw State University

SCHOLARLY PROJECTS AND THE SCHOLARSHIP OF TEACHING

Regardless of one's faculty status, often the most difficult step in academic publication is developing or identifying content for scholarly work. Considering the range of contingent faculty positions we described earlier in this chapter, drawing from current coursework is not feasible for those not enrolled in graduate programs, and with limited resources and full-time schedules pieced together on multiple campuses, opportunities to read and fully engage with current scholarship may be limited. Yet the voices of contingent faculty—their experiences and insights—are essential to scholarship in our field as illustrated in the groundbreaking Boyer Commission Report (1998), sponsored by the Carnegie Research Foundation. This oft-cited work, *Reinventing Undergraduate Education: A Blueprint for America's Research Universities*, argues that research universities must shift their missions to include a more integrated view of the traditional triumvirate of faculty responsibilities: research, teaching, and service. The document also demands a more collaborative and synergistic relationship between teachers and students—particularly undergraduate students. In the wake of the Boyer Report, institutions of higher learning have reevaluated their commitment to teaching and reexamined the role that intellectual inquiry and research plays in instruction. The effects of this report are far reaching, and the implications for revising the traditional expectations of research, teaching, and service are great. With backing from the prestigious Carnegie Foundation, research institutions are now encouraged to more carefully integrate faculty responsibilities, keeping the needs of undergraduates and those who teach them in mind. For contingent faculty, who primarily teach undergraduates students, the Boyer mandates offer opportunities for establishing a higher profile within departments and suggest new ways to blend intellectual inquiry and research with instruction. We think this reconfiguration of traditional responsibilities holds great promise for disseminating and publishing scholar/teacher research and pedagogical experiences.

Essential to discussions of scholarship in Rhetoric and Composition, particularly in light of the Boyer model, and to our vision for creating a space for contingent faculty in academic publication is the scholarship of teaching. Blending scholarship and teaching, "allows educators to grow professionally and intellectually, to share their ideas with peers, and to become better teachers through the reflective and critical processes of writing for public readership" (Casanave and Vandrick 2003, 1). For contingent faculty, creating intersections between teaching and scholarly work makes scholarship more feasible, diversifies the perspectives from which we understand teaching and professional work, and allows "knowledge making and professionalization [to] come into better balance" (Bishop 1993, 210). "Attention to the scholarship of teaching can promote individual and collective development while also challenging the field of composition to take a more visible place in conversations about how to assess and improve upon postsecondary teaching" (Minter and Goodburn 2002, xix), and begins to improve, in turn, the ways that we recognize, mentor, and reward contingent faculty.

Using the Boyer model as framework, Richard Gebhardt (1997, 37) offers four approaches to teaching-focused scholarship that allow other teacher-scholars to see how current scholarship may improve their teaching in practical ways. As one of the few scholars in this discussion of academic publication to even mention *where* ideas may stem from, he suggests, "if you work at being a publishing teacher-scholar (or *scholar-teacher*, if you prefer) for whom both composition scholarship and good teaching are important, you may discover article ideas fairly often as you organize courses, read scholarly articles, prepare syllabi, listen to conference papers, and talk with students about their writing" (Gebhardt 1997, 38). Within a sustained discussion of scholarly work, we want to make academic publication accessible and essential for *all* teachers who fulfill various roles in our changing academic landscape.

FILLING A NICHE

In *Writing and Publishing for Academic Authors,* published in 1997, Todd Taylor argued, "The result of the job crunch has *not* meant less scholarship and more teaching, rather, it has meant *more* of both–much more" (Moxley and Taylor 1997, 221). Nearly a decade and a half later, in light of our current economic crisis, Taylor's words continue to ring true and perhaps more so, since many teachers are even less supported now— without travel funds, professional development opportunities, research resources, and, in some cases, office space. Rhoades tells us that the solution to many contingent faculty problems lies in "enabling the positions of qualified contingent faculty members to be converted into tenure-eligible appointments (and part-time positions into full time)" (Rhoades 2008), but we realize the limitations of writing one's way out of a contingent position, particularly given the high teaching and service demands associated with these positions. McMahon and Green bluntly explain, "English departments in particular depend upon contingent faculty to teach writing, and the labor-intensive work of teaching four or five or six sections of first-year writing to 150 students or more each semester is not conducive to publication" (McMahon and Green 2008, 18).

How can we create a new vision of scholarly work that takes into account these realities and continues to energize and to foster growth among our best teachers? First, we must support initiatives that connect professional development with opportunities for scholarship both for tenured and tenure-track faculty as well as contingent teachers, workshops, and initiatives that focus on other alternate forms of publication; and offering teacher-scholars supportive communities in which they can share ideas, address the current questions in the field, and seek opportunities for collaboration. Second, we must expand our notions of who *can* and *should* join scholarly discussions in light of who is doing much of the teaching in rhetoric and composition. Although collections such as Gary A. Olson's (2002) *Rhetoric and Composition as Intellectual Work* offer professionals in Rhetoric and Composition a theoretical treatise on work already taking place in the field, notably absent in these conversations on the teaching of writing are voices from the two-year college, and, more important we argue, the voices of contingent faculty across institutions. Third, we must illustrate how scholarship can be tied to the work that we are already doing, work that allows all teachers to actively fulfill the vision of the Boyer model and that helps them to see scholarship in genres beyond books or journal articles alone. Although existing scholarship offers practical strategies on how to write articles, conference presentations, dissertations, books, and even cover letters, guiding novice teacher-scholars on precisely how these ideas come to fruition gets little attention. Right or wrong, publishing still offers a viable means for advancement—even in the current employment climate—but that work cannot be done by contingent faculty working in isolation.

> I love the validation of seeing my words on the printed page, but as a full-time instructor and part-time graduate student publishing quality work is a Sisyphean task. I'll get fired up about a hot topic in a class, research it to death, collect all of the data I need, and then the push to synthesize my ideas evaporates into the daily grind of teaching, grading, and class work. I have found great success with scheduling a writing session with a mentor. If I set a regular date to meet with someone I hold in high esteem for their professional skills and position, I will never show up empty-handed. For example, I asked my master's program director to work on an article with me. We meet every week at Panera Bread. He walks me through the steps of crafting quality work but more important holds me accountable for producing the actual writing. Much like meeting with a therapist you are paying a lot of money to solve your problems, meeting with my mentor obligates me to work hard and to write. His time is valuable. My relationship with him is valuable. I don't want to screw it up!
>
> Mary Helen Ramming, Georgia Perimeter College

ESTABLISHING A COMMUNITY OF SCHOLARS

Some of our most rewarding teaching and learning experiences as academics have come from mentoring relationships and from the professional development opportunities in which we have taken part both as participants and leaders. These occasions to share our best practices, discuss teaching challenges, and engage in discussions that blend theory and practice can foster connections with colleagues and set the stage for intellectual inquiry. While support does exist on some campuses for contingent faculty, Writing Program Administrators and campus Centers for Teaching Excellence are generally the most important resources for organizing these initiatives. In the following sections, we draw from scholarship on mentoring and professional development and from our own experiences to offer examples of sustainable models of scholarship that are both ethical and allow contingent faculty to publicize reflective pedagogical practice.

Writing Program Administrators (WPAs) as Facilitators

Given the number of contingent faculty who continue to teach most first-year writing courses, it is WPAs who most often recognize the extent to which many contingent faculty are unsupported and even discouraged from participating in research and creative activity and who can benefit from opportunities to connect with colleagues and build networks of support. Although it was 1995 when Kristine Hansen wrote about the continued exploitation of first-year writing faculty (as many others have), her concerns regarding the number of teachers hired on part-time contracts in English and writing programs as well as the need for professional development opportunities remain significant today. In the place of job security and sustained support for continued education and scholarship, the initiatives we offer below allow writing program administrators and directors of general education programs an opportunity to connect all teachers to the program in significant ways and to acknowledge the expertise that participants bring to the table, expertise that is worth sharing and developing. Ellen Strenski suggests, for example, that opportunities for professional development facilitated by the WPA can help to make part-time teachers more valuable to the department and more marketable for other positions, highlighting unique experience and innovative pedagogy (Strenski 1995, 97). Contrary to the common belief that development initiatives should consist of training alone, they should instead become "opportunit[ies] for reciprocal exchange, learning, and knowledge production" (Willard-Traub 2008, 434) and should be faculty-driven and -organized, allowing the WPA to act as a promoter for "grassroots" efforts to create a more meaningful experience for willing participants (Carpenter 2002, 160–61).

Ideally, this kind of professional development should "avoid devaluing lore" and should allow both experienced and novice teachers to share and to learn side-by-side (Hansen 1995, 32). In this way, "WPAs . . . work to raise the status of part-time faculty by valuing what they know and creating opportunities for them to publicly share their knowledge," and, in turn, create an ongoing cycle of training and professional development without requiring large budgets that typically are unavailable for contingent faculty (Hansen 1995, 34). While these strategies may be supported by institutional grants, many of the initiatives discussed within this chapter are particularly useful to untenured WPAs with few resources to facilitate professional development opportunities for their staffs. Although the WPA may not have the resources—or authority if untenured—to call for immediate improvement of the status of contingent faculty in their programs, these initiatives can help to establish connections and collegiality and validate the work of all who teach in a program regardless of faculty status.

In some cases, initiatives may constitute a form of traditional mentoring between new and experienced teachers intended to share best practices for the classroom. For example, the WPA may institute weekly mentoring events sponsored primarily by contingent faculty that include a call for proposals and the submission of abstracts for workshops and presentations by interested faculty. Presentations may address best practices for peer response, strategies for promoting small and large group discussion, use of non-fiction texts in the writing classroom, and other topics specifically suited to the program goals and outcomes. These presentation proposals then can be vetted by a small committee, perhaps even returned for revision and resubmission, and selected submissions can be slated for presentation advertised to the department at large. The goal of this kind of initiative is twofold: (1) to help contingent faculty learn the ropes of submitting their work for publication and methods for presenting their research/best practices to an interested audience, and (2) to create a scholarly environment for composition faculty to exchange ideas. In addition to the collective benefit for the program, individual presenters also can list these workshops on their CVs, and these less formal presentations certainly can serve as fodder and preparation for more formal conference presentations. This opportunity to make teaching public not only works to validate the presenters' experience and contribution to the program, but also allows them to engage in scholarly activity without additional funding. Again, with the increase in contingent and teaching-focused appointments across campuses, these presentations allow new teachers to benefit from the expertise of experienced faculty and help to foster community within the program.

MODELS OF PROFESSIONAL DEVELOPMENT AND SCHOLARSHIP

In considering both the pressure to engage in scholarly activity and the impact of shrinking budgets and heavier course loads, we offer the following examples of initiatives that connect professional development with opportunities for scholarship aimed at tenure-track faculty as well as contingent teachers. We argue that these initiatives should promote collaboration and mutual growth, and should offer both support for teaching and an arena for scholarly work.

Workshops

Considering the number of contingent faculty teaching first-year writing and general education courses at many colleges and universities, emerging literacies and digital media often make ideal topics for professional development. Networked—or computer-supported—classrooms and fully online learning are becoming the standard on many college campuses, and those teachers who are comfortable with and versed in using technology in the classroom certainly make themselves more marketable and may create for themselves teaching opportunities that require fewer visits to multiple campuses on which they teach. Furthermore, contingent faculty who are experienced in using technology in pedagogically effective ways become important resources on whom WPAs and department chairs may call to train others. In departments fortunate enough to have a wealth of technology resources such as computer classrooms for writing courses, teacher technology stations, digital cameras, camcorders, digital voice recorders, etc., contingent faculty typically do not have the time to experiment with these resources when they are already engaged in carrying heavy teaching loads. Participants in these kinds of workshops should be invited to explore strategies for using digital media in the classroom and provided the opportunity to *play* with the technology, receive hands-on training, and create assignments and class activities for a course taught during a future term. Ideally, this work should be supported by a modest stipend and/or lunch and snacks.

In an effort to allow contingent faculty to connect with colleagues within the department/program, these workshops can be open to tenured/tenure-track faculty in the department as well, likely serving as one of the few opportunities these teachers will have to share ideas with one another and to collaborate with colleagues whom they have never met. This kind of workshop can succeed in drawing contingent teachers into current and ongoing discussions in the field and allowing them to consider how theory blends with practical classroom application. Beyond a focus on technology, the workshops may address topics such as assessment, peer review, response to student writing, reading in the writing classroom, etc. and should be organized by faculty—both tenure-track and contingent—with the support of the WPA. Since these workshops are open to all who teach within the program, they succeed in bringing together faculty of various ranks and specializations and draw contingent faculty into sustained pedagogical discussions. Furthermore, contingent faculty who participate in these workshops are able to both improve their teaching and showcase their work. This opportunity to become an expert or go-to faculty member within the department has the potential to increase morale and prompt teachers to share their work in public venues.

Service as Intellectual Inquiry

In addition to organizing the more traditional writing program/first-year writing committee on which all writing teachers may serve, WPAs also may identify experienced teachers among contingent faculty to facilitate orientation for new hires or to offer best practices that can be documented in print (as a handbook) or as digital resources for all faculty. This work can be included on CVs and later used in support of performance reviews. Beyond distribution among faculty at the local university, digital resources may be published and made public online. Furthermore, contingent faculty—those who most often are teaching first-year writing courses—should be called upon to participate in assessment and program review and can strive to make this work public with other members of assessment teams. These findings and reflections become important not only for other members of home departments or institutions in determining what is taking place in a program, but also for others in the profession who are searching for models of effective program review. The guidelines and documents designed and collated by this kind of assessment committee not only become public as they are enforced by the department/college, but also may serve as the basis for presentations at professional conferences and the foundation for publications.

Writing Groups

Given that the book is still regarded as the standard for publication at many schools, it is no surprise that some institutions offer professional development opportunities and sustained support for faculty who are working on long-term projects. However, these kinds of workshops also can become more widely useful when focused on journal articles, conference presentations, and other forms of scholarship. Whether limited to members of one department or open to the campus community as a whole, the larger purpose for workshops and initiatives of this kind is to offer teacher-scholars supportive communities in which they can share and generate ideas, address current questions in the field, and seek opportunities for collaboration while working on drafts of their own work. Works in Progress (WIP) groups, where faculty exchange/critique articles and ideas fall under these categories. Faculty may meet one day a week, perhaps over lunch, to talk about teaching concerns and new composition scholarship, and beyond the increased sense of camaraderie among teachers who may rarely find opportunities to come together in this way, these sessions also may lead to the formation of conference panels and foster the drafting and revision of other forms of scholarship.

Furthermore, writing groups model, on a local level, initiatives by professional organizations to promote publication and professional development among contingent faculty. For example the Coalition of Women Scholars in the History of Rhetoric and Composition (CWSHRC) recently instituted a publication workshop that will meet at two national conferences—the Conference on College Composition and Communication and the FemRhet conference—and invites interested participants to submit drafts of works in progress prior to the conference dates and then brings together emerging scholars with published authors to discuss their work. The experienced writers are selected from a wide range of fields, including composition and administration, and while many contingent faculty do not have available resources to travel to national conferences, those in the vicinity of the region can attend relatively cheaply. This commitment to publishing and mentoring over a period of time and divided between two conferences has the potential to reach many contingent faculty.

> For the past five years I have facilitated a writing group for non-tenured faculty, including assistant professors and contract faculty. We meet every two weeks, twelve months a year. Approximately one week before each meeting two or three members of the group send drafts of their writing projects to the entire group. Before the meeting everyone reads the drafts and writes comments, questions, and line editing in the margins. During the meeting each member of the group asks questions and offers suggestions focused on content; other members of the group discuss each question and suggestion so that the writer has options for addressing them, including the option of ignoring a suggestion. We don't discuss line editing because the writer can see that when peers hand marked-up manuscript copies to the writer.
>
> The writing group has had several benefits. First, when writers know that their manuscripts will be discussed on a particular date, that has served to keep writers on task with their writing. Second, members of the writing group report that the feedback has helped them submit better quality manuscripts to journal and book editors. Third, because the group includes faculty from multiple disciplines, members have sometimes developed interdisciplinary research projects.
>
> Duane Roen, Arizona State University

Local Conferences

WPAs can also create opportunities for scholarly work through local, department or college sponsored conferences. For example, at Kennesaw State University, the WPA and members of the first-year writing program instituted precisely this kind of public event—a departmental conference—that allows all who teach in the writing program to share their expertise in a formal venue. According to Daniell, Davis, Stewart, and Taber:

We thought the professional framework of a conference—a deadline for a written proposal, formal papers, timed presentations, someone to chair the event, and time for a question-and-answer session – would distinguish this event from composition committee discussions, hallway conversations, and generic faculty development opportunities on campus. By reinventing the academic conference at our local institution, we eventually discovered that the event was pivotal in disturbing traditional faculty roles and fostering community within our program. (Daniell et al. 2008, 451)

Ideally, this kind of conference should bring together instructors of all ranks who teach a variety of courses yet do not always have the opportunity to share teaching strategies with one another. Not only will the conference value lore but it also offers contingent faculty another opportunity to connect with colleagues from across ranks and specializations and engage in "current academic conversations in [the] department and in [the] profession" (Daniell et al. 2008, 453). Similar to the workshops described above, conference themes may include research and first-year writing, teaching writing with technology, reading in the writing classroom, strategies for general education literature courses, and other topics that meet the specific needs and showcase the strengths of individual programs and departments.

Furthermore, since the conference is local, participants do not require travel funds and faculty simply can attend as audience members, contributing to discussions, benefitting from shared scholarly work, and offering support for their colleagues. Drawing from these scholarly discussions, presenters may take feedback that they receive during the conference and make revisions to their work that later may be presented in regional or national venues or submitted for publication. Conference organizers and participants also may explore the potential for publishing the conference proceedings (digitally, in print, or both) as well as inviting participants to develop a special issue of a teaching journal. "As a general rule . . . instructors who reflect on their own practice, who participate in dialogue about teaching, who write about their ideas, who present their ideas to real audiences will gain confidence in themselves and in their own abilities" (Daniell et al. 2008, 463), reminding us again, of the need to bring many voices into these ongoing pedagogical exchanges.

When I was a master's student at Wayne State University (WSU), I had intense curiosity regarding how conferences were run. Not surprisingly, I enthusiastically answered a faculty call to graduate students and contingent faculty to help co-coordinate the Youth Xchange (Y/X) conference, a nationally recognized, annual American Studies program undergraduate/graduate conference hosted at WSU. As coordinators, we held diverse positions within the English Department as graduate students, faculty, contingent faculty, and an undergraduate advisor. We also used the idea of "inclusiveness" to guide decisions we made about the Y/X conference, meaning that we valued perspectives from a range of university positions and educational institutions because they enriched our understandings of what it means to interpret "America"—a central goal of the conference, and of the American Studies program at WSU. This mindset yielded a conference theme that accommodated a variety of interests (ranging from how "American globalism" impacts the environment to how it impacts literary genres); many presentation style choices for presenters (from the traditional academic "reading" to multi-media presentations); and a myriad of ways for possible presenters to discover the conference (through local and national listservs, print and electronic flyers, and instructor presentations at regional institutions). Our means of designing the conference echoed the kinds of presentations we hoped to and did attract (such as explorations of battles on the local/global borderline). I have carried this mindset and associated strategies to my continued work on local and national conferences (in service-learning and in my field of Rhetoric and Writing).

Jessica Rivait, Michigan State University

SEEKING OUT COMMUNITIES

In *Writing for Scholarly Publication,* Anne Sigismund Huff offers a very personal overview of the writing and publication process drawn from her struggle to be published after completing her PhD. Returning often to conversation metaphors, Huff argues that professional fields are marked by ongoing dialogues in which we must participate. Essential to this process she explains is participation in a community of writers: "Your chances of getting advice will increase significantly if you can establish a continuing connection with a small set of people who will converse about your field of inquiry. . . and make an ongoing effort to read your attempts to participate in that community" (Huff 1999, 11, 12). Other scholars note that "working jointly with a colleague whose work complements one's own can create a relationship in which genuine peer teaching and learning can take place" (Hedgcock 2003, 119). For example, for the last fifteen years, the Coalition of Women Scholars in Rhetoric and Communication has hosted a Wednesday night discussion of contemporary issues in the field (presented by both experienced and emerging scholars) followed by a one-hour mentoring session at the national Conference on College Composition and Communication. The mentoring tables/discussions (now co-led by an experienced and newer scholar) address a wide range of topics of interest to faculty at various places in their careers, such as: writing program administration, managing home and work, writing the thesis/dissertation, writing conference abstracts and book proposals, putting together an edited collection, preparing for the job market, negotiating promotion, establishing mentoring programs at your institution, civic engagement, grant writing, applying to graduate school, etc.

Beyond formal conferences and initiatives sponsored by WPAs or national organizations, faculty can seek out mentorships or partnerships with colleagues, both those who have experience in scholarly publication and those with whom they share teaching interests. Often these collaborations occur among graduate students and faculty mentors as students begin to find their scholarly voices. Given that faculty across ranks are often engaged in teaching that overlaps in significant ways, these partnerships may very easily exist among contingent faculty and with tenured/tenure-track faculty who share teaching and research interests and who wish to engage in collaborative inquiry.

Faculty Learning Communities

Prompted by the success of student learning communities on many campuses, a growing number of colleges and universities are also applying this model—formally and informally—to faculty success as well. Generally organized at the department level, these Faculty Learning Communities (FLCs) identify as their primary goal the facilitation of conversations among faculty (across ranks) who rarely have opportunities to discuss their work. Typically, these colleagues will meet a few times over the course of a semester to discuss best practices and to share teaching strategies for a variety of courses; in some cases, members of these groups may even organize open house days during which they invite colleagues to visit their classrooms to see many of these teaching activities in action. Beyond prompting us to open the doors of our classrooms and fostering new connections, these informal communities allow colleagues to identify common teaching and research interests and to maintain a collaborative web of support.

In addition to informal groups in which participants may share best practices and project drafts and discuss current scholarship, over one hundred institutions have implemented formal FLC programs guided by the Ohio Learning Network (OLN) Learning Community Initiative (a project supported by grants from the Department of Education, FIPSE, and Ohio Board of Regents). According to the website for the initiative:

> A *faculty learning community* (FLC) is a group of trans-disciplinary faculty, graduate students and professional staff . . . 8 to 12 is the recommended size) engaging in an active, collaborative, yearlong program with a

curriculum about enhancing teaching and learning and with frequent seminars and activities that provide learning, development, transdisciplinarity, the scholarship of teaching and learning, and community building. (Cox 2009)

Often, faculty funding through campus centers for teaching excellence may provide support for more formal work of this kind. Similar to programs on other campuses, the Center for Excellence in Teaching and Learning (CETL) at Kennesaw State University, for example, offers a number of funding initiatives designed to "cultivat[e] an institutional culture that encourages, values, and rewards ongoing professional development that advances faculty effectiveness" (KSU 2009b). Among these is the Faculty Learning Communities Program (FLCP) "designed to bring together small groups of faculty (no more than six) who are interested in focusing on a particular teaching and learning initiative for some extended period of time (e.g., a full semester or an academic year). Faculty are encouraged to submit proposals to establish a Faculty Learning Community on a topic that advances excellence in teaching and learning at KSU. Topics might be something specifically related to a department or discipline or one that crosses disciplines and departments" (KSU 2009a).

These funded projects not only foster collaboration among faculty—often faculty across disciplines—but also provide up to $750 for supplies as well as travel funds of $750 for the coordinator(s) and $500 for each participant. For contingent faculty who typically are not provided with support for scholarship and professional development, this type of initiative makes scholarly activity more feasible and is one step toward publicizing effective teaching. This kind of initiative may be an ideal opportunity for faculty to explore the growing impact of online distance learning on their campuses while promoting collective inquiry among faculty.

CONCLUSION

While all of these initiatives are grounded in improving teaching, they also begin to expand our notions, mentioned earlier, of who *can* and *should* join scholarly discussions in light of who is doing much of the teaching on our campuses—particularly in rhetoric and composition. They offer opportunities to collaborate, to build communities, and to discover among colleagues webs of support that are sustainable and foster intellectual exchange. For administrators who are faced with shrinking budgets and an ever-growing need for excellent teachers, many of these initiatives provide opportunities for professional development and allow new teachers to learn from those colleagues who are already doing excellent work. Furthermore, these initiatives are in compliance with NCTE "Statement on the Status and Working Conditions of Contingent Faculty." Section 4 of this document, "Respect and Recognition," is particularly pertinent to establishing a community among contingent faculty. This section states that contingent faculty "should have access to most, if not all, of the resources and services that are available to tenure-line faculty, including mentoring programs, support of scholarly work, support for travel, and so on" ("Position Statement on the Status, 2010"). This section goes on to stipulate that contingent faculty members should have opportunities "to participate in professional development activities" ("Position Statement on the Status, 2010"). We certainly agree and hope that our practical ideas for creating community among contingent faculty will offer ways to put NCTE's ethical guidelines into practice.

REFERENCES

American Association of University Professors. 2009. "Contingent Faculty." *American Association of University Professors.* http://www.aaup.org/AAUP/issues/contingent/.

Bishop, Wendy. 1993. "Students' Stories and the Variable Gaze of Composition Research." In *Writing Ourselves into the Story: Unheard Voices from Composition Studies,* ed. Sheryl I. Fontaine and Susan Hunter, 197–214. Carbondale, IL: Southern Illinois UP.

Carpenter, William J. 2002. "Professional Development for Writing Program Staff." In *The Allyn and Bacon Sourcebook for Writing Program Administrators,* ed. Irene Ward and William J. Carpenter, 156–165. New York: Longman.

Casanave, Christine Pearson, and Stephanie Vandrick, eds. 2003. *Writing for Scholarly Publication: Behind the Scenes in Language Education.* Mahwah, NJ: Lawrence Earlbaum Associates.

Cox, Milton D. 2009. "What is a Faculty and Professional Learning Community?" *Website for Developing Faculty and Professional Learning Communities (FLCs): Communities of Practice in Higher Education.* http://www.units.muohio.edu/flc/whatis.php.

Dalton, Margaret Stieg. 2006. "A System Destabilized: Scholarly Books Today." *Journal of Scholarly Publishing* 37 (July): 251–69.

Daniell, Beth, Laura Davis, Linda Stewart, and Ellen Taber. 2008. "The In-House Conference: A Strategy for Disrupting Order and Shifting Identities." *Pedagogy* 8(3): 433–45.

Gebhardt, Richard C. 1997. "Scholarship and Teaching: Motives and Strategies for Writing Articles in Composition Studies." In *Publishing in Rhetoric and Composition,* ed. Gary Olson and Todd W. Taylor, 35–46. Albany, NY: SUNY Press.

Hansen, Kristine. 1995. "Face to Face with Part-Timers: Ethics and the Professionalization of Writing Faculties." In *Resituating Writing: Constructing and Administering Writing Programs,* ed. Joseph Janangelo and Kristine Hansen, 23–45. Portsmouth, NH: Heinemann.

Hedgcock, John. 2003. "Reflections on Coauthorship and the Professional Dialogue." In *Writing for Scholarly Publication: Behind the Scenes in Language Education,* ed. Christine

Pearson Casanave and Stephanie Vandrick, 113–127. Mahwah, NJ: Lawrence Earlbaum Associates.

Huff, Anne Sigismund. 1999. *Writing for Scholarly Publication.* Thousand Oaks, CA: Sage.

Kennesaw State University. 2009a. "Faculty Learning Communities." *CETL: Center for Excellence in Teaching and Learning.* http://cetl.kennesaw.edu/faculty-funding/faculty-learning-communities.

Kennesaw State University. 2009b. "Mission." *CETL: Center for Excellence in Teaching and Learning.* http://www.kennesaw.edu/cetl/aboutus/mission.html.

McMahon, Deirdre, and Ann Green. 2008. "Gender, Contingent Labor, and Writing Studies." *Academe Online* (November–December). http://www.jstor.org/stable/40253262.

Minter, Deborah, and Amy M. Goodburn. 2002. *Composition Pedagogy and the Scholarship of Teaching.* Portsmouth, NH: Boynton/Cook Heinemann.

Moxley, Joseph M. 1997. "If Not Now, When?" In *Writing and Publishing for Academic Authors.* 2nd ed., ed. Joseph M. Moxley and Todd Taylor, 3–18. Lanham, MD: Rowman and Littlefield.

Moxley, Joseph M., and Todd Taylor, eds. 1997. *Writing and Publishing for Academic Authors.* 2nd ed. Lanham, MD: Rowman and Littlefield.

Olson, Gary, and Todd W. Taylor. 1997. *Publishing in rhetoric and composition.* Albany, NY: SUNY Press.

Olson, Gary A, ed. 2002. *Rhetoric and composition as intellectual work.* Carbondale, IL: Southern Illinois UP.

"Position Statement on the Status and Working Conditions of Contingent Faculty." 2010. Developed by the College Section Steering Committee. National Council of Teachers of English. http://www.ncte.org/positions/statements/contingent_faculty.

"Report of the MLA Task Force on Evaluating Scholarship for Tenure and Promotion." 2007. *Profession* 63:9–71. http://www.mlajournals.org/loi/prof.

Rhoades, Gary. 2008. "The Centrality of Contingent Faculty to Academe's Future." *Academe Online* (November–December). http://www.jstor.org/stable/40253261.

Savage, William W., Jr. 2003. "Scribble, Scribble, Toil and Trouble: Forced Productivity in the Modern University." *Journal of Scholarly Publishing* 35 (1): 40–6. http://dx.doi.org/10.3138/jsp.35.1.40.

Strenski, Ellen. 1995. "Recruiting and Retraining Experienced Teachers: Balancing Game Plans in an Entrepreneurial Force-Field." In *Resituating Writing: Constructing and Administering Writing Programs,* ed. Joseph Janangelo and Kristine Hansen, 82–99. Portsmouth, NH: Heinemann.

The Boyer Commission on Educating Undergraduates in the Research University. 1998. "Reinventing Undergraduate Education: A Blueprint for America's Research Universities."

Willard-Traub, Margaret K. 2008. "Writing Program Administration and Faculty Professional Development: Which Faculty? What Development?" *Pedagogy* 8:433–45.

13
EXPERIENCING OURSELVES AS WRITERS
An Exploration of How Faculty Writers Move from Dispositions to Identities

William P. Banks and Kerri B. Flinchbaugh

In working with faculty writers over the last decade, we have found that many have sought out popular texts on "how to write" in order to increase their productivity or help them be "better" at writing. Texts like Elbow's famous *Writing Without Teachers* (1973) (and later *Writing with Power* [Elbow 1981]) continue to make the list of those texts that would-be writers turn to for help or inspiration, as do more recent favorites like Anne Lamott's *Bird by Bird* (1994) and Natalie Goldberg's (2005) *Writing Down the Bones*. When we read these texts, as well as many of the research-based texts discussed later in this chapter and throughout this book, we see accomplished writers talking to others whom they address as *fellow writers*. But if these folks saw themselves as writers, would they be turning to these books in the first place?

In the context of this collection, we might ask the question, "Do faculty really see themselves as writers?" Would seeing themselves as writers help them increase productivity? The work we have done with faculty—both teachers of writing intensive courses across the disciplines and faculty working on specific projects for publication—has suggested time and again that these faculty do not see themselves primarily as *writers* but as teachers/professors and researchers. Scholars may be intensely curious about the world and conduct any number of studies or experiments that grow from that curiosity and still not see themselves as writers. Teachers can read voraciously and share their learning with a room full of students or their colleagues and not see themselves as writers. For us, seeing oneself as a writer is a key element to being successful

DOI: 10.7330/9780874219029.c013

in planning, drafting, revising, editing, and publishing your research, to conquering the many stumbling blocks suggested in the research on faculty writers.

In this chapter, we will attempt to examine several texts that, while not incorrect or misguided in their inquiry or advice, tend to be written about/for a presumed subject—the writer—who may not exist in large numbers on our campuses. The University Writing Program at East Carolina University, following the ideas established in previous scholarship and writing guides, has attempted a number of projects with faculty in order to help them to be more productive writers and teachers of writing. Despite our best efforts in conducting workshops, projects, institutes, and interventions, we found that they seemed to have little impact with increasing faculty writing productivity—until we revised them to shift the focus toward helping faculty to identify as writers. Using the Professional Writers Program (PWP) and the Writing Across the Curriculum Academy (WAC Academy) as examples, we showcase how two specific interventions at our university have been revised in order to help faculty more effectively make a shift in their self-perceptions from "researchers who write" or "teachers who write" to "writer-researchers" and "writer-teachers." Ultimately, we argue against the idea that any single project or initiative can effect the types of change we value in faculty writer productivity.

BEYOND DISPOSITIONS: REFIGURING FACULTY ETHOS

In many of the texts used to encourage writers, we have seen a marked focus on observable dispositions (physical activities). Underlying these texts is the assumption that by embodying different behaviors, we may come to be something different as well. These sorts of dispositions are most readily apparent in the advice we've seen from writing gurus, some of which has been studied by Boice (1994; 1996). For example, Brande's (1934, 58) *Becoming a Writer* encourages readers to change their writing habits, for in doing so, "you will find yourself getting your results far more quickly and with less 'backwash.'" Another solution may be simply to get up early and start writing: "what you are actually doing is training yourself," writes Brande, "in the twilight zone between sleep and the full waking state, simply to *write*" (66). Elbow (1973, 3) encourages writers to "do freewriting exercises regularly. At least three times a week," but for those who are "serious about wanting to improve [their] writing," Elbow tells them, "the most useful thing [they] can do is to keep a freewriting diary" (9). Essential to these endeavors is to "start writing and keep writing" (25). Meanwhile, Lamott (1994, 16-17) encourages the writers in her workshops to give themselves "short assignments," to "write down as much as [they] can see through a one-inch picture frame." And, in perhaps one of our favorite visual metaphors for silencing those voices that stop our writing, Lamott suggests that we "close [our] eyes and get quiet for a minute, until the chatter starts up. Then isolate one of the voices and imagine the person speaking as a mouse. Pick it up by the tail and drop it into a mason jar. Then isolate another voice, pick it up by the tail, drop it in the jar. And so on" (27).

We hear these ideas and we enjoy them as writing teachers and faculty developers. In fact, in professional development events, we frequently quote from Elbow and Lamott, or provide copies of their texts in order to help reluctant or timid faculty to understand where their blocks may be coming from or what behaviors can help them move past the blocks. But we also recognize that the texts may resonate with us because we already think of ourselves as writers; in short, we see ourselves as the writers that Elbow and Lamott invoke in their language. And as writing teachers, we have found these texts useful because they buttress the identities we want student-writers to take on. Faculty writers, who come from a host of disciplines and often share stories of frustration with writing, seem different to us, which is why we have turned to scholars like Robert Boice in order to help us rethink our work with faculty in the professional development we offer.

Boice has listed several types of "interventions" in the work of faculty he understood as "procrastinators" or "blockers," interventions that share traits with the advice offered by Elbow and Lamott. In *Procrastination and Blocking: A Novel Practical Approach,* Boice (1996, 87-88) offers "ten fundamental rules of efficacy that proved most effective" at helping extreme procrastinators and blockers toward greater fluency. Some of those include

- *Waiting*—for Boice, "[w]aiting helps writers (and teachers) develop patience and direction for writing by tempering rushing."
- *Starting even if the writer isn't "ready"* as this "coaches writers in systematic ways of finding imagination and confidence."
- *Working in short regular bursts,* which is about "maintaining a regular habit of brief sessions."
- *Stopping* as a "means [of] halting in [a] timely fashion" so that the writer doesn't overdo it at a single sitting.

These and the other pieces of advice that he offers, are part of a larger problem that research demonstrates is common among blocked or procrastinating writers: a fear of letting go. Each of these interventions encourages writers to "let go," to allow for the process of writing to work itself out, for habits of mind and body to develop so that subsequent writing events are more productive and meaningful, less agonizing or frustrating. After all, faculty "who wait until they are ready and undistracted tend to do very little writing" (Boice 1990, 15). These are extremely useful suggestions/observations, and we often provide them to faculty and students alike, but in such contexts as one-and-done professional development events, they can appear to faculty as somewhat hollow or simply palliative. Like maxims, they sound good and true, but can be difficult to implement in one's own life. The faculty listen, but they don't *experience* these changes; in fact, they can't in the limited space of the one- to two-hour workshop. What was missing in our workshops and professional development events was the constitutive and reflective space that faculty needed to embody a new writerly *ethos*.

Our work with faculty writers in various contexts has encouraged us toward a different sort of intervention, one based not so much in dispositions as one based on a rhetorical refiguration of writerly identity. Specifically, grounded in work that rhetorical scholars have done on *ethos*, we see ways of rethinking "dispositions" in terms of identity formations and change. Likewise, we believe in being "up front" about this desire to shift identities: rather than engage faculty in activities intended to change their behaviors and identities and not make that clear, we see this as an opportunity to talk with faculty about why they do or do not see themselves as writers. While theories of identity and subjectivity remain complex and vexed, we think that *ethos* provides a space for valuing the complexity of identities and subjectivities available to contemporary faculty as well as a way for discussing our "selves" such that faculty can more easily see and experience some of the choices available to them. Such a shift moves faculty from hearing/reading about successful writers and writing strategies toward an embodiment of those ideas, an experiential method for effective change.

One reason we do not use the discourse of identity is that we do not want to be stuck—even we the writers of this piece, who see ourselves as writers—as thinking in terms of fixity or exclusion, which is part of the baggage that term brings with it. Instead, consider the language that Elbow and Sorcinelli (2006, 19) use to describe the faculty that they invite to their Writing Place: "Professors write things. If they don't write things, they don't get to be professors. Yet few professors experience themselves as 'writers.'" Experience themselves—not "are" writers, but "experience themselves" as writers. This subtle but meaningful distinction aligns with our own thinking: college faculty *are* writers (the action)—that's unavoidable. From syllabi to letters of recommendation to exams or reports, even those faculty who are not actively publishing scholarship in refereed journals are still involved with writing. Yet that fact does not necessarily make faculty more prolific as publishing writers. One problem with identity discourses, of course, is that they function based on categorical fixity, in this case the either/or-ness that is bound up in our cultural imagination with the idea of the writer. Brodkey (1996, 59) notes that we often carry around an image of the writer like the one even she, an accomplished scholar and writer, is vexed by "when I picture writing, I often see a solitary writer alone in a cold garret working into the small hours of the morning by the thin light of a candle. It seems a curious image to conjure, for I am absent from this scene in which the writer is an Author and the writing is Literature."

Tellingly, it does not matter that Brodkey herself is excluded from such a romantic image, as are most faculty writers, writers whose "day jobs" are usually more about instruction, committee work, and research/data gathering than pondering deep thoughts in a picturesque tower. Excluded or not, we can carry that image with us. If only we had more time, more uninterrupted time, fewer distractions—then we, too, could be a writer. This image of the writer, and its persistence, hurts those writers who cannot identify in such a way, operating as J. K. Rowling's (1997, 213) fictional Mirror of Erised: it shows us an image we want to see rather than one that actually exists, and as Dumbledore tells Harry Potter, people "have wasted away before it . . . not knowing if what it shows is real or even possible."

Ethos provides a language and theory for disrupting simple identity categories with faculty and helping them to think of how we "experience" or "perform" particular selves at particular moments for particular outcomes. In short, *ethos* is a rhetorical self, a self we choose based on current exigencies. Typically, when writing and rhetoric teachers think about *ethos*, they see it as the presentation of self in the text, the textual evidence of "good character" (*arête*), "good sense" (*phronesis*), and "good will" (*eunoia*) (Kinneavy and Warshauer 1984, 171–190). Writers establish these traits in academic discourse through how they handle the history of a topic, how they treat their source materials, how they create bridges between what the readers know and what the writers know, how they use appropriate language, etc. But, historically, *ethos* has also had other connotations, growing out of a tradition that links thought/self with speech/action. For classical rhetors, it wasn't simply that one put on a mask (persona) or pretended, as an actor might, but that in such performances, the doer might also experience a shift in self-perception.

Swearingen (1984, 115), for example, argues that our current concept of *ethos* as primarily interior demonstrates a tragic misreading of the classical concept: our "modern concept of *ethos*, to the extent that it emphasizes candid self-expression, is a post-Romantic paradigm of an inward-looking, reflective self . . . a derivative of the Cartesian subject." Similarly, by bringing psychoanalytic theories to rhetoric, Alcorn (1984, 5) has suggested that *selves* are "an effect of learning": our "selves do not emerge as they choose to do things with rhetoric," but instead they "are the effects of rhetoric, a sort of epiphenomena constituted by an interplay of social, political, and linguistic forces. There is no inner entity, the self, that chooses its character. Instead, the self reflects the particular character of larger social forces that determine its nature and movement."

If we understand *ethos* as the ability of the individual to "put on" certain kinds of self, or certain identities, at certain times, and for certain effects, while simultaneously recognizing that those "put ons" also impact how these individuals come to understand themselves, then we can begin to think of *ethos* as a productive lens for helping faculty to disrupt certain debilitating notions of the writer that function in our collective imaginations. Like the doctor at our medical school who, despite having published over three hundred articles and chapters in scholarly journals and books, still thinks of himself as a "bad writer," many faculty persist in the notion that they are not writers (which seems always to imply "good writers"); this construct prevents them from thinking of their writing in positive and empowering ways. In the professional development projects that we have developed at our university, we have wanted to find ways to help faculty "come to experience themselves" as writers. Rather than simply *being* a writer or *not being* a writer, faculty in these projects are approached in ways that encourage them to adopt "writer" as one of their *ethoi*, or roles, or identities (Castells 1996, 6). In their research on programs similar to the ones we discuss below, Grant and Knowles (2000, 8) have found the same need as we, to move faculty toward embracing a sense of self as writers:

> This other struggle has to do with the kinds of imaginative spaces women can find for themselves in their subject positions as academics. More than simply a talent or caprice of the individual, imagining is understood here to be a socially constructed capacity to *be*, a form of subjectivity which hails us and offers us a way to act. To be able to imagine ourselves as a writer (in our mind's eye), and to find pleasure in and attachment to being this writer, is crucial to "be(com)ing" a writer. Marking the word in this way underscores the potentially transformative relationship between what we do and how we understand ourselves.

As faculty begin to adopt this *ethos*, they make the move from researchers or teachers who have to write (to get jobs, gain promotion and/or tenure, secure external grants, etc.) toward writer-researchers and writer-teachers, and perhaps, eventually, to faculty who can embrace themselves as writers.

PROFESSIONAL WRITING PROGRAM

More than a decade ago, the Brody School of Medicine's Academic and Faculty Development Program and East Carolina University's Writing Program collaborated to develop a project for offering discipline-specific writing and publication support, faculty development, and space to discuss writing. We began this program because we realized, despite the compelling reasons to publish the medical research being conducted, publication outputs at the university were only around 25 percent. Although innovations in research and education in schools of medicine and the venues from which they can be disseminated are consistently increasing, not submitting these innovations for publication is more commonplace than one may expect (Simpson, McLaughlin, and Schiedermayer 2000, 62). Many good ideas are simply not being shared. Common obstacles for writing and publication include writing-related anxiety (Lee and Boud 2003, 187), a lack of confidence about writing for scholarly publication (Berger 1990, 69), a lack of time and momentum (Boice and Jones 1984, 568), or trouble selecting a topic of wide appeal (Steinert et al. 2008, 281). Scholarly writing, however, is a critical skill for doctors in academic medicine. While change is constant in the way physicians practice medicine, teach classes, and engage in research, the written word remains the primary mode for communicating that research to others, a reality that affects the partnership between Brody School of Medicine and the University Writing Program.

In order to support writing in the health sciences, Brody started a series of medical writing workshops run by the Director of the University Writing Program, who was also a tenured faculty member of the English Department. Likewise, the UWP provided a medical writing consultant to work one-on-one with faculty that evolved into what is now the Professional Writing Program (PWP). Much like Elbow and Sorcinelli (2006), we quickly shifted from simply offering workshops to offering space, but in this case, the space was primarily an opportunity for faculty with a project to work with a highly-trained writing consultant. Many writers, especially academics early in their writing careers, lack confidence in their ability and find professional support and encouragement to be helpful (Baldwin and Chandler 2002, 9). The PWP is open to any faculty members engaged in research and writing at any stage of the writing process, meeting with them to discuss specific projects with the goal of not only improving that piece of writing but also improving the writer's overall skills.

During writing consultations, writers engage in conversation about their processes, strengths, weaknesses, and experiences with writing and publication. Grounded in research on writing, the consultant emphasizes the importance of equal and interactive discourse, the awareness that knowledge is a result of such discourse, and the notion that writers gain agency and voice by negotiating a "middle space" between their own experience and the expectations of the discourse community (Wallace and Ewald 2000, 87). We work with writers to assist them in navigating through the process of moving from research to writing, writing to revision, and revision to publication, providing methods to make what is "messy" in our minds "neat" in our writing (Elbow 2000, 87). One goal of this "middle space," of course, is to bring out the self-as-writer so that it merges with the self-as-researcher and the self-as-teacher that tend to dominate faculty self-perceptions (Alcorn 1984, 5). Because just as many unproductive or beginning academics experience a disconnect between their image of writing and accomplishing their writing goals or tasks, bridging that gap helps facilitate productivity (Eodice and Cramer 2001, 118).

Since 2007, the PWP has conducted over 240 writing consultations with individual writers. During the 2010–2011 academic year, the writing consultant held eighty-nine writing consultations. Forty-five of the consultations involved articles for professional journals while five were grant proposals. The remainder consisted of abstracts, book chapters, case studies, article proposals, or resumes. In a recent survey of these writers, we found that 93 percent of those who had writing consultations with the PWP had succeeded in their publication efforts. The remaining 7 percent were still waiting for a reply from the journal, leaving no fruitless publication efforts. In a separate satisfaction survey, writers refer to the PWP as "an excellent and valuable program" and "a valuable resource," citing the appreciation of "palatable suggestions."

Given this program's youth, it's hard to make large claims about its success in helping the faculty to rethink their senses of self-as-writers. However, early response is quite positive: of those faculty who have worked with the writing consultant more than once, there has been a marked change in how they approach the consultation sessions, with the faculty writers taking a more active part in the conversation, coming with larger chunks of text written, and exhibiting greater confidence in themselves as writers and researchers. Several writers, in fact, claim they have "turned a corner" in their thinking about themselves as writers and about writing more generally. One writer, for example, wrote very little for a couple of years and suffered multiple rejections on manuscripts, rejections that he saw as indicative of his inability to write. After his first article from the PWP was published, his confidence grew dramatically, and he approached his next couple of projects with greater investment. Now, this writer publishes one or two articles per year and relies less and less on the writing consultant.

WAC ACADEMY

The WAC Academy is a six-week institute held each spring; we invite ten instructors of writing intensive (WI) courses from across the university to meet once a week to discuss topics related to writing instruction, share writing-related teaching strategies they have used successfully in helping their students become better writers and thinkers, and collaborate on demonstrations of inquiry-based projects involving writing. The academy's new slogan "Writers Teaching Writing" is a reflection of the transformative method of professional development that the academy strives to achieve.

Modeled on the National Writing Project's Summer Institute, the WAC Academy encourages participants to gain a better understanding of writing processes, assessment issues, teaching methods, and new literacy technologies. Through its activities, readings, writings, and reflections, participants develop more effective writing curricula and assignments to take into their classroom, improving students' writing abilities by improving their own teaching of writing. The Academy also aims to expand the role of WI course instructors within the university by providing opportunities beyond the Academy for its participants to provide professional development programs to other WI instructors. We want our "graduates" to consider themselves a WAC resource within their departments and disciplines. We attempt to structure the Academy to foster innovation in teaching strategies, promote practice in writing skills and processes, and enable the sharing of knowledge and skills gained.

Each Academy meeting begins and ends with time for a focused free-write on a topic related to the week's discussion that participants keep in daybooks (Brannon et al. 2008). Daybooks also become invaluable as spaces for faculty to respond to readings, reflect on activities, sketch, doodle, even collect and archive handouts from the other participants. One activity we began using to encourage faculty to reflect on their writer selves and evoke an image of their mental model of self-as-writer also engages their artistic selves: draw your writing process. Writers are asked to consider the last formal writing project they worked on—an article, grant, syllabus, or research proposal—something that required multiple drafts. Individually, they determine the steps that went into writing the finished product, each tool, collaboration, experiment, or reading. The steps may be linear or recursive, may spiral or meander, or follow some other pattern entirely. Then, using the art supplies provided, the faculty create a visual representation of their writing processes.

Processes vary, often demonstrating through metaphor how writers, writing, and discipline interconnect. Some have represented themselves as a chef in a kitchen, baking composition pie. Others have been cross-sections of a cell—nucleus, cytoplasm, and membrane—deconstructing and then coming back together to evolve into a species. Some are geometric shapes that progress in a straight line while others are a frantic funnel. But among all the stick figures, Ferris wheels, bulls' eyes, arrows, music notes, question marks, and gold stars is the resemblance of what happens in each of us from the time we are tasked with a writing project until we are finished. And these drawings are the starting points for our conversations about who we are as writers. In pairs or as a whole group, we discuss the pieces that compose our processes, how our processes compare, the nature of process depending on genre, context, and exigency, and what our processes say about ourselves as writers and thinkers. Our drawings are an opportunity for us to reflect on the social and psychological influences that affect our writing lives—the obstacles, motivators, and rituals—and in some beginning ways, we come to see ourselves as we are, as a member of a community of academic writers (Dunn 2001; Geller 2005, 5–24). Surrounded by others who are actively researching, writing, and learning, we are encouraged to see ourselves as writers who are also researching, teaching, learning, and contributing. Once faculty are able to identify this part of themselves in this group, their experience may be similar to that of Grant and Knowles (2000, 16), who "found the experience [of the faculty writing group] resonated beyond itself, so that when we sat alone later to write there was still sometimes a sense of being with the group." They also underscore the idea that "writer" is an *ethos* we choose and refigure depending on context and exigency.

Activities like drawing our writing processes are just one aspect of the academy as the bulk of each week is spent engaging in the participants' inquiry presentations and in discussing and writing about research and scholarship on writing across the curriculum. Inquiry presentations provide an important space for discussion and exploration of a writing issue, writing idea, or writing activity participants have done or are considering doing with their students. We encourage them to use this time to get feedback from their colleagues, examine the inquiry from different points of view, harvest ideas for this activity or others, and share their own thoughts. Likewise, the other faculty serve as respondents, which offers them space to write, reflect on, and discuss different aspects of teaching writing. The WAC Academy provides an opportunity for faculty to push out from their different disciplinary mindsets and see how writing functions across disciplines. Each meeting closes with time to write and reflect on the meeting and explore any questions that may linger or be emerging in the writer's mind with another focused freewrite. With each focused freewrite, we work to build our "freewrite muscles" (Elbow and Sorcinelli 2006, 21), muscles that can assist us best at times when we are stuck or confused, and ones that let us exercise the voice that is unique to us. As Boice (1990, 21) has noted, writers who have opportunities to understand and practice writing "build the confidence to face writing problems as understandable, manageable problems."

In order to encourage the participants to "experience themselves as writers," we also ask them to take an aspect of what they've learned, connect it to their own classroom practice, and write an article for publication either in our own WAC Newsletter or another venue. We encourage faculty at our institution to share their insights about teaching writing in their disciplines in journals that value such contributions, journals such as *Across the Disciplines*; *International Journal of Critical Pedagogy*; *Research in Higher Education*; *Pedagogy, Culture, and Society*; or *Radical Teacher*. We offer our assistance and support at any point in the process. With these pieces of writing, and based on what we've learned about faculty writers in the PWP, we hope faculty will see their writing intensive courses and their teaching as spaces for making knowledge, and we hope they will come to see the WAC Newsletter as a space for sharing that knowledge with their colleagues. For faculty who have not seen pedagogical inquiry as a professional option, this alone opens doors for them as writers. Again and again, we work with faculty who have been conditioned not to see pedagogical inquiry as research or scholarship, which seems truly problematic for faculty writers; if we want them to see *writer* as part of their identities, we should not so quickly close off inquiry around and writing about what often makes up the largest portion of our work: teaching. With the WAC Academy, we encourage faculty to invest in sharing their disciplinary and pedagogical knowledge with audiences they may not have considered writing to before (e.g., graduate students who are just starting out, early-career faculty), as well as faculty like themselves (e.g., those interested in teaching and learning and writing). As we point out in the Academy, we all struggle to be effective teachers: we need more discourse and discussion, not less.

While the WAC Academy focuses primarily on how faculty across the disciplines can more effectively teach writing intensive courses, rather than on how faculty can become stronger writers, the faculty who have participated have helped us to see the obstacles that often stand between faculty and productive writing habits, obstacles that come through in how they teach and understand writing. Faculty routinely share their own "rigid rules" for writing—for themselves and for their students—as well as the "inflexible plans" they have adopted over the years, strategies that have led to writer's block and apprehension (Rose 1980; Daly 1985; Daly and Miller 1975). Through the WAC Academy, we have been able to get these on the table, demonstrate that they are not as idiosyncratic as writers might think, and find methods for overcoming them. By focusing initially on students and teaching, the faculty have found ways to approach their own anxieties about writing. This refiguring of faculty perceptions of student writers, coupled with their experiences in the WAC Academy, provides the foundation for individual transformations; working together, we enjoy time, space, and a supportive and engaged cohort of peers to accomplish this work.

REVISING THE PROGRAMS

While much of our focus in the WAC Academy and the PWP involves providing time and space for writers to make connections and attempt shifts in frames of mind, we wonder if we have been making enough deliberate attempts to identify how and in what ways these times/spaces are being used by the writers and ourselves? A useful frame for identifying and discussing a possible tension that exists in both programs is offered by Geller (2005, 8). Much of our day, Geller points out, is measured in fungible time: calendars, hours, deadlines, to-do lists, and other units of temporal measurement. The tension arises when these units prevent our accessing epochal time, during which it is not a clock that defines the time but rather events and individual or social rhythms.. Fungible time, Geller notes, could be explained as, "Let's have lunch tomorrow at noon. That is my lunch hour," while epochal time would be eating when we get hungry and stopping when we are full or done eating. Within our contexts of institutional time, it is often difficult to access the epochal time that can be so valuable for not only productive writing but also for achieving the shift to writer-teacher or writer-researcher. If we successfully encourage a shift in our concerns away from the demands and duties that are a large portion of faculty life to the "fluidity and possibility of epochal time," (9) we can create a space for writers to reflect, write, connect, relate, learn, and, we hope, see themselves and each other in new ways. But how often do we make this happen within the PWP and WAC Academy? And what are some strategies that can help faculty and ourselves accept the harness and utilize this epochal time in and outside of the programs we offer?

For example, while one intention of our use of daybooks in the WAC Academy was to encourage writers to embrace epochal time in writing, reflecting, and eventually coding[1] (Brannon et al. 2008; Finley 2010), we feel it failed to function in this manner as well as it could. Daybooks, a staple in our yearly Tar River Writing Project's Summer Institute (http://www.trwp.org), provide a space for engaging epochal time in writing, which is one reason we have tried to use them in the WAC Academy. We have noticed SI participants quickly discover these possibilities in the space their daybooks provide—writing, drawing, reflecting, exploring, and discovering in them during the daylong meetings and also during their free time before and after meetings and on the weekends. But while the Summer Institute is an everyday event meeting for eight hours a day for four weeks, the WAC Academy meets only once a week for two or three hours. These time differences make the possibilities of daybook use more difficult to sustain. While participants tend to use them in our weekly meetings, they are rarely used outside of that space, in part, we believe, because they do not have sustained practice with them. While the WAC Academy carves out a lot of space in the semester, the use of the daybook (or the failure really to use them) has shown us that the Academy still does not provide the type of epochal space it needs for the faculty to make use of daybooks themselves, making them less likely to make use of the books in their classes.

Likewise, despite being built around notions of mutuality and process, we know that the one-to-one sessions typical of the PWP are invariably over-determined by fungible time (e.g., publishing and tenure deadlines). They also run the risk of asymmetry, because the writer may

---

1. Coding reflects an inquiry orientation for reviewing daybooks in order to see themes emerge while the writer engages the past and the present with an eye toward what might be happening.

come to see the consultant as a "subject supposed to know" (Brooks 1991; Trimbur 1987), projecting onto the consultant more knowledge about writing than is appropriate if, as in this case, we want the faculty member to experience him/herself as a writer. It takes the faculty in the PWP a long time to invest in the writing consultant enough to trust that person; too often, the faculty member is just looking for someone to "fix" things. Since the projects being worked on tend to emerge as deadline-based writing events, the faculty writers we have worked with sometimes lack an investment in reseeing themselves or their writerly *ethoi.* Rather, they work to finish a project quickly and move on to something else. There are few writers we have seen consistently throughout the years or who have continued to seek the help of the PWP consultants after the immediate project has finished, which may also suggest that the faculty writer used this successful experience to establish a foundational identity as a writer, one who may not need a "consultation" to write. At it's worst, when the faculty writer is least invested in the process, we have seen resistance based on the fact that the consultant is not from the discipline and thus is perceived as having nothing constructive to say beyond remarks about editing and formatting.

In some ways, it is our work with groups of faculty in the WAC Academy that has shown us how problematic these issues in the PWP can be. The academy participants, working together as a group, move quickly beyond issues related to their disciplinary silos and varying levels of experience with teaching writing, finding the various types of knowledge in the room intensely helpful. These faculty are not motivated by an external deadline of any sort, and know that they have six weeks to work together to figure out new ways for teaching writing in their own courses. Their success or failure will, in many ways, be their own; there are no chairs or senior faculty in the institute who sit in positions to evaluate their work.[2] Where these faculty have tended to slow or falter, however, has been the final step: writing up their teaching for the WAC Newsletter or a pedagogical journal. In part, these faculty have lacked the immediacy of an external deadline for such a project, which the PWP faculty know all too well, or they have tended to see themselves primarily as teachers, not as writer-teachers who can and should share their

---

2. We try not to have multiple faculty from the same department, as well, because we don't want the faculty in the Academy to feel that they have to perform for the peers whom they have to work most closely with. Occasionally, we'll have a pair of faculty from the same department apply together; they see this as a way to support each other, in which case we worry less that they will serve as judgmental eyes that prevent each other from speaking and writing candidly about topics.

best practices with other teachers.

Both the PWP and the WAC Academy have worked well together for helping us to see faculty writers engaging with writing in different ways, ways that have shaped much of our thinking about how we want to revise both programs in order to support faculty as writers. Structurally, we are working to revise the PWP into a group-based, yearlong project with specialized writing support from the University Writing Program. While we do not plan to abandon completely the consultation sessions we offer faculty, we recognize that these do little to help with long-term fluency or to encourage faculty to resee themselves in relation to their writing. Instead, taking a note from the WAC Academy, we plan to build small, manageable writing groups that start each fall through an application-based process. We want to create a space, like the WAC Academy, where self-selection and a desire to work on projects encourages faculty writers to work together and disrupt some of the power-issues that we've found in a more tutor-based type of PWP. We have also begun to use National Writing Project–inspired "writing into the day" and "exit slips" in order to engage faculty writers metacognitively; faculty write to reflect on their writing, what they're learning about themselves as writers, and what they need to be more effective or productive writers.

Likewise, the WAC Academy, while focusing productively on helping teachers to teach writing in upper-division courses, has struggled to push faculty into seeing themselves as writers or to embrace writer as one of their identity markers. As with the PWP, we see the WAC Academy as needing more direct reflective writing and discussion meant to engage faculty in conversations about how their senses of self-as-writer and, hopefully, having an impact on how they teach writing to their students. In part, given the value our institution places on pedagogical scholarship and the scholarship of engagement, we see this move as one that faculty can invest in because the local rewards will be meaningful: pedagogical scholarship/writing counts in our university's economy of tenure, promotion, and reward.

Both the PWP and the WAC Academy have helped us to see faculty writers from different positions and in doing so, we've come to value the complexities inherent in any intervention intended to support faculty as writers and to envision more fully that "complex network of relationships" inherent in scholarly writing (Crosby 2003, 626). Simple dispositional shifts, while useful to the extent that they may produce immediate pieces of writing, do not help establish the sort of communities of writers that Grant and Knowles (2000, 15) have suggested is necessary in order to "overcome some of our deep resistances" and, ultimately, to move past some of the "pragmatic obstacles" that hamper productive writing. However, we believe that combining dispositions with reflection may lead to the sort of shifts in *ethos* that may help reluctant faculty to embrace reseeing themselves as writers-who-teach and writers-who-research. We also recognize that assessing this impact requires the sort of longitudinal study we're just now beginning in our program.

Ultimately, these shifts in self-perception and self-efficacy may translate into significant changes in behavior that can impact both institutional mission and the work of higher education. As we know, graduate school and the tenure process tend to work against the creation of a holistic person who can integrate teaching, research, and service effectively. Graduate students are consumed by the need to read and experiment, or to join successful faculty/research projects in apprenticeship positions. Likewise, new faculty worry about conducting and publishing the type of research that will impress tenure committees. In such a context, it's hard for teaching and service to gain any footing, which can be true even at small universities and liberal arts colleges with Research I aspirations. We believe that projects like WAC Academy encourage faculty to revise their ideas about "what counts" in the professional economies of higher education, not to supplant disciplinary research, but to see such inquiry as equally valid and needed. Such a shift can impact the departments in which these faculty work. While this sort of change is slow, we think it's needed, in large part because higher education should be more responsive to calls for improving instruction, not less. Our own institution prides itself on a mission of regional service and engagement; we think the WAC Academy and PWP encourage faculty to embrace this mission through the scholarship of engagement and the scholarship of teaching and learning (SOTL) (Boyer 1990).

The most important thing we have taken away from the WAC Academy and the PWP, as well as other work with faculty-writers, is that we cannot expect a "silver bullet" approach to be successful. We do not believe any single project, activity, or workshop can effect more productive faculty writers; the variables that lead to under-production, writer's block, and poor self-efficacy are simply too numerous and complex. By working to help faculty writers refigure their relationship to writing and by embracing that change as a programmatic goal, however, one that weaves through nearly all of our workshops, events, project, academies, and programs, we believe we have a better chance of meeting faculty writers where they are so that they can begin to experience themselves as writers in divergent contexts. For if writing is the meta-discipline, as Murphy et al. (1998, 31) has argued, we should engage writing and writers as frequently and flexibly as possible, taking each opportunity we have to help faculty *see* themselves as writers. Only through changing our programmatic and professional development culture can we hope to engage a broader range of faculty and to break down some of the myths about writer/writing that get in the way of faculty productivity.

REFERENCES

Alcorn, Marshall W. 1984. "Self-Structure as a Rhetorical Device: Modern Ethos and the Divisiveness of the Self." In *Ethos: New Essays in Rhetorical and Critical Theory*, ed. James S. Baumlin and Tita F. Baumlin, 3–35. Dallas: Southern Methodist University Press.

Baldwin, Claire, and Genevieve E. Chandler. Jan-Feb 2002. "Improving faculty publication output: the role of a writing coach." *Journal of Professional Nursing* 18 (1): 8–15. http://dx.doi.org/10.1053/jpnu.2002.30896. Medline:11859488.

Berger, Raymond M. 1990. "Getting Published: A Mentoring Program for Social Work Faculty." *Social Work* 35 (1): 69–71.

Boice, Robert. 1990. *Professors as Writers: Self-Help Guide to Productive Writing.* Stillwater, OK: New Forums Press.

Boice, Robert. 1994. *How Writers Journey to Comfort and Fluency: A Psychological Adventure.* Westport, CT: Praeger.

Boice, Robert. 1996. *Procrastination and Blocking: A Novel Practical Approach.* Westport, CT: Praeger.

Boice, Robert, and Ferdinand Jones. 1984. "Why Academicians Don't Write." *Journal of Higher Education* 55 (5): 567–82. http://dx.doi.org/10.2307/1981822.

Boyer E. L. 1990. *Scholarship Reconsidered: Priorities of the Professoriate.* Princeton, NJ: Carnegie Foundation for the Advancement of Teaching.

Brande, Dorothea. 1934. *Becoming a Writer.* New York: Harcourt, Brace and Company.

Brannon, Lilian, Sally Griffin, Karen Haag, Tony Iannone, Cynthia Urbanski, and Shana Woodward. 2008. *Thinking Out Loud on Paper: The Student Daybook as a Tool to Foster Learning.* Portsmouth, NH: Heinemann.

Brodkey, Linda. 1996. *Writing Permitted in Designated Areas Only.* Minneapolis: University of Minnesota Press.

Brooks, Jeff. 1991. "Minimalist Tutoring: Making the Student Do All the Work." *Writing Lab Newsletter* 15 (6): 1–4.

Castells, Manuel. 1996. *The Rise of the Network Society.* Oxford: Blackwell.

Crosby, Christina. 2003. "Writer's Block, Merit, and the Market: Working in the University of Excellence." *College English* 65 (6): 626–45. http://dx.doi.org/10.2307/3594274.

Daly, John A. 1985. "Writing Apprehension." In *When a Writer Can't Write: Studies in Writer's Block and Other Composing-Process Problems*, ed. Mike Rose, 43–83. New York: Guilford Press.

Daly, John A., and Michael Miller. 1975. "The Empirical Development of an Instrument of Writing Apprehension." *Research in the Teaching of English* 9:242–9.

Dunn, Patricia A. 2001. *Talking, Sketching, Moving: Multiple Literacies in the Teaching of Writing.* Portsmouth, NH: Boynton/Cook.

Elbow, Peter. 1973. *Writing without Teachers.* New York: Oxford.

Elbow, Peter. 1981. *Writing with Power: Techniques for Mastering the Writing Process.* New York: Oxford.

Elbow, Peter. 2000. *Everyone Can Write: Essays toward a Hopeful Theory of Writing and Teaching Writing.* New York: Oxford.

Elbow, Peter, and Mary Deane Sorcinelli. 2006. "The Faculty Writing Place: A Room of Our Own." *Change: The Magazine of Higher Learning* 38 (6): 17–22. http://dx.doi. org/10.3200/CHNG.38.6.17-22.

Eodice, Michele, and Sharon Cramer. 2001. "Write On! A Model for Enhancing Faculty Publication." *Journal of Faculty Development* 18 (4): 113–21.

Finley, Todd. 2010. "The Importance of Student Journals and How to Respond Effectively." *Edutopia*. Last modified August 1, 2010. http://www.edutopia.org/blog/ student-journals-efficient-teacher-responses.

Geller, Anne Ellen. 2005. "Tick-Tock, Next: Finding Epochal Time in the Writing Center." *Writing Center Journal* 25 (1): 5–24.

Goldberg, Natalie. 2005. *Writing down the Bones: Freeing the Writer Within*. Boston: Shambhala.

Grant, Barbara M., and Sally Knowles. 2000. "Flights of Imagination: Academic Women Be(com)ing Writers." *International Journal for Academic Development* 5 (1): 6–19. http:// dx.doi.org/10.1080/136014400410060.

Kinneavy, James L., and Susan C. Warshauer. 1984. "From Aristotle to Madison Avenue: Ethos and the Ethics of Argument." In *Ethos: New Essays in Rhetorical and Critical Theory*, ed. James S. Baumlin and Tita F. Baumlin, 171–190. Dallas: Southern Methodist University Press.

Lamott, Anne. 1994. *Bird by Bird*. New York: Anchor.

Lee, Alison, and David Boud. 2003. "Writing Groups, Change and Academic Identity: Research Development as Local Practice." *Studies in Higher Education* 28 (2): 187–200. http://dx.doi.org/10.1080/0307507032000058109.

Murphy, James J., James Berlin, Robert J. Connors, Sharon Crowley, Richard Leo Enos, Victor J. Vitanza, Susan C. Jarratt, Nan Johnson, and Jan Swearingen. 1988. "The Politics of Historiography." *Rhetoric Review* 7 (1): 5–49. http://dx.doi. org/10.1080/07350198809388839.

Rose, Mike. 1980. "Rigid Rules, Inflexible Plans, and the Stifling of Language: A Cognitivist Analysis of Writer's Block." *College Composition and Communication* 31 (4): 389–401. http://dx.doi.org/10.2307/356589.

Rowling, Joanne K. 1997. *Harry Potter and the Sorcerer's Stone*. New York: Scholastic.

Simpson, Deborah E., Chris McLaughlin, and David Schiedermayer. May 2000. "Writing 'blitzes' for medical educators." *Academic Medicine* 75 (5): 555. http://dx.doi. org/10.1097/00001888-200005000-00087. Medline:10824839.

Steinert, Yvonne, Peter J. McLeod, Stephen Liben, Linda Snell, Yvonne Steinert, Peter J. McLeod, Stephen Liben, and Linda Snell. 2008. "Writing for Publication in Medical Education: The Benefits of a Faculty Development Workshop and Peer Writing Group." *Medical Teacher* 30 (8): e280–85. http://dx.doi. org/10.1080/0142159080233720. Medline:18484455.

Swearingen, C. Jan. 1984. "Ethos: Imitation, Impersonation, and Voice." In *Ethos: New Essays in Rhetorical and Critical Theory*, ed. James S. Baumlin and Tita F. Baumlin, 115–148. Dallas: Southern Methodist University Press.

Trimbur, John. 1987. "Peer Tutoring: A Contradiction in Terms?" *Writing Center Journal* 7 (2): 21–8.

Wallace, David L., and Helen R. Ewald. 2000. *Mutuality in the Rhetoric and Composition Classroom*. Carbondale: Southern Illinois University.

14

IMAGINING COAUTHORSHIP AS PHASED COLLABORATION

William Duffy and John Pell

All writers will tell you that they write to connect; we simply add one more, very important connection to that process: the connection with each other.

—Kate Ronald and Hephzibah Roskelly

In a time of dwindling institutional budgets, the idea of academic departments and university programs using their limited resources to support faculty writing sounds like a luxury from a bygone era. As departments and programs try to do more with less, many faculty members are left to navigate the challenging terrain of writing and publication on their own. Yet most of us know that regardless of one's disciplinary field, writing is difficult work that often requires external motivations. While it is true that some universities offer workshops or sponsor writing retreats to provide the proverbial kick needed to start a writing project, these measures do not always alter the perceptions of faculty who believe writing is an activity that should be pursued alone. While it goes without saying that a successful academic career depends (at least in part) on the ability to work well in isolation, having regular access to and accountability from one's peers often helps to scaffold and invigorate a scholar's intrinsic motivations for writing.

Is it possible to provide the external motivation faculty writers often need to move forward with their scholarship while simultaneously providing support that enhances their confidence as writers? Moreover can this kind of provision be achieved with little, if any, formal institutional support?

As faculty writers ourselves, we have answered this question in the affirmative by engaging in the practice of collaborative writing,

DOI: 10.7330/9780874219029.c014

specifically what we call *phased collaboration*. Phased collaboration is the name we give to our orientation toward coauthorship and those practices of collaboration that serve both a utilitarian function (we get work done) and a conceptual function (we are encouraged to assess and improve our writing practices). Over time, we have come to recognize how phased collaboration allows us to discover ideas and compose texts that neither one of us could produce individually. The "could" in the previous sentence has nothing to do with individual ability, inborn talent, or old-fashioned effort; rather it signals the simple fact that one's vision is always partial, which is to say there is always a horizon of insight that limits what one person can see at any given time. In terms of writing, this horizon is manifested in our capacities to intervene in and enhance the ways we read, think, and compose—actions that for many academic writers (as well as for our students) sometimes get entrenched with routine and convention. But as the aphorism goes, two minds are better than one, and thus collaboration has and continues to influence the writing we undertake as full-time faculty who are expected to maintain active research agendas.

Now as faculty members of different departments, across the country from each other, collaboration offers a benefit that we never fully recognized when we had the luxury of walking into each other's offices as graduate students and teaching colleagues. Namely, collaboration provides us with an organic support structure that encourages us to pursue scholarship while honing our writing craft. Such a support structure emerges as a result of the unique experience collaborators share experimenting with the work of coauthorship. Specifically, the type of collaboration we are discussing is entered into voluntarily, with those whom we wish to partner. Thus the demands to produce are simultaneously the demands to honor a partnership, which is to say collaborative writing encourages authors to attend to their own writing in order to uphold their commitments to a partner.

The idea that collaboration helps support one's writing by introducing a relationship with another is seldom discussed; after all, there aren't many pocket guides for cowriters. Yet this is precisely what many novice collaborators require: ideas about how to conceptualize the work of coauthorship as a means of facilitating their shared development as academics. This is what we hope to offer here, a conceptual framework for imagining the work of coauthorship that encourages writers to experiment with writing that can genuinely be called collaborative. But as we will make clear below, there is no surefire model or step-by-step process for collaborative writing that can be served up as a blueprint for new coauthors to follow. Moreover for teachers and scholars who are genuinely curious about the possibilities of collaborative writing in their own scholarship, we imagine this kind of direct instruction is at best ingratiating and at worst condescending. With that said, our intention is to present phased collaboration not only as a viable method for text production—as a way to actually start and finish a writing project—but also as a critical intervention in the epistemological work of writing itself.

Critically pursued for its epistemological benefits, collaborative writing can result in texts greater than the sum of their individual parts. The reason for this is because the real value of collaborative writing is located in the reflexive work collaborators navigate when communicating with each other about not only what to write, but also how best to write it. Process and product emerge like sister skyscrapers impossible to divorce from view; where there is one there is the other.

To encourage faculty writers to experiment with collaborative writing and assume its risks, we offer the concept of phased collaboration as a recursive heuristic for conceptualizing the practical mechanics of collaborative writing itself. The value of phased collaboration is located in how it encourages coauthors to take advantage of one another's presence as a resource throughout the writing process. In the third section of this chapter we discuss phased collaboration in detail as well as offer advice for how to use it in practice. In the next section, however, we first want to distinguish between the concepts of coauthorship and collaborative writing in order to make clear that employing collaboration as a support mechanism for writers requires a conceptually rich and theoretically astute definition of collaboration capable of defending such a position.

WHAT DOES IT MEAN TO WRITE COLLABORATIVELY?

The purpose of this essay is to promote collaborative writing as a generative practice among teaching and research faculty. If it is not already clear, we have been careful about our use of the term "collaborative writing" in relationship to its partner concept, "coauthorship." While conventionally these terms are often used interchangeably to signal when more than one author contributes to the composition of a text, we think it is valuable to share how we have come to parse these terms since what we promote is the latter as a means for doing the former. In short, we believe that collaborative writing tends to enrich the experience of coauthorship.

Ever since Michel's Foucault's (1977) seminal essay "What is an Author?," scholars have concluded that the concept of authorship as a proprietary designation, one that denotes intellectual ownership, is a relatively modern invention. As legal scholar Martha Woodmansee explains, "The notion that the writer is a special participant in the production process—the only one worthy of attention—is of recent provenience. It is a by-product of the Romantic notion that significant writers break altogether with tradition to create something utterly new, unique—in a word, 'original'" (Woodmansee 1995, 16). As an extension of this poststructuralist critique, scholars working in feminist theory have recently promoted collaboration as a challenge to rigid definitions of individual agency. Patricia Sullivan notes how the university was "founded on epistemological assumptions that either denied or displaced the generative and creational roles of women." As a result, the standard practice in academic research "places the onus of invention, discovery, creativity, and originality on an individual knower who must somehow transcend the web of relationships—both intellectual and personal—that ground his or her work and give it significance and meaning" (Sullivan 1994, 20, 25). Jane Danielewicz and John McGowan explain that academic research is often characterized "as an individual possession and/or burden." As they put it, "All that is open to public view are the products: the written works, the lines on the *vita* and the annual report, the student evaluations" (Danielewicz and McGowan, 2005, 168). Taken together, these scholars promote coauthorship as a practice for enacting resistance to myths about the primacy of individual genius in the hierarchy of academic labor and its systems of punishment and reward.

But the politics of coauthorship continue to muddy the practice of collaboration as a legitimate method for text production in academia, especially in the humanities. Holly Laird notes that beginning in the 1980s, inquiry into coauthorship usually focused on methodology, "how did writers collaborate, and how could the investigator sort out their contributions (a query that turned the collaboration into a matter of two writers writing individually, one better than the other)" (Laird 2001, 347). Unfortunately not much has changed for academic coauthors who still must answer interrogations from tenure and promotion committees that wish to identify the individual contributions of collaborative writers.[1] In "Rhetoric, Feminism, and the Politics of Textual

---

1. It is our experience that most faculty writers can cite at least one personal anecdote about a friend or colleague (if not themselves) who was forced to negotiate the politics of collaboration before a professional committee of some type. Lunsford and Ede (1990) share narratives to this end in "Rhetoric in a New Key," and Yancey and Spooner (1998) discuss the challenge of assigning by-lines to collaborative work in "A Single Good Mind." Day and Eodice (2001) shape the first chapter of *(First Person)²*

Ownership," Andrea Lunsford evidences that feminists still have yet to dismantle the hierarchy of textual ownership that dictates the superiority of "radical individualism" in conceptions of authorship that permeate academic work, especially in the humanities (Lunsford 1999, 529). Lunsford poses a challenge to all academics, one rooted in revising the rhetoric of authorship itself. She says we must create "a contemporary grammar and vocabulary capable of recognizing—and re-valuing-rhetorical practices that until very recently have been defined, if not as writing 'crimes,' then certainly as suspiciously collaborative misdemeanors" (541). As academic cowriters ourselves, we believe part of this rhetorical re-visioning of collaboration requires bringing a nuanced understanding to the terms *coauthorship* and *collaborative writing*, not to privilege one over the other but to demonstrate the complexity of collaboration as a rhetorical practice.[2]

For us, coauthorship simply denotes when two or more writers claim ownership over the composition of a single text. In this way coauthorship is a neutral term, one that tells us only that multiple individuals have contributed to a text, not what is the configuration of those individuals in relationship to one another and to the writing that has been produced. As we all know, coauthorship occurs frequently both in and out of academia, and the degree to which individual coauthors contribute to a composition is always dependent on context. For this reason, it is impossible for coauthorship to mean the same thing from one instance to the next. The stigma that has historically been associated with coauthored scholarship, especially in the humanities, comes from the assumption that coauthored texts require less investment and less rigor—in short, less scholarship—than single-authored texts. Many coauthors will testify to the contrary, however, and for good reason. For example, in Kami Day and Michele Eodice's book-length study of academic coauthorship (which looks at coauthors from across the

---

around their experience as graduate students attempting to write a coauthored dissertation. For an interesting discussion about collaboration, feminism, and academic labor, see Evelyn Ashton-Jones and Dene Kay Thomas's (1990) interview with Mary Belenky in the journal *JAC* in which the latter argues why collaborative writing should count more than single-authored texts when it comes to tenure and promotion.

2. In writing studies scholarship, coauthorship and collaboration have been studied in contexts ranging from the first-year writing classroom to corporate environments. For book-length studies related to collaborative writing in practice, see Spear (1988); Ede and Lunsford (1990); Day and Eodice (2001). Two collections of essays related to the theory and practice of collaborative writing were published in the early 1990s, *New Visions in Collaborative Writing* (Forman 1992), and *Writing With* (Reagan, Fox, and Bleich 1994).

disciplines) many of the coauthors they interview testify that the relationship they foster with one another is what makes the writing process more enjoyable and effective. Indeed, successful coauthors who continue to write together usually do more than simply divvy up the parts of a writing project; they pursue acts of collaboration that enhance their engagement while producing a composition.

Consequently we suggest that successful coauthors often collaborate with one another. To use a term forwarded by Lisa Ede and Andrea Lunsford, they foster "dialogic" discourse that directs how they articulate ideas, something that gives their writing both a voice and point of view that is unique to the collaboration that produced it. For this reason, we call collaborative writing an inventive process and reflexive relationship through which two or more writers synthesize their individual perspectives to create a new, shared voice through which to compose texts.

While we believe this description reflects a fair assessment of our own collaborative writing practices and those of the coauthors we have studied, we want to present the idea of collaborative writing in a way that invites academic writers from a variety of backgrounds to adapt this approach to fit their own unique experiences and circumstances. We therefore have identified three basic qualities that inform the collaborative interaction effective coauthors foster with one another. While certainly not exhaustive, the following descriptions represent our initial contribution to developing a new rhetoric for collaborative writing, one that answers the call Lunsford puts forward; vocabulary coauthors can draw upon to name and thus shape their collaboration as it develops.

First, collaborative writers practice reflexive dialogue, that process through which one discourser uses his own ideas and observations to play off the ideas and observations of another discourser. Donna Qualley defines reflexivity as "the act of turning back to discover, examine, and critique one's claims and assumptions in response to an encounter with another idea, text, person, or culture." But is also involves "a commitment to both attending to what we believe and examining how we came to hold those beliefs *while we are engaged in trying to make sense of an other*" (Qualley 1997, 3, 5 emphasis in original). Used to inform the work of collaborative writing, Qualley's definition of reflexivity underscores how an individual writer must balance the perspective of another alongside her own. It also requires one to understand how her own habits, strengths, and patterns as a writer can be brought into a productive relationship with the habits, strengths, and patterns of another writer. As Day and Eodice (2001, 128) suggest, "the importance of talk is even clearer when writers collaborate; their thinking is audible and several pools of knowledge combine in a virtual space to create deep lakes of possibility from which choices of what is to be written down are made." For this reason, what usually remains a private negotiation for writers— the shaping of how best to articulate an idea into text—is what makes collaborative writing such a valuable epistemic practice in its own right.

What we are describing as collaboration's reflexive impulse signals a way to talk about the inventive potential of collaborative writing, what we suggest is the second quality of effective collaboration. Invention is in a certain sense the *raison d'être* of writing; we create texts because we want to share ideas, explore questions, foster curiosity, and explain the things around us. As Janice Lauer notes, the term invention encompasses whatever "strategic acts" we pursue to compose something. "Such acts include initiating discourse, exploring alternatives, framing and testing judgments, interpreting texts, and analyzing audiences" (Lauer 2004, 2). Coauthors who want to enhance the collaborative dimension of their work attempt to engage as many of these strategic acts together.

Third, and finally, effective collaborative writing tends to be continuous, which is to say collaborative writers value the products of their collaboration in conjunction to the sustaining potential of the collaboration itself. As with any disciplined practice, the craft of collaborative writing improves as coauthors develop their skill from one project to the next. What makes any practice disciplined is of course the deliberation that marks how practitioners reflect on, test, and take risks with their craft. In one of their earliest coauthored texts, Ede and Lunsford attempt to describe their writing process as follows: "If you can imagine the words *talk . . . write . . . read . . . talk . . . write . . . talk . . . read . . .* written in a large looping spiral – that comes closest to a description of the process as we know it" (Ede and Lunsford 1983, 152). We think this image of a spiral randomly dotted with conversation, writing, and reading describes how coauthors build continuity into their collaboration. Accordingly, collaborative writers can certainly expect to coauthor successful texts even though with continued experience the purpose of collaboration gets located in the reflexive space they construct for inquiry and invention, space they can continually return to as new projects arise.

THE WORK OF PHASED COLLABORATION

If collaboration enriches the experience of coauthorship, what are the practices that make such enrichment possible? We want to conclude our argument in favor of collaborative writing by describing how we have come to discuss the practices that make coauthorship collaborative—what gives it its reflexive, inventive, and continuous quality. To this end we have developed the concept of *phased collaboration* to describe the recursivity of collaborative practices writers may choose to employ. Phased collaboration simply names a holistic view of collaborative writing, one that reminds us how "discourse is a unitary process" (Yarbrough 2005, 491). Every element of collaboration influences to varying degrees how coauthors approach their writing. Moreover for writers to foster the inventive space that makes collaboration possible, they must first orient themselves toward the process of writing with another.

The notion of phased collaboration developed for us as we tried to understand the struggles we experienced as coauthors who wanted to collaborate. During early attempts of composing this current essay, for example, we found ourselves frustrated by what felt like a lack of development in the central arguments we wanted to make. We would sit, often in the same room, rehashing pieces of the essay, hoping that our conversations would lead to greater clarity in our writing. Looking back, however, we realize that while we may have been together in terms of proximity, we were sometimes miles apart conceptually. As coauthors we wanted to share meaning with each other, but we wrongly believed that the best articulations of ideas would simply present themselves if we talked about them enough.

We reminded ourselves that this view of coauthorship only works when there exists a clear outcome for a particular text. It is easy, after all, to fit the pieces together if you have a clear view of the final image. What happens, though, when you and your coauthors do not have a clear direction for a particular piece of writing? The answer lies in being attuned to the phases of your collaboration. Rather than always assuming that coauthors will find their way through difficult moments in the writing process by examining new material, or asking one more research question, or following the next step in the process, phased collaboration reminds writers that reflexively assessing the process thus far often leads to new insights and direction.

In many ways successful collaboration occurs when writers reorient themselves toward each other and approach the prospect of collaborative writing as an opportunity to discover new ideas. As collaborators Duane Roen and Stuart Brown note, there is "more up front design that goes into collaboration" (quoted in Day and Eodice 2001, 127), and we would argue this notion of design is better understood as a type of conceptual stance one takes toward writing with another person. That is, successful collaboration is not wholly dependent on erecting proper scaffolding, but instead requires that writers approach their work with an orientation toward writing that encourages continual reflection and assessment.

The terms that follow describe the work of phased collaboration. These terms do not name discrete elements of the composing process, nor do they name frameworks that must be in place in order to write. Instead these are intended to be used heuristically as rules of thumb coauthors can draw on to maintain an environment amenable to invention. For new and even experienced coauthors, these phases can be used to identify and thereby productively exploit the actual practices that work most effectively for each set of collaborators.

Approaching

When writing together we first spend time discussing how we are approaching the project at hand. To approach something suggests a spatial metaphor, and indeed, we often remind ourselves that we are about to "enter into" (rather than "begin," which suggests the start of an ordered process) an inventive and collaborative space. Approaching reminds us that while our first inclination will be to divide our labor, such decisions will only hamper the possibility of invention since it assumes that writers already know the outcome their labor will produce.

So rather than jumping in head first with writing, approaching reminds us to account for the rhetorical space that will influence our work. Certainly writers must know the type of writing they want to produce—a journal article, a conference paper, a report to their department—but writers must also consider the other limitations on their time and talents. This suggestion may seem like a no-brainer, but to discuss with someone else that you will have a difficult time managing the collaboration because of family commitments or prior professional responsibilities requires a certain level of trust with your fellow writers. In other words, approaching as a heuristic tells us that writing together entails a certain degree of intimacy, a quality of professional relationship not often discussed in faculty writing workshops or seminars. Moreover, approaching suggests that maintaining an inventive, reflexive space demands that writers remain aware that a number of external forces shape our thinking and thereby inform the ideas that emerge while working together.

Examples of approaching practices:

> *Coordinate your efforts:* Identify from the onset your goals as well as
> your restraints. How much time can each writer devote to the proj-
> ect? In what environments is writing most productive? What other

commitments will you have to balance? Be sure to build in time so you can occasionally recoordinate your efforts as the project develops.

Assess resources: Each collaborator brings unique abilities and experiences to a writing project. Talk about what each of you can do well, in addition to where you sometimes struggle as writers. The point is to be attuned to one another's particular skill sets. For example, in our own collaboration we've realized how to draw on each of our strengths when explaining abstract ideas. John has a talent for articulating practical examples, which is something that always comes hard for Will. But on the flip side, Will is fairly adept at explaining ideas in simple terms (just not with the illustrations!), while John has a tendency to lean on disciplinary jargon if he's not careful. In this way you can assess your resources as you approach writing with a coauthor.

Generate questions: The most successful coauthors are those who pay attention to the questions that get raised throughout a collaboration. As you identify and assess logistical demands, it is important to notice the various lines of inquiry that emerge as the collaboration takes shape. Do you see avenues to narrow your project? How are you each coming to understand the primary claim that your writing makes? Have you identified how this writing is going to fit into the venue you have selected for it? Make sure to begin the habit of recording these questions and how you answer them because they often provide the means through which coauthors reestablish direction and maintain focus.

Listening

Once we have accounted for the needs of each other and the particularities of the project, we begin to articulate the direction we feel is most appropriate for the writing. We call this the listening phase because we believe effective collaborative writers listen to each other as a strategy for cultivating a shared voice through which to write. Listening is a productive metaphor because it stresses the necessity of allowing space for your ideas and voices to intermingle with the ideas and voices of your collaborator(s). Krista Ratcliffe offers a helpful way for thinking about the kind of listening effective collaborative writers engage. She suggests that writers should strive to "stand under" another's ideas (Ratcliffe 2005, 28). This play on words highlights how collaborative writers should position themselves in relationship to one another. "Standing under" refers to a deliberate attempt to see your partner's ideas as important and valuable to your own thinking, not simply as a means of sharpening and clarifying a singular vision for the writing at hand.

Emphasizing listening as a phase of collaboration reminds us that ideas emerge in the confluence between speakers. As noted above, reflexivity tells us that our ideas and points of view are influenced by encounters with others, and as such listening as a phase of collaboration means more than simply trying to understand another person or idea; it signals that collaboration, objects of inquiry continually take on new meanings as writers interact to produce a text.

Examples of listening practices:

Locate Assumptions and Identify Positions: Spend time talking about what you already know about the topic, as well as any assumptions and expectations you have. Being deliberate about this initial dialogue allows collaborators to anticipate the new observations and tentative conclusions they will generate. Moreover, pay attention to those places where you disagree. These differences will create opportunities for inventing new ideas.

Track Dialogue: Never underestimate the value of taking thorough notes during conversations. One of the most important ways that collaborators listen to each other is through note taking, jotting down questions as well as each other's words as you engage in dialogue. Notes help us track each other's ideas and how they develop through conversation. We find it helpful to return to these notes as we write the text, even if our ideas have changed, because this reflection fosters awareness about how our ideas have developed over time.

Time-Lapsed Reflection: It is sometimes valuable to step away from the immediacy of collaboration and allow time to help ideas grow. What we call time-lapsed reflection simply names a deliberate strategy collaborative writers can use to conceptualize their work. This strategy is especially useful if a meeting is not as productive as you had hoped. In short, put some time and space between your meetings, but use this time to individually reflect on the plans or outlines already generated. For us, we often take the notes we created while tracking dialogue and then add individual commentary after several days have passed. This opens up new spaces for intervention during the next meeting.

Transcribing

The actual work of rendering words into text can be the hardest part of collaborative writing. We use the idea of transcribing to describe this third phase of collaborative writing because it highlights that coauthored composition is, at its core, both a process of transcription (putting words on paper) and interpretation (the process of coming to shared meaning). Collaborative writing can be difficult and it is during the transcribing phase where collaborators most often get frustrated. Like other types of writing, collaborative writing requires practice and patience, which usually means the more drafts coauthors produce and the more revisions they make, the more comfortable they become with the process of writing together.

Nevertheless the actual writing act that collaborative writers engage can often be difficult, but just as when you write individually, there is no right or wrong way to get words on the page as collaborators. The trick is to practice with different drafting strategies and see what works best for you and your coauthor(s). Thus transcribing looks different for each group of writers. While it is certainly possible for partners to share a single computer, composing each word together, a more realistic model would probably locate collaborators taking turns speaking while the other types. Of course, given the constraints of life, collaborators may find that they need to compose apart from each other. For example, after taking notes one of us might rewrite the introduction of a text and then together we will revise this revision "together" while video chatting (see "strategic free-writing" below). Nevertheless we encourage writers to spend at least some time together experimenting with the transcribing process because such interactions serve as a powerful illustration of the dynamic nature of two or more voices merging into one.

Examples of transcribing practices:

Speaking/Transcribing: This is really the most basic strategy for getting words onto the page: one partner speaks while another partner writes. At first this might feel a little awkward, but with practice this sense of awkwardness will lessen, especially if partners take turns in these roles. In our experience, coauthors will soon notice a rhythm developing, and often the person transcribing actually edits and revises the words being spoken because they anticipate the direction of their partners' thoughts.

Strategic Free-Writing: All writers, including collaborative writers, experience writer's block. One way to work through these blockages and continue the work of transcribing is to identify the problem areas of a text, the places where ideas remain unformulated. Once identified, coauthors individually free-write in response to these ideas or problem areas. More often then not collaborators, as a result of their individual free-writing, will locate new avenues of inquiry through which ideas might develop, avenues that would not have been possible to locate without previous interactions with one's coauthor.

Talk to the Text: Another invaluable strategy for developing the quality of your written work is to "talk to the text" as the draft emerges. This might take the form of collaborators either individually or as a group reading through a draft while making comments in the margins that signal places where ideas could be clarified, developed, or maybe even dropped. Talking to the text emphasizes that the written document is a shared production. Rather than focusing on what each person has contributed, which might prompt collaborators to over-emphasize their individual efforts, talking to the text encourages writers to acknowledge the draft as representative of their shared voice.

CONCLUSION

In the end, our hope for prospective coauthors is that they will experiment with collaborative writing as a means to grow their "double-voiced relationships consciously," to echo Kate Ronald and Hephzibah Roskelly (2001, 259). For faculty encountering the pressures of publication for the first time, collaboration can provide a means of remaining attentive to the work of writing while nurturing a partnership that could potentially last for a career. The aim of most faculty writing support is to create opportunities for writers to assess their needs, identify venues for publication, and create accountability, all worthy goals but ultimately limited by the provisional nature of workshops and seminars. Collaboration, however, includes these aims and provides an exigency that workshops and seminars cannot approximate: our responsibility to each other.

Finally, the examples of rhetorical practices we have offered for engaging the phases of collaboration are just that, examples. They are the practices that have emerged in our own work together as collaborators, and we name them here simply to demonstrate that when collaborative writers attend to the reflexive nature of their work together, it becomes possible to reflect on your own best practices and name them as such. The practices that work best for you and your collaborators will emerge with practice and over time, of course, but know that *naming* what you do as collaborative writers is possible. In fact, when you begin to identify your best practices together, this usually signals the moment when coauthorship becomes collaborative.

REFERENCES

Ashton-Jones, Evelyn, and Dene Kay Thomas. 1990. "Composition, Collaboration, and Women's Ways of Knowing: A Conversation with Mary Belenky." *Journal of Advanced Composition* 10 (2): 275–92.

Danielewicz, Jane, and John McGowan. 2005. "Collaborative Work: A Practical Guide." *Symploke* 13 (1–2): 168–81. http://dx.doi.org/10.1353/sym.2006.0014.

Day, Kami, and Michele Eodice. 2001. *(First Person)²: A Study of Co-authoring in the Academy.* Logan. Utah State University Press.

Ede, Lisa, and Andrea Lunsford. 1983. "Why Write . . . Together?" *Rhetoric Review* 1 (2): 150–7. http://dx.doi.org/10.1080/07350198309359047.

Ede, Lisa, and Andrea Lunsford. 1990. *Singular Texts/Plural Authors: Perspectives on Collaborative Learning.* Carbondale: Southern Illinois University Press.

Forman, Janice, ed. 1992. *New Visions of Collaborative Writing.* Portsmouth, NH: Boyton/ Cook Heinemann.

Foucault, Michel. 1977. "What Is an Author?" In *Language, Counter-Memory, Practice: Selected Essays and Interviews*, ed. Donald Bouchard, trans. Donald Bouchard and Sherry Simon, 124–27. Ithaca: Cornell University Press.

Laird, Holly A. 2001. "'A Hand Spills from the Book's Threshold': Coauthorship's Readers." *PMLA* 116 (2): 344–53.

Lauer, Janice M. 2004. *Invention in Rhetoric and Composition.* West Lafayette, IN: Parlor Press.

Lunsford, Andrea. 1999. "Rhetoric, Feminism, and the Politics of Textual Ownership." *College English* 61 (5): 529–44. http://dx.doi.org/10.2307/378972.

Lunsford, Andrea, and Lisa Ede. 1990. "Rhetoric in a New Key: Women and Collaboration." *Rhetoric Review* 8 (2): 234–41. http://dx.doi.org/10.1080/07350199009388896.

Qualley, Donna. 1997. *Turns of Thought: Teaching Composition as Reflexive Dialogue.* Portsmouth, NH: Boynton/Cook Heinemann.

Ratcliffe, Krista. 2005. *Rhetorical Listening: Identification, Gender, Whiteness.* Carbondale: Southern Illinois University Press.

Reagan, Sally Barr, Thomas Fox, and David Bleich, eds. 1994. *Writing With: New Directions in Collaborative Teaching, Learning, and Research.* Albany: State University of New York Press.

Ronald, Kate, and Hephzibah Roskelly. 2001. "Learning to Take It Personally." *Personal Effects: The Social Character of Scholarly Writing,* ed. Deborah Holdstein and David Bleich, 253–66. Logan: Utah State University Press.

Spear, Karen. 1988. *Sharing Writing: Peer Response Groups in English Classes.* Portsmouth, NH: Boynton/Cook.

Sullivan, Patricia. 1994. "Revising the Myth of the Independent Scholar." In *Writing With: New Directions in Collaborative Teaching, Learning, and Research,* ed. Sally Barr Reagan, Thomas Fox, and David Bleich, 11–29. Albany: State University of New York Press.

Woodmansee, Martha. 1995. "On the Author Effect: Recovering Collectivity." In *The Construction of Authorship: Textual Appropriation in Law and Literature,* ed. Martha Woodmansee and Peter Jaszi, 15–28. Durham, NC: Duke University Press.

Yancey, Kathleen Blake, and Michael Spooner. 1998. "A Single Good Mind: Collaboration, Cooperation, and the Writing Self." *College Composition and Communication* 49 (1): 45–62. http://dx.doi.org/10.2307/358559.

Yarbrough, Stephen. 2005. "On the Very Idea of Composition: Modes of Persuasion or Phases of Discourse?" *JAC* 25:491–512.

15
EXPERIENCING THE BENEFITS OF DIFFERENCE WITH- IN MULTIDISCIPLINARY GRADUATE WRITING GROUPS

Elena Marie-Adkins Garcia, Seung hee Eum, and Lorna Watt

This chapter explores the experiences of three participants in Michigan State University's (MSU) Graduate Writing Groups (GWGs). We were involved in one writing group for two semesters in the 2009–2010 academic year. This group provided us with a unique space for learning new ways of being graduate students and what it will mean for us to become faculty—experts in our own fields and professors who will teach and mentor graduate students. Much of what we gained aligns with existing research on writing groups—that conversations with other writers about our work aids in developing stronger written products and that frequently meeting with the same people can foster a sense of community and belonging. We observed that the combination of peer-to-peer collaborative conversation and cross-disciplinary interaction were essential to the particular learning outcomes of our group. In this chapter, we argue that multidisciplinary graduate writing groups in higher education provide a unique professional and personal development space, the kind of academic space that should be a more explicit component to graduate education. Based on our personal experiences, offered here as individual testimonials and reflections, and using a collective voice that contextualizes, situates, and makes arguments about our individual stories by drawing on existing scholarship on collaborative learning, mentoring, and multi/interdisciplinary interaction as connected to graduate student education and professional development, we make two main claims: (1) Graduate student-only writing groups offer the potential for peer-mentoring, which we believe is one way students can feel the sense

DOI: 10.7330/9780874219029.c015

of community, belongingness, and support necessary to move successfully through the degree process; and (2) They provide the opportunity
to engage in multidisciplinary discussions that can help combat disciplinary entrenchment, can help participants develop enthusiasm for
approaching writing with a multidisciplinary consideration and become
teachers of writing in their varied disciplines, and, perhaps most important, can help participants grow as confident disciplinary experts. We
conclude with advice regarding GWGs for graduate students, writing
program administrators, and chairs and deans, arguing that such groups
can and should be implemented at any college with graduate programs.

> *Elena:* I am a PhD candidate in Michigan State University's Rhetoric and
> Writing program. In my second year, I decided to facilitate a graduate
> writing group. Seung hee and Lorna were two of the three members
> who made up this group.
>
> My academic, research, and teaching interests all involve writing,
> and so the GWGs seemed like an interesting new arena to work in.
> Facilitating a GWG has expanded my academic interests into the realm
> of graduate education and professionalization. The experiences I had
> sparked a desire to work toward more explicit writing instruction for
> graduate students across disciplines.
>
> *Seung hee:* I am a student in the PhD program for Music Therapy at
> Michigan State University. My main research interest is Multicultural Music
> Therapy. Within this broad research area I also focus on Community
> Music Therapy and Feminist Music Therapy. I have two reasons for partici-
> pating in the GWGs. First, as an international student, I am able to learn
> more about and practice the American academic communication meth-
> ods of my discipline. Second, I enjoy learning about diverse writing styles
> from others who are studying in different disciplines from my own.
>
> *Lorna:* I earned my MS in Michigan State University's Department of
> Plant Biology and the Ecology, Evolutionary Biology, and Behavior
> Program. My studies focused on evolutionary ecology, in particular how
> new species evolve and how adaptation is involved in the steps that occur
> during speciation. My principle work in our GWG was on my writing pro-
> cess, and my experiences there surprisingly encouraged me to consider
> writing more for audiences outside my discipline.

STARTING AT THE BEGINNING: MICHIGAN STATE
UNIVERSITY'S GRADUATE WRITING GROUPS

The Writing Center at Michigan State University hosts graduate writing
groups in which a writing center consultant, usually a PhD student, facilitates groups of three to six graduate students. The GWGs meet each
week for two hours, having read each others' work before coming to the
group meeting. At MSU, the groups are organized based on discipline

(generally by humanities, social sciences, and natural sciences) and then based on research methods (quantitative, qualitative, mixed methods) so that members have enough similarity for the groups to function smoothly. However, this homogenous group make up rarely occurs. With almost every group over the past several years, the realities of time constraints and scheduling have trumped disciplinary anchoring, and students have been placed together based on weekly availability, leading to highly diverse membership.

The Writing Center, on its website, lists for potential writing group members the following benefits:

- A sense of accountability (via required weekly writing)
- Resources on academic and disciplinary writing conventions
- Regular spoken and written feedback on your writing
- Scholarly community while you conduct independent research
- Opportunities to talk about research, teaching, and the job search
- Practice with peer response strategies and mentoring skills.

This list addresses issues of accountability, resources, and community as the positive attributes writing group participation provides, attributes not uncommon to writing groups in and outside academia. To help accomplish these goals, the MSU Writing Center appoints a writing-center-experienced graduate student as the graduate writing group coordinator. This coordinator appoints and trains facilitators for the groups, and it is the job of the facilitators to model ways of responding to writing. Like the work in the Writing Center, the facilitators primarily focus on modeling response to global, or higher order, concerns, rather than responding to correctness of content or grammar. The MSU GWGs value this approach for all writing groups, but we have found it to be especially useful in multidisciplinary groups.

At their core, GWGs are formed to provide a space within which graduate students can learn and talk about writing, and for us this group certainly provided a great deal of practical learning opportunities. It was a space for learning new writing strategies and approaches without a classroom or direct instruction model. The strategies we shared added an important dimension to our group in that we knew there would be a chance to learn something new about writing each week.

> *Elena:* As facilitor, I tried to establish an atmosphere for learning, experimenting, questioning, and sorting out thoughts. I also tried to make sure I shared my own knowledge regarding writing strategies and approaches. I made copies of book sections on revision; I found online sources that discuss organizational structures and mapping strategies; during weeks

in which there wasn't much of the group members' writing to discuss, I walked the members through rhetorical analyses of well-written texts. I felt responsible to share my disciplinary knowledge with the group.

Lorna: The results of our work in the writing group were not always visible, and I took care to notice when I was learning despite making no visible progress on the page. My writing process has totally changed, which is growth I couldn't possibly measure in pages. I now have crayons in my shower to ensure I can record my ideas no matter when they occur. I didn't have the chance to make the kind of progress with my writing anywhere else but in my graduate writing group. For me it wasn't so much about the actual writing, but bigger ideas about the process of writing that were only highlighted by our diversity.

Seung hee: The writing group for me was a kind of class or a place where I learned lessons about writing. I know that the main point is for students, especially American students, to share their writing and support each other; it is more for community and relationships. Our group especially provided such community and good relationships, but it also provided much more. I took notes, I recorded our meetings, I asked questions about the writing we were talking about because I was learning different ways of thinking about writing. I learned new ways to put ideas together. And so it was like a class I attended each week—I prepared ahead of time like a class and listened to our meetings later like a class—but I didn't feel the pressure that I would in an actual class. I could focus on learning rather than producing something that would be graded.

Though we clearly gained more knowledge about writing and learned ways to improve our work, coming together each week to collaboratively learn was a key to the positive gains. Our GWGs follow an approach based on the conversational nature of our writing center consulting— that collaborative conversation helps to improve both processes and products (Bruffee 1997, 2001; A. Lunsford 1995; Highberg, Moss, and Nicolas 2004; George 1984; Payan 1979; Hawley 1979; Mezeske 2005; and Vygotsky 1986). The term collaboration contains many meanings: rather than developing texts together (Ede and A. Lunsford 1983; A. Lunsford and Ede 1986, 2003), within weekly group meetings we talked through members' work, together forming an understanding of the work and collaboratively improving the communicated meaning. We engaged in an approach to collaboration that sees knowledge "as mediated by or constructed through language in social use" (A. Lunsford, 1995, 37), so when we met together each week we were constructing knowledge—knowledge about our writing, our research, and ourselves.

In this kind of collaborative environment we also developed deeply personal and fulfilling connections—the sense of belonging to a community. For many students, graduate work is rife with feelings of fear and self-doubt, the state of mind often termed "impostor syndrome." The result is often isolation, attempting to work, struggle, and doubt alone as we fight to survive a uniquely harsh rite of passage. In our writing group, however, we recognized that we did not have to be alone and that our hardships were also being faced by others. Institutional mentoring is often seen as the best way to combat such isolation, providing the "protégé with a knowledgeable guide who will lead her through the system and thus aiding in retention and completion (L. Lunsford, 2012, 253-4,). In the following discussion of mentoring, we argue that spaces like the GWGs offer students an environment of peer-mentoring, a "safe" alternative to hierarchical mentoring by faculty because it is institutionally assessment-free; thus, it is a facet of mentoring that should be a component of all graduate education.

MENTORING: TRADITIONAL AND PEER-BASED

One of the most personally fulfilling benefits we gained from our writing group was the opportunity to interact with peers. We were able to mentor and be mentored by each other. Such peer mentoring is not an uncommon benefit to any peer learning community; in fact, it is often cited as one of the primary benefits of graduate writing groups (Thomas, Smith, and Barry 2004; Highberg, Moss, and Nicolas 2004; Barry, et al. 2004). We do not intend to argue that existing mentoring structures, such as the more traditional advisor and committee mentoring we have received, are not an essential component to graduate education. What we do claim is that these structured mentoring relationships are often not enough to meet all of our needs. Mentoring in graduate school needs to happen in multiple environments, and we all quickly learned that our GWG provided such a resource.

Most of our mentoring has been located in a more traditional mode of mentoring—that of experienced faculty giving their knowledge to us as novice graduate students. Fishman and A. Lunsford (2008, 28) summarize the traditional view of mentoring as follows: "Regarded as a novice, a mentee is someone who undergoes an extended process of initiation and assimilation in order to learn duty and obedience alongside the rudiments of a discipline and/or profession. Construed as an apprentice, a mentee is not only a student or pupil (roles associated more with childhood than with professionalization), but also someone socially as well as intellectually subservient to a master or mentor."

Such a master-apprentice approach is also called "grooming mentoring," which be "severely constrained by its hierarchical, power-laden, and dyadic nature" (Haring 1999, xi). As graduate students, we often find ourselves in such a master-novice dichotomy with our professors, and we tend to behave accordingly.

> *Seung hee:* In my PhD program at MSU, I have what I feel is a strained relationship with my advisor, my official mentor. I feel a great deal of stress and anxiety when I meet my advisor for two main reasons: my cultural background and my English language difficulties.
>
> Regarding my cultural background: In the South Korean educational system, the hierarchy is very rigid, so the relationship between student and teacher is one of authority and submissiveness. I bring this cultural practice with me to my meetings with my advisor here in the U.S.
>
> Regarding my difficulties with English: I have to work hard to hide my lack of English ability, which often means I cannot ask important questions or express my real thoughts because I don't know how to explain those ideas in English. I have to work hard to only say things I know are correct so that my advisor does not judge me negatively if I say something incorrectly.
>
> I always feel that I am evaluated by my advisor as a graduate student, with my abilities always in question. These two issues make forming a friendly relationship with my advisor very difficult, basically impossible.

> *Elena:* My relationships with my current mentors—my committee—are positive and I feel strong academic support from them, but we do not have the close, personal, emotional connection that some of the scholarship on positive mentoring relationships discusses. I know that a reason for this is my own hesitation to become emotionally invested in a person who has authority over me, as I have had negative experiences with that in the past.
>
> However, after some pretty severe emotional turmoil during one of my comprehensive exams, I forced myself to seek out help. I was pleased with the responses I received, and it feels great to have mentors who care about me and my success, but I still hesitate to risk going out for drinks regularly or calling and texting socially. I sense that I am a student rather than a colleague, even if that gut feeling might be my own creation, my own distrust.

Faculty members represent the authority of the academy, and we want to prove to our gatekeepers that we can "acquire enough convention to be read as 'in'" (Ashley and Lynn 2003, 4). Given the gatekeeper roles our faculty mentors play, we present our knowledge rather than seeking to learn, we don't easily or confidently share our early, messy, uncertain work nor our hesitations, fears, or insecurities (Snively, Freeman, and Prentice 2006; Fawcett 1999). We are worried about being seen for what we think we really are: imposters who cannot actually do the work being asked for and who do not belong in graduate school.

We recognize that not all structured mentoring involves the kind of anxiety that we have felt, so we investigated other models. We appreciate recent scholarship on graduate education that advocates an "ethic of care"

(Ashe and Ervin 2008), presenting arguments for healthy, balanced, co-mentoring relationships that are based on reciprocity: both mentor and mentee are supported and inspired by each other (Fishman and Lunsford 2008; Miles and Burnett 2008; Downs and Goldstein 2008; Haring 1999; Liu, et al. 2008). Though we admire and desire such relationships, we also recognize that, as Miles and Burnett (2008, 116) state, "hierarchy is always present in mentoring," and the reality is that our experiences with hier-archical mentoring are steeped in issues of authority, comfort, support, and trust. When hierarchy is at play, whether overt or subtle, it can block opportunities for more collaborative, intimate relationships to develop. We feel that such close relationships need to form within graduate school in order for us to stay sane and healthy.

For some students, GWGs are one of the few, if not only, spaces in which they can develop such mentoring friendships. As an important contrast to hierarchical, structured mentoring, our Center's GWGs are based on the common composition and writing center tenet that peer learning interaction adds an essential dimension to education. When it comes to learning how to not only be mentored but to actually mentor, the peer environment of our writing group provided us the opportunity to practice explicit mentoring with each other. Cahill, et al. (2008, 157) explain this same practice, in relation to their own work in graduate writing groups: "When we bring our work to the group, we come to be mentored, and when we read and comment on the work of our fellow grad students, we mentor them." By understanding that we were prac-ticing mentoring with each other, we were able to test and try on men-toring personalities in the relative comfort and experimental nature of our writing group, without the pressure to be successful that more struc-tured mentoring brings with it.

> *Lorna:* Through the lens that the group provides a safe place, we mentored each other, we learned from each other, and we taught each other. That helped us to form a space outside of the direct influence of our official mentors. We also had a place to practice at being the kinds of scholars and experts, the kinds of professionals, we want to be rather than what others in our disciplines sometimes say we should be.

> *Seung hee:* Speaking and writing in English are difficult, and so I don't really have a way to talk about my ideas, except for through the Writing Center and especially in a graduate writing group. Our group was very helpful because even though I was a little stressed and nervous because of my lan-guage barrier, the other members were open and accepting of my ideas, feedback, and questions. They allowed me the time to think through my ideas and helped me figure out ways to explain what I was thinking.

Elena: When I am teaching, I am the clear authority in the classroom—I'm in charge—and when I'm writing center consulting, I'm doing my best to remain a peer—to refrain from being in charge. But in the writing group I had to fit myself somewhere in the middle. I had to learn to teach without dominating, to mentor without teaching, to be a peer without actually sharing my own writing. While I made my mistakes, certainly, I also learned ways to mentor and how to switch between types of mentoring roles.

Both roles of mentoring—mentor and mentee—played out in our GWG, and a strong sense of community and friendship formed through our experimental mentoring interactions. Ashe and Ervin (2008, 90) might call such interactions "friendships of play" encouraging "openness and risk-taking, seek[ing] to counter the 'hyperindividualism' of exclusive [mentoring] relationships." The play of our group lowered our typical barriers, allowing us to experience moments of belonging, moments of being within a space where we felt safe and smart. When we mentored each other, we also expanded our mentoring abilities and experienced a variety of mentoring styles. Now, in our present positions as graduate students and in our future roles as official faculty mentors, we will likely have more understanding of student needs, being more flexible and effective than we might have been otherwise.

MULTIDISCIPLINARITY

Thus far we have looked to add our three voices to existing scholarship on writing groups, and peer-based graduate student writing groups in particular. In the rest of the chapter, we extend these conversations by asserting that multidisciplinary graduate writing groups are important spaces for cross-disciplinary interactions to occur. In our specific experience, the multidisciplinary nature of the group encouraged us to grow as writers, teachers of writing, and burgeoning disciplinary experts. Together we had a rare opportunity to move beyond the boundaries of our departments and were thus exposed to ways of thinking, researching, and writing (Clary-Lemon and Roen 2008; González 2001, 1625) that varied significantly from what we had grown accustomed to.

By bringing disparate disciplines together in a collaborative spirit, writing groups like ours can mitigate learning and production homogenization. Joe Moran (2010, 16) has recently addressed the potential of multi/interdisciplinary interaction, arguing that it "can form part of a more general critique of academic specialization as a whole, and the nature of the university as an institution that cuts itself off from the outside world in small enclaves of expertise." Because our weekly meetings were first and foremost a place to talk about our writing, we learned a great deal from our different individual and disciplinary writing styles, conventions, practices, approaches, and strategies. By socially, collaboratively discussing the writing brought into our meetings, we noticed what Ken Hyland (2004, 3) points out about disciplinary discourses: "It is how [disciplines] write rather than simply what they write that makes the crucial difference between them." In our role as readers we became learners, learning from a diverse range of backgrounds, and this learning provided the most concrete and visible growth for all of us.

> *Lorna:* Because of the make-up of the group, the way we ended up talking about writing became the greatest benefit. We decided early on, with Elena's input, that we weren't going to focus on things like grammar or content accuracy. Instead we focused on asking questions about the connections and ideas in our writing. When I was asked important questions that I couldn't answer it made me realize that I wasn't doing the ground work for writing: I wasn't showing the relevance of information, I wasn't clearly explaining vocabulary, etc. By asking me questions about what I was taking for granted, I started to see my own work in new ways. The challenge to communicate with my peers outside my discipline revealed my difficulty with writing. I was taking the disciplinary ideas for granted and I needed to study the logic of my ideas.

While such ideal learning didn't and doesn't always occur easily, Lorna's challenge and her revelation, isn't uncommon to multidisciplinary discussions of writing (Harris 2001, 2002; Moran 2010; Trimbur 1997; Vygotsky 1986). This occurred specifically because we were readers unfamiliar with each other's disciplinary assumptions and uncomfortable with—or even sometimes clueless about—disciplinary jargon. In fact, we were full of our own expectations and assumptions regarding what is appropriate in academic writing.

> *Lorna:* When I get help from my disciplinary peers, we make very few considerations about writing. First of all, my disciplinary groups are not explicitly about writing, but about findings and experiments, research and ideas. Second, the writing must be done in a particular way, so there are very few considerations about it. I am lucky if I can find someone who (a) will talk about writing, and (b) knows how to.

> *Seung hee:* Through our writing group I greatly improved my sense of academic writing and what "good writing" might mean. I think that the strong diversity of the group helped this. I not only learned how to make my own writing better, I also learned how to respond to other people's writing in useful ways. I started to realize just how useful my writing group was when I was able to give helpful comments to other music education

students during department-wide readings of papers in progress. The writing group taught me how to talk about writing in useful ways, and now I am much more confident expressing any of my concerns and asking questions in this arena.

The immediate benefits we experienced as student writers are clearly presented in our above statements, but a more substantial and longer-lasting boon developed. Through the discussions of disciplinary-diverse texts, the learning of new and interesting writing strategies, and the sharing of the fears of judgment associated with our scholarship we also grew into better teachers of writing. Writing across the curriculum (WAC) and writing in the disciplines (WID) initiatives embrace the belief that writing needs to be taught across a college campus, not just within first year writing courses and not just assigned to students without explicit writing instruction. When department chairs or college deans demand such initiatives to be implemented, this places most of the pressure on writing program administrators (WPAs); and it seems that one of the greatest assets in that pursuit is an enthusiastic faculty member (McLeod and Soven 1991). Our experiences with the writing group inspired a focus on writing that will serve us well when we become faculty ourselves, for we will be those willing faculty members who teach (rather than just assign) writing in our classes and who push other faculty in our disciplines to place more importance on writing instruction. McLeod and Soven (1991, 29) explain that "WAC begins with faculty development" and that such an initiative needs to "involve key faculty at the decision-making level," but where does such faculty come from? We feel confident claiming that if more graduate students—those individuals who will be the higher education faculty of the future—are involved in multidisciplinary graduate writing groups, there will be a larger base of faculty across disciplines who can already talk about writing in ways that WPAs so often desire.

Lorna: Sharing and exploring our internal conversations about disciplinary style led each of us to consider the impacts of broadening our own writing. What would happen if I tried a different style? Would I be rejected for publication? Why? What are the reasons why the sciences require a specific style? Were there venues in which I could try other styles? The last answer was yes. A visiting speaker from the American Association for the Advancement of Science had in fact called researchers to contribute more editorials and articles to popular press. Without contact with other disciplines in a space dedicated to writing, I would not have heard his call as clearly.

Elena: I see that the WPAs I work for and with try to communicate what many in our fields believe to be best practices in writing instruction. I see them struggle to reach across the campus to faculty who are already too busy, hoping that those faculty members will make the time to attend writing pedagogy workshops. It seems like a constant battle. In my writing group, though, that battle seems to have been won. We already have the kinds of conversations that occur in such faculty workshops.

Writing across the curriculum and writing in the disciplines efforts are not just about encouraging faculty to think about their own writing—reconsidering their own assumptions, processes, and rhetorics (though this is all certainly part of WAC/WID initiatives)—it is about the teaching of writing to students. Adams (2002, 3) writes that "teaching is the responsibility that demands the most immediate attention and consumes the most time and energy of new faculty." She adds that "recent curricular changes in undergraduate education include emphasis on multicultural, international, interdisciplinary, and service learning . . . [and new faculty] may also be asked to teach writing." And if Adams is correct in that most graduate programs provide little to no teacher training regarding these expectations, then clearly there needs to be some way that gap is fulfilled. Multidisciplinary graduate writing groups can provide a way for graduate students to gain exposure to and practice with a variety of writing strategies, ways to talk about writing that they can bring with them when they become faculty in other institutions.

Elena: Based on my own student experiences and the feedback I've heard from students over nearly a decade of writing center consulting, it's clear to me that many instructors and professors across disciplines assign writing but often don't know how to talk about or teach it. Writing assignments are given with knowledge assumptions already made and peer response is assigned with the expectation that students know how to talk about writing with each other. In our group we used approaches based on writing center and composition pedagogies, approaches that value questions over corrections, audience considerations, and the making visible of knowledge assumptions. When I presented a new writing concept or strategy that the group members were curious about, I did my best to present my knowledge to them in ways that were useful to them as both writers and writing teachers. I found that I was learning how to be a WAC WPA within the safe, small boundaries of our group.

Lorna: I use many of the group's techniques for giving feedback as a teacher with my students. I have realized that in the sciences we assign writing and we grade writing, but we don't teach it, passing an insidious buck. I was frustrated one semester recently when I had to assign and grade writing without the time or training to teach it. I remembered that the questions I was asked about my writing in the GWG forced me to examine my own work, notice the choices that I made, develop my ideas, and write them deliberately. With only my interactions in the group as a guide for teaching my students how to write, I decided to switch from making nitpicky comments to asking questions and making demands for clarification. I think my comments surprised some students, but there were fewer complaints, which I interpreted as evidence of their reflection and an overall better teaching approach.

Seung hee: I don't have my own classes to teach right now, but I am planning on teaching when I leave MSU and find a job in South Korea. I want to continue my research in music therapy, but I also want to teach music therapy students, even develop music therapy programs and curriculum. It will be important for me when I teach to make sure my students learn how to write in a South Korean academic style and in American English academic style. Both will be important for music therapy students, particularly at the graduate level, since most of the music therapy discipline is located in the United States and Europe, and most international music therapy conferences are conducted in English. While the writing groups and the writing center were places where I learned how to improve my own writing, they also provided experiences that taught me how to talk about writing with others. Responding in the writing group to other members' work instead of just focusing on my own writing has been extremely important practice for me and my future as a scholar and professor.

GAINING DISCIPLINARY EXPERTISE BY ROLE-PLAYING AS EXPERTS

Graduate school is often discussed as being a transitional space, a space in-between student and professional (Nicolas 2008; Mattison 2008; Tirabassi, Zenger, and Gannett 2008). To grow professionally we present at conferences, develop publications, learn research practices—all culminating in a thesis or dissertation that "proves" we are ready to face the road ahead. However, "research has clearly documented the impact of the mismatch between graduate training and the multiple academic responsibilities facing new faculty" (Adams 2002, 1). The transition from student to professor tends to occur over a brief time-span of a few months, and in that time PhD students move from the positionality of a novice or apprentice—learning how to be scholars—to an expert or master—teaching new students who take our place in the novice role. But how do we learn to make such a drastic shift? How do we move from a lifetime of being students to possibly being in charge of an entire program for an unfamiliar institution (Adams 2002, 5)? In order to make these monumental moves into faculty positions, we need to practice what it means to be an expert, to display confidence in ourselves and our work.

Multidisciplinary graduate writing groups meet this need directly—they are key resources for developing professional academic identities and practicing at being experts within our own fields. In this group we were allowed to experiment, to try on and play out expert identities without fear of judgment or being told our claims, arguments, data, or interpretations are wrong. Because each of us was the only person in the room from our disciplines, we were each the only person who really knew what we were talking and writing about. The freedom the writing group space provided was a relief from the seemingly constant sense of being assessed that existed within our departments.

> *Lorna:* Sometimes when my GWG peers probed a specific passage of mine, their question was really about my discipline's style. Justifying and explaining that style to them required that I consider it myself. This occurred often, so I spent a lot of time in our meetings evaluating my discipline, exploring its approaches to communication, its philosophies about practice, and the boundaries of other disciplines. As a graduate student, I rarely practice that in other settings. The multidisciplinary writing group allowed me to develop mastery of my discipline, both by studying it and explaining it.

> *Seung hee:* I felt in the group that it was the only place where I have really played with the idea of being an expert. I am hesitant around faculty, but with the group I was more comfortable. I actually felt like I had control and authority over my own ideas, that I owned my ideas and my writing. I was the person with the final say about how I wanted my writing to be or how a term needed to be defined. I had to figure out how to explain my ideas myself.

> *Elena:* I think the similarity of all of us being grad students created the safety that allowed the members to take ownership of their work. Though I didn't bring my own writing in to receive feedback from the group, and though my job as facilitator led me to take a back seat to what group members discussed, there were important moments when I had to step up and practice displaying my own expertise. As the Writing Center representative and a writing studies scholar, I was asked to share my knowledge regarding writing strategies, especially about process and revision strategies that would help the members grow as writers. I could not rely on the traditional writing center mantra that consultants are not, should not be seen as, and should not claim to be, academic writing experts: my role as facilitator of the group told the members that's exactly what I was. This was actually great for me because if I'm going to run a writing center, a writing program, or some other WPA initiative in the near future, a writing expert is exactly what I will need to be.

If we see disciplines as social discourse communities (Hyland 2004) and the practices we learn as bringing us closer to being fully accepted members of our communities, then we are being constructed by our academic disciplines through the particular approaches of our departments. In our group, though, we each embraced our special expertise, giving us a rare feeling of "making" the knowledge of our disciplines (for the other group members) rather than only being "the object of this making" (Lauer, et al. 2008, 34). When we had to present our disciplinary knowledge we experienced "making" in ways that, as Barry, et al. (2004, 219) claim regarding their own multidisciplinary writing group, we "could not have as 'mere' students." As with our group, their multidisciplinary group required its members to recognize assumptions they were making and the disciplinary beliefs they were presenting. When recognizing such assumptions in a multidisciplinary group, when questioned by differently-disciplined experts-in-training, we found a need to negotiate our thinking with the ideas of others and stand up for the epistemologies of our disciplines when they were challenged by contradicting ways of thinking. Though we argue that GWGs challenge our existing disciplinary thinking, we also know one of the strongest benefits from our group was that we gained confidence in our own disciplinary knowledge through the expert-role-playing that our group encouraged.

CONCLUSION

Our experiences demonstrate the unique benefits that can be gained through participation in multidisciplinary graduate writing groups. Our group was a safe space within which we could mentor each other as we shared new ways of seeing and talking about writing, and we experimented with our burgeoning roles as scholars. Our hope is that we have provided strong enough arguments to encourage the implementation of and participation in graduate writing groups in a wide variety of institutions. We want to offer graduate students, WPAs, and chairs and deans a list of takeaways that might aid in the creation of GWGs.

Takeaways for Graduate Students

Unfortunately, GWGs tend to be seen as academic luxuries, something to engage in when there is time; or they are seen as a need-based service, to provide poor writers with writing instruction. We do not want GWGs to be seen in such ways, so we encourage all current graduate students to consider the following benefits of participation:

- Peer mentoring: The GWGs provide a chance to mentor and be mentored at a peer level, which can help graduate students develop mentoring skills, allows them to be mentored without the authority involved in faculty mentoring, and provides comfort and safety in mentoring.
- Multidisciplinarity: GWGs provide a unique opportunity to take on the role of disciplinary expert, allowing graduate students to practice

explaining their work in a safe and judgment free setting. They can struggle through defining key terms or explaining the "so what" of their work without anyone to contradict the claims presented. By communicating disciplinary practices in a multidisciplinary setting, students engage in the kinds of conversations they are likely to have when they graduate and move into academic or non-academic careers.

- Focus on writing and writing practices: In the GWGs students discuss writing in a focused, comfortable environment with individuals from multiple disciplines. Such conversations lead to better understanding of discipline's own writing conventions but also expose students to a variety of writing practices and tendencies. Finally, by learning about different approaches to writing process, graduate students can work on developing their own most effective writing processes.

Takeaways for WPAs

Writing program administrators are often tasked with developing programs that will help students and faculty focus more directly on their own writing as well as how they teach writing in their classes. WPAs also strive to foster a community of writing on their campuses. Such programs require time, effort, and resources that are scarce. Therefore, we offer these takeaways regarding GWGs:

- Graduate student writing instruction: We have noticed throughout our graduate educations (not just at MSU) that there is little institutional effort to teach writing at a graduate level. Perhaps there are dissertation workshops or support groups, but actual instruction is expected to come from advisors and committees. Developing writing groups open to all grad students can help meet the very intense need of grad students for writing support and assistance.
- A relatively easy initiative: We understand that many cross-campus writing initiatives are costly, so we want to express clearly that GWGs are fairly easy to establish and fund. The components of the GWG program at MSU are a graduate student support coordinator (a grad student hired through the Writing Center), graduate student facilitators with writing center experience, and a brief training session for new facilitators that focuses on transporting one-on-one consulting into a group setting.
- Seeding future multidisciplinary discussions about writing: When graduate students have participated in multidisciplinary writing groups, they have learned how to respond to writing productively; therefore, when these students become faculty, they will bring these approaches with them. Graduate writing groups serve double-duty as support and future faculty professional development.

Takeaways for Chairs and Deans

We understand that academic support resources are limited, and in graduate programs, committees and advisors provide much of the writing instruction for students, and writing centers tend to bear the brunt of writing support. However, graduate students need a variety of support sources. Below, we present arguments for why graduate writing groups should be one of those sources:

- Success with high-stakes writing: From our own experience, we know that coursework is not where students get stuck, it's the high-stakes writing (exams and dissertations) that cause the problems. In courses students have consistent structure and feedback, but once that structure is gone, many students flounder and are not productive. Graduate writing groups reestablish regular structure, accountability, and feedback. In addition, the student-only environment that holds high potential for friendships can allow the work to feel less daunting, less impossible.

- Encourage cross-disciplinary interaction: Academic interdisciplinarity is becoming an important component of higher education; as Christina González writes: "Another way in which universities are attempting to meet students' needs for research training is through interdisciplinary programs that emphasize professional development" (González 2001, 1625). However, intense programs can be costly and take a great deal of time to develop and establish. In graduate writing groups, which are fairly easy to put into place, students engage in interdisciplinary conversations that can lead to collaborative projects (like ours).

- Student support: A major goal of college administrators is providing student support to improve retention and completion rates. Graduate writing groups are one such method of support for graduate students, and their low cost and ease of implementation make them a smart choice. Providing resources to WPAs, writing centers, and graduate colleges, though, is essential.

Our final argument, then, is that there is a more explicit consideration of multidisciplinary graduate writing groups as an institutionalized aspect of graduate writing education. Increasingly, arguments are being made for interdisciplinarity, for cross-disciplinary scholarship and projects, and for more explicit consideration of the power of writing and the importance of writing instruction. GWGs such as our own should be places to begin these initiatives. Our writing group played an integral part in our transitions from being caught up and confused by our disciplines to being confident multidisciplinary thinkers. This—exactly what academia needs—is what we will take with us to institutions around the world.

REFERENCES

Adams, Kathrynn A. 2002. *"What Colleges and Universities Want in New Faculty."* Preparing Future Faculty. Sponsored by the Association of American Colleges and Universities and the Council of Graduate Schools.

Ashe, Diana, and Elizabeth Ervin. 2008. "Mentoring Friendships and the 'Reweaving of Authority." In *Stories of Mentoring: Theory and Praxis*, ed. Michelle F. Eble and Lynée Lewis Gaillet, 83–97. West Lafayette, IN: Parlor Press.

Ashley, Hannah, and Katy Lynn. 2003. "Ventriloquism 001: How to Throw Your Voice in the Academy." *Journal of Basic Writing* 22 (2): 4–26.

Barry, Terri Trupiano, Julie Galvin Bevins, Elizabeth Demers, Jami Blaauw Hara, M. Rini Hughes, and Mary Ann K. Sherby. 2004. "A Group of Our Own: Women and Writing Groups: A Reconsideration." In *Writing Groups Inside and Outside the Classroom*, ed. Beverly J. Moss, Nels P. Highberg, and Melissa Nicolas, 207–27. Mahwah, NJ: Lawrence Erlbaum Associates.

Bruffee, Kenneth A. 1997. "Collaborative Learning and the 'Conversation of Mankind." In *Cross-Talk in Comp Theory*, ed. Victor Villanueva, Jr., 393–414. Urbana, IL: NCTE.

Bruffee, Kenneth A. 2001. "Peer Tutoring and the 'Conversation of Mankind." In *The Allyn and Bacon Guide to Writing Center Theory and Practice*, ed. Robert W. Barnett and Jacob S. Blumner, 206–218. Boston: Allyn and Bacon.

Cahill, Lisa, Susan Miller-Cochran, Veronica Pantoja, and Rochelle L. Rodrigo. 2008. "Graduate Student Writing Groups as Peer Mentoring Communities." In *Stories of Mentoring: Theory and Praxis*, ed. Michelle F. Eble and Lynée Lewis Gaillet, 153–158. West Lafayette, IN: Parlor Press.

Clary-Lemon, Jennifer, and Duane Roen. 2008. "Webs of Mentoring in Graduate School." In *Stories of Mentoring: Theory and Praxis*, ed. Michelle F. Eble and Lynée Lewis Gaillet, 178–192. West Lafayette, IN: Parlor Press.

Downs, Doug, and Dayna Goldstein. 2008. "Chancing into Altruistic Mentoring." In *Stories of Mentoring: Theory and Praxis*, ed. Michelle F. Eble and Lynée Lewis Gaillet, 149–152. West Lafayette, IN: Parlor Press.

Ede, Lisa, and Andrea Lunsford. 1983. "Why Write . . . Together?" *Rhetoric Review* 1 (2): 150–7. http://dx.doi.org/10.1080/07350198309359047.

Fawcett, Emily. 1999. "'Like, it was, you know what I mean?': Conversational vs. Presentational Speech in Student Academic Discourse." In *Working with Student Writers: Essays on Tutoring and Teaching*, ed. Leonard A. Podis and JoAnne M. Podis, 73–83. New York: Peter Lang.

Fishman, Jenn, and Andrea Lunsford. 2008. "Educating Jane." In *Stories of Mentoring: Theory and Praxis*, ed. Michelle F. Eble and Lynée Lewis Gaillet, 18–32. West Lafayette, IN: Parlor Press.

George, Diana. 1984. "Working with Peer Groups in the Composition Classroom." *College Composition and Communication* 35 (3): 320–6. http://dx.doi.org/10.2307/357460.

González, Christina. 31 Aug, 2001. "Undergraduate research, graduate mentoring, and the university's mission." *Science* 293 (5535): 1624–6. http://dx.doi.org/10.1126/science.1062714. Medline:11533483

Haring, Marilyn J. 1999. "Forward from the Field." In *New Directions in Mentoring: Creating a Culture of Synergy*, ed. Carol A. Mullen and Dale W. Lick, xi–xii. New York: Falmer Press.

Harris, Muriel. 2001. "Collaboration Is Not Collaboration Is Not Collaboration: Writing Center Tutorials vs. Peer-Response Groups." In *The Allyn and Bacon Guide to Writing Center Theory and Practice*, ed. Robert W. Barnett and Jacob S. Blumner, 272–287. Boston: Allyn and Bacon.

Harris, Muriel. 2002. "'What Would You Like to Work on Today?': The Writing Center as a Site for Teacher Training." In *Preparing College Teachers of Writing: Histories, Theories,*

Programs, Practices , ed. Betty P. Pytlik and Sarah Liggett, 194–207. New York: Oxford University Press.

Hawley, Isabel L. 1979. "Critique of Groups for Composition Classes." In *Classroom Practices in Teaching English, 1979-1980: How to Handle the Paper Load,* ed. Gene Standford and the Committee on Classroom Practices, 119–23. Urbana, IL: NCTE.

Highberg, Nels P., Beverly J. Moss, and Melissa Nicolas. 2004. "Introduction: Writing Groups as Literacy Events." In *Writing Groups Inside and Outside the Classroom,* ed. Beverly J. Moss, Nels P. Highberg, and Melissa Nicolas, 1–10. Mahwah, NJ: Lawrence Erlbaum Associates.

Hyland, Ken. 2004. *Disciplinary Discourses: Social Interactions in Academic Writing.* Ann Arbor, MI: The University of Michigan Press.

Lauer, Janice, Michele Comstock, Baotong Gu, William Hart-Davidson, Thomas Moriarty, Tim Peeples, Larissa Reuer, and Michael Zerbe. 2008. "Their Stories of Mentoring: Multiple Perspectives on Mentoring." In *Stories of Mentoring: Theory and Praxis,* ed. Michelle F. Eble and Lynée Lewis Gaillet, 33–51. West Lafayette, IN: Parlor Press.

Liu, Lu, Irwin Weiser, Tony Silva, Janet Alsup, Cindy Selfe, and Gail Hawisher. 2008. "It Takes a Community of Scholars to Raise One: Multiple Mentors as Key to My Growth." In *Learning the Literacy Practices of Graduate School: Insiders' Reflections on Graduate Education,* ed. Christine Pearson Casanave and Xiaoming Li, 166–183. Ann Arbor, MI: The University of Michigan Press.

Lunsford, Andrea. 1995. "Collaboration, Control, and the Idea of a Writing Center." In *St. Martin's Sourcebook for Writing Tutors* , ed. Christina Murphy and Steve Sherwood, 36–42. Boston: Bedford/St. Martin's.

Lunsford, Andrea, and Lisa Ede. 1986. "Why Write . . . Together: A Research Update." *Rhetoric Review* 5 (1): 71–81. http://dx.doi.org/10.1080/07350198609359137.

Lunsford, Andrea, and Lisa Ede. 2003. "Rhetoric in a New Key: Women and Collaboration." In *Feminism and Composition: A Critical Sourcebook,* ed. Gesa E. Kirsch, Fay Spencer Maor, Lance Massey, Lee Nickoson-Massey, and Mary P. Sheridan-Rabideau, 256–262. Boston: Bedford/St. Martin's.

Lunsford, Laura. 2012. "Doctoral Advising or Mentoring? Effects on Student Outcomes." *Mentoring and Tutoring: Partnerships in Learning* 20 (2): 251–70.

Mattison, Michael. 2008. "Just Between Me and Me: A Letter to Myself About Being a Graduate Student Tutor and Administrator." In *E)Merging Identities: Graduate Students in the Writing Center,* ed. Melissa Nicolas, 11–25. Southlake, TX: Fountainhead Press.

McLeod, Susan H., and Margot Soven. 1991. "What Do You Need to Start—and Sustain—a Writing-Across-the-Curriculum Program?" *WPA: Writing Program Administration* 15 (1–2): 25–33.

Mezeske, Barbara A. 2005. "How I Conquered Peer Review." In *More Ways to Handle the Paper Load: On Paper and Online,* ed. Jeffrey N. Golub, 57–62. Urbana, IL: NCTE.

Miles, Katherine S., and Rebecca E. Burnett. 2008. "The Minutia of Mentorships: Reflections about Professional Development." In *Stories of Mentoring: Theory and Praxis,* ed. Michelle F. Eble and Lynée Lewis Gaillet, 113–128. West Lafayette, IN: Parlor Press.

Moran, Joe. 2010. *Interdisciplinarity.* New York: Routledge.

Nicolas, Melissa. 2008. ""Introduction: (E)Merging Identities; Authority, Identity, and the Place(s)." In *Between." In (E)Merging Identities: Graduate Students in the Writing Center,* ed. Melissa Nicolas, 1–8. Southlake, TX: Fountainhead Press.

Payan, Irene. 1979. "Peer Proofreading." In *Classroom Practices in Teaching English: How to Handle the Paper Load,* ed. Gene Standford and the Committee on Classroom Practices, 124–5. Urbana, IL: NCTE.

Snively, Helen, Traci Freeman, and Cheryl Prentice. 2006. "Writing Centers for Graduate Students." In *The Writing Director's Resource Book,* ed. Christina Murphy and Byron L. Stay, 153–64. Mahwah, NJ: Lawrence Earlbaum Associates.

Thomas, Sharon, Leonora Smith, and Terri Trupiano Barry. 2004. "Shaping Writing
   Groups in the Sciences." In *WritingGroups Inside and Outside the Classroom*, ed. Beverly
   J. Moss, Nels P. Highberg, and Melissa Nicolas, 76–93. Mahwah, NJ: Lawrence
   Erlbaum Associates.
Tirabassi, Katherine E., Amy A. Zenger, and Cinthia Gannett. 2008. "Songs of Innocence
   and Experience: Graduate Student Administrators Negotiate Positions of Power." In
   (E)Merging Identities: Graduate Students in the Writing Center, ed. Melissa Nicolas, 65–85.
   Southlake, TX: Fountainhead Press.
Trimbur, John. 1997. "Consensus and Difference in Collaborative Learning." In *Cross-Talk
   in Comp Theory*, ed. Victor Villanueva, Jr., 439–456. Urbana, IL: NCTE.
Vygotsky, Lev S. 1986. *Thought and Language. Revised Edition.* Ed. Alex Kozulin.
   Cambridge, MA: MIT Press.

16

THE PROMISE OF SELF-AUTHORSHIP AS AN INTEGRATIVE FRAMEWORK FOR SUPPORTING FACULTY WRITERS

Carmen Werder

Who is the self that teaches?
I cannot know in another being what I do not know in myself.
—Parker Palmer

The literature on educational development demonstrates a generation-long interest in advancing what is typically the most valued dimension of the academic trinity: scholarly publication. Even at research-intensive institutions that esteem the role of teaching in faculty lives, scholarly production tends to be privileged. Given this imperative, many institutions have judiciously developed programs for the primary purpose of advancing faculty scholarly productivity. Much of the attention in this growing body of literature focuses on the practical benefits of these development programs. Many articles and guidebooks address time management as a key to productivity, as evidenced by titles such as *Writing Your Journal Article in Twelve Weeks: A Guide to Academic Publishing Success* (Belcher 2009). The language of volume and expedience marks this pointed interest in highlighting production above other goals. Given the sweeping budget reductions across higher education, when faculty often find themselves with increasing class sizes and workloads but with decreasing time available to pursue scholarship, this highly practical focus makes good sense. Topics such as managing time and aligning personal writing goals with departmental expectations are the hallmarks of these programs. In this scheme, program developers tend to define success primarily in terms of the number of publications that result from participation and the extent to which participating faculty advance their individual scholarly publishing agenda.

DOI: 10.7330/9780874219029.c016

I appreciate this practical focus. In facilitating faculty writing groups at my own institution (Western Washington University), I have devoted considerable energy to assisting faculty in identifying ways to manage their time more effectively and to minimize distractions (Werder and Hoelscher 2010). However, while the utilitarian benefits of this approach for productivity seem obvious, if it is the only consideration, we risk putting an exclusive focus on short-term tips and strategies, rather than on long-term processes.

I do not mean to say that developers have only been interested in immediate gains to productivity. A distinct thread in the literature points to the value of faculty writing groups not only for advancing scholarship, but also for nurturing "better teaching" (Fassinger, Gilliland, and Johnson 1992). Boice (1995, 416, emphasis mine) describes successful writing groups as ones that result in both prolific writing and in more effective teaching because "both depend on similar kinds of collegial supports and on *self*-management; both need good starts, and each can augment the other." Furthermore, Boice prompts a lingering question here in using the term "self-management"—for what does it mean to support faculty writers not only in managing their time, but in managing *themselves?*

In addition to promoting productivity and enhanced teaching, faculty writing programs have also expanded to ground support in the scholarship of teaching and learning (SoTL). For example, Elon University's annual Faculty Writing Residency, represents one such program that focuses specifically on supporting faculty publishing on teaching and learning. In addition to advancing productivity, enhancing pedagogy, and fostering the scholarship of teaching and learning, many faculty writing programs also feature an explicit goal of developing communities of practice. As Elbow and Sorcinelli (2006, 19) acknowledge, "Professors-as-writers programs create a sense of intellectual stimulation and community that helps break down the isolation of many faculty scholars and teachers." This emphasis on the social dimension has even included students in the mix. Arguing for a reciprocal relationship that provides for interconnected cycles of co-mentoring, Mullen, Whatley and Kealy (2000) describe a program that features faculty-student support groups. Because of my work in partnering with students on the scholarship of teaching and learning (Werder et al. 2010), I have been particularly interested in creating mixed writing groups that include students. The Scholarship of Teaching and Learning residency that we have launched (titled "Landscapes of Learning") brings together mixed groups of students, faculty, and staff publishing individual and collaborative research on teaching and learning.

The multiple benefits of faculty writing support structures—with their array of models and goals—seem clear. However, despite the clear merits of all these results—increased production, enhanced pedagogy, deeper learning, and stronger collegiality—something seems to be missing in the discussion. We developers have created a generous repertoire of structures to enact this work, but what is the common theoretical base? What mental model might help hold all the pieces and practices together? What overall conceptual framework might accommodate these common and diverse approaches, one that will do what Geller emphasizes in the introduction to this volume: "value both the individual scholar and the collective effort of writers working together." I have come to see the promise of self-authorship as a potentially powerful integrative framework for working with faculty writers.

I originally encountered the theory of self-authorship in the process of conducting a research project on personal metaphors as a Carnegie Fellow in 2005–06. In analyzing the individual metaphors that students in my classes were using for themselves as learners and communicators, I turned to the theory of self-authorship to help explain why students found the process of generating and then analyzing metaphors-for-self such a significant learning experience—one that they often reported as transformative (Werder 2010). The self-authorship theory enabled me—and them—to understand how personal metaphors assisted in recognizing how the way they perceived their sense of self in relation to others and to their views of knowledge generated an overall self-definition and the resulting sense of agency to author their own lives.

First formulated by Robert Kegan (1994) and refined, as well as elaborated on and applied, most prominently by Marcia Baxter Magolda (2001a, 2001b, 2004, 2008, 2010), the self-authorship theoretical model has proven to be capacious and enduring with many applications to instructional and student affairs settings. Defined as "the internal capacity to define one's beliefs, identity, and social relations" (Baxter Magolda 2008, 269), this multi-dimensional construct has proven to have an abundant explanatory usefulness. This utility results in part because it assumes an interactive dynamic involving three distinct dimensions: the **cognitive** (how one makes meaning), the **interpersonal** (how one views oneself in relation to others), and the **intrapersonal** (how one views one's sense of identity).

At first blush, the notion of extending the construct of self-authorship from student development to faculty development might seem presumptuous or at least unnecessary. Surely, faculty have already journeyed from external to internal self-definition. Certainly, they have already become authors of their own lives. And yet if we use Baxter Magolda's (2001b) frame for understanding self-authorship in its various phases, we can see how faculty might benefit from guidance when they find themselves questioning their internal voices.

I contend that these three spheres of self-authorship—especially when understood as an interrelated construct—can provide a powerful lens for conceptualizing how faculty writers can move beyond simply advancing their immediate writing projects/research agenda to becoming more aware of how they make meaning when composing, how they construct their audiences, and how they represent their own writerly voices. In the rest of this chapter, I will explore how the theory of self-authorship, so influential in understanding and fostering undergraduate learning and so fundamental to the scholarship of teaching and learning and its penchant for "going meta" (Hutchings and Shulman 1999) has the potential to also serve as an integrative framework for supporting faculty writers.

Let us look first at the overall self-authoring process. In describing the development of self-authorship, Baxter Magolda (2001b, 40) postulates four, though not necessarily discrete, stages:

- External Foundations—when outside authority is in the foreground of our belief system
- Crossroads—a place of discontent, a felt need to work toward self-definition
- Becoming Author of One's Life—a time of reconstructing beliefs about knowledge, self, and others
- Internal Foundations—a shift from developing own beliefs about knowledge, self, and others to enacting those beliefs

While one might assume that all faculty have moved beyond the External Foundations stage, I wonder how many of our faculty find themselves back in that place when they (re)situate themselves in the academy as new/untenured faculty. I think of the faculty participant in the first writing group I facilitated who referred to the process of writing for tenure review as a "soul crunching" experience. With this image, he evoked excruciating pain in the very essence of being. As a junior faculty member, he pointed to the way that external forces (his departmental T & P criteria) were exerting an almost unbearable pressure on his spirit, suggesting that his own beliefs were under siege. His language suggests a turning point when other voices were displacing his own. In fact, faculty writers often say they are having trouble "finding their own voices" when faced with the perceived rigid expectations of scholarly production.

Perhaps, as developers, we need to consider these comments not simply as passing moments of stress but as places of deep discontent, where faculty are working toward self-definition. Or perhaps they are in a transition period moving between a Crossroads stage to Becoming Author of One's Life stage—attempting to reconstruct their own beliefs about knowledge, self, and others in the face of competing voices.

If we conceive of self-authorship as a developmental process involving oscillation, then it is not surprising that faculty would have times of recomposing themselves. Baxter Magolda (2001b, 2004) has demonstrated with her twenty-year longitudinal study that the majority of college students do not approach the Crossroads stage until *after* finishing college, so we might well wonder at what stage our faculty are when they come to us. Moreover, even though faculty may have passed well beyond the Crossroads stage before starting their first academic positions, we might assume that at least some junior faculty may be experiencing a new crossroads where they are finding the need to redefine themselves no longer as doctoral students or newly granted PhDs, but as full-fledged members of the professoriate. And what of limited term/adjunct faculty? To what extent have they moved to the edges of the Crossroad stage where they have the rhetorical agency to pursue their own research/professional pathways when securing ongoing employment is often the overriding concern?

While I know of no studies that have been done to show how faculty might gauge their self-authorship development, if seems logical that each momentous move in the academy (e.g., from non-tenured to tenured status or assistant to associate professor) could very well entail a new professional and personal crossroad where faculty look to reconstruct their beliefs about knowledge, themselves, and their relationship to others. And to what extent have the faculty we're supporting passed into the Internal Foundations stage where they move from not only developing beliefs about knowledge, self, and others but also enacting them? Given how tenure serves as the official rite of passage for so many faculty, do they rely on receiving it as sanction for moving to this fully realized, self-authored stage?

As Baxter Magolda (2008) has characterized this self-authoring development for undergraduates, it is often marked by stages of alternative periods of equilibrium and disequilibrium—a state of flux that many faculty at my institution similarly describe in talking about their own professional journeys. Here's how one third-year faculty member characterized this sense of unnerving oscillation on an opening survey: "When I was first hired, I had a really firm research agenda and writing plan, but somehow my clarity has blurred. Now I'm not sure that I can really add much to what's already been said. Scary." This expressed uneasiness may reflect a cognitive/interpersonal/intrapersonal disequilibrium that many faculty experience, an implicit uneasiness that requires more than simply some strategies for time management. Moreover, since self-authorship relies on self-perception—one faculty member might recognize a significant turning point where another might not. And if one understands self-authorship as a life-long journey, and I do, then all faculty could benefit from this kind of ongoing tripartite development.

COGNITIVE DEVELOPMENT

Given the epistemological maturity of faculty, based on their confident beliefs about the source(s) of knowledge being grounded in their own disciplines, it seems likely that the epistemological dimension of self-authorship would be fairly stable by the time they secure faculty positions. While faculty beliefs about how to make meaning may be open to change given their penchant for learning new ideas and sources of knowledge, generally they would certainly be more likely than undergraduates to have a firm epistemological grounding. And, yet, participating in an exchange that pushes cognitive dissonance—such as a cross-disciplinary conversation afforded by faculty writing groups—might disrupt that cognitive confidence and prompt a crossroads in beliefs about knowledge making. For example, I think of a communication faculty member who noted after our summer writing residency how much she had been influenced by conversations with a secondary science education colleague. She said that the science education professor's manuscript draft about the importance of schooling children in the materiality of the natural world had dramatically affected her thinking about the ecology of knowledge. She said that his use of ecological language had given her a new way to think about and talk about her own research and that she was now pursuing more of an ecological approach as a result.

This encounter seemed to constitute what Baxter Magolda (2001b) terms a "provocative moment"—a turning point where one's belief system about the source of knowledge (or about the interrelationships between knowledge sources) shifts. So it is certainly possible that junior and even senior faculty can be moving in their cognitive development to recognizing new sources of knowledge. If, as Palmer and

Zajonc (2010) have asserted, "collegial conversations" (especially those occurring across disciplines) have the potential to transform higher education, perhaps Baxter Magolda would say that they do so, in part, because they foster "provocative moments" where faculty view another's meaning-making beliefs, a new view that results in modifying or extending their own. In terms of implications for practice: If the goal is to foster self-authorship, then inviting faculty to exchange drafts across disciplinary boundaries represents an important activity, not simply to encourage a sense of community, but also to prompt cognitive growth as part of a self-authoring process. Affording faculty a chance to find readers from disciplines beyond their own increases the possibility that they will experience a useful epistemic crossroad.

Of course, the collegial conversations that happen in faculty writing groups can also prompt diametrically opposed views resulting in a different kind of cognitive influence. I recall a memorable conversation I overheard between a physics professor and a journalism professor about what they count as compelling evidence in their own and in their students' writing. Thinking of expert testimony (in the form of direct quotations) as valid evidence was simply beyond the pale for the physics faculty member, and in the process of explaining why, she strengthened her own convictions about the authority of empirical evidence—as grounded in her own cognitive belief system in the sciences. And the same was likely true for the journalism professor who clarified his own epistemological roots in the process of talking about evidence. While the conversation may have functioned to advance self-authorship in terms of deepening epistemic beliefs, it may have also advanced the participating faculty members sense of how their beliefs relate to others (both the cognitive and interpersonal domains). As some self-authorship researchers (Creamer, Baxter Magolda, and Yue 2010) suggest, development in one of the three dimensions can lead to development in another.

INTERPERSONAL DEVELOPMENT

While it may be likely that the cognitive dimension of self-authorship development in faculty may be relatively stable, the **interpersonal** dimension—how one views oneself in relation to others—is quite likely more in flux. Certainly, much of the tension inherent in the movement from assistant to associate professor relies on the uncertainty of how colleagues view one another's scholarship. Depending on the clarity of the tenure and promotion expectations and the openness of the communication channels within a department, faculty frequently express feelings of vulnerability in their writing groups about how colleagues view their scholarship. Unfortunately, for some, it is only when they are actually up for formal review that they discover their colleagues do not value their work as worthy scholarship.

I recall two assistant professors from the same department in a writing group who gained an increasingly uneasy understanding of their department's faulty communication channels when they talked with faculty from other departments. At the prodding of their writing colleagues, they asked their department chair for further clarification of the expectations and, in the process, one discovered an obvious skepticism about her scholarship on teaching and learning (a path she had already traveled extensively as a result of her engagement with service-learning). While the discovery was unnerving at the time, the information proved crucial in her professional journey because she was able to cite examples from other colleagues in her writing group who were also doing similar scholarly work when she constructed her tenure and promotion application. The information she gained as a result of the writing group conversations enabled her to understand better the legitimacy of her own scholarship and to place it in relationship to others both in her own department and also at the university and even in the academy more generally. Viewing this gain in terms of the interpersonal dimension of self-authorship helps clarify how faculty writing group conversations have the potential not only to develop a support group generally, but also specifically to help faculty writers see their scholarship not in isolation, but in relationship to others both in their departments and disciplines as well as outside of them.

INTRAPERSONAL DEVELOPMENT

While both the cognitive and interpersonal dimensions of the self-authorship construct are extremely useful in understanding what I've observed in faculty writing groups, it is the **intrapersonal** dimension that I suspect might be the most significant aspect of how the self-authorship construct can ground our work with faculty writers. Call it "rhetorical agency" or a strong sense of "professional identity," faculty writers need it in order to prove themselves as legitimate scholars to others. Unfortunately, given the realities of typical departmental dynamics, the colleagues who could optimally affirm a colleague's disciplinary-based scholarship may not be in a position to give it. Either because they are in an evaluative situation (on a review committee) or because they are simply too busy pursuing their own scholarship, colleagues within the same department are not typically well positioned to respond to each other's scholarship while it is in the works, and it is *during* the composing process that writers most need affirming response. The courage to keep writing often comes from the small encouragements along the way, and writing groups can provide the affective boost to sustain faith in our writerly selves.

Furthermore, strengthening one's sense of professional identity requires detailed information, not merely sweeping acknowledgments of worth. I think of the countless times I have responded to drafts from writers in our faculty writing series about what I understand their claims to be and can see and hear their expressions of delight—and relief. Like our students, many of them say they didn't know what they were trying to say until it was paraphrased for them. I recall one theater arts faculty member who was writing on a topic that he worried might be too mundane. After reading his draft and summarizing his claim, he grinned broadly and said, "You seem to think this idea is worth writing about. What a relief." Later, he wrote to say the piece had been accepted by a peer-reviewed journal and attributed his success to the writing series saying that he had gained a new sense of him*self* as a scholar from his participation.

Unfortunately, the opportunities to gain detailed information about one's identity as a scholar seem sparse in typical academic journeys. Since so much academic scholarship on most topics is addressed to limited audiences, faculty writers may receive little acclaim even after their work is published. Instead, faculty seem aware mostly of their deficits. Because I work with faculty from across campus, I write many letters of recommendation for colleagues. In the process, I hear about their (practically always) successful tenure and promotion stories. But rarely do I hear any real joy along with the results. Countless times, they say, yes they received tenure/promotion/rehire, but are now painfully aware of what they have not done and all the goals still unreached. Faculty writing groups can often provide the affirmation needed to sustain a scholarly writing identity and a sense in one's potential to learn and grow.

A concern with this intrapersonal dimension of self-authorship helps shed light on why certain activities associated with faculty writing groups tend to serve as best practices. As already suggested, providing pointed reader response that includes detailed information about what is working and why, can work wonders for helping writers understand what they have to offer that is distinctive, and for strengthening how they view themselves as scholars. Just as undergraduates benefit from a pedagogy that avoids dwelling on deficits, so too can faculty benefit from a deliberate effort to pause on the successes in their drafts and understand their effectiveness. The self-authorship approach to development reflects what O'Meara, Terosky, and Neumann (2009) advocate as a "narrative of growth," where faculty continue to learn not merely out of some contextual imperative or institutional calamity (as in a "narrative of constraint" where external forces mandate the movement), but more because they want to grow and develop as teachers and scholars. This impulse toward self-actualization is very much in keeping with the movement toward self-authorship. So instead of interpreting the faculty member's comment about "soul crunching" as simply a passing complaint, we developers can turn to the concept of self-authorship in recognizing that this faculty member may have been delayed in the External Foundations stage where he was unable to view his own scholarly agency—effectively slowing the cognitive development needed to extend his knowledge and view his interpersonal development in relation to other scholars. In other words, stalling in this key area of self-authorship development (the intrapersonal) can also delay development in the other two spheres as well.

PROMISING PRACTICES FOR ADVANCING SELF-AUTHORSHIP

If we accept the self-authorship model as a sound theoretical base for working with faculty writers and thus embrace its three dimensions as an interrelated construct where enhancing one dimension can enhance others, what are some practices we might implement? Taking a cue from Baxter Magolda (2001b) who advocates four sets of practices for advancing the intrapersonal dimension of self-authorship (experience, reflection, integration, and application)—I suggest that the one most relevant to faculty writing groups is reflection. Perhaps because of the fast pace of so many faculty lives, providing as many opportunities as possible for faculty writers to stop and reflect not only on what they are writing, but also on how and why represents a significant set of practices to consider. Because self-authorship attends in a particular way to the "how" of our beliefs, this meta-cognitive work represents an essential component if self-authorship is the goal. Here are three specific activities to consider in prompting this necessary kind of reflective work: eliciting personal metaphors, facilitating dialogue with students, and using the language of self-authorship.

Although asking faculty to consider what personal metaphors they would choose for themselves as scholars/writers tends to be particularly useful at the first gathering of a writing group—it can be a stimulating activity at any point. A three-part sequence is helpful: Ask participants to list some words or phrases others have used to describe them as schol-ars/writers or ones they would use to describe themselves; complete a sentence frame that prompts a personal metaphor, and then explain to others why this personal metaphor seems apt. To elicit optimal meta-phors, I invite participants to complete this frame after they generate a list of words/phrases about themselves: "When I'm at my best as a scholar, I am a/an _____because _____." If partici-pants are having difficulty coming up with a personal metaphor, give examples. For instance, one faculty member decided that she was a "wolf" as a writer because she had to sniff out every single inch of the lit-erature before she felt comfortable recording a single word of her own. In telling others in her writing group why she chose this personal meta-phor, she became more conscious of her composing process and later in the development series noted that she felt more forgiving of the time she took to read the literature, and once when she didn't have a draft quite ready for exchange said confidently, "I'm still *wolfing* around." Asking faculty to reflect in writing about the metaphors they would choose for themselves as scholars/writers pushes them to focus on the intrapersonal dimension—on their writerly selves.

Another practice that can fruitfully stimulate both the intrapersonal and the interpersonal dimensions is to identify times during faculty writ-ing work sessions for participants to enter into dialogue with students. Hosting writing residencies that include undergraduate/graduate stu-dent writers and scheduling some dialogue time together provides an organic way for faculty writers to talk about their scholarly writing with students. Not only does the exchange provide the faculty writers a chance to articulate their ideas more clearly, it can help translate the scholarship into teaching terms and into language meaningful to stu-dents. In this way, the dialogue helps faculty writers develop both intrap-ersonal and interpersonal dimension by clarifying their writerly goals at the same time that they can re-situate themselves them as faculty writers who are also in learning relationships.

A third, more global, practice and one that can productively be used at the beginning and throughout a development series is to present the self-authorship model and to use the language of its three dimensions in framing all the activities. Giving faculty this language can help them name for themselves what they are doing during their composing and why. Having the language can also serve to remind them that developing as faculty writers involves development in all three dimensions and in a sense remind them that they can aspire to whole lives. Hodge, Baxter Magolda, and Haynes (2009) intimate why it might be so important to have this conceptual model and its attendant language for working with faculty when they describe the danger for those undergraduates who "trust others more than they trust themselves" (18)—suggesting an ongoing danger of the interpersonal dimension eclipsing the intrapersonal one. The same danger exists for faculty who may become too reliant on academic expectations for scholarship and forget about sustaining a secure internal sense of self (the interpersonal capacity).

While I am increasingly drawn to the notion of self-authorship as an integrative framework for structuring support for faculty writers, I recognize the challenges in assessing development in these terms. The primary method for assessing self-authorship for undergraduates has been the qualitative measure of interviews (Baxter Magolda and King 2004, 2007), a method that has distinct disadvantages: interviews (including transcribing and training others) are time-consuming, and the results are not conducive to comparison (Pizzolato 2007; Creamer, Baxter Magolda, and Yue 2010). However, there is evidence that a new quantitative instrument (a career decisions survey) that Creamer, Baxter Magolda, and Yue (2010) have created and tested, results in a valid and reliable measure of all three self-authorship dimensions. What is especially promising about the resulting matrix is that it has the potential to pinpoint which activities and experiences contribute to self-authorship development and to show small, incremental advances associated with educational activities of short duration (such as a summer writing residency). Additional research is needed to demonstrate that the dimensions of self-authorship can be assessed sufficiently, but this possibility holds great promise for assessing development efforts for faculty writers. Capturing the growth narratives for faculty writers using the tri-part lens of self-authorship would be immensely useful especially if recorded over time in the way that Baxter Magolda has done it for undergraduates. While Wildman (2004) suggested the value of using self-authorship for framing faculty development initiatives, no one seems to have tapped self-authorship as a way of fostering and tracking professional growth.

By recasting the immediate outcomes of productivity, pedagogy, and collegiality into the desired long-term and expansive goal of self-authorship, we can more readily account for why certain practices seem to have more enduring benefits and to envision others in an overarching theoretic model. Faculty writing groups that make no deliberate attempt to develop self-authoring capacities may be missing an essential component of professional development, as well as overlooking an organic way to support faculty and student writers together. Baxter Magolda (2007) has contended that self-authorship is the single most important goal of an undergraduate education, and perhaps the same could be said for professional development. Without the self-authorship conceptual framework, development activities might end up as short term fixes, rather than the transformational experiences they could be, leaving participants in formula-following, pat modes of thinking, rather than in promoting fully self-authored faculty members who can compose not only their scholarly writing, but their whole lives.

REFERENCES

Baxter Magolda, Marcia. 2001a. "A Constructivist Revision of the Measure of Epistemological Reflection." *Journal of College Student Development* 42:520–34.

Baxter Magolda, Marcia. 2001b. *Making Their Own Way: Narratives for Transforming Higher Education to Promote Self-Development.* Sterling, VA: Stylus.

Baxter Magolda, Marcia. 2004. "Learning Partnerships Model: A Framework for Promoting Self-Authorship." In *Learning Partnerships: Theories and Models of Practice to Education for Self-authorship*, ed. Marcia Baxter Magolda and Patricia M. King, 37–62. Sterling, VA: Stylus.

Baxter Magolda, Marcia. 2008. "Three Elements of Self-Authorship." *Journal of College Student Development* 49 (4): 269–84. http://dx.doi.org/10.1353/csd.0.0016.

Baxter Magolda, Marcia. 2010. "The Interweaving of Epistemological, Intrapersonal, and Interpersonal Development in the Evolution of Self-Authorship." In *Development and Assessment of Self-authorship: Exploring the Concept across Cultures*, ed. Marcia Baxter Magolda, E. G. Creamer, and P.S. Meszaros, 25–43. Sterling, VA: Stylus.

Baxter Magolda, Marcia, and Patricia M. King. 2004. *Learning Partnerships: Theories and Models of Practice to Education for Self-authorship.* Sterling, VA: Stylus.

Baxter Magolda, Marcia, and Patricia M. King. 2007. "Interview Strategies for Assessing Self-Authorship: Constructing Conversations to Assess Meaning Making." *Journal of College Student Development* 48 (5): 491–508. http://dx.doi.org/10.1353/csd.2007.0055.

Belcher, Wendy Laura. 2009. *Writing Your Journal Article in Twelve Weeks: A Guide to Academic Publishing Success.* Thousand Oaks, CA: Sage Publications.

Boice, Robert. 1995. "Developing Writing, Then Teaching, Amongst New Faculty." *Research in Higher Education* 36 (4): 415–56. http://dx.doi.org/10.1007/BF02207905.

Creamer, Elizabeth G., Marcia Baxter Magolda, and Jessica Yue. Sept/Oct 2010. "Preliminary Evidence of the Reliability and Validity of a Quantitative Measure of Self-Authorship." *Journal of College Student Development* 5 (5). http://muse.jhu.edu/login?auth=0&type=summary&url=/journals/journal_of_college_student_development/v051/51.5.creamer.html. http://dx.doi.org/10.1353/csd.2010.0010.

Elbow, Peter, and Mary Deane Sorcinelli. Nov/Dec 2006. "The Faculty Writing Place: A Room of One's Own." *Change: The Magazine of Higher Learning* 38 (6): 17–22. http://dx.doi.org/10.3200/CHNG.38.6.17-22.

Fassinger, Polly, Nancy Gilliland, and Linda Johnson. 1992. "Benefits of a Faculty Writing Circle: Better Teaching." *College Teaching* 40: 53–56.

Hodge, David C., Marcia B. Baxter Magolda, and Carolyn A. Haynes. 2009. "Engaged Learning: Enabling Self-Authorship and Effective Practice." *Liberal Education* 95 (4): 18–23.

Hutchings, Pat, and Lee Shulman. September/October 1999. "The Scholarship of Teaching: New Elaborations, New Developments." *Change* 31 (5): 10–5. http://dx.doi.org/10.1080/00091389909604218.

Kegan, Robert. 1994. *In Over Our Heads: The Mental Demands of Modern Life.* Cambridge, MA: Harvard University Press.

Mullen, Carol A., April Whatley, and William A. Kealy. 2000. "Widening the Circle: Faculty-Student Support Groups as Innovative Practice in Higher Education." *Interchange: A Quarterly Review of Education* 31 (1): 35–60. http://dx.doi.org/10.1023/A:1007682713733.

O'Meara, Kerry Ann, Aimee LaPointe Terosky, and Anna Neumann. 2009. "Faculty Careers and Work Lives: A Professional Growth Perspective." *ASHE Higher Education Report* 34 (3): 1–221. San Francisco: Jossey-Bass.

Palmer, Parker. 2007. *The Courage to Teach: Exploring the Inner Landscape of a Teacher's Life.* San Francisco: Jossey-Bass.

Palmer, Parker, and Arthur Zajonc. 2010. *The Heart of Higher Education: A Call to Renewal; Transforming the Academy through Collegial Conversations.* San Francisco: Jossey-Bass.

Pizzolato, John E. 2007. "Assessing Self-Authorship." In "Self-Authorship: Advancing Students' Intellectual Growth," edited by P. S. Meszaros, special issue *New Directions for Teaching and Learning* 109: 31–42.

Werder, Carmen. 2010. "Fostering Self-Authorship for Citizenship: Telling Metaphors in Dialogue." In *Citizenship across the Curriculum,* ed. Michael B. Smith, Rebecca Nowacek, and Jeffrey L. Bernstein, 54–72. Bloomington, IN: Indiana University Press.

Werder, Carmen, and Karen Hoelscher. October 1, 2010. "Time Out to Write." *Inside Higher Ed.* http://www.insidehighered.com/advice/hoelscher/werder2.

Werder, Carmen, Luke Ware, Cora Thomas, and Erik Skogsberg. 2010. "Students in Parlor Talk on Teaching and Learning: Conversational Scholarship." In *Engaging Student Voices in the Study of Teaching and Learning,* ed. Carmen Werder and Megan M. Otis, 16–31. Sterling, VA: Stylus.

Wildman, T.M. 2004. "The Learning Partnerships Model: Framing Faculty and Institutional Development." In *Learning Partnerships: Theory and Models of Practice to Educate for Self-Authorship,* ed. M.B. Baxter Magolda and P.M. King, 245–268. Sterling, VA: Stylus.

AFTERWORD

Michele Eodice

In the act of "making a book"—in this case, *Working with Faculty Writers*—we have enacted our own call to "work with faculty writers." Anne and I worked closely with each writer or writing team (forty-four in all) to develop chapters. The process reinforced our beliefs about supporting the faculty writer: writers need and want truly helpful feedback that provokes revision; writers want to sense movement, progress, which regular communication can foster; and even solo authors want to feel they are among other writers in community. Reviewing each chapter draft several times and composing notes for authors sharpened our mindfulness and improved our own thinking and talking about writing. E-mail back from authors confirmed their excitement about the project, and they readily acknowledged the value of the exchange. This work has been a real pleasure to engage in.

As the collection emerged, we pledged that the finished product would offer two things, at the very least: first, a sense of the scope and depth of programs already working with faculty writers, with the inclusion of all types of institutions and writers in mind; and second, bringing together, for the first time, a collection of persuasive stories of these representative and successful programs so that readers might find in them new or renewed support and guidance for their own efforts. This collection should also put the kibosh on any doubts that our institutions should offer support to all of our writers, including faculty. No school should feel support is unnecessary. Like the motive for creating a writing center for all students, the motive for building such programs is not remediation; this support demonstrates a commitment to what many of our mission statements promise and value: lifelong learning. This is about development, growth, and improvement.

We imagine our readers will be those who already cross institutional boundaries—teaching center directors, writing program directors, deans, chairs—and they will span the disciplines as well. A real strength of this collection is that it does not plant this work with faculty writers in one location. And while most support programs originated from teaching centers or writing programs or from a collaboration between the two, we can only guess at how these programs will be offered (or outsourced) in the future. No matter who sponsors the support, it will likely be "mutually beneficial" (Schick et al. 2012, 45) because all the participants and facilitators learn from the experience. What is learned can be surprising. For one thing, empowering faculty to place themselves in contexts that will activate their own professional development can become a pathway to improving the teaching of writing across the disciplines. Hearing from and talking with colleagues from a department far, far away from your own opens such possibilities; the more we interact, the better we can "decode disciplinary conventions" (Schick et al. 2012, 60), thus clearing the way for a more comprehensive understanding of the demands on students and the need to craft our learning outcomes and assignments to make sense of those demands.

FUTURE FILE

The programs described in this collection privilege proximal ways of working with writers—around tables, through consultations, at retreats, up in tree houses. Any number of these admirably high touch/low tech efforts can likely work on your campus. At the same time, higher education priorities are shifting, writing itself is changing shape in modality, and scholarly contributions are due for an exciting transformation as we exploit the powers of the digital world. But the future of scholarly writing and writers can be enhanced by retaining the values of high touch/low tech in new environments with new demands. For example, what happens best to faculty writers (according to them) happens in person: building community, sharing drafts, engaging in peer review, celebrating. But several technologies will make it more possible to apply high touch to digital collaboration and online community-generated peer review, and to make way for the mega accessible through "the inevitability of open access" (Lewis 2012). One of Anne's graduate students, Laura Lisabeth, was introduced to these ideas by one of the pioneers, Kathleen Fitzpatrick. Following a visit by Fitzpatrick to her campus, Lisabeth (2012) wrote this in her blog: "One of Dr. Fitzpatrick's most thought provoking ideas was the need to move out of the 'filter then publish' process of academic publishing and into a 'publish then filter' one, which certainly challenges ownership of intellectual thought."

And Fitzpatrick (2009) writes in her own blog of the concept, that was originated by Clay Shirky (2008):

> It's those readers, after all, who are the article's true peers, not the two or three editor-selected reviewers who now give the article the up-or-down vote. It makes no sense for the labor of the same small set of reviewers to be drawn upon again and again when there's the potential for more broadly and fairly distributing that work. And it makes no sense for article publishing to be subject to the crazy delays that now hold a lot of work hostage, first waiting for the peer reviews to come in, and then waiting for the journal's backlog of accepted articles to clear out. Why shouldn't readers be able to read and respond to that work right away, and why shouldn't that reading and response *constitute* the article's peer review?

Future faculty will need to be thinking about this now. I would venture that one of the most important subjects to be studied, or at least to be familiar with, is the future of publication. To catch up, or even get in front of these issues, Preparing Future Faculty programs and other events for graduate students could include discussions of the expectations for scholarly writing and the ways in which their work will be created, evaluated, and disseminated in the future. In our annual Camp Completion for dissertation writers across the disciplines, we facilitate productivity individually with writers while enacting a collective discourse about the ways knowledge gets made and disseminated. Those new to high stakes research and creative activity have more questions than we can imagine about how this work gets done. We all need to participate in what I think is one of the most engaging and complex topics of the next generation.

WORKPLACES

According to Robert Boice, "The most basic skills of writing are more a matter of how to work than how to write" (Boice 1995, 418). There is little to dispute the main claim of Boice's research—that with changes in habits and attitudes, most faculty could "learn to make writing *painless, efficient,* and *successful*" for themselves (3). His research on how faculty writers work (or don't work) effectively is referred to again and again by those who want to repair a writing problem of their own. What it takes for that to happen has been designed and delivered by consultants, counselors, psychotherapists, deans, and mentors and is variously called nagging, nudging, supporting, coaching, and the proverbial kick in the pants (or tenure pressure). But procrastination, writer's block, and dysphoria (Flaherty 2004) continue to emerge as issues for individual faculty writers, and Boice (2012) recognizes these as the key habits and attitudes that must be reformed to reach fluency through practice.

So, if our efforts are going to focus on "how to work," they must be supported by the places where our work takes place. Our workplaces are still primarily brick and mortar campuses, filled with learners, teachers, researchers, and administrators who all write to earn. William Savage, a professor on my campus, has written extensively and bluntly in reference to expectations for publication: "This forced productivity contributes mightily to the frenetic life on the modern campus, where nothing—teaching, research, writing, thinking—is allowed to occur at a leisurely pace" (Savage 2003, 43). How can we mentor our faculty toward productivity without diminishing the quality of life offered by more time to think, talk, and walk around our campuses? The metrics for success may seem to be changing too often, and campus leadership needs to provide ballast. According to Sharon Cramer, an experienced administrator, chairs and department members need to examine their own assumptions about scholarly productivity out loud, in front of junior faculty, assumptions that continue to privilege the myth of the solitary author and to reinscribe habits and dispositions that separate writers and writing from the everyday work of the academy. Cramer calls on chairs to enjoin their departments to signal support, not just by singling out the struggling writers, but by creating a community of practice that takes time to reflect on what research and writing mean to the department, the discipline, the institution. In this way, a department moves from using the "language of complaint" about faculty productivity to using a "language of commitment" to each other's work by asking about research agendas, reading drafts, and celebrating writing accomplishments (Cramer 2006, 537). Another leader on her own campus, Elizabeth H. Boquet (2009), offers this challenge:

> How might we really help all members of a college or university community to make the best use of the resources available to them (libraries, writing centers, teaching excellence centers) to promote a culture of campus writing that extends beyond the classroom and becomes part of the fabric of the university? Consider a writing model more consonant with the innovative teaching and learning occurring institutionally, one that acknowledges campus learning goals as well as individual concerns about factors such as time and expertise.

Cramer and Boquet above offer calls to action for departments and campuses. My final call to action is this: it will be more and more imperative for faculty to turn toward each other—not inward, not isolated with a screen and device. In turning toward and forming communities, faculty of all types can together consider some of the pressing questions of the coming years in regards to publication, intellectual property, knowledge repositories, academic labor, and the digital commons. Institutional leadership must get behind these communities in tangible and visible ways. It won't matter much whether this attention to faculty writers is offered by a writing program or teaching center, so the chapters here offer various configurations of program delivery, understanding that local culture and context are the arbiters of successful implementation. Take this book and run with it . . .

REFERENCES

Boice, Robert. 1995. "Developing Writing, Then Teaching, amongst New Faculty." *Research in Higher Education* 36 (4): 415–56. http://dx.doi.org/10.1007/BF02207905.

Boice, Robert. Sep 2012. "An alternative to thought suppression?" *American Psychologist* 67 (6): 498. http://dx.doi.org/10.1037/a0028999. Medline:22963421

Boquet, Elizabeth H. 2009. *Faculty Writing and Reflection.* Fairfield, CT: Fairfield University.

Cramer, Sharon. 2006. "Learning the Ropes: How Department Chairs Can Help New Faculty Develop Productive Scholarship Habits." *Reflective Practice* 7 (4): 525–39. http://dx.doi.org/10.1080/14623940600987155.

Fitzpatrick, Kathleen. 2009. "The Cost of Peer Review and the Future of Scholarly Publishing." *Mediacommons: A Digital Scholarly Network* (blog). http://mediacommons. futureofthebook.org/content/cost-peer-review-and-future-scholarly-publishing.

Flaherty, Alice. 2004. *The Midnight Disease: The Drive to Write, Writer's Block, and the Creative Brain.* New York: Mariner Books.

Lewis, David W. 2012. "The Inevitability of Open Access." *College & Research Libraries* 73, no. 5 (September): 493–506.

Lisabeth, Laura. 2012. "'Undo Expectations': Dr. Kathleen Fitzpatrick Brings her Thoughts on Writing in the Digital Age to St. John's University." HASTAC (blog). http://hastac.org/blogs/lauralissju/2012/09/29/undo-expectations-dr-kathleen-fitzpatrick-brings-her-thoughts-writing-d

Savage, William W., Jr. 2003. "Scribble, Scribble, Toil and Trouble: Forced Productivity in the Modern University." *Journal of Scholarly Publishing* 35 (1): 40–6. http://dx.doi.org/10.3138/jsp.35.1.40.

Schick, Kurt, Cindy Hunter, Lincoln Gray, Nancy Poe, and Karen Santos. 2012. "Writing in Action: Scholarly Writing Groups as Faculty Development." *Journal on Centers for Teaching and Learning* 3:43–63.

Shirky, Clay. 2008. *Here Comes Everybody: The Power of Organizing without Organizations.* New York: Penguin Books.

ABOUT THE CONTRIBUTORS

ANNE ELLEN GELLER is associate professor of English and director of Writing Across the Curriculum in the Institute for Writing Studies at St. John's University in Queens, New York.

MICHELE EODICE is associate provost for academic engagement and director of the writing center at the University of Oklahoma.

CHRIS ANSON is university distinguished professor and director of the Campus Writing and Speaking Program at North Carolina State University. He has published 15 books and more than 100 journal articles and book chapters and has spoken widely across the United States and in twenty-seven other countries. He is currently chair of the Conference on College Composition and Communication. For more information, please visit www. ansonica.net.

BRIAN BALDI serves as the organizational lead for the University of Massachusetts Center for Teaching & Faculty Development's scholarly writing and new chair programming and assists with the Mellon Mutual Mentoring Initiative and other faculty development programs.

WILLIAM P. BANKS is director of the University Writing Program and associate professor of rhetoric and writing at East Carolina University, where he teaches graduate and undergraduate courses in writing, research, and pedagogy. His published articles on history, rhetoric, pedagogy, writing program administration, and sexuality have appeared in several recent books, as well as in *College Composition and Communication, College English,* and *Computers and Composition.*

A. JANE BIRCH is assistant director for faculty development at the Brigham Young University Faculty Center. Since founding the annual semester-long Scholarship Workshop, she has directed the program for fourteen years and sponsored more than 1,200 participants. She loves seeing how passionate the participants are about how much this program increases their scholarly productivity.

ROBERT BOICE is Professor Emeritus at SUNY Stony Brook and author of more than 200 journal articles, chapters, and books. He lives in the remote mountains of Western Carolina, where he tries to follow the Buddhist path. In his clinical practice as a writing therapist he has helped hundreds of writers, especially women and underrepresented academics, survive dissertation and tenure rituals.

ANN BRUNJES received her MA and PhD in English from New York University and is currently associate professor of English at Bridgewater State University. She served as BSU's founding director of the Office of Teaching and Learning from 2008–2012 and collaborated with BSU colleagues to establish the annual Teacher-Scholar Institute.

LISA CAHILL is associate director of Arizona State University's University Academic Success Programs, which provides writing and subject tutoring, supplemental instruction, peer mentoring, and summer transition programs. With research interests in writing in the disciplines/writing across the curriculum and high school writing centers, she oversees the writing center model across four campuses.

SUSAN CALLAWAY has a PhD in composition and rhetoric and is associate professor and director of the Center for Writing and of the Faculty Writers Program at the University of St. Thomas in St. Paul, Minnesota. Her current research focuses on writing centers and the impact of service learning on writing consultants' intercultural maturity.

ANGELA CLARK-OATES is the course manager for and teaches in the Writers' Studio in the School of Letters and Sciences at Arizona State University. She is the former coordinator of the ASU Writing Center–Downtown Phoenix campus, where she also designed and implemented ASU's first online writing tutoring program. Her research is focused on how writing identities are shaped by peers, teachers, and institutions.

MANUEL COLUNGA-GARCIA works with the Center for Global Change and Earth Observations at Michigan State University. He is interested in the interactions between human and natural systems. His current research is on the impact of global trade on the environment with emphasis on invasive species in terrestrial systems.

MICHELLE COX, a former WAC director, is now a multilingual specialist at Dartmouth College. She has co-edited several collections, including *WAC and Second Language Writers: Research towards Developing Linguistically and Culturally Inclusive Programs and Practices.* Her scholarship focuses on writing pedagogy, second-language writing studies, and writing program administration.

WILLIAM DUFFY teaches courses in writing, rhetoric, and literacy studies at Francis Marion University, where he also serves as assistant director of composition. He primarily studies the overlap between rhetoric and ethics, and his work has appeared in *Rhetoric Review, Enculturation,* and several edited collections.

VIOLET DUTCHER is professor of rhetoric and composition and writing program director at Eastern Mennonite University. Her research interest is in literacy practices, particularly within Amish communities. With the support of the Young Center for Anabaptist and Pietist Studies, she is currently working on a book-length project that examines literacy practices within Amish communities.

VIRGINIA FAJT is a veterinary clinical pharmacologist and has been in the Department of Veterinary Physiology and Pharmacology at Texas A&M University since 2005. She teaches undergraduate, graduate, and professional students and collaborates on research about teaching and the clinical use of drugs in veterinary species.

PETER FELTEN is assistant provost and executive director of the Center for Engaged Learning and the Center for the Advancement of Teaching and Learning and associate professor of history at Elon University.

KERRI B. FLINCHBAUGH is currently serving as the assistant director of East Carolina University's Writing Program, coordinating programmatic assessment and working closely with faculty writers and writing instructors. She is also working on a PhD in discourse and rhetoric and serving on the leadership team for the Tar River Writing Project.

JENNIFER FOLLETT has taught writing and worked in writing center administration for fifteen years. As assistant director of the Temple University Writing Center, she advises faculty on their writing and on teaching writing in different disciplines. She is completing a dissertation about emotion in writing center sessions through Indiana University Pennsylvania.

GERTRUDE FRASER, vice provost for faculty recruitment and retention at the University of Virginia, conducts research and writes on faculty careers. She established the university's Professor as Writers Program. Her book *African American Midwifery in the South: Dialogues of Birth, Race, and Memory* was published by Harvard University Press.

LYNÉE LEWIS GAILLET, director of the Writing Studio and Lower Division Studies, is professor of English at Georgia State University. She teaches a wide range of undergraduate and graduate courses in the history of rhetoric; writing theory, practice, and administration; and archival research methods.

ELENA MARIE-ADKINS GARCIA is a 2013 graduate of Michigan State University, whose dissertation focuses on the writing practices of her father, a thirty-seven-year factory machine operator. Her chapter in this book reflects her dedication to studying and improving graduate student educational experiences.

FRAN I. GELWICK is associate professor in wildlife and fisheries sciences. Her research and teaching focuses on aquatic community ecology, fisheries management, and ecological assessment.

TARA GRAY serves as associate professor of criminal justice and as the founding director of the Teaching Academy at New Mexico State University. She hosts five different kinds of writing groups on her home campus and has presented Publish and Flourish workshops to 5,000 participants in more than thirty US states and in Guatemala, Mexico, Canada, and Saudi Arabia.

CLAUDINE GRIGGS is the writing center director at Rhode Island College, and her publications include three nonfiction books and twenty articles. Griggs earned her BA and MA in English from California State Polytechnic University, Pomona, and now lives in Warwick, Rhode Island.

LETIZIA GUGLIELMO is associate professor of English and assistant director of composition at Kennesaw State University and also teaches in the Gender and Women's Studies Program. Her research and writing focus on feminist rhetoric and pedagogy, multiliteracies, digital media in the writing classroom, and the intersections of feminist action and digital communication.

EVA KASSENS-NOOR, assistant professor of urban and transport planning in the School of Planning, Design, and Construction at Michigan State University, holds a joint appointment with the Global Urban Studies Program and is an adjunct professor in the Department of Geography. She holds a PhD in urban planning and an SM in transportation from MIT and the Diplom-Ingenieur in business engineering from the Universität Karlsruhe. Her research centers on resilience, sustainability, and large-scale urban planning projects triggered by global forces.

WEN LI is assistant professor of electrical and computer engineering at Michigan State University. She received her PhD (2008) and MS (2004) in electrical engineering from the California Institute of Technology. Her research interests include BioMEMS, micro/nanosensors, and microsystem integration and packaging technologies.

DEANDRA LITTLE is associate professor and associate director of the Teaching Resource Center at the University of Virginia, where she also teaches courses in US literature. Her research and publications focus on effective educational development practices, including consultations, graduate student professional development, writing, and teaching with visual images.

VERÓNICA LOUREIRO-RODRÍGUEZ, a native of Galicia (Spain), received her PhD in Spanish linguistics from the University of California, Davis. Currently, she is assistant professor in the Department of Linguistics at the University of Manitoba (Winnipeg, Canada). Her publications are in the areas of Galician and Spanish sociolinguistics and Galician rap.

LAURA MADSON is associate professor and director of the graduate program in psychology at New Mexico State University. She enrolled in Tara Gray's Publish and Flourish workshop in 1997 and integrates the accompanying book into the mentoring program she conducts for all incoming graduate students in psychology.

PRUDENCE MERTON is associate director in the Dartmouth Center for Advancement of Learning, where she provides professional development in teaching and course design. She also teaches a first-year writing course at Dartmouth and in the graduate program in higher education administration at New England College. Her degree is in adult education.

JANICE C. MOLLOY studies relationships between human capital and firm performance. Her doctorate is from the Fisher College of Business at the Ohio State University and her MBA is from the University of Rochester. She is assistant professor of human resource management at Michigan State University.

JESSIE L. MOORE is associate director of the Center for Engaged Learning at Elon University and associate professor of English. Her research interests include multi-institutional research structures, writing transfer, second language writing, and faculty development, particularly as it relates to the teaching and practice of writing.

GEORGIANNE MOORE is associate professor at Texas A&M University in ecosystem science and management and received her BS from Georgia Tech and PhD from Oregon State. Her research explores the role of vegetation in the water cycle. She conducts research in Texas and Costa Rica and teaches ecological restoration classes.

MARÍA IRENE MOYNA is associate professor of the Department of Hispanic Studies at Texas A&M University. She has published more than twenty articles in linguistics journals and collections. She is the author of *Compound Words in Spanish: Theory and history* (2011), and co-editor of *Recovering the US Hispanic Linguistic Heritage* (2008). Most recently, she served as associate editor of the sixth edition of the *University of Chicago Spanish Dictionary* (2012).

JOHN PELL is director of the University Writing Program and chair of the Writing Across the Curriculum Committee at Whitworth University in Spokane, Washington. He wrote his essay for this volume while at Stanford University.

LORI SALEM is assistant vice provost at Temple University, where she has been the director of the Writing Center since 1999. Her research on faculty and writing appears in the *Journal of Writing Program Administration* and has been presented at CCCC, WPA, and IWCA.

ELLEN SCHENDEL is professor of writing and director of the Fred Meijer Center for Writing and Michigan Authors at Grand Valley State University. Her scholarship focuses on writing program administration, assessment, and writing center pedagogy. She recently co-authored the book *Building Writing Center Assessments that Matter* (USUP).

TRIXIE G. SMITH is director of the Writing Center at Michigan State University and core faculty in rhetoric and writing and the Center for Gender in Global Contexts. Her teaching and research combine issues of gender and activism with writing center theory and practice, WAC, and teacher mentoring.

MARY DEANE SORCINELLI is associate provost for faculty development, director of the Center for Teaching and Faculty Development, and professor of educational policy at the University of Massachusetts Amherst. She is interested in the role of faculty development programs in helping faculty improve their own writing as well as their students' writing.

MICHAEL STRICKLAND teaches in both the English and environmental studies departments at Elon. He directs the Elon Community Garden and teaches a gardening course, as well as a wide range of writing courses, from environmental and scientific rhetoric to travel writing.

LORNA WATT studied the origins of biodiversity and college science education at Michigan State University. She is currently self-employed in the San Francisco Bay Area.

CARMEN WERDER directs the Teaching-Learning Academy, Writing Instruction Support, and the Learning Commons at Western Washington University, where she also teaches civil discourse. She was a 2005 Carnegie Scholar and has written and presented widely on the scholarship of teaching and learning. She helped develop a faculty writing group model at WWU, where she has facilitated many faculty writing cohorts.

JUNG H. YUN is director of new faculty initiatives at the Center for Teaching and Faculty Development at the University of Massachusetts Amherst, where she develops programs for orientation, mentoring, tenure preparation, and time management. She holds degrees from Vassar College, the University of Pennsylvania, and UMass Amherst.

JILL ZARESTKY, MS, is a senior lecturer in mathematics at Texas A&M University. She studied mathematics and computer science at the University of Tennessee, Knoxville, and the University of Texas, Austin. She specializes in student-centered learning practices, applying reflective writing to mathematics education, and mathematics-based art.

INDEX